CONT

HAPPINESS
AND THE
FULFILLED
LIFE

365 Motivational
Meditations

Graham Albert Logan
MMed Sc, BSc Hons, Dip Th, Dip Pastoral

To all those on the hunt for
lasting happiness and the fulfilled life.

ACKNOWLEDGMENTS

To my publishing team at Kindle Book Publishing, thank you for your expertise and outstanding work in preparing this book for publication. Your dedication and skill have been invaluable throughout this process.

To those friends and family members who encouraged me to, "Keep going."

This book was completed as a result of their encouragement.

"Never underestimate a word of encouragement." Author

PREFACE

Happiness and the Fulfilled Life is the culmination of over two years of painstaking research and writing. The reader is invited to think more deeply about what happiness and the fulfilled life really means for them, and what it could look like in the future. Such a vast subject demands a kaleidoscopic approach, and this thought-provoking book does just that, taking in 12 dimensions throughout the year, one for each month. The nature of the dimensions allows for some overlap of the wide variety of material.

January: The Historical Dimension: *Hic habitat felicitas (Here dwells happiness)*

February: The Philosophical Dimension: *Everyone has a philosophy of life*

March: The Physical Dimension: *All truly great thoughts are conceived while walking*

April: The Psychological Dimension: *The mind matters and here's how it works*

May: The Emotional Dimension: *Getting a handle on our emotional life*

June: The Spiritual Dimension: *To be spiritually dead is to be diabolically alive*

July: The Relational Dimension: *We all have a strong need for connectivity and belonging*

August: The Attitudinal Dimension: *The attitude of gratitude makes us happier*

September: The Biblical Dimension: *The unfolding drama of redemption*

October: The Cultural Dimension: *The spirit of the age*

November: The Musical Dimension: *Music is the literature of the heart, it reaches into our soul*

December: The Practical Dimension: *Practical steps for the journey of life*

The reader is provided with short, daily motivational meditations, and these only take a couple of minutes to read. However, the in-depth and insightful observations provide a wealth of knowledge that will yield much food for thought for the serious seeker of happiness and the fulfilled life. Each day is set out in the following format:

- **A motivational idea:**
  Kaleidoscopic ideas are designed to kickstart your daily focus on the subject.

- **A memorable quote:**
  A wide variety of quotes are used from a range of sources and influencers.

- **A journaling suggestion:**
  The reader is invited to journal each day and is given a journaling suggestion to provoke both positive and critical thinking. (Note: *"Journaling is the act of expressing your deepest thoughts and feelings by putting words to your inner life and then putting these words on paper."* Coach Zone)

- **A memo for meditation:**
  All memos for meditation are taken from the Bible. The author takes a Christian approach to the subject, but this is juxtaposed with a wide range of world views and beliefs from which we can learn much. Commonalities are highlighted, and where they diverge, the reader is invited to give careful consideration to these in their thinking and journaling.

THE HISTORICAL DIMENSION

January 1

Motivational Idea: The beginning of happiness

Before we dive into our motivational meditations, what is your personal history of happiness? When did you first feel happy? What makes you happy? Have you found this seemingly elusive experience? If you were to write a book on your history of happiness, what would it contain? And how many chapters or pages would it have? Any or many?

What is most important to the author is to find happiness and experience the joy of a fulfilled and flourishing life. Today we *expect* to be happy! Yet it's only within the past two hundred years that human beings have begun to think of happiness as not just an earthly possibility but also as an earthly entitlement. We seek happiness, we may even demand it, yet the question has to be asked: is happiness possible in this day and age? We live in a world of fear, stress and dis-ease, yet 'happiness gurus' are everywhere with their guaranteed method of obtaining happiness. However, with each 'flavour of the month', most people still seem to be on the lookout, though some seem to have given up. The advertising experts tell us we need their product to be happy and marketing campaigns feed the instantaneous gratification mentality, 'I want it all and I want it now.'

The philosopher Bertrand Russell, whom we shall meet under The Philosophical Dimension, considered happiness as something to find by conquest. He concluded that one of the reasons people are anxious, upset or depressed is because life is meaningless. Who hasn't asked the question, *'What's it all about?'* or, *'What's the point?'* Russell went on to say that the first secret of happiness was to simply be interested in new experiences. That sounds like a good idea and there must be some merit in it, but it does lend itself to the conundrum that such happiness will tend to be ephemeral and fleeting, and we will simply seek out another experience and another. A happy flourishing, fulfilled life is worth aiming for – and one that's authentic! And so we begin.

Memorable Quote:

"When we get what we want, we are temporarily happy and fulfilled. But the reason for happiness is not because we got what we wanted, but because for a brief period of time, we stopped wanting, and thus got a measure of temporal happiness." Adapted

Journaling Suggestion:

What gives me happiness and fulfilment?

Memo for Meditation:

"Where there is no [wise, intelligent] guidance, the people fall [and go off course like a ship without a helm], But in the abundance of [wise and godly] counsellors there is victory." Proverbs 11:14

January 2

Motivational Idea: *Hic habitat felicitas* (Here dwells happiness)

The desire for happiness is not new. Take the example of the baker from Pompeii who lived 2,000 years ago. The inscription found above his shop read, *'Hic habitat felicitas,'* meaning, here dwells happiness. The owner of the bakery had served in his 'happy' shop and probably died in the eruption of Vesuvius which destroyed the city in AD79. We may wonder what happiness meant to the Pompeiian baker, and how the Roman idea of happiness helps us in our quest today. The Romans looked to Felicitas, the goddess of good luck, success and prosperity, and Fortuna, the goddesses, of chance, fate and fortune. They each had temples in Rome so that those seeking divine favours could place their offerings and make vows to them. Felicitas also featured on Roman coins, suggesting a connection to financial prosperity. Coins with Felicitas were minted by emperors, for example, Felicitas Augustia was the golden coin of the emperor Valerian, suggesting he was the happiest man favoured by the gods. By claiming Felicitas, the baker may have been hoping for financial prosperity and the happiness to accompany it, helped by the goddesses, of course. He would either have lived through the earthquake of AD62 or died in it. Fellow Pompeians rebuilt the city. There was always the dread of what might happen against the backdrop of political turmoil in Pompei and disquiet in the Roman Empire itself. Life was filled with instability and looming disaster. Perhaps the plaque was an attempt to combat these fears.

We are not unlike the baker and his circumstances are not dissimilar to the world in which we live. We may not have to worry about Vesuvius if we don't live in the region of that still extremely active volcano, but we live in a world of wars with the threat of a nuclear catastrophe. At the time the baker was serving in his bakery, the followers of 'The Way' were turning the world upside down. The first followers of Jesus were known as 'The Way,' a name that echoes Jewish *halakha*, the way of life enshrined in the Torah, as well as the disciple's belief that Jesus was 'The Way' to God the Father. Theirs was a life of faith; they did not believe in fate or luck, nor did they trust in goddesses or money, but in Jesus, the only way. For them, security was found in the Most High, as was *Hic habitat felicitas.*

Memorable Quote:
"If you are living your life with a 'fate' mentality, I encourage you to switch to 'faith' instead. Get those faith juices flowing and start exercising those faith muscles. Don't sit by and watch your life float by as if you are a bystander; partner with God and expect His very best. THAT is His destiny for you."

Journaling Suggestion:
How I see my destiny in the light of a faith-based life or a fate belief system.

Memo for Meditation:
"Whoever dwells in the shelter of the Most High will rest in the shadow of the Almighty. I will say of the LORD, 'He is my refuge and my fortress, my God, in whom I trust.'" Psalm 91:1-2.

January 3

Motivational Idea: The Michelin Man - Happy Travelling

As a boy, I remember seeing the Michelin man outside a garage on my way to school. He always looked happy! But what's the story behind Bibendum, commonly referred to as the Michelin Man, a humanoid figure made of tyres and the mascot of the Michelin Tyre Company? The original Michelin Man was introduced at the Lyon Exhibition of 1894 where the Michelin Brothers had a stand. He is one of the oldest trademarks in the world and still on active duty. The Michelin Man is white because rubber tyres are naturally white. It was not until 1912 that carbon chemicals were mixed into the white tyres, which turned them black. By adding carbon, tyres became more durable.

Michelin also began reviewing restaurants so that more people would travel further distances in their cars to eat at these restaurants. This in turn would wear down their tyres faster, and force them to buy more. The star system that Michelin uses goes up to three and is broken down by whether or not it's worth driving to the restaurant. One star: *"A very good restaurant in its category."* Two star: *"Excellent cooking, worth a detour."* Three star: *"Exceptional cuisine, worth a special journey."* So it was happy histories all round. Michelin were happy with their sales trajectory and motorists were happy too, travelling with good safety tyres and eating in good restaurants. We may not all have Michelin tyres or even own a car, or eat in star-rated restaurants but we are all on the road of life, a busy road with bends and curves, hills and dales, and fast lanes, too. It's staggering when you see pictures posted by police of people with bald, defective tyres putting lives at risk. Faith in that which is defective and dangerous? How can we travel safely on the road of life and in the right direction? What's our faith in? There is a spiritual lesson here. When the rubber hits the road, we need to know who we can trust and direct us. We, too, can be happy travellers and satisfied souls as we travel on our journey. Take Jesus with you on your life's journey and feed on His word. Good company and good food – and don't forget to check your tyres!

Memorable Quote:

"Life in Christ is like travelling on a road with a predetermined destination. You are not the driver, Jesus is, and God provided the route on this one time trip. He plotted everything, the date and the time of your

travel and arrival. There will be stops and delays along the way, but remember this, at the bottom of a traffic light is always a green light." Anon

Journaling Suggestion:
What's my soul food?

Memo for Meditation:
"How sweet are your words to my taste, sweeter than honey to my mouth!" Psalm 119:103
"Sweeter also than honey and the drippings of the honeycomb." Psalm 19:10

January 4

Motivational Idea: Learning from the longest running study on happiness

The longest running study of happiness originated during the Great Depression. In 1938, researchers at Harvard measured the physical and mental health of 268 sophomores and, for 80 years, tracked these men and some of their descendants. Unfortunately, women weren't in the original study because the college was still all-male. Their main finding? *"Close relationships, more than money or fame… keep people happy throughout their lives."* This includes both a happy marriage and family, and a close community of supportive friends. Importantly, the relationships highlighted in the study were those based on love, care and equality, rather than abuse and exploitation. These ties protect people from life's discontents, help to delay mental and physical decline, and are better predictors of long and happy lives than social class, IQ, or even genes. That finding proved true across the board among both the Harvard men and the inner-city participants. This is also true in Biblical teaching on flourishing as a whole-of-life philosophy.

C S Lewis discovered that true happiness could only be found in a relationship with God. When he entered into this relationship, it changed his life. Lewis said, *"To believe in God and to pray, were the beginning of my extroversion. I had been taken out of myself."* After he embraced faith, Lewis broadened his circle of friends. He was drawn more and more to the writers and scholars at Oxford who shared his faith. The 'Inklings Group' began and this included his friend Tolkien. Lewis said, *"To belong to a group of real friends is to be armed against influences from without. The public opinion within the group may be tiny, but it matters more than the opinion of ten thousand outsiders."*

Motivational Quote:

"The surprising finding is that our relationships and how happy we are in our relationships has a powerful influence on our health. Taking care of your body is important, but tending to your relationships is a form of self-care too. That, I think, is the revelation." Robert Waldinger, Director of Study, Psychiatrist at Massachusetts General Hospital, and Professor of Psychiatry at Harvard Medical School.

Journaling Suggestion:

A relational focus today - building healthy relationships brings happiness.

Memo for Meditation:

"Happy are the people whose God is the LORD." Psalm 144:15.
"Rejoice in the Lord always. I will say it again: Rejoice! Let your gentleness be evident to all. The Lord is near." Philippians 4:5,6
"And let us not neglect our meeting together, as some people do, but encourage one another, especially now that the day of his return is drawing near." Hebrews 10:25

January 5

Motivational Idea: How to build a life and enhance happiness

Just as the Great Depression motivated Harvard's study, the global Covid pandemic inspired social scientist Arthur C Brooks to launch, in April 2020, a weekly column on happiness titled, *How to build a life.* The column aims to give us the tools we need to construct a life that feels full and meaningful – a flourishing life. Brooks blends cutting-edge research in behavioural science and neuroscience with philosophy and various wisdom traditions, including scripture. He teaches people from all walks of life how to have a better, happier life, and how to build it. The way Brooks sees it, happiness is a combination of enjoyment, satisfaction and purpose. His thinking comes from years of research from which he developed a number of equations resulting in four pillars that support his findings: family, faith, friends and work.

Brooks says that people have an inalienable right to pursue happiness but are not always good at the pursuit. Instead of putting their energy into the 'four pillars,' they chase the 'four idols' of money, power, pleasure and the admiration of others. This is the way most of society lives and Brooks admirably has made it his life's mission to turn the tide and to reorient society from these false idols, to help people live better and be kinder to one another during these fearful and terrifying times in the world's history. The Harvard Magazine referred to Brooks as, 'the happiness revolutionary,' and there is certainly a lot we can learn from him. He also writes from personal experience, having accomplished so much as a musician, among other things, but he found he wasn't thriving. Now he not only teaches happiness, he models happiness.

As a devout Catholic, Brooks believes in the importance of faith. However, he is aware that many do not believe and so he suggests that, *"Faith is anything transcendent that helps you escape the boring sitcom that is your life."* It can be meditation, it can be music, it can be anything that taps into that deep spiritual need in all of us. One would beg to differ with Brooks on this matter, and while music and other things can inspire us, we need our faith to be firmly rooted in the transcendent God of eternity Himself to live the truly flourishing life, in Jesus the God-Man.

Memorable Quote:
"Let your life reflect the faith you have in God. Fear nothing and pray about everything. Be strong, trust God's word, and trust the process."
Germany Kent

Journaling Suggestion:
Brooks says happiness is a combination of enjoyment, satisfaction and purpose. Flourishing is derived from investing in these and not the 'four idols' of money, power, pleasure and the admiration of others.

Memo for Meditation:
"But without faith it is impossible to [walk with God and] please Him, for whoever comes [near] to God must [necessarily] believe that God exists and that He rewards those who [earnestly and diligently] seek Him."
Hebrews 11:6

January 6

Motivational Idea: One man's history - how will you be remembered?

You really can make a difference to others in the way you live. Sam Magill from Banbridge, Co Down, was born on this day in 1924. He lived to see his 100th year and he is fondly remembered by all who knew him as *'Sam, the man with that big broad smile!'* He could drive but didn't, he preferred to walk. The reason being, he had a real passion and a deep compassion for others. He loved to meet people and engage with them, which he could better do on foot. He could not do enough for his family and all those around him. If a helping hand was needed, Sam was there with a warm word and an encouraging smile. Sam's open secret was his devotion to the Bible. His Bible was falling apart because it was so well used. He recorded in his notes that he was born again on 25th October 1945 and for over 77 years he walked with Jesus. His passion was for Jesus and his compassion for others stemmed from this passion. He exemplified what a true Christian really is. He found authentic happiness and, boy, did he show it! That's how he is remembered by all who knew him. His story is truly memorable!

Memorable Quote:
"When I was young, my ambition was to be one of the people who made a difference in this world. My hope is to leave the world a little better for having been there." Jim Henson, creator of *The Muppets, Fraggle Rock* and more

Journaling Suggestion:
What life story am I writing? Is it time for a new chapter?

Memo for Meditation:
"The reputation of the righteous becomes a sweet memorial to him, while the wicked life only leaves a rotten stench." Proverbs 10:7

January 7

Motivational Idea: Confucius, happiness and self-transformation

Confucius was named Kongqiu in 551 BC at his birth near Qufu, in eastern China. It is believed his family may have been aristocratic, but fell on hard times. Perhaps, like many, it was his life experiences that propelled Confucius into the joy of study. We find that the Analects (a collection of literary extracts) of Confucius focused not only on book learning, but also on social relationships. His passion was the great virtue of humanity and learning about humanity, and trying to emulate this great virtue in our lives. He also found great joy in the company of fellow travellers on the great path of *dao*; *dao* means 'a way' or 'a path'. He used the term *dao* to speak of the way human beings ought to behave in society and saw it as an ethical or moral way.

Confucius detests those who unfailingly do the right thing for the sake of social approbation, and not self-cultivation. Instead of 'rejoicing in virtue' these people steal virtue and use it as a cloak. Confucius was perhaps the earliest figure to argue that we have the power to transform ourselves. He insisted that his followers had the power to become a *junzi*, or noble person, a title which originally referred to a son of the aristocracy. It didn't matter who your parents were – if you did not cultivate your humanity, you were not worthy of the title.

In Confucianism, the ideal personality is the *sheng*, translated as 'saint' or 'sage'. Since sagacity is hard to attain, he used the term *junzi* which more individuals could achieve by acting according to proper conduct. The junzi embodies humanity, one who possesses a totality of the highest human qualities, always helping others. We all know that self-transformation is possible. However, the teaching of Jesus shows us that we need spiritual new birth to experience ultimate transformation.

Memorable Quote:
"Change is something we all need. It is an ongoing part of life. With its constant flux, life demands adjustments for our schedules and plans.

Essentially, change is the new norm. We need constant transformation, but real change starts with new life, not just a new leaf, and living a new life." Adapted

Journaling Suggestion:
Confucian transformation compared to Christological transformation.

Memo for Meditation:
"Anyone who belongs to Christ is a new person. The past is forgotten, and everything is new." 2 Corinthians 5:17
See what great love the Father has lavished on us, that we should be called children of God! And that is what we are! The reason the world does not know us is that it did not know him." 1 John 3:1

January 8

Motivational Idea: Buddhism – happiness in purposelessness?

Buddha, the former prince Siddhartha Gautama, emphasised that purposelessness is good because of the devastation of disappointment. His journey led him to conclude that we suffer because we desire things that are impermanent. Purposelessness is also seen as good because it brings emancipation through emptiness. Experiencing emptiness means the present is lived free from anxiety, selfish desire and ignorance, with nothing gained or lost. Recognizing that life comes to us empty and without inherent purpose means not only freedom from attachment but also freedom for creativity, like that of an artist. Buddhist awareness of the immediate 'thusness' of all existence is seen as the way to nirvanic joy. Christianity, on the other hand, gives the opposite answer about our human existence.

We have been created by God for a purpose, and this purposefulness is good and permanent as it is found in knowing God the Creator. We fallen humans can be restored to our intended purpose through God, remaking us into the likeness of Jesus, the Divine Son of God who added to Himself a human nature and lived among us, being and showing us what it meant to be a true human. It was Jesus's sacrificial death on the cross that brought about justification and life (Romans 5:18) for us, being united with Him in His death and resurrection (Romans 6:5). Rather than emptiness, life is lived in all its fullness. (John 10:10).

Now that we can be restored to Christlikeness and union with God in Christ, all of creation has reason to be hopeful that it, too, will experience restoration when He returns as He promised. You have a real purpose! Be creative!

Memorable Quote:
"Why do humans exist? What is our ultimate purpose? A person will arrive at wildly different answers depending on whether they've been spending more time under the cross of Christ or under the 'Bodhi Tree'. On the one hand, there is Christianity's robust sense of purposefulness, as humans were created by God for a purpose — eternal life in union with God. On the other hand, there is Buddhism's view that life is fundamentally impermanent and ultimately without purpose." Daniel McCoy

Journaling Suggestion:
A life of purposefulness or purposelessness.

Memo for Meditation:
"I keep my eyes always on the Lord. With him at my right hand, I will not be shaken. Therefore, my heart is glad and my tongue rejoices; my body also will rest secure, because you will not abandon me to the realm of the dead, nor will you let your faithful one see decay. You make known to me the path of life; you will fill me with joy in your presence, with eternal pleasures at your right hand." Psalm 16:8-11

January 9

Motivational Idea: Epicureanism and the 'pleasure principle'

Epicurus (341-270 BC) was a moderate, and not a hedonist, viewing life's highest goals as physical and intellectual pleasure, and emotional calm. *"Nature's wealth is easy to procure,"* he said, *"but the wealth of vain fancies recedes to an infinite distance. When we say pleasure is the end and aim, we do not mean the pleasures of the prodigal or the pleasures of sensuality. By pleasure we mean the absence of pain in the body and of trouble in the soul. It is not an unbroken succession of drinking-bouts and of revelry; it is sober reasoning and banishing those beliefs through which the greatest tumults take possession of the soul."*

Epicurus believed the gods to be almost infinitely distant limited beings made from the same atomic stuff as humans, who, in their divine equanimity, didn't care about evil and had no real effect on the world. Death for humans is seen as the end, total cessation of existence, no after-life, no divine punishment. *"Death, therefore, the most awful of evils, is nothing to us, seeing that, when we are, death is not come, and, when death is come, we are not."*

We can see these ideas reflected today in similar guise, relax, enjoy life, don't worry so much, and don't be too bothered about God. No accountability and no judgement after death. We are just made of atoms destined to disintegrate at death. Paul met Epicureans on Mars Hill in Athens (Acts 17.16-34). When he spoke of Jesus and the resurrection of the dead, some laughed, but others brought him to the Areopagus to talk further and some believed. There were stoics there, too.

Memorable Quote:
"Ultimately, what Epicureanism taught was a 'fulfilled' life free from pain, hunger, distress, worry—and God. Considering the gods the Greeks knew—violent, lusty, and capricious super-humans—they maybe aren't to be condemned for seeking to cast off the deities. But the Epicureans didn't understand that a fulfilled life can't happen without the Creator-God who loves us and saved us. It is good to have bread and friends. It is better to have the Bread of Life (John 6:35,48) and the Friend who made the ultimate sacrifice for us." John 15.13-15, taken from *Got Questions*

Journaling Suggestion:
The basis of a fulfilled life from the Epicurean viewpoint and the Christian perspective.

Memo for Meditation:
"When they heard Paul speak about the resurrection of the dead, some laughed in contempt, but others said, 'We want to hear more about this later.' That ended Paul's discussion with them, but some joined him and became believers." Acts 17:32-34b.

January 10

Motivational Idea: Stoicism and the cardinal virtues

Stoicism is popular with many readers today and is well worth knowing. Many have referred to the similarities with Christianity and that certainly is the case. So, we will give a bit of time to stoicism over the next few days and learn more about its commonalities with Christianity and also where it diverges. The Stoics referred to the four corners known as the cardinal virtues. It was their belief that these virtues led to a better, happier and a more fulfilled and flourishing life. The four virtues of stoicism are: courage, temperance, wisdom and justice. These are great virtues to aspire to and to build one's life foursquare upon, up to a point. The Stoics were interested in what is termed 'eudaimonia' – a life worth living, or a flourishing life. For its exponents, Seneca, Epictetus and Marcus Aurelius, the point of philosophy was the application of the four virtues of stoicism in practical ethics – it was a study of how to best live life.

Courage is the ability to act in situations where we feel fear. It is not the absence of fear, it is the ability to act despite fear. Temperance can mean moderation, but is more akin to self-discipline or self-control. For Marcus Aurelius, the most important virtue is justice, how to act well in relation to other people, the interactions, and the obligations of being a human being. Wisdom, though, stands out as the virtue around which all the other cardinal virtues revolve. Like Aristotle, the Stoics were concerned with applying virtue in real life, and without wisdom that was difficult. Practical wisdom meant using philosophy to understand how to act and respond in all situations, good and bad. Much food for thought here.

Memorable Quote:

"To achieve this, we have to apply the four cardinal virtues. We need temperance and courage to pursue our own interests. We need justice out of concern for other people's interests and finally, we need wisdom to deal with the inevitable conflicts. And although these are discreet virtues, they are also unified... it is difficult to have one virtue and not the others."
Tim Lake

Journaling Suggestion:

Living a life of courage, temperance, wisdom and justice in my world.

Memo for Meditation:
"He has told you, O mortal, what is good; And what does the LORD require of you except to be just, to love, and to diligently practise kindness (compassion), and to walk humbly with your God setting aside any overblown sense of importance or self-righteousness." Micah 6:8

January 11

Motivational Idea: Stoicism

The first rule – control. *Who* is in control?

Stoic philosophy is one of the few ancient schools of philosophy that people can apply to their day-to-day lives. Such is its practicality and simplicity that it provides a framework on which to build a resilient and constructive personal philosophy of life, and help to answer the basic question of stoicism, namely, *"How can we live a good life?"* The first stoic rule is: accept what you can and cannot control. This is one of the most fundamental principles of stoicism, having the ability to distinguish between what you can control and what you cannot. Epictetus said, *"There is only one way to happiness and that is to cease worrying about things which are beyond the power of our will."* He elaborates further: *"The chief task in life is simply this: to identify and separate matters so that I can say clearly to myself which are externals not under my control, and which have to do with the choices I actually control. Where then do I look for good and evil? Not to uncontrollable externals, but within myself to the choices that are my own."*

The argument is, if we get this right, we are in a position to remove the ability of external forces outside our control to impact our peace of mind, and we're free to focus our efforts on the areas of life we can control; this essentially makes us far more resilient and effective as individuals. On the other hand, to get this wrong we are allowing things in the world around us to influence our well-being, our peace of mind is shattered and we are pulled in all directions by anything around us that captures our attention. Many seek to practise this approach to life, and some can even attain this level of stoical maturity. However, given the world we live in, it seems it's becoming increasingly difficult to achieve, especially when our social media gives us up-to-date news and video footage from around the world in nanoseconds. This points up one of the inherent differences between Christianity and stoicism: stoics think of human reason and virtue as being necessary and sufficient for a flourishing life. It's about self-reliance. Christianity, by contrast, acknowledges that faith in God is necessary, and that reason or virtue are insufficient because of the inherent flaws in our human nature. The answer is Christ-reliance.

Memorable Quote:
"Faith is a living, daring confidence in God's grace, so sure and certain that a man could stake his life on it a thousand times." Martin Luther

Journaling Suggestion:
Self-improvement or Spirit empowerment?

Memo for Meditation:
"The LORD is my light and my salvation; whom shall I fear? The LORD is the strength of my life; of whom shall I be afraid?" Psalm 27:1

January 12

Motivational Idea: Stoicism

The second rule – accept fate

For the stoic, the second rule applies in the unravelling of life events. It's referred to as the concept of Amor Fati, or love of fate. Epictetus said: *"Do not seek for things to happen the way you want them to; rather, wish that what happens happen the way it happens: then you will be happy."* Nietzsche said, *"My formula for greatness in a human being is amor fati. That one wants nothing to be different, not forward, not backwards, not in all eternity. Not merely bear what is necessary, still less conceal it...but love it."* Nietzsche, the ultimate determinist, linked Amor Fati to the concept of eternal recurrence. If you were to have to repeat the same actions as in the past, you would do them the same way. In other words, be at one with your fate and give your actions the weight of eternity. Instead of resisting fate, fighting it tooth and nail, learn to accept and love it. Nietzsche was, however, critical of stoicism for seeking to preserve scope for moral responsibility whilst living in a deterministic universe. Stoics tend to believe that fate and free-will are compatible (a form of compatibilism).

It has been argued that the basic flaw in Amor Fati is that one cannot truly love one's fate in the face of existential crisis. We cannot truly love painful situations. Fate that involves suffering cannot merit a similar response. We cannot truly love to remain in pain. Instead, we truly love to immediately liberate ourselves from that very painful circumstance of our life. Therefore, the love that Amor Fati demands cannot be seen as true love. For the Christian, fate is not fatalistic, life is not an outcome of a predetermined course of events. God gives us the freedom to make choices that control our destiny. Our temporal destiny, in large part, is also based on our choices. Our eternal destiny is based on the choices we make now.

Christians see life's events from the perspective that God is the author and sustainer of our life, find our joy in relationship with Him, and look to Him continually in total dependence. We are not made to navigate life without God, rather we are to gain God's peace and His sustaining and healing power to navigate through life's terrain, and its darkest moments, too.

Memorable Quote:
"Are you fate-driven or are you faith-driven?"

Journaling Suggestion:
How am I navigating life's terrain, and do I need to change?

Memo for Meditation:
"For I know the plans I have for you declares the Lord, plans to prosper you and not to harm you, plans to give you a hope and a future." Jeremiah 29:11

January 13

Motivational Idea: Stoicism

The third rule – accept death

Stoics employed the principle 'Memento Mori,' meaning, 'Remember you must die'. This was not morbid; rather, it was designed for beauty, gratitude and fulfilment of life. The reminder of death can enable us to appreciate life. The awareness that we have a limited time on earth to experience the activities of life for a finite number of times can create an intense feeling of gratitude in the moment; it can also incentivise us to stop taking things for granted, avoid petty arguments, and ignore minor annoyances, and instead become more deliberate with our days because it's a limited resource.

The realisation of our mortality can help us focus on what's important. Marcus Aurelius said, *"You could leave life right now. Let that determine what you do and say and think."* Solomon's take on this was: *"Better to go to the house of mourning than to go to the house of feasting, for that is the end of all men; And the living will take it to heart. Sorrow is better than laughter, for by a sad countenance the heart is made better."* Ecclesiastes 7:2-3. The Psalmist David prayed, *"So teach us to number our days, That we may apply our hearts unto wisdom. Return, O LORD, how long? And let it repent thee concerning thy servants. O satisfy us early with thy mercy; That we may rejoice and be glad all our days."* Psalm 90:17.

Memorable Quote:
"MAN IS UNWILLING to consider the subject of death. The shroud, the mattock and the grave, he labours to keep continually out of sight. He would live here always if he could; and since he cannot, he at least will put away every emblem of death as far as possible from his sight. Perhaps there is no subject so important, which is so little thought of. Our common proverb that we use is just the expression of our thoughts, "We must live." But if we were wiser we should alter it and say, "We must die." C H Spurgeon, based on Deuteronomy 32:29

Journaling Suggestion:
Being aware of my own mortality can incentivise me to live the abundant life here and now – life to the full (John 10:10) and then forever. This mortal will put in immortality.

Memo for Meditation:
"Don't let the excitement of youth cause you to forget your Creator. Honour him in your youth before you grow old and say, 'Life is not pleasant anymore.' Remember him before the light of the sun, moon, and stars is dim to your old eyes, and rain clouds continually darken your

sky...Remember him before the door to life's opportunities is closed and the sound of work fades. Now you rise at the first chirping of the birds, but then all their sounds will grow faint... Here now is my final conclusion: Fear God and obey his commands, for this is everyone's duty." Ecclesiastes ch12.

January 14

Motivational Idea: Stoicism

The fourth rule – accept that happiness is your responsibility

Epictetus said, *"If you want something good, get it from yourself."* Yet one of the things that blocks all routes to growth is that we blame others for our problems, and take no responsibility; we are off the hook and it's the road to no town. In the long run, an inability to accept responsibility generally means an inability to accept that we need to do something different, so as the years go by, instead of growing we stagnate and the same problems abide year after year. So, if we get it right we can move on. The inherent problem we face is that it is all about self, the god of self. That's where Christianity comes in to rescue us from ourselves. The memo for the day from Peter elaborates on this with an insight that can only come from above.

Memorable Quote:
"If we serve the god of self, we cannot know God. As long as we are looking inward we cannot see the One who is above us, and who invites us to know Him."

Journaling Suggestion:
Avoiding stagnation and living to please God.

Memo for Meditation:
From Simon Peter, a servant and apostle of Jesus Christ: *"I write this to you whose experience with God is as life-changing as ours, all due to our God's straight dealing and the intervention of our God and Saviour, Jesus Christ. Grace and peace to you many times over as you deepen in your experience with God and Jesus, our Master. Everything that goes into a life of pleasing God has been miraculously given to us by getting to know,*

personally and intimately, the One who invited us to God. The best invitation we ever received! We were also given absolutely terrific promises to pass on to you – your tickets to participation in the life of God after you turned your back on a world corrupted by lust. So don't lose a minute in building on what you've been given, complementing your basic faith with good character, spiritual understanding, alert discipline, passionate patience, reverent wonder, warm friendliness, and generous love, each dimension fitting into and developing the others. With these qualities active and growing in your lives, no grass will grow under your feet, no day will pass without its reward as you mature in your experience of our Master Jesus. Without these qualities you can't see what's right before you, oblivious that your old sinful life has been wiped off the books. So, friends, confirm God's invitation to you, his choice of you. Don't put it off; do it now. Do this, and you'll have your life on a firm footing, the streets paved and the way wide open into the eternal kingdom of our Master and Saviour, Jesus Christ." 2 Peter 1:1-11

January 15

Motivational Idea: Stoicism

The fifth rule – accept that life is change

We live in a world of change and the fifth rule of stoicism makes sense: we need to accept that things change and we need to change, yet change can be terrifying. Marcus Aurelius said, *"Frightened of change? But what can exist without it? What's closer to nature's heart? Can you take a hot bath and leave the firewood as it was? Eat food without transforming it? Can any vital process take place without something being changed? Can't you see? It's just the same with you, and just as vital to nature."*

We tend to resist change because we like things to fit into our mental framework of how things should be. Change and unfamiliarity risks destabilisation and perhaps that is why some people live in the past. Given that change is inevitable, if we don't learn to be flexible in the face of change, it has the potential to break us, hence the wisdom of the fifth rule. It's a familiar phrase, 'people hate change'. But is that really true? It's not entirely true. We enjoy familiarity and routines but most people welcome new things, new adventures, new technology

21

and, *'We should go to that new coffee shop.'* Oh yes! Perhaps it's not change that we resist so much as being changed ourselves. It's not that we don't *like* change, we just don't *want* to change.

Change is at the heart of Christianity. To become a Christian, we accept the truth that we need to change. We know we are broken people whom God can make new through Christ. Not only us as individuals, but we believe that God is going to make *all* things new. There is also a cosmic change coming. God not only wants to change a person's non-Christian status to that of Christian, but He also wants to change and develop those who are Christians to change and grow to be more like Jesus – the truly flourishing life.

Memorable Quote:
"We can often fall into a dangerous complacency as Christians. Content to simply have an identity as a Christian, we fail to rigorously and tenaciously pursue this Christ-likeness. But the Holy Spirit and the Word of God unsettle us with a holy discontentment. Here, aware of our nonconformity to Christ, we are prodded forward in sanctification. We see that it's God's will and his work to make us more like Christ." Erik Raymond

Journaling Suggestion:
My current status and the positive changes needed to live a fulfilled life.

Memo for Meditation:
"This means that anyone who belongs to Christ has become a new person. The old life is gone; a new life has begun!" 2 Corinthians 5:17

January 16

Motivational Idea: Life, liberty and the pursuit of happiness

The unanimous Declaration (The Declaration of Independence) of the thirteen United States of America, July 4 1776, includes the following: *"We hold these truths to be self-evident, that all men are created equal, that they are endowed by their Creator with certain unalienable Rights, that among these are Life, Liberty and the pursuit of Happiness."* Thomas Jefferson took the phrase *"pursuit of happiness"* from John Locke (1632-1704), a major English philosopher, and incorporated it into his famous statement of a people's inalienable right to "Life, Liberty, and the pursuit of Happiness." This inalienable right to the pursuit of happiness has led millions down many roads, and indeed many cul-de-sacs, too. It has been assumed that for Jefferson, the "pursuit of happiness" was really a euphemism for the pursuit of wealth. From this perspective, Jefferson's vision of happiness was seen as the 'rags to riches' version of the good life. Jefferson stated he was an Epicurean, who has been regarded as an 'egoistic hedonist'. However, it is argued that he was not a proponent of the 'rags to riches' view of happiness. Far from it. He was what one writer has referred to as the 'riches within rags' view of happiness. Simply put, if you cultivated close friendships, limited your desires to the essential necessities of life, and rejoiced in the moment, happiness was yours to keep. What are we in pursuit of today?

Memorable Quote:
"If Jefferson really was an Epicurean, the third of his unalienable human rights is much more than a veiled glorification of the rat race."

Journaling Suggestion:
Rejection of over-indulgence helps our peace of mind.

Memo for Meditation:
"But godliness with contentment is great gain. For we brought nothing into the world, and we can take nothing out of it. But if we have food and clothing, we will be content with that. Those who want to get rich fall into temptation and a trap and into many foolish and harmful desires that plunge people into ruin and destruction. For the love of money is a root of all kinds of evil. Some people, eager for money, have wandered from the faith and pierced themselves with many griefs. But you, man of God, flee from all this, and pursue righteousness, godliness, faith, love, endurance and gentleness." 1 Timothy 6:6-11

January 17

Motivational Idea: What's in a name?

We come across many names in the recorded history of Israel. More often than not, each name has a specific meaning. One example of this is that of an ancient biblical name, Gaddiel, of the house of Zebulun. He was one of the spies sent to Canaan prior to the crossing of the River Jordan. His name means *Goat of God; the Lord my happiness.* You can read all about it in Numbers, chapter 13. Basically, 12 spies were sent, and two came back with a glowing and positive report. However, 10 came back with a negative report. When Israel heard of the Nephilim living in the land and the words of Gaddiel and his fellow spies *("We seemed like grasshoppers in our own eyes"),* they were terrified and were not going anywhere. A journey of 11 days turned into the wilderness wanderings of forty years. This man, goat of God, The Lord is my happiness, certainly did not live up to his name; his attitude was that of seeing a problem in every solution, his happiness was not in God; if it had been, his report would have been the same as Caleb and Joshua. Caleb tried to quiet the people as they stood before Moses. *"Let's go at once to take the land,"* he said. *"We can certainly conquer it!"* Caleb's name means 'wholehearted' and he lived up to his name. The name Jesus also has an amazing meaning: 'God is salvation – God who saves His people from their sins, and He does live up to His Name.'

Memorable Quote:
Go forth today knowing that in God is your source of strength and happiness.

Journaling Suggestion:
Count my blessings. *"Man likes to count his troubles rather than his happinesses."* Fyodor Dostoevsky

Memo for Meditation:
"Look! He has placed the land in front of you. Go and occupy it as the LORD, the God of your ancestors, has promised you. Don't be afraid! Don't be discouraged!" Deuteronomy 1:21

January 18

Motivational Idea: Seligman and the peaks of lasting fulfilment

Martin Seligman, born in 1942, is known as the father of Positive Psychology, where happiness is viewed as having three dimensions to cultivate. For us to appreciate what he calls 'the pleasant life', we need to learn to appreciate basic pleasures such as companionship, the natural world and our physical needs. In order to achieve 'the good life', we need to discover our unique virtues and strengths, and then use these creatively to enhance our lives. Modern theories of self-esteem suggest that we need to discover value within ourselves for life to be satisfying. One of the best ways of discovering this value is by nourishing our unique strengths in contributing to the happiness of our fellow humans. Consequently, the final stage, 'the meaningful life', is where we find a deep sense of fulfilment by employing our unique strengths for a purpose greater than ourselves.

Seligman's theory reconciles two conflicting views of human happiness: the individualistic approach, which emphasises that we should take care of ourselves nurturing our own strengths, and the altruistic approach, downplaying individuality and emphasising sacrifice for the greater purpose. From a Christian perspective, positive psychology strives for what God designed humanity to enjoy but goes further. Christianity ministers to our deepest needs. God created us; He loves us, seeks our good, and wants us to flourish in a relationship with him, of worship, love and grateful receptivity. However, Christianity also teaches that we have turned from our Creator to find fulfilment without him, so we are disordered by sin, suffering and damage. Nevertheless, God has revealed in the Bible a new way of spiritual and psychological healing through Jesus Christ and the highest peaks of lasting fulfilment.

Memorable Quote:
"We discover in the Bible the inspired beginnings of a psychology focused on the most important things in life: God as the ultimate beauty, goodness, and truth of the universe; what's most wrong with human beings; what divine restoration looks like; the basics of ethics and spirituality; and communion with God and neighbour as the highest goals of life."

Journaling Suggestion:
Finding fulfilment in a pleasant, good and meaningful life in God's way and plan.

Memo for Meditation:
"You will show me the path of life; In Your presence is fullness of joy; At Your right hand are pleasures forevermore." Psalm 16:11.

January 19

Motivational Idea: the transformational power of positive emotions

Barbara L. Fredrickson began studying positive emotions in 1998. Her foundational research led her to develop a theory on positive emotions called Broaden and Build Theory. Her research defines positivity and how it can transform people's lives. At that time, research showed an approximate 3:1 ratio of positivity as being ideal in terms of high-functioning teams, and relationships. (This is sometimes referred to as the Losada Ratio). Fredrickson explains how experiencing positive emotions to negative emotions in this approximate ratio leads people to achieve optimal levels of well-being and resilience. This scientific discovery was groundbreaking in beginning the discussions on how a positive state of mind can enhance relationships, improve health, relieve depression, and broaden the mind. The theory also suggests that negative emotions serve the opposite function of positive ones. When threatened with negative emotions like anxiety, fear, frustration or anger, the mind constricts and focuses in on the imposing threat (real or imagined), thus limiting one's ability to be open to new ideas and build resources and relationships.

Fredrickson draws on the imagery of the water lily to beautifully illustrate her theory: *"Just as water lilies retract when sunlight fades, so do our minds when positivity fades."* The work of Fredrickson and her colleagues has had a great impact on the science of happiness. For Christians, we know that the even greater news is that we human beings who long for lasting love can know and experience a greater love, the agape love of God in a personal relationship with Him. It's a love that is unconditional and never wanes. The Apostle John tells us about this in our memo for today. We need human love, but we also need to embrace Divine love.

Memorable Quote:
"Love is a momentary upwelling of three tightly interwoven events: First, a sharing of one or more positive emotions between you and another; second, a synchrony between you and the other person's biochemistry and behaviours; and third, a reflective motive to invest in each other's well-being that brings mutual care." Fredrickson

Journaling Suggestion:
Being a recipient of a love that never fails.

Memo for Meditation:
"God showed how much he loved us by sending his one and only Son into the world so that we might have eternal life through him. This is real love—not that we loved God, but that he loved us and sent his Son as a sacrifice to take away our sins. Dear friends, since God loved us that much, we surely ought to love each other. No one has ever seen God. But if we love each other, God lives in us, and his love is brought to full expression in us." 1 John 4:9-12

January 20

Motivational Idea: Finding the true meaning of life

Viktor Emil Frankl (1905-1997) was concerned with satisfaction and fulfilment in life: *"Striving to find meaning in one's life is the primary motivational force in man."* Frankl was an Austrian neurologist, psychiatrist and Holocaust survivor, who devoted his life to studying, understanding and promoting 'meaning'. In his book, *Man's Search for Meaning,* Frankl tells his story of how he survived the Holocaust by finding personal meaning in the experience, which gave him the will to live through it. Frankl pointed to research indicating a strong relationship between 'meaninglessness' and criminal behaviours, addictions and depression. Without meaning, people fill the void with hedonistic pleasures, power, materialism, hatred, boredom, or neurotic obsessions and compulsions. Frankl also said that some may also strive for 'Supra Meaning', the ultimate meaning in life, a spiritual kind of meaning that depends solely on a greater power outside of personal or external control. Corrie ten Boom, another Holocaust survivor, believed in the sovereignty of God and rejoiced in her hope as a believer in Christ.

Suffering does not bear witness to 'human potential', but to the gospel, to Christ's death on the cross, and resurrection, His victory over sin and death. The 'ultimate meaning' of suffering is not left to idle speculation about some higher level of life; this brings little comfort (or none). God has revealed much of His plan and purposes for man. He has given us the history of man, the account of creation, man's fall into sin, and God's glorious plan of redemption that has been fulfilled in the life of Christ. He has given the believer an assurance of the future hope of glory, eternal life with Him. He has revealed to man that history will one day be consummated, with the return of Christ and the final overthrow of all evil. Frankl's system contains no hint of this glorious hope, but rather leaves man to his own hopelessly inadequate imaginations and bearing his own burdens.

Memorable Quote:

"Worrying is carrying tomorrow's load with today's strength – carrying two days at once. It is moving into tomorrow ahead of time. Worrying doesn't empty tomorrow of its sorrow, it empties today of its strength."
Corrie ten Boom, *The Hiding Place*

Journaling Suggestion:
Embracing the God of hope in the everyday experiences of life.

Memo for Meditation:
"In this you greatly rejoice, though now for a little while, if need be, you have been grieved by various trials, that the genuineness of your faith, being much more precious than gold that perishes, though it is tested by fire, may be found to praise, honour, and glory at the revelation of Jesus Christ." 1 Peter 1:6, 7

January 21

Motivational Idea: A joy beyond comprehension

Corrie ten Boom, the joyful hero of the Holocaust, concentration camp survivor, and author was born in Haarlem in the Netherlands, on 15th April 1892. Her grandfather, Willem ten Boom, had opened a watchmaker's shop there in 1837. In 1844, he began a weekly prayer service to pray for the Jewish people, who even then experienced discrimination in Europe. Willem's son Casper continued that tradition. When her mother died in 1921, Corrie apprenticed as a watchmaker. In 1922, she was named the first woman in Holland to be licensed as a watchmaker. Over the years, the ten Booms took care of many refugee children and orphans. Corrie taught Bible classes and Sunday school, and was active in organising Christian clubs for Dutch children. During the German Blitzkrieg across Europe in May 1940, Corrie turned their home into a safe haven for people trying to escape the Nazis. The hideout worked well for nearly four years, but on 28th February 28 1944 an informant betrayed the operation to the Gestapo. Several members of the ten Boom family were arrested, and Corrie and her sister Betsie ended up in Ravensbruck concentration camp near Berlin. Living conditions were brutal, with meagre rations and harsh discipline. Even so, Betsie and Corrie conducted secret prayer services in their barracks, using a smuggled Dutch Bible. The women voiced prayers and hymns in whispers to avoid the attention of the guards. On 16th December 1944, Betsie died at Ravensbruck of starvation and lack of medical care. Two weeks after Betsie's death, Corrie was released from the camp, thanks to claims of a 'clerical error'. Shortly after her release, all of the other women in her age group at Ravensbruck were executed. From the 1950s through the 1970s, Corrie ten Boom travelled to 64 countries, speaking about the joy she found in her Saviour and preaching the Gospel of saving grace and forgiveness in Jesus Christ her Lord. Her 1971 book, *The Hiding Place*, became a best-seller, and in 1975, World Wide Pictures released a movie version. One of her most famous phrases is *"Never be afraid to trust an unknown future to a known God."*

Memorable Quote:
"... [we] must tell them what we have learned here. We must tell them that there is no pit so deep that He [God] is not deeper still. They will listen to us, Corrie, because we have been here." Betsie's last words

Journaling Suggestion:
Finding good role models; who is mine? Consider Corrie ten Boom as a good role model.

Memo for Meditation:
"You are my hiding place; you will protect me from trouble and surround me with songs of deliverance." Psalm 32:7

January 22

Motivational Idea: A train journey that led to an inspired life

Corrie ten Boom, the watchmaker's daughter, tells that as a small child she heard a word that she didn't understand. When she wrote the

English version of her book, she chose to translate it as 'sexsin'. Here's what she reveals about what her father told her when she sat next to him in a train compartment: *"I suddenly asked, 'Father, what is sexsin?' He turned to look at me, as he always did when answering a question, but to my surprise he said nothing. At last he stood up, lifted his travelling case off the floor and set it on the floor. 'Will you carry it off the train, Corrie?' he said. I stood up and tugged at it. It was crammed with the watches and spare parts he had purchased that morning. 'It's too heavy,' I said. 'Yes,' he said, 'and it would be a pretty poor father who would ask his little girl to carry such a load. It's the same way, Corrie, with knowledge. Some knowledge is too heavy for children. When you are older and stronger, you can bear it. For now you must trust me to carry it for you."* Casper ten Boom was indeed a wise father. Life is like a train journey. As Len Magee used to sing, *"The train goes down the track, there ain't no turning back, life is just the same, there ain't no two way lane; when you reach the end and eternity just begins, which station will your train be in?"*

Corrie took quite a journey in her lifetime, a journey she records in her book, *The Hiding Place.* But she learned a lesson that day that stood her in good stead in the bitter and sweet experiences of life. She learned that a greater Father than Casper, her Heavenly Father, could be trusted to carry her burdens. She placed her faith in God, knowing in the unknowing that God would never let her down and in the end the full picture would be made known. *"All things work together for good to those who know God and are called according to His purpose."* (Romans 8:28). No wonder she lit up the room with her joyous serene presence as Jesus shone upon her and through her.

Memorable Quote:
"When a train goes through a tunnel and it gets dark, you don't throw away the ticket and jump off. You sit still and trust the engineer." Corrie ten Boom

Journaling Suggestion:
Innocence is worth protecting. And we have a Father who carries our burdens.

Memo for Meditation:
"See how very much our Father loves us, for he calls us his children, and that is what we are! But the people who belong to this world don't

recognize that we are God's children because they don't know him. Dear friends, we are already God's children, but he has not yet shown us what we will be like when Christ appears. But we do know that we will be like him, for we will see him as he really is. And all who have this eager expectation will keep themselves pure, just as he is pure." 1 John 3:1-3

January 23

Motivational Idea: talking the walk of life

In the 19th century, walking for pleasure grew in popularity with city dwellers heading into the open countryside to get away from pollution and the stresses of daily life. Hills of happiness! Eventually, the Ramblers Association was officially created in 1935, and since then they have been doing everything, they can to make sure everyone everywhere can enjoy nature on foot. The first mention of waking in the Bible is a fascinating glimpse into how things were at the beginning of the world. The first humans *"heard the sound of the LORD God as He was walking in the garden in the cool of the day."* (Genesis 3:8). Rather than enjoy the immediate presence of God, they tried to hide because they had sinned. From that day to this, the Creator of the universe has been seeking to walk with humankind. He provided a way back to fellowship at the cross when Jesus took our sins upon Himself. The cross is the central event in world history: *"all before looked forward from the day of the promise."* (Genesis 3:15), and all history now looks back to the day God made a way for us to walk with Him in fellowship. The Bible refers time and time again to this walk. God said to Abraham: *"I am God Almighty; walk before me, and be blameless."* (Genesis 17:1-2). David could say, *"Even though I walk through the darkest valley, I will fear no evil, for you are with me; your rod and your staff, they comfort me."* (Psalm 23). In the Gospel of Matthew, we read, *"One day as Jesus was walking along the shore of the Sea of Galilee, he saw two brothers—Simon, also called Peter, and Andrew—throwing a net into the water, for they fished for a living. Jesus called out to them, 'Come, follow me, and I will show you how to fish for people!' And they left their nets at once and followed him."* (Matthew 4:18-20). And throughout the New Testament, we are exhorted to walk with God. *"So I say, walk by the Spirit, and you will not gratify the desires of the flesh."* (Galatians 5:16).

Being a rambler in the countryside can be a wonderful happy experience of getting away from it all, yet the actual word 'ramble' means proceeding without a specific goal, purpose or direction. We are invited to walk with God not to get away from it all but to walk by faith through the pollution and stresses of everyday life, with a goal and a destination that's sure. It's literally the walk of life! Do the walk of life with God.

Memorable Quote:
"Those who walk with God always reach their destination." Henry Ford

Journaling Suggestion:
Taking the walk of life with God – what does it look like and what does it mean?

Memo for Meditation:
"...Walk humbly in the company of your God." Micah 6:8.

January 24

Motivational Idea: Happiness in the upside-down kingdom

Tucked away in the Book of Isaiah (700BC), we find a beautiful prophetic poem. *"How beautiful upon the mountains are the feet of Him who brings good news, who publishes peace, who brings good news of happiness, who publishes salvation, who says to Zion, 'Your God reigns.'"* (Isaiah 52:7). The powerful Northern Babylonian Kingdom had utterly destroyed Jerusalem; God's temple lay in ruins and many were carried into exile. So, what's the 'good news'? Yet the watchman speaks of one with beautiful feet, denoting a beautiful message. In spite of everything, the good news is that God still reigns. Fast forward to Jesus announcing the good news of the kingdom, the Euangelion, the Gospel! The people heard Him joyfully as He proclaimed the Gospel of repentance and forgiveness of sins in the kingdom of love and grace. The religious leaders were not happy with this upside-down kingdom; they looked for a king who would destroy all their enemies. So, they killed the king and He allowed them to because of His sacrificial love. He died to destroy the powerful enemies of sin and death, and rose again.

Jesus, the eternal king, restores peace to us by the blood of His cross, and the world will only know real peace when the Prince of Peace returns. This is the good news! He is the soon-to-come king, to rule and reign on this earth. Every wrong will be made right and every injustice dealt with by the court of divine justice.

Today, Jesus calls us to give our allegiance to Him, to proclaim Him our king and announce this good news to the world. In reality, this is the right way up kingdom; it's the world's kingdoms that are upside-down with corruption, sin and evil. Which king will you give allegiance to today? Which kingdom will you choose to serve? It is staring us in the face – look around you, look up! Our redemption draws near! The King is coming! Get ready to be ready!

Memorable Quote:
"Jesus went throughout Galilee, teaching in their synagogues, proclaiming the good news of the kingdom, and healing every disease and sickness among the people." Matthew 4:23.

Journaling Suggestion:
Jesus is my king, I give my allegiance to Him, and will serve Him henceforth for ever!

Memo for Meditation:
"Listen! Your watchmen lift up their voices; together they shout for joy. When the LORD returns to Zion, they will see it with their own eyes. Burst into songs of joy together, you ruins of Jerusalem, for the LORD has comforted his people, he has redeemed Jerusalem. The LORD will lay bare his holy arm in the sight of all the nations, and all the ends of the earth will see the salvation of our God." Isaiah 52:8-10.

January 25

Motivation Idea: World history and the importance of hope

'The Day of the Lord' is a biblical term used to describe the end of the world; Armageddon, the apocalypse, Jesus on a white horse, and other incredible images are found in the Book of Revelation. Babylon also features. To understand the imagery, we have to go back to the book of

Genesis. God's creation is in perfect harmony, and humans have been given power to rule over the world on His behalf. A mysterious unhuman character (Satan) appears and offers them a promise: *"You can define good and evil on your own terms and put yourselves in the place of God."* They went for it and so we have a world history of broken relationships, violence and huge problems. Humans have to protect themselves and fight for survival and death is used as a weapon to gain power. It all leads to the story about the building of the city of Babylon (Hebrew, aka Babel). They all come together to elevate themselves to the place of God. God knows how devastating this would be, a whole united world culture defining good and evil as if they themselves were God. So, God confused their language and scattered them. From here on in, Babylon becomes an icon for the biblical story; it's an image that represents humanity's corporate rebellion against God, and people the world over began to redefine what they believed to be good and evil. The pharaoh of Egypt illustrates this evil in his treatment of the immigrant Israelites. But God delivered them and every year since, the Israelites have celebrated 'The Day' of liberation with the Passover and the sacrificial lamb meal. Israel eventually came into the land, had their own kings, faced new threats from other kingdoms, and looked forward to God's deliverance from their enemies; they again looked for 'The Day' of deliverance and placed their hope in God. World events today point to the return of Jesus Christ, the Messiah; then Israel will recognise Him but we need to be ready today for The Day of the Lord.

Memorable Quote:
"On the Day of the Lord—the day that God makes everything right, the day that everything sad comes untrue—on that day the same thing will happen to your own hurts and sadness. You will find that the worst things that have ever happened to you will in the end only enhance your eternal delight. On that day, all of it will be turned inside out and you will know joy beyond the walls of the world. The joy of your glory will be that much greater for every scar you bear. So live in the light of the resurrection and renewal of this world, and of yourself, in a glorious, never-ending, joyful dance of grace." Timothy Keller

Journaling Suggestion:
Hope and history rhyme in the divine – in Jesus.

Memo for Meditation:
"Blessed are those who hope in the Lord." Psalm 1:1

January 26

Motivational Idea: The Day of the Lord in world history and the choices we make

When Israel entered the land (1450 BCe), they looked to God for 'The Day' of deliverance from their enemies. Sadly, their history is one of succumbing to the power of evil and a downward spiral of deterioration and departure from God. Some kings were downright evil and some were good, but the underbelly of the nation was a cesspit of violence, evil and debauchery, just like the nations around them. Some prophets were good and some were evil, and spoke only to tickle the ears of their leaders. A false sense of security ensued. When we delve into the year 750 BC, we come across a prophet called Amos. He pronounces God's judgement on the nations surrounding Israel and calls upon Israel to repent, to turn back to God and find peace and flourishing in Him. There was a way back to harmony and happiness, and God would empower them to resist evil, but they would not listen. Amos then uses the term, 'The Day of the Lord,' but Israel gets a massive shock because the prophet is proclaiming a day of judgement against them. *"Woe to you who long for the day of the LORD! Why do you long for the day of the LORD? That day will be darkness, not light..Will not the day of the LORD be darkness, not light— pitch-dark, without a ray of brightness?"* (Amos 5:18-20). And so, from here on in, the history of Israel is one of captivity and exile, dominated by powerful kingdoms like Babylon. All hope is not lost, however, because Amos refers to a future 'Day of the Lord' when those who repent can experience recovery from the chaotic mess we have made of our world and live in a harmonious relationship with God in a restored world, at peace and with the total absence of evil.

Memorable Quote:
"For the LORD of Heaven's Armies has a day of reckoning. He will punish the proud and mighty and bring down everything that is exalted." Isaiah 2:12.

Journaling Suggestion:
Learning the lessons that Amos teaches: repentance and living in harmony with God.

Memo for Meditation
"'The days are coming,' declares the LORD, 'when the reaper will be overtaken by the ploughman and the planter by the one treading grapes. New wine will drip from the mountains and flow from all the hills, and I will bring my people Israel back from exile. They will rebuild the ruined cities and live in them. They will plant vineyards and drink their wine; they will make gardens and eat their fruit. I will plant Israel in their own land, never again to be uprooted from the land I have given them,' says the LORD your God." Amos 9:13-15

January 27

Motivational Idea: World history and the upside-down kingdom

Jesus was born into a world where the Jews were under the jackboot of Roman oppression. The religious leaders were in cahoots with the oppressors for their own financial gain, but longed to be rid of Rome. The Messiah, as they understood Messiahship, was needed to do the job. Dr Luke, in his historical record, states that, *"He went throughout every city and village, preaching and shewing the glad tidings of the kingdom of God: and the twelve were with him."* (Luke 8:1). The religious leaders' ears pricked up and they sent their cronies to find out more. *This could be it; if Jesus is proclaiming the kingdom, then our deliverance may be at hand.* Other insurrectionists had appeared but to no avail. Jesus might be different! He could be the one the prophets predicted. Then to their total dismay they realised that His kingdom was one of love and forgiveness. When Jesus confronted the religious class and not only challenged them but told them in no uncertain terms they were *"A brood of vipers, whitened sepulchres full of dead men's bones,"* that was it. Even early on in His ministry, they plotted to kill Him. They hated His kingdom manifesto and they were appalled that He said He was the Son of God, making Himself equal with God.

When Jesus overturned the tables of the money men in the temple and told them they had made His Father's house a den of thieves, that was the final straw. His 'fate' was sealed as far as they thought, but there was a bigger plan unfolding; they were totally blind to the scriptures they claimed to know, blinded by self-interest to the extent that they could not accept this crazy self-denial stuff the teacher from Galilee was peddling. They thought He was mad. His was the upside-down kingdom.

Memorable Quote:
"You must make your choice: either this man was, and is, the Son of God, or else a madman or something worse. You can shut him up for a fool, you can spit at him and kill him as a demon; or you can fall at his feet and call him Lord and God. But let us not come with any patronising nonsense about his being a great human teacher. He has not left that open to us. He did not intend to."

Journaling Suggestion:
I believe that Jesus is the Christ, the Son of living God and I am His servant.

Memo for Meditation:
"Again, the high priest asked him, 'Are you the Christ, the Son of the Blessed?' Jesus said, 'I Am. And you will see the Son of Man seated in the place of power at God's right hand and coming on the clouds of heaven.'" Mark 14:61,62.

January 28

Motivational Idea: World history and the King lifted up

The plot was hatched. Jesus was going to die. They had Judas lined up as the arch betrayer. Yet as is often the case, things are not always what they seem. The backstory, prophesied in the Old Testament, was that Jesus was destined to die, it was why He came into the world. He was born to die! This was the divine plan to redeem humanity! There was a greater problem than the Romans; in fact, it was the problem of humanity's rebellion against God and included every Jew and every Gentile – *us*!

In Jerusalem, Jesus was going to have a showdown with that unhuman being (Satan) and all his hellish forces. All the evils of the world were going to be unleashed on Jesus and the ultimate weapon that can be used against humanity – death – was going to be the result. After a mock trial, Jesus was lifted up, not on a throne but on a cross, nailed to a Roman gibbet. The enemy of humanity must have initially thought, *"We have Him now - this is the end of Jesus!"* But in the act of sacrifice, Jesus exhausted all the powers of hell, sin and death. He died and the blood flowed down from His body, and His beautiful feet, with this beautiful message, the Good News of the Gospel: *"Blessed are the feet of Him who brings good news."*

The Passover was a commemoration of liberty and freedom from slavery – Jesus was our Passover lamb who was sacrificed for us. *"Behold the Lamb of God that takes away the sin of the world."* Oh how He loves us and forgiveness is offered to a rebellious fallen world! His body was placed in a borrowed tomb with a 24-hour guard. But three days later, He rose triumphantly from the dead. Death is defeated and Jesus the risen king offers us the way back to God; He offers us life – eternal life!

Memorable Quote:
"The children of Adam fall into two groups, those who belong to the kingdom of God and those who belong to the kingdom of the world. To the kingdom of God belong all who believe in Christ and live under Him, for Christ is King and Lord in the kingdom of God." Martin Luther

Journaling Suggestion:
Rescued from the kingdom of darkness and an inheritor in the kingdom of light.

Memo for Meditation:
"Giving joyful thanks to the Father, who has qualified you to share in the inheritance of his holy people in the kingdom of light. For he has rescued us from the kingdom of darkness and transferred us into the Kingdom of his dear Son, in whom we have redemption through his blood, even the forgiveness of sins." Colossians 1:12-14

January 29

Motivational Idea: The building programme

Since Jesus went back to heaven two thousand years ago, the world has kept building new versions of Babylon: the symbol of rebellion against God. Just look at the world around you; have you ever seen so much disquiet, so much hatred and polarisation? Absolute despair on the faces of millions flash across our social media, the innocents caught up in wars as despots play games in power manoeuvres with people's lives, death being their ultimate weapon. Most of us live lives of quiet desperation. It doesn't make sense, and it wouldn't unless we had a clear revelation inspired by the God who made the world. He has set out His redemption plan in the Bible.

The unhuman creature, the deceiver, Satan, knows his time is short and he is busy with his armies causing as much mayhem and destruction as he can. Yet Jesus is building His kingdom now and millions follow Him today. His kingdom of light counteracts the dark kingdom of the world. Jesus said, *"I will build my church and the gates of hell will not prevail against it."*

We are called to be followers of Jesus and to take the good news of the Gospel to the very gates of hell and tell people that Jesus is coming back soon, and to get ready to be ready! We don't know the date but we see the signs all around us (Matthew ch24). We have been given the Holy Spirit and we have the promise that the One who lives in us is *'greater than the one in the world.'* In this evil age in which we have been placed, God is at work and He is in control, and if we take the time to listen to Him, He will teach us our part in kingdom-building. One day, when this world comes to an end, suffering, sin, death and hell will be banished for good, and we will live forever in the new heavens and new earth.

Memorable Quote:
"Be energised and incentivised to spread the Gospel in your sphere of influence."

Journaling Suggestion:
Understanding the signs of the times from the Bible (see Matthew 24)

Memo for Meditation:

"A final word: be strong in the Lord and in his mighty power. Put on all of God's armour so that you will be able to stand firm against all strategies of the devil. For we are not fighting against flesh-and-blood enemies, but against evil rulers and authorities of the unseen world, against mighty powers in this dark world, and against evil spirits in the heavenly places. Therefore, put on every piece of God's armour so you will be able to resist the enemy in the time of evil. Then after the battle you will still be standing firm." Philippians 6:10-13.

January 30

Motivational Idea: The Day of the Lord will come as a thief in the night

The Book of Revelation describes the Day of the Lord and how the world will end. It describes the return of Jesus, the king of kings and lord of lords. His kingdom will come on earth to end evil once and for all. He is portrayed as coming on a white horse, symbolising His authority as the rightful king. The white horse also represents final victory over the kingdom of this world that has rejected His salvation. As the Passover lamb, He opened up a new and living way to anyone who wants to escape the evil Babylonian world system. He is described as having a robe stained in blood. Whose blood does it symbolise? It's His own blood! It's the blood of the lamb. It is by His own blood He obtained eternal redemption for us. He is also described as having a sharp two-edged sword coming out of His mouth. This signifies His absolute authority as He comes to judge the world. He will hold everyone to account on the final day of judgement.

Today, the Day of the Lord is an invitation to accept Christ and follow Him. To live that new creation life, and resist the Babylonian culture where humankind is in rebellion against God. The Day of the Lord is also a promise that one day soon the world will be free from all sin and corruption, from all suffering and death. Jesus is coming soon, and the Day of the Lord also serves as a warning because we are either in the kingdom of Christ or the kingdom of the world. All the signs point to His imminent return. One day He will plant His feet on the Mount of Olives and He will take Jerusalem as the rightful eternal

Davidic king and Israel will recognise Him and bow before their Messiah. You need to bow before Him today as your Lord and Saviour, or one day you will have to bow before Him as the Judge.

Memorable Quote:
"Look, he is coming with the clouds," and "every eye will see him, even those who pierced him"; and all peoples on earth "will mourn because of him." So shall it be! Amen." Revelation 1.6.

Journaling Suggestion:
The Day of the Lord is my incentive to live a fulfilled and purposeful life for the King and His Kingdom.

Memo for Meditation:
"Then I saw heaven opened, and a white horse was standing there. Its rider was named Faithful and True, for he judges fairly and wages a righteous war. His eyes were like flames of fire, and on his head were many crowns. A name was written on him that no one understood except himself. He wore a robe dipped in blood, and his title was the Word of God." Revelation 19:11,12

January 31

Motivational Idea: The consummation of world history

Jesus is coming back again. He promised this!

Memorable Quote:
"I will come again." John 14

Journaling Suggestion:
Living in the light of the Lord's return. I'm getting ready to be ready!

Memo for Meditation: The Day of the Lord is coming
"I want you to remember what the holy prophets said long ago and what our Lord and Saviour commanded through your apostles. Most importantly, I want to remind you that in the last days scoffers will come, mocking the truth and following their own desires. They will say, "What happened to the promise that Jesus is coming again? From before the

41

times of our ancestors, everything has remained the same since the world was first created." They deliberately forget that God made the heavens long ago by the word of his command, and he brought the earth out from the water and surrounded it with water. Then he used the water to destroy the ancient world with a mighty flood. And by the same word, the present heavens and earth have been stored up for fire. They are being kept for the day of judgement, when ungodly people will be destroyed. But you must not forget this one thing, dear friends: a day is like a thousand years to the Lord, and a thousand years is like a day. The Lord isn't really being slow about his promise, as some people think. No, he is being patient for your sake. He does not want anyone to be destroyed, but wants everyone to repent.

The Day of the Lord will come as unexpectedly as a thief. Then the heavens will pass away with a terrible noise, and the very elements themselves will disappear in fire, and the earth and everything on it will be found to deserve judgement. Since everything around us is going to be destroyed like this, what holy and godly lives you should live, looking forward to the day of God and hurrying it along. On that day, he will set the heavens on fire, and the elements will melt away in the flames. But we are looking forward to the new heavens and new earth he has promised, a world filled with God's righteousness.

And so, dear friends, while you are waiting for these things to happen, make every effort to be found living peaceful lives that are pure and blameless in his sight. And remember, our Lord's patience gives people time to be saved. You already know these things, dear friends. So be on guard, then you will not be carried away by the errors of these wicked people and lose your own secure footing. Rather, you must grow in the grace and knowledge of our Lord and Saviour Jesus Christ. All glory to him, both now and forever! Amen." 2 Peter 3:2-15a, 17, 18

THE PHILOSOPHICAL DIMENSION

February 1

Motivational Idea: Everyone's a philosopher

We are all philosophers! We all have a philosophy of life. It may not be the kind of hyper-intellectual mental workout of the academic, and don't be bamboozled by the multiplicity of ideas formulated by various schools of thought and the jargon that goes with it. When we break it all down, it's about these questions: What is real? (metaphysical); How do I know? (epistemological); How should I live? (ethical); What am I? (human nature); and, What's the point? (teleological). Our philosophy of life is based on all these things and more, and is like an architect's plans for a building. It makes us who we are, what we believe, what we base it on, how we behave, how we view ourselves, and finding our purpose for living on planet earth.

We need to make some sense of life in order to have some coherence to it all. We tend to live by our ideas, but we rarely stop to examine the ideas we have and where they come from. Like it or not, we are unwittingly influenced by many of the ideas of the great philosophical thinkers from down the centuries who struggled with the same questions and from their search came up with how they made sense of the world. So, if you thought that you had no interest in philosophy, you need to think again. It's like your heart beat – it's there and you may not be aware of it, but it's there if you are alive, and so is your philosophy.

You might hear someone say, *"I am not interested in philosophy, I just want to be happy."* But that is stating a philosophical idea of being happy. Our philosophies have been constructed on the anvil of life and all the experiences and influences we have encountered. Solomon, one of the wisest men who ever lived, whom we will consider tomorrow, devoted himself to making sense of life. He found it all to be utterly meaningless; even wisdom was just another vanity if it was not being pursued in the context of knowing God and living a life that pleases Him.

Memorable Quote:
"Good philosophy must exist, if for no other reason, because bad philosophy needs to be answered." C S Lewis

Journaling Suggestion:
Reflect on my philosophy of life and where it comes from.

Memo for Meditation:
"Now, LORD my God, you have made your servant king in place of my father David. But I am only a little child and do not know how to carry out my duties. Your servant is here among the people you have chosen, a great people, too numerous to count or number. So give your servant a discerning heart to govern your people and to distinguish between right and wrong. For who is able to govern this great people of yours?" 1 Kings 3:7-9.

February 2

Motivational Idea: The best philosophy book in the world

If the Bible was a university, we would have 66 courses of study. The textbook for the philosophy class would be the book of Ecclesiastes, written by the philosophy professor, Solomon. The *qoheleth* – the teacher – presents two philosophical paths: life without God, and life with God. The prologue sets out the basic philosophical problem: everything in life seems meaningless. This is the enigma of life. Solomon then recounts his philosophical journey and his search for the answer to the age old question: *Is there any meaning to life?* He then takes us through the things that have perplexed humankind down the centuries: the transient nature of life, injustice, oppression, loneliness, irreverence, inequality and obscurity.

He also asks how we can live wisely with philosophical integrity. To understand all this we need to see that this is life without God. Then comes the epilogue. He makes an appeal to his philosophy students to choose the right and the best philosophy. He resolves the puzzle of life that without God, life cannot and does not and never will make sense. Solomon looked back to his earlier life – a life in a relationship with God. God gave him great wisdom, yet he strayed and went his own godless way; he had it all and tried it all, and found it all to be meaningless, chasing after the wind. He then realised that this selfish hedonistic philosophy made his life totally empty and devoid of any meaning. He returned to God and found all the answers in Him, and wrote the best philosophy book in the world; it's God's word to us today.

Memorable Quote:
"Solomon started strong, strayed, encountered a disillusionment he couldn't explain and with which he could not live; and he learned the lesson of the ages. The only working philosophy that really works is to acknowledge our Creator, fear God and keep His commandments, and follow our Lord Jesus Christ to the ends of the earth–and on to Heaven."
Robert J Morgan

Journaling Suggestion:
Read the book of Ecclesiastes at one sitting (45-50 minutes), and note your takeaways from it.

Memo for Meditation:
"The teacher searched to find just the right words, and what he wrote was upright and true. The words of the wise are like goads, their collected sayings like firmly embedded nails—given by one shepherd. Be warned, my son, of anything in addition to them of making many books there is no end, and much study wearies the body. Now all has been heard; here is the conclusion of the matter: Fear God and keep his commandments, for this is the duty of all mankind. For God will bring every deed into judgement, including every hidden thing, whether it is good or evil." Ecclesiastes 12:9-14

February 3

Motivational Idea: Good philosophy and the flourishing life

What is philosophy?

The Department of Philosophy at Florida State University answers: *"Quite literally, the term "philosophy" means, 'love of wisdom'. In a broad sense, philosophy is an activity people undertake when they seek to understand fundamental truths about themselves, the world in which they live, and their relationships to the world and to each other. As an academic discipline philosophy is much the same. Those who study philosophy are perpetually engaged in asking, answering, and arguing for their answers to life's most basic questions. To make such a pursuit more systematic academic philosophy is traditionally divided into major areas of study.'*

Metaphysics: the study of the nature of reality, of what exists in the world, what it is like, and how it is ordered. Philosophers wrestle with such questions as: *Is there a God? What is truth? Do people have free will?*

Epistemology: the study of knowledge and is primarily concerned with what we can know about the world and how we can know it. The questions here are: *What actually is knowledge? Do we really know anything? How do we know what we know? Can we be justified in claiming to know certain things?*

Ethics: concerned with behaviour and asks: *What is good? What is right? Is morality objective or subjective? How should I behave towards others?*

Logic: this aspect of philosophy is about the arguments or reasons given for the answers to the questions above. Logic is employed to consider the construct of arguments, and logicians ask things like: *What constitutes good or bad reasoning? How can we know if a piece of information is good or bad?*

Great thinkers down through the centuries have grappled with all these questions and we can learn from all of them, but we need to seek out good philosophy that enables us to flourish and be on the lookout for bad philosophies that are detrimental to our spiritual wellbeing. The Apostle Paul was not anti-philosophy, but rather anti-bad philosophies (Colossians 2:8). All highbrowed thinking must be brought before the courtroom of biblical philosophy.

Memorable Quote:
"The person who claims to have no need of philosophy is the one most apt to be fooled by it." Dr William Lane Craig

Journaling Suggestion:
Take a dive into biblical philosophy and its teaching on the flourishing life.

Memo for Mediation:

"The reverent fear of the Lord [that is, worshipping Him and regarding Him as truly awesome] is the beginning and the preeminent part of wisdom [its starting point and its essence], and the knowledge of the Holy One is understanding and spiritual insight." Proverbs 9:10

February 4

Motivational Idea: The greatest philosopher – a whole-life philosophy

One of the oldest churches ever uncovered in Dura-Europos, Syria, has a fresco depicting Jesus wearing the philosopher's robe; Jesus, the greatest philosopher. This was part of the ancient understanding of Jesus, and that a huge part of His mission on earth was to teach God's comprehensive wisdom for life. Jesus' teaching is described in the New Testament as 'wisdom', the Greek term *sophía* from which we get 'philosophy', the 'love of wisdom'. The philosophy of Jesus relates to every aspect of our lives including our desires, habits and behaviour. Adherence to His philosophy enables us to decompartmentalise and rediscover biblical Christianity as a whole-life philosophy, one that addresses our greatest human questions and helps us live meaningful and flourishing lives. Jesus, the only saviour who was crucified for our salvation and raised from the dead for our justification, is also our great philosopher for our sanctification, and we need to listen to Him as revealed in the scriptures. Jesus the philosopher gives us the answers on how to find meaningful happiness.

Philosophy is about ultimate reality, how we can know it and then live in the light of it. The creator is the ultimate reality, the mind behind the logic of the universe. We can know something about God through reason, but we can only know Him personally if He discloses Himself to us, and that's what happened in the incarnation, Immanuel, God with us. When we live in accordance with His revealed wisdom, His philosophy, we find ourselves living in harmony with ultimate reality, God Himself. This is how many Christians in ancient times thought about Christianity and Jesus – philosophy from the greatest philosopher ever, the great creator Himself.

Memorable Quote:

"We need to recover the lost biblical image of Jesus as the one true philosopher who teaches us how to experience the fullness of our humanity in the kingdom of God. Jesus teaches us what is good, right, and beautiful and offers answers to life's big questions: what it means to be human, how to be happy, how to order our emotions, and how we should conduct our relationships." Jonathan T Pennington

Journaling Suggestion:

Discovering or rediscovering biblical Christianity as a whole-life philosophy, from Jesus the greatest philosopher.

Memo for Meditation:

"That they may know the mystery of God, namely, Christ, in whom are hidden all the treasures of wisdom and knowledge. I tell you this so that no one may deceive you by fine-sounding arguments. For though I am absent from you in body, I am present with you in spirit and delight to see how orderly you are and how firm your faith in Christ is. So then, just as you received Christ Jesus as Lord, continue to live in him." Colossians 2:2b-6.

February 5

Motivational Idea: The Greatest Philosophy

Justin Martyr was born around 100 AD at Flavia Neapolis (modern Nablus) in Samaria. Well-educated, he studied at various schools of philosophy in Alexandria and Ephesus. His quest for answers led him to Stoicism, then Pythagoreanism, and then Platonism. He was deeply moved by the faithfulness of Christian Martyrs and a conversation with a follower of Jesus changed his life. In his own words, *"Straightaway a flame was kindled in my soul, and a love of the prophets and those who are friends of Christ possessed me."*

As a Christian, Justin continued to wear the robe of a philosopher. He said that Christianity was the greatest philosophy and that other philosophies had a partial grasp of truth. He debated with all kinds of people and opened a school of Christian philosophy at Ephesus, and then later at Rome. After a debate with the Cynic philosopher Crescens, he was arrested and falsely charged with unlawful religious practices. He was found guilty and, refusing to renounce Christianity, was put to death by beheading. Six of his students, one of them a woman, were also martyred.

Three of Justin's works have survived, and in these he defends Christianity as the only true creed, that good Christians make good citizens and do not undermine the foundations of a good society based on slander or misunderstanding. He writes of Trypho, a Jew, and how they discussed the Jewish people and their place in history, and about Jesus as the promised Messiah. A principal question was whether belief in the deity of Christ can be reconciled with the monotheism of the Old Testament. They parted friends, with Trypho saying, *"You have given me food for thought. I must consider this further."* When Justin had been converted, the man he spoke to had talked about Jesus as the fulfilment of the promises made through the Jewish prophets. For Justin, the philosophy of Christ was not some bolt from the Johannine blue, it was written and prophesied about throughout the Old Testament.

Motivational Quote:
"Almighty and everlasting God, who found your martyr Justin Wandering from teacher to teacher, seeking the true God, and revealed to him the sublime wisdom of your eternal Word: Grant that all who seek you, or a deeper knowledge of you, may find and be found by you; through Jesus Christ our Lord, who lives and reigns with you and the Holy Spirit, one God, for ever and ever." Justin Martyr (prayer)

Journaling Suggestion:
Start searching the scriptures for myself using a good reading plan. Evidence search!

Memo for Meditation:
"[The Bereans] received the Word with all eagerness, examining the Scriptures daily to see if these things were so." Acts 17:11.

February 6

Motivational Idea: The counter-cultural life-changing philosophy of reframing

Great teachers have the ability to simplify and explain the most complex and seemingly incomprehensible subjects. Jesus, the greatest teacher, in His famous Sermon on the Mount encapsulates His philosophy in eight short counter-cultural statements. *"Blessed are the poor in spirit for the kingdom of heaven belongs to them."* (Matthew 5:3).

We need a reframing to take place, not only a cognitive reframing but a spiritual one. We must acknowledge that we are spiritually bankrupt and destitute, we have nothing to offer. Stop the straining and striving, and acknowledge we are nothing and we have nothing, and embrace Jesus as Lord and Saviour. When we place our lives in His life, something miraculous happens – we are born anew! This radical counter-cultural redemptive philosophy of Jesus is life-changing. Many great philosophers have missed it, or in their arrogance and self-aggrandisement choose to ignore it. But we have a God-created need in our very souls and the message brought to us in the incarnational philosophy of the Son of God is to bow humbly at His feet, acknowledging our fallen condition and receiving Him into our hearts. In His kingdom, we can grasp the deep things of God which cannot be understood otherwise.

Sartre in *Being and Nothingness* espoused a life of freedom without God, a life of useless passion. Jesus on the other hand shows us that our being and nothingness is transformed in the reframing of our lives in the freedom of the kingdom, and we can live a flourishing life of fulfilment and usefulness for God – *and* it has eternal rewards. There is a sense in which we need constant reframing to remain humble before Him. (Luke 14:11, AMP)

Motivational Quote:

"Jesus the philosopher proclaimed his own authoritative view on the nature of true happiness in the 'Beatitudes'," addressing a major topic in ancient philosophy. He described what it means to be a whole and virtuous person (in Greek, teleios, one of Aristotle's favourite words) and sharply contrasted the two ways of the "fool" and the "wise person" (the phronimos one, another Greek favourite) by showing their varying outcomes of destruction and flourishing." Jonathan T Pennington

Journaling Suggestion:
Reframing my life in the context of the counter-cultural redemptive philosophy of Jesus is life-changing.

Memo for Meditation:
"[Jesus] Who, being in very nature God, did not consider equality with God something to be used to his own advantage; rather, he made himself nothing by taking the very nature of a servant, being made in human likeness. And being found in appearance as a man, he humbled himself by becoming obedient to death— even death on a cross!" Philippians 2:6-8

February 7

Motivational Idea: A robust philosophy of life needs a clear understanding of human nature

The only way to construct a robust philosophy for life is to have a clear understanding of human nature. The first statement from God about man's nature is the crucial one: Genesis 1:26–31 tells us that God made man and woman, *"In the image of God."* Humans were created to be like God — apart from having His power or omniscience. The ways in which humans are like God (but not God) include our capacity for a 'right' relationship with God, ability to reason, creativity, sociability, dominion over creation, and freedom of choice. The Fall, however, changed all that in profound ways. Genesis 3 tells us of the sin of Adam and Eve, their expulsion from the Garden, and the fundamental alteration in their nature. Sin entered into the world and that perfect relationship with God was broken.

Yesterday, we considered the philosophy of Jesus as presented in the Sermon on the Mount. Being poor in spirit acknowledges our spiritual bankruptcy. Jesus builds on this with His next beatitude statement, *"Blessed are they that mourn for they shall be comforted."* (Matthew 5:4.). Given the human condition, Jesus' promise to comfort those who mourn sin could scarcely be more counterintuitive. Given the *'spirit of our age'*, it could scarcely be more counter-cultural. Jesus uses the strongest Greek word to express mourning. The world views this grieving of sin as regressive and constricting, but for the believer it's the pathway to joy and freedom – to be forgiven and wrapped in the comfort and love of God. Jesus meets repentance with comfort, not condemnation. No longer do we need to fear but *trust*. Acknowledging the depths of our sinful nature brings us to an end of ourselves but experiencing infinite mercy, grace, love and comfort takes us into the joy of the Lord.

Memorable Quote:
"Sin in the late-modern West is not grieved. It's not disapproved of. It's not merely tolerated. It is celebrated. Our society doesn't mourn sin; it mourns those who mourn sin. Yet we can succumb to similar tendencies, can't we? No doubt one reason we fail to mourn sin is because we underestimate it. We assume it's little more than a cosmic parking ticket. But sin is not trivial; it is treason, an insurrection against heaven's throne. We have never committed a small sin because we have never offended a small God." Matt Smethurst

Journaling Suggestion:
I acknowledge my sinfulness and grieve before God, receiving His mercy and love.

Memo for Meditation:
"Against you, you only, have I sinned and done what is evil in your sight; so you are right in your verdict and justified when you judge." Psalm 51:4.

February 8

Motivational Idea: A philosophy of life that espouses meekness

Jonathan T Pennington observes: *"The experience of modern philosophy is that it asks big questions but doesn't provide answers. It leaves a person lost, uncertain and ambivalent. You remember just enough to screw you up for the rest of your life."* Pennington goes on to state that this is not the whole story: *"This life screwing up is not what philosophy used to do. This common modern experience of philosophy - irrelevant at best and destructive at worst - is a radical change from how humans have understood and been affected by philosophy over the last three thousand years."*

Biblical philosophy was not concerned about whether chairs exist when we leave the room, it was a guide by which humans could experience true happiness; it declared Jesus as Lord, Saviour, Redeemer, God – the great philosopher. This understanding has been lost. The reasons for this we will consider another day, but it needs to be realised afresh that the true philosophy of life is Jesus the philosopher and Christianity. Christianity is not just a set of doctrines but a divine whole-life philosophy for happiness and the flourishing life. Jesus, the Alpha and Omega, the beginning and the end, the philosopher for all of life, tells us in Matthew 5:5: *"Blessed are the meek for they shall inherit the earth."* This turns modern philosophy on its head. The world works on the basis of power and influence. Christ's kingdom operates on the basis of humility and meekness. In kingdom life, we live by grace, not judgement; God's power, not our own. Meekness is not weakness. Greek *praeis* means 'gentle', 'unpretentious'. Jesus our Lord and Master, our philosopher, is our perfect role model. As a man He depended on God the Father's strength and restrained His limitless power. We model our lives on Him and find that this is the pathway of happiness on earth. We are called to be His disciples and to go with His good news, the Gospel, and make disciples. We have His philosophy for life to teach and to live out today.

Memorable Quote:
"Nothing is more powerful than meekness. For as fire is extinguished by water, so a mind inflated by anger is subdued by meekness. By meekness we practise and make known our virtue, and also cause the indignation of our brother to cease, and deliver his mind from perturbation." John Chrysostom

Journaling Suggestion:
Learning meekness from the Master Philosopher, Jesus Christ.

Memo for Mediation:
"Blessed [inwardly peaceful, spiritually secure, worthy of respect] are the gentle [the kind-hearted, the sweet-spirited, the self-controlled], for they will inherit the earth." Matthew 5:5.

February 9

Motivational Idea: A philosophy of life satisfaction

We all have a soul hunger and thirst for something. U2 sang, *I Still Haven't Found What I'm Looking For.* We may not be able to name it specifically, but high on the agenda for most is the chief desire for happiness and life satisfaction. Pink Floyd captured the conundrum of our human condition in their powerful song, *High Hopes.* *"Encumbered forever by desire and ambition/there's a hunger still unsatisfied/ our weary eyes stray to the horizon/though down this road we've been so many times."*

Jesus in His fourth statement in the Sermon on the Mount says: *"Blessed are those who hunger and thirst for righteousness, for they will be satisfied."* Matthew 5:6. Jesus the philosopher king offers righteousness to all who will make Him Lord and Saviour. He declares us righteous even though we are sinful. Jesus imparts to us His righteousness and He enables us to live righteously. It is only in this relationship with God that we find what we have been looking for. Only God can satisfy the cravings of the hungry soul and slake our unquenchable soul thirst. Here is the eternal unchanging philosopher God showing us how we can be truly satisfied. Adam and Eve rebelled, and so have we. Jesus came to bring us back to our first love, to renew and restore our broken relationship with God. Jesus suffered physical hunger, and after 40 days of fasting, was tempted by the devil to turn stones into bread. Jesus answered the devil by quoting from the book of Deuteronomy (8:3). Jesus told him, *"No! The Scriptures say, 'People do not live by bread alone, but by every word that comes from the mouth of God."*

Our philosopher God has given us His manual for living abundantly. Here is satisfying food and drink for our souls, and we are invited to the banqueting table of our Saviour and philosopher king each day! *"For He satisfies the longing soul, and the hungry soul He fills with good things."* (Psalm 107:9).

Memorable Quote:

"How prompt we are to satisfy the hunger and thirst of our bodies; how slow to satisfy the hunger and thirst of our souls!" Henry David Thoreau

Journaling Suggestion:

Satisfying my soul hunger and thirst: How and why?

Memo for Mediation:
"But as for you, continue in what you have learned and have become convinced of, because you know those from whom you learned it, and how from infancy you have known the Holy Scriptures, which are able to make you wise for salvation through faith in Christ Jesus. All Scripture is God-breathed and is useful for teaching, rebuking, correcting and training in righteousness, so that the servant of God may be thoroughly equipped for every good work." 2 Timothy 3:14-17.

February 10

Motivational Idea: The philosopher of philosophers teaches on mercy

Many philosophers, including Aristotle, saw mercy as a vice rather than a virtue, a form of pathological defect excusable only in the elderly and children. The philosopher of philosophers, Jesus Himself, however, taught differently and His measureless wisdom is stated succinctly in the fifth beatitude: *"Blessed are the merciful for they shall obtain mercy."* (Matthew 5:7). For Jesus, the most basic metaphysic is that there is a God of love and mercy, and that's the animating principle of the universe. And the wise life, the authentic life, the life in sync with ultimate reality is the life of love and mercy toward others. Mercy is not getting what we *do* deserve; grace is getting what we *don't* deserve.

God is a graceful and merciful God and in Jesus we are the recipients of God's mercy, instead of death, He gives us life, instead of punishment, He gives us forgiveness, instead of dishonour, He gives us honour, in the place of shame, He gives us grace, instead of our sins' consequences, He treats us in terms of the consequence of Jesus' action for us in His life, death and resurrection. Since we are the recipients of the mercy of God we are to show mercy. Mercy is one of the characteristics Jesus expects of those of us in the kingdom of God. We have obtained mercy! *"What does the Lord require of you? To act justly, and to love mercy and to walk humbly with your God."* Micah 6:8.

Memorable Quote:
"His mercy is so great that He doesn't just forgive us when we fail, He erases any record of our failure. He doesn't just reduce our sentence -

eternal punishment - He eliminates it and sets us free." Craig Groeschel

Journaling Suggestion:
As a recipient of divine mercy, am I merciful, and who do I need to show mercy to?

Memo for Meditation:
"Among whom all of us also formerly lived out our lives in the cravings of our flesh, indulging the desires of the flesh and the mind, and were by nature children of wrath even as the rest... But God, being rich in mercy, because of his great love with which he loved us, even though we were dead in transgressions, made us alive together with Christ – by grace you are saved! – and he raised us up with him and seated us with him in the heavenly realms in Christ Jesus, to demonstrate in the coming ages the surpassing wealth of his grace in kindness toward us in Christ Jesus. For by grace you are saved through faith, and this is not from yourselves, it is the gift of God; it is not from works, so that no one can boast. For we are his workmanship, having been created in Christ Jesus for good works that God prepared beforehand so we may do them." Ephesians 2:3-10.

February 11

Motivational Idea: The great philosopher talks on purity

Purity for many philosophers was the virtue of benevolence, acting without any traces of selfish motives, and intentions free from self-interest and egotism, power, control or coercion. Jesus, however, takes purity to the highest heights of heaven and to the deepest depths of the human heart. The heart of the matter is the matter of the heart. The heart is crucial in our understanding of the philosophy of Jesus. What we are in the deep recesses of our hearts is what He is concerned about most. Jesus came into the world not because we have some bad habits, but because we have such impure and sinful hearts. We can try and clean up our act, which is very admirable, but that is not enough. In Psalm 51:2, David asks God, *"Wash me thoroughly from my iniquity, and cleanse me from my sin."* In verse 3, David expresses his guilt when he writes *"my sin is ever before me."* But David is optimistic that God will forgive all of his sins when he writes *"... wash me, and I shall be whiter than snow."* This is the purity we need – transformation from the inside –

and then we seek to walk in purity. John wrote in 1 John 1:7-9: *"But if we walk in the light as He is in the light, we have fellowship with one another, and the blood of Jesus Christ His Son cleanses us from all sin. If we say that we have no sin, we deceive ourselves, and the truth is not in us."* The pure in heart will see God, (Matthew 5.8.) but what does it mean to see God? This means to be in His presence, to be awestruck by His glory and the joy and sweet satisfaction of being in a close and intimate relationship with Him. The psalmist writes: *"My heart says of you, seek His face! Your face, LORD, I will seek. Do not hide your face from me, do not turn your servant away in anger; you have been my helper. Do not reject me or forsake me, O God my Saviour. Though my father and mother forsake me, the LORD will receive me."* (Psalm 27:8-10).

Memorable Quote:
"The heart is what you are, in the secrecy of your thought and feeling, when nobody knows but God. And what you are at the invisible root matters as much to God as what you are at the visible branch. 'Man looks on the outward appearance, but the Lord looks on the heart.' (1 Samuel 16:7) From the heart are all the issues of life." John Piper

Journaling Suggestion:
Ways for keeping my heart pure. (See Psalm 119:9.)

Memo for Meditation:
"Who may ascend onto the mountain of the Lord? And who may stand in His holy place? He who has clean hands and a pure heart, Who has not lifted up his soul to what is false, Nor has sworn [oaths] deceitfully. This is the generation [description] of those who diligently seek Him and require Him as their greatest need, Who seek Your face, even [as did] Jacob. Selah." Psalms 24:3-4.

February 12

Motivational Idea: The philosophy of peace

"Blessed are the peacemakers for they shall be called the children of God." (Matthew 5:9). This is the seventh beatitude Jesus taught in His Sermon on the Mount. To understand what He means, we must trust in Jesus, the prince of peace. *"He made peace for us through His blood shed*

on the cross." (Colossians 1:20). Not only has He made peace, He gives to us His peace in a world of fear (see John 14:27).

Peacemakers in the context of the kingdom are those who promote God's peace. Peace is taken from the word *shalom* which can be defined as total or complete wellbeing. Jesus our great philosopher is saying that those who put their faith in Him will have *shalom* and share in the characteristics of God, and bring the message of peace and reconciliation to others. We are children of God by virtue of what Jesus has done for us, and this is evidenced in our seeking to live peacefully and promote peace in a world where it is sadly lacking. We are given new hearts through Jesus and reflect His peace. Our desire is to promote the peace He has given us and share that peace with others – we walk in the ways of peace, a peace that passes all understanding. *"Do not be anxious about anything, but in everything by prayer and supplication with thanksgiving let your requests be made known to God. And the peace of God, which surpasses all understanding, will guard your hearts and your minds in Christ Jesus."* (Philippians 4:6,7).

Memorable quote:
"Make me a channel of your peace/Where there is despair in life let me bring hope/Where there is darkness only light/ And where there's sadness, ever joy." Sebastian Temple

Journaling Suggestion:
Living as a channel of peace in the places bereft of peace.

Memo for Meditation:
For Christ's love compels us because we are convinced that one died for all, and therefore all died. And He died for all, that those who live should no longer live for themselves but for Him who died for them and was raised again. So, from now on, we regard no one from a worldly point of view. Though we once regarded Christ in this way, we do so no longer. Therefore, if anyone is in Christ, the new creation has come: The old has gone, the new is here! All this is from God, who reconciled us to himself through Christ and gave us the ministry of reconciliation: that God was reconciling the world to Himself in Christ, not counting people's sins against them. And He has committed to us the message of reconciliation. We are therefore Christ's ambassadors, as though God were making His appeal through us. We implore you on

Christ's behalf: be reconciled to God. God made Him who had no sin to be sin for us, so that in Him we might become the righteousness of God.

February 13

Motivational Idea: The great philosopher speaks on persecution

The beatitudes are not valued in today's culture. Rewards are not given to the 'Most Pure in Heart' or 'Most Poor in Spirit'. The culture today dismisses such character traits as ancient and outdated. Not so for Jesus; He adds a double one in the eighth beatitude for those who endure suffering, not because of their own stupidity or fanaticism, but because of their loyalty to Him. *"Blessed are those who are persecuted for righteousness' sake, for theirs is the kingdom of heaven. Blessed are you when they revile and persecute you, and say all kinds of evil against you falsely for My sake. Rejoice and be exceedingly glad, for great is your reward in heaven, for so they persecuted the prophets who were before you."* (Matthew 5:11-12.)

Jesus brings insults and spoken malice into the sphere of persecution. We cannot limit our idea of persecution to physical opposition or torture. Early Christians were grossly misunderstood and were charged with treason because they would not honour the Roman gods. They were charged with revolutionary fanaticism because they believed, and rightly so, that Jesus would return and bring an apocalyptic end to all history. They were also accused of immorality because of the gross deliberate misrepresentation of the weekly Love Feast (we know it as The Lord's table or Communion), and they were even believed to be cannibals because of the deliberate misrepresentation of this practice. Today, more than 200 million Christians in over 60 countries are being deprived of basic human rights because of their adherence to Jesus and His whole-life philosophy. Jesus says: *"Rejoice and be exceedingly glad."* Literally, *"leap for joy."* Why? Because the persecuted will have great reward in heaven, in good company with the prophets.

Memorable Quote:

Quote on the word 'rejoice': *"A strong word of Hellenistic coinage, from to leap much, signifying irrepressible demonstrative gladness... It is the*

joy of the Alpine climber standing on the top of the snow-clad mountain."
F F Bruce

Journaling Suggestion:
Loyalty is to Jesus, whatever the cost.

Memo for Meditation:
"But whatever were gains to me I now consider loss for the sake of Christ. What is more, I consider everything a loss because of the surpassing worth of knowing Christ Jesus my Lord, for whose sake I have lost all things. I consider them garbage, that I may gain Christ and be found in him, not having a righteousness of my own that comes from the law, but that which is through faith in Christ—the righteousness that comes from God on the basis of faith. I want to know Christ—yes, to know the power of his resurrection and participation in his sufferings, becoming like him in his death, and so, somehow, attaining to the resurrection from the dead." Philippians 3:7-11.

February 14

Motivational Idea: Great philosophers from the past

We are influenced by some of the great thinkers of past centuries. Great thinkers such as Plato, Socrates and Aristotle, along with the later stoics like Seneca. These men, along with many others, were concerned about the big questions of existence, and, with great energy, boundless persistence and abundant mental labours they sought with deep insightful thought in a very practical way to help people to live lives that were flourishing and good. They sought to provide ways to deal with our emotions, to build good societal relationships, and to find true happiness. This was the engine that drove their philosophical systems. We admire them and we can learn from these great thinkers. We will meet some of them in the coming days as we continue in our reflections on the philosophical dimension of happiness.

Today, everyone has their influencers and their gurus about how to find joy and happiness in life and how to make the most of it. Social media is awash with influencers, but who do we look to? Who are our key influencers? Certain unhelpful influencers and influences came to bear upon ecclesiastical circles over the centuries, the product of which is that most people today, including many Christians, don't get the fact that Jesus is not only Lord and Saviour, He is also the greatest philosopher. If Jesus is who He says He is, then He is our go-to influencer!

We need to ensure that His wisdom, teaching and philosophy for all-of-life is the benchmark for our consideration of all other influencers and all other philosophical systems. Learn from the rest and bow to the best!

Memorable Quote:

"Philosophers have been shaping the world and our school of thought for thousands of years and are still very much relevant in our world today. The greatest philosophers of all time have left us with abundant resources that help us understand the human psyche and the world around us." The University of People

Journaling Suggestion:

Jesus' all-of-life philosophy for all-of-life, and what it means to me. (See John 17:17)

Memo for Meditation:

"Dear friends, do not believe every spirit, but test the spirits to see whether they are from God, because many false prophets have gone out into the world. This is how you can recognize the Spirit of God: Every spirit that acknowledges that Jesus Christ has come in the flesh is from God, but every spirit that does not acknowledge Jesus is not from God. This is the spirit of the antichrist, which you have heard is coming and even now is already in the world. You, dear children, are from God and have overcome them, because the one who is in you is greater than the one who is in the world." 1 John 4:1-4.

February 15

Motivational Idea: The laughing philosopher and lessons on cheerfulness

Democritus, an endearing character, is known as the laughing philosopher because of his emphasis on cheerfulness. He was born in an ancient Greek town called Abdera in 460 BCE and lived into his nineties, a prolific writer of over seventy works, of which only a few fragments remain. His relentless curiosity led him to come up with many theories. His big theory on happiness finds its roots in his ethics and a concern with 'euthymia', which means possessing a happy spirit. *"Happiness resides not in possessions, and not in gold, happiness dwells in the soul. The soul is the house of happiness."* Happiness is seen as a state of mind; it is not found in external circumstances. It should be our highest and noblest goal, living a balanced life with moderation in all things. Democritus emphasised avoiding gluttony, excess alcohol and promiscuity. He teaches us to cut the cord of unrealistic expectations. *"By desiring little, a poor man makes himself rich."* Democtrius knew how to tame his expectations and lead a simple, happy and fulfilling life. One of the biggest killjoys in life is unrealised expectations. We are trapped, and these expectations turn into debilitating obsessions. We can learn a lot from Democritus. He did not believe in God. He came up with his famous atomic theory of eternal atoms interacting through random collisions. He saw the universe as being governed by natural laws rather than by divine power. Around the time of his theorising, a prophet called Malachi was writing, not about atoms but about the eternal God who created the atom, the same God that Paul presented in his Areopagus message to the philosophers in Acts 17. Malachi prophesied that God would send the Messiah 400 years later. For Democritus, happiness is found in the self; for Malachi, lasting joy and happiness is found in the eternal God, its true source revealed in Jesus Christ, the Son of Righteousness with healing in His wings.

Memorable Quote:
"If we are happy only with possessions of material goods, we are doomed to have small blinks of satisfaction - a surrogate of happiness - because the effects fade soon and we'll need another dose to feed our addiction. It's so sad to live in perennial captivity, shaped by massive marketing forces pushing us to consumerism and to find a meaning only in buying things."

Journaling Suggestion:
Reassess my understanding of lasting happiness and its true source.

Memo for Meditation:

"But for you who fear my name, the Sun of Righteousness will rise with healing in his wings. And you will go free, leaping with joy like calves let out to pasture. Malachi 4.2. God is the true source of happiness, strength, hope, and wisdom. Those who are in His favour will always have these things." Psalm 144:15

February 16

Motivational Idea: Socrates: *"The unexamined life is not worth living."*

Socrates lived in Athens in Greece his entire life (469-399 BC), teaching that *"the unexamined life is not worth living."* He was the first known figure in the West to argue that happiness is attainable by human effort. This was abhorrent to the Greeks since happiness was seen as a gift of the gods to the favoured. The 'Socratic method' consisted of a process of questioning to expose ignorance and enhance knowledge.

His student, Plato, recorded his Three Dialogues on Happiness: the Euthydemus, the Symposium, and the Republic.

The Euthydemus is concerned with two things: firstly, happiness is what all people desire since it is always the end (goal) of our activities, and, secondly, it is an *unconditional* good. Happiness does not depend on external things, but rather on how those things are *used* – for the good of others! He's seen as the first 'positive psychologist', considering what brings out the best in human nature and the importance of wellbeing.

In the Symposium, he considers how Eros can be harnessed to pursue the higher things of the mind. This is the realisation of the pure love of beauty itself.

In the Republic, he wants to prove that the just person is happier than the unjust person. Virtue and happiness are inextricably linked.

Socrates paid the ultimate price in his honest search for truth. He was convicted of 'corrupting the youth' and sentenced to die by hemlock poisoning. He took the cup gladly, such was his brief in the eternal value of the soul. He saw death not as the end but as a release from the limitations of the body. There was no fear of wandering aimlessly in ghost-like existence in Hades, the common Greek belief.

Socrates had remained faithful to his commitment to rational inquiry by professing his belief in a personal God who is all-knowing, all-powerful, and benevolent.

Memorable Quote:
"If... man's life is ever worth the living, it is when he has attained this vision of the soul of beauty. And once you have seen it, you will never be seduced again by the charm of gold, of dress, of comely boys, you will care nothing for the beauties that used to take your breath away...and when one discerns this beauty one will perceive the true virtue, not virtue's semblance. And when a man has brought forth and reared this perfect virtue, he shall be called the friend of God, and if ever it is capable of man to enjoy immortality, it shall then be given to him." Socrates (212d)

Journaling Suggestion:
"The unexamined life is not worth living." I will keep a close watch on how I live before God. (See 1 Timothy 4:16)

Memo for Mediation:
"For God is sheer beauty, all-generous in love, loyal always and ever." Psalm 100:5
"For what shall it profit a man, if he shall gain the whole world, and lose his own soul?" Mark 8:36

February 17

Motivational Idea: Plato and the allegory of the cave

In this famous philosophical allegory, Plato describes a group of prisoners who from birth have been in the depths of a cave. Chained and unable to move, they can only see the wall in front of them. Behind them at a distance, fire illuminates the wall and in the middle there is a corridor from which men use objects so that the fire projects shadows onto the wall that the prisoners can see. One of the men breaks free of his chains and is told to stand up and turn around – to convert. He moves forward and is dragged out of the cave. He is blinded by the light, but eventually he sees everything clearly. This is real reality, but his friends are in the cave and he has to go back to help them to break free. He does so, but as he enters the depths of the cave, he is blinded by the darkness. They think he is crazy and decide this is dangerous talk, and if anyone tries to escape again, they will kill them.

This story is an allusion to Socrates' effort to help men to reach the truth and their failure in doing so, only to be condemned to death himself. The story brings together a series of common philosophical themes, namely that truth exists independently of individuals' opinions; the presence of deceptions keeps us from truth and the change needed in accessing truth. It may take time to know the truth, and once you know it, there is no going back, and having the truth may be perceived as dangerous to the blind. For Plato, a life committed to the knowledge of the truth from which virtue flows will result in happiness and self-fulfilment.

The following quote tells of C S Lewis 'seeing the light'.

Memorable Quote:
"You must picture me alone in that room in Magdalen, night after night, feeling, whenever my mind lifted even for a second from my work, the steady, unrelenting approach of him whom I so earnestly desired not to meet. That which I greatly feared had at last come upon me. In the Trinity Term of 1929 I gave in, and admitted that God was God, and knelt and prayed: perhaps, that night, the most dejected and reluctant convert in all England. I did not then see what is now the most shining and obvious thing; the divine humility which will accept a convert even on such terms. The prodigal son at least walked home on his own feet. But who can duly adore that Love which will open the high gates to a prodigal who is brought in kicking, struggling, resentful, and darting his eyes in every direction for a chance of escape? The hardness of God is kinder than the softness of men, and his compulsion is our liberation." C S Lewis

Journaling Suggestion:
Application of this allegory to my life today as I embrace the absolute truth.

Memo for Mediation:
"Jesus said, 'And you will know the truth, and the truth will set you free.'"
John 8:32

February 18

Motivational Idea: Aristotle and the four levels of happiness

Aristotle takes the view that not only do we strive for happiness but that we only strive for it for its own sake. So, everything we do, we do in order to feel happy.

Aristotle distinguishes between four levels of happiness, thus indicating that this elusive concept is much more complicated than it first seems; or is it?

Level one is referred to as *Laerus* – happiness from material things and objects. The word *laerus* can mean lucky or happy; this level of happiness is all about sensual gratification and is based on things which are external. It is about instant gratification and the idea of a hedonistic lifestyle. *Laerus* tends to be intense and short-lived. We all know the pleasure of going out for a nice meal, taking a holiday, or buying your favourite music artist on vinyl and listening to it on the turntable for the very first time. They give us pleasure and it makes us feel happy. However, if we only live our lives for such short-lived experiences, life can be empty and shallow and meaningless most of the time. We rush from one short-lived experience to another. This can be a recipe for disaster and this addiction to instant gratification can lead us into all kinds of other addictions; we find that life is one of *unhappiness* most of the time, and we languish rather than flourish. The human condition, our desires and cravings can lead to giving free reign to what Freud would have referred to as the instincts of the id: addictions to alcohol, drugs, sex, shopping, the next thing, the latest gadget and so forth. There is a limit to all these 'pleasures'.

Memorable Quote:

"Happiness is the meaning and purpose of life, the whole aim and end of human existence... happiness depends upon ourselves." Aristotle

Journaling Suggestion:

Stop chasing the wind, seek true wisdom's path, and happiness will find you.

Memo for Meditation:
"A person can do nothing better than to eat and drink and find satisfaction in their own toil. This too, I see, is from the hand of God, for without him, who can eat or find enjoyment? To the person who pleases him, God gives wisdom, knowledge and happiness, but to the sinner he gives the task of gathering and storing up wealth to hand it over to the one who pleases God. This too is meaningless, a chasing after the wind." Ecclesiastes 2:24–26.

February 19

Motivational Idea: Embracing self-acceptance and avoiding self-absorption

Aristotle refers to level 2 as *Felix:* ego gratification. Happiness from competition, comparison and contrast. This kind of happiness derives from those feelings you get when you win the match, get a promotion at work and are admired by others. Some people also thrive on such admiration and seek it out. When you take to social media, you find a lot of famous people like to show us their latest acquisition or even their new hair style; some try to keep their youthful beauty with cosmetic surgery and Botox, and whatever else will give them that appeal and admiration they crave. Much of it may be a marketing ploy to obtain more royalties, but it would seem the golden goose of admiration is prevalent. However, this kind of happiness can be short-lived and can lead to the very antithesis of happiness, and cause deep frustration and a sense of worthlessness. Then there is always the danger of being attacked by others for an excessive focus on self-absorption. *Look at me!* People become cynical, and the popularity the self-absorbed person once enjoyed can soon dissipate. Do people who are self-absorbed enjoy self-acceptance? One wonders because self-absorption is one thing, but self-acceptance is another. The reality is, the person who is self-absorbed is lacking in authentic self-love; they feel empty on the inside and need to validate their self-worth from external objects, usually people, but possessions may feature highly as well. Authentic self-love generates self-worth. To be in a relationship with God and experience His unconditional *agape* love is the epitome of worth and value, unworthy yet we are of infinite worth and value beyond measure.

Memorable Quote:
"Be yourself, everyone else is taken." Oscar Wilde (allegedly)

Journaling Suggestion:
Being myself and finding my true worth in God.

Memo for Meditation:
"So be content with who you are, and don't put on airs. God's strong hand is on you; he'll promote you at the right time. Live carefree before God; he is most careful with you." 1 Peter 5:6-7.

February 20

Motivational Idea: Making the world a better place

Aristotle refers to level 3 as *Beatitudo* – happiness from helping others and making the world around us a better place to be. I have seen first-hand over a period of twenty-two years working in the mental health arena the desire of many staff and volunteers to support and empower service users to live their best lives. People showing empathy, compassion and downright goodness to others, making their world a better place. It would not be too strong a word to say 'showing love' to their fellow human beings. What we can say about this level of happiness is that we move away from ourselves and focus on the wellbeing of others. So, what we find at this level is that our own happiness flourishes in the process of helping others. One would not be unjustified in saying that this level of happiness is bound to be more lasting and provide a deeper, more meaningful experience than what we get from the previous levels when the focus is on ourselves.

The English poet John Lydgate (ca. 1370-1449) was one of the most prolific, versatile writers of the Middle Ages. He spent much of his early life as a monk at the Benedictine abbey of Bury St Edmunds. Having left the monastic life, he travelled widely throughout Europe, his measure of humanity expressed in one of his inspirational proverbs: *"You can please some of the people all of the time, you can please all of the people some of the time, but you can't please all of the people all of the time."* Such a reality can lead to our unhappiness due to disappointment, displeasure and other negative reactions from our fellow human beings. People can be fickle and we risk being hurt in our genuine desire to reach out to others to help improve their lives and wellbeing. However, it is worth it to seek to make the world a better place and the happiness we derive from helping others should not be displaced or diluted when we face the odd individual who may be 'happy' in their misery.

Motivational Quote:
"Never worry about numbers. Help one person at a time, and always start with the person nearest you." Mother Teresa

Journaling Suggestion:
Consider how you can meaningfully and effectively help the people you meet today.

Memo for Meditation:
"Abandon every display of selfishness. Possess a greater concern for what matters to others instead of your own interests." Philippians 2:4

February 21

Motivational Idea: Finding sublime, ultimate, perfect happiness

Aristotle's level 4 is *Sublime Beatitudo*: ultimate, perfect happiness. This level of happiness is said to be the most difficult to describe. For Aristotle, to reach this level one has called off the search for fullness and perfection. One way of looking at this level is to see it as the optimal balance between the other levels and then something more. The world of psychology has considered this to be the desire for ultimate happiness and the experiences of a connection to the universe or something of a transcendent nature. The word 'transcendence' seems to capture the essence of this level of happiness, and some find its fulfilment in spirituality or religion. However, for others the need for such connection is found in philosophical thought, in the arts, or in science. Undergirding such pursuits are the endeavours of the human soul to find the answers to some of the big questions of life, our human existence and the origin of the universe. Some have concluded there is no definitive answer to it all, it can only be subjective. Or is it? The secret of happiness isn't the great mystery of the universe. Happiness comes when we seek God and obey Him in faith. But happiness seems elusive to such a lot of people. So many books have been written about finding happiness because so many people are still searching for it. The last place on earth or heaven for that matter that human beings tend to look for happiness is in God. The things in our lives that lead to our misery and unhappiness are all things that happen outside of God's will for our lives – our pride, selfishness, unforgiveness and deeply ingrained patterns of a host of besetting sins. However, the things that lead to this ultimate level of happiness are all part of knowing, following and obeying God. Inside His perfect will, we find authentic happiness in His love, loving relationships, unselfishness, a sense of awe and wonder filled with gratitude.

Motivational Quote:
"Do not let your happiness depend on something you may lose. If love is to be a blessing, not a misery, it must be for the only Beloved who will never pass away." C S Lewis

Journaling Suggestion:
Seek God today and every day, and build a relationship with Him and find in Him perfect happiness.

Memo for Meditation:
"Paul said, 'For my determined purpose is that I may...progressively become more deeply and intimately acquainted with Him, perceiving and recognizing and understanding the wonders of His Person more strongly and more clearly.'" Philippians 3:10.

February 22

Motivational Idea: Augustine of Hippo and the joy of truth

Augustine's works are both voluminous and monumental; he is one the greatest thinkers and philosophers who ever lived. *"Gaudium de veritate,"* or *"The joy of truth,"* (See Confessions, X, 23). Here we have Augustine's way of contributing to the perennial discussion on the definition of happiness. The topic of happiness is found throughout his many writings; his thought processes started where most philosophers in the ancient world would have started – human beings seek happiness. Once we have food, safety and shelter, we want the joy of bliss, wellbeing and flourishing. The problem is that we can't agree on a definition of happiness. Then there is the added difficulty of how we get it. How can we parse out the false and the true happiness?

Augustine, like other philosophers, goes with the idea of wanting something and getting it. Yet we all know people who, when they get what they want, are still not happy, and we may have had the same experience. Augustine then considers that happiness must mean something good, and this means to be indestructible and permanent – something that cannot be taken away. This brought Augustine to the view that happiness cannot be found in created things. Created things are fleeting and fragile, and we will eventually lose them. The knowledge that we can lose what we have means that we cannot rest securely, and we may live in fear. This process of thinking brought Augustine to the view that since only God is eternal, only He can impart happiness. The person who has God lacks nothing because we have the fullness and the plenitude of God. This is true wisdom and we can live in the joy of this truth. Since Jesus Christ is the wisdom of God (1 Corinthians 1:24), to be united with Christ, the one who is fully God and fully man, we enter into His wisdom and happiness. He who has Christ has happiness. The love of God is poured into our hearts by the Holy Spirit (Romans 5:5); we are cleansed from emptiness and folly. The Spirit exhorts us to seek God, to dwell far from wrong desires and thirst for Him who, *"flows out to us from the very fount of truth."*

Memorable Quote:
"Accordingly, two cities have been formed by two loves: the earthly by the love of self, even to the contempt of God: the heavenly by the love of God, even to the contempt of self. The former, in a word, is the glories of itself, the latter in the Lord." Augustine

Journaling Suggestion:
I seek the truth. (Jesus, the wisdom of God, and in finding the truth I find true happiness.)

Memo for Meditation:

"I am the Way, the Truth, and the life. No one comes to the Father except through me." John 14:6

February 23

Motivational Idea: Augustine and the Trinity of Love

Augustine's philosophical inquiries led him to place great emphasis on a number of important beliefs, and these included the need for each individual to have a relationship with God, the personal creator God. This viewpoint was also accompanied by the belief that humanity is in a helpless and hopeless condition. Augustine shows us that the human race is united in sinful rebellion against God and cannot save itself. Those who come under the conviction of the Holy Spirit and having met with Christ have learned that they must trust him completely and not rely on their own efforts, qualities or inheritance for their salvation.

Augustine did something that nobody before him had managed; he brought two things together, the Trinity of Love – the Triune God – and the love of God. *"The Bible does not teach us that God needed the creation in order to have something to love, because if that were true, he could not be fully Himself without it. So Augustine reasoned that God must be love inside Himself. To His mind, the Father is the one who loves, the Son is the one who is loved (the "beloved Son" revealed in the baptism of Jesus), and the Holy Spirit is the love that flows between them and binds them together. It is in the Spirit, moreover, who binds believers to God and makes us partakers by adoption of that love which is intrinsic to the Trinity's being."* (Gerald Bray).

Augustine further taught that God created the world for a purpose. The fact that He placed his own triune image in Adam – who was intended to be the crowning glory of his creation – teaches us that God's otherwise mysterious act had a reason that we cannot fully understand or appreciate. What we do know is that He enacted His great plan of redemption for Adam's fallen race, loving and calling out a people to Himself who will enter into His fullness in eternity and experience complete happiness which begins here and now as our happiness and flourishing is found in God.

Memorable Quote:
"The reader of these reflections of mine on the Trinity should bear in mind that my pen is on the watch against the sophistries of those who scorn the starting-point of faith, and allow themselves to be deceived through an unseasonable and misguided love of reason." Augustine of Hippo, The Trinity

Journaling Suggestion:
Embracing the redemptive love of the Triune God for me, and loving Him above all else.

Memo for Meditation:
"And may you have the power to understand, as all God's people should, how wide, how long, how high, and how deep His love is. May you experience the love of Christ, though it is too great to understand fully. Then you will be made complete with all the fullness of life and power that comes from God." Ephesians 3:18,19.

February 24

Motivational Idea: Augustine and supreme authority

Augustine taught that the word of God is to be found in the Bible and nowhere else. He had a concept of the Bible as a single, overarching message from God. Augustine's sense of the bigger picture is of great importance because there is a constant temptation to take Bible verses out of context. There is also a temptation to introduce human traditions that are not in the Scriptures and make them tests of orthodoxy.

Augustine's method of interpretation was designed to prevent aberrations like these. He believed without hesitation that God is the Bible's author and accepted both its inspiration and its inerrancy. The writing of Scripture is God's initiative alone and that He determined what was to be written in the pages of Holy Scripture. Augustine had become convinced of the truth but wrestled with his old life. This scripture had a profound impact upon him: *"Let us conduct ourselves becomingly as in the day, not in revelling and drunkenness, not in debauchery and licentiousness, not in quarrelling and jealousy. But put on the Lord Jesus Christ, and make no provision for the flesh, to gratify its desires."* (Romans 13:13–14). Here, Augustine found the power to overcome the fears and doubts that had plagued him for so long. However, the power did not come from himself. The power came from the word of God in Scripture. Here, we discover one of the most important differences between God's word and mere human words: God's word contains in itself the power to accomplish the very things it declares. Unlike the latest philosophy or self-help book, which may have good advice but leaves us to do the work. God's word is able to make happen exactly what it proclaims. This opens up for us a whole new way of reading Scripture, a way in which we expect God's word to accomplish in us the very thing we are reading, just like Augustine.

Memorable Quote:
"For I confess to your Charity that I have learned to yield this respect and honour only to the canonical books of Scripture: of these alone do I most firmly believe that the authors were completely free from error...when I read other authors, however eminent they may be in sanctity and learning, I do not necessarily believe a thing is true because they think so, but because they have been able to convince me, either on the authority of the canonical writers or by a probable reasons which is not inconsistent with the truth." Letters 82:3, Augustine to St Jerome.

Journaling Suggestion:
Record your prayers, prompted by reading God's word and hearing what He is saying to you.

Memo for Meditation:
"All Scripture is inspired by God and is useful to teach us what is true and to make us realise what is wrong in our lives. It corrects us when we are wrong and teaches us to do what is right." 2 Timothy 3:16.

February 25

Motivational Idea: What authority do you choose for the flourishing life?

From Augustine right up to the present day, many people still believe in the infinite personal living creator God, who is both transcendent and immanent, and that He speaks to us through His word, the Bible, which is the supreme and final authority in all matters of faith and doctrine. The Bible gives us the revelation of God, the way of salvation, His philosophy on the flourishing life, and the wisdom to embrace such a way of life, experiencing a happiness and a joy that the world cannot give. Yet for many, the rise of the 'enlightenment' – known as the Age of Reason and developed in the early-to-mid-17th century – changed everything. The rise of rationalism, empiricism and scepticism saw a new found authority with an emphasis on the primacy of reason and strict scientific method. Materialistic humanism came to the fore, placing man at the centre of all things and the watchword was 'reason'. Man is supreme and the consciousness of the individual is the source and centre of truth.

Francis Schaffer said of this Age of Reason: *"The utopian dream of the enlightenment can be summed up in five words: reason, nature, happiness, progress and liberty. It was thoroughly secular in its thinking."*

The Kantian view is that you need to deny knowledge to make way for faith. Hegel came to the view that nothing is true in the absolute sense. Hume, the father of modern scepticism, opened the door to chronic hopeless scepticism about everything. This age led not to *"reason, nature, happiness, progress and liberty"* at all but to a cul-de-sac of gross ignorance and darkness, not a utopian dream but a horrible nightmare!

Ironically, science and faith are not diametrically opposed at all. Newton developed the theory of gravity, the laws of motion which became the basis for physics, and he saw God as the masterful creator whose existence could not be denied in the face of the grandeur of creation. God's word cannot be denied, either. Do we choose the mess of man which elevates human reason and denies divine revelation, or the message of the Master, Jesus Christ Himself, fully God and fully man, the perfect man revealed in the Bible?

Memorable Quote:
"Well, here's another nice mess you've gotten me into!" Laurel and Hardy's best-known catchphrase.

Journaling Suggestion:
 The Bible is the supreme and final authority in all matters of faith and doctrine.

Memo for Meditation:

"Although they claimed to be wise, they became fools and exchanged the glory of the immortal God for images made to look like a mortal human being and birds and animals and reptiles." Romans 1:22-23

February 26

Motivational Idea: Bertrand Russell and the quest for happiness

Bertrand Russell, one of the greatest thinkers of the 20th century, believed that happiness was something that did not just come to us – it had to be achieved. In his book, *The Quest for Happiness,* he spends more time looking at unhappiness because, for Russell, we need to know what unhappiness is and its causes before we can set out on our quest for happiness. One of the main reasons for unhappiness is meaninglessness. We need to find meaning outside of our daily struggles and routines, and boredom is the opposite of happiness. We need to escape from psychological misery and find interests that are as wide as possible. Happiness is achieved by effort. He referred to Byronic unhappiness: this denotes the person who is self-obsessed, having a broody personality, proud, moody, cynical and defiant; a person who is unhappy and proud to be so. A wide range of interests will give us what he called a 'zest' for life, and we will derive pleasure from engaging with the world rather than the malady of misery when we don't engage and withdraw into ourselves.

Russell was also a vocal atheist, arguably the foremost atheist of the 20th century, and ironically a militant defender of scepticism. He wrote about why he was not a Christian and this was based on two categories. Firstly, he did not accept belief in God and immortality, nor that Jesus was God. Secondly, he argued that if everything has a cause, then God must have a cause; if there can be anything without a cause, it just might as well be the world as God. The world could just have been there – that could have been the uncaused cause. However, this is a straw man argument. Put simply, everything that *begins* to exist has a cause; the universe *began* to exist, therefore the universe has a cause. The laws of thermodynamics indicate that the universe could not have always existed, it had a cause. God is eternal and he made it and designed it for human habitation. Design indicates a designer who made us and made us for a life of happiness and joy in knowing Him in the revelation of His beloved Son, co-equal and co-eternal with the Father. Embrace Him!

Memorable Quote:

"A low view of God is the cause of a hundred lesser evils. A high view of God is the solution to ten thousand temporal problems." A W Tozer

Journaling Suggestion:

The answers are found in you, Oh God. Teach me your truth and your way. Amen.

Memo for Meditation:

"But all who are hunting for you—oh, let them sing and be happy. Let those who know what you're all about tell the world you're great and not quitting. And me? I'm a mess. I'm nothing and have nothing: make something of me. You can do it; you've got what it takes— but God, don't put it off." Psalm 40:17.

February 27

Motivational Idea: Moses the philosopher

Philo of Alexandria (ca 20BC-50AD), a Jew, trained as a Greek philosopher, and argued that Moses was a great philosopher. One of the big issues in philosophy is metaphysics, which considers the nature of the universe and how it works. It's concerned about being, nature, identity and cause. What is reality? These big questions are exactly what Moses answers in his writings. He wrote about the great mysteries of the universe as well as the laws of God for humanity's wellbeing. When we consider his writings on creation, we find what Jonathan T Pennington (JTP) calls the *"metaphysic extraordinaire"*, and what sets the Bible metaphysic apart is the radical claim that there is one God, the ultimate reality, when most ancient peoples were polytheists (belief in many gods).

The reality is that the Bible answers the fundamental questions of philosophy. JTP states, *"Was Philo right that Moses was a philosopher? Yes! And Moses is not alone in the Old Testament. Moses and his writings are the foundation of the rest of the Bible for a great truth that we have forgotten in modern times - that the Hebrew*

Scriptures present themselves as a work of divinely revealed ancient philosophy."

Sadly, modern philosophy has made a distinction between 'reason' and 'revelation', between 'philosophy' and 'faith'. These should not be divided and differentiated as being polar-opposites. We can read the word of God philosophically, and hold to both reason and revelation as well as both philosophy and faith. It has been allowed to be a false separation for many who have been opposed to the reality of revelation and the need for faith in God. So let us approach the Bible with renewed confidence, embracing His revelation with both reason and faith, acknowledging that God is the God of infinite wisdom declared in His revealed philosophy which is inexhaustible in its treasures yet simple enough in its message for our children and grandchildren, with a depth that will keep us on the edge of our philosophical seats forever. But we need to live it out on earth.

Memorable Quote:
"What is happiness/flourishing? What is goodness? And what is reality? The Bible presents us with answers to these fundamental, philosophical questions. In the Bible, God is the ultimate reality and one is a good person and truly well off when one is in a right relationship with God. The Bible is addressing precisely the same questions as traditional philosophy."

Journaling Suggestion:
I am going to read and study the inspired Scriptures as divine philosophy for life.

Memo for Meditation:
"In the beginning God created the heavens and the earth." Genesis 1:1.

February 28

Motivational Idea: The New Testament is a philosophy book

Philosophers had biographies written to show what they taught and how to live. This was well established when Jesus came on the scene of time. The biography of a philosopher contained a record of their teachings and wise sayings, stories that revealed their character and encouraged people to become their disciples. Jesus the philosopher is revealed in His biographical Gospels. He used wisdom tools to explain his teaching, i.e. 60 parables (35% of his teaching method), and He used 'aphorisms' – short, pithy memorable wisdom sayings. This was a common technique used by philosophers. And so Jesus' wisdom and teachings as a prophetic philosopher and sage prophet are recorded in the Gospels. As for the rest of the New Testament, JTP notes that, *"Again we find that the 23 books naturally and consciously interact with the Greco-Roman world into which Christianity had arrived."* (See quote below).

Jesus is the true prophetic philosopher but He is the Son of God who became man, died for our sins, was raised for our justification, and is coming back for those who have put their faith and trust in Him, to make everything right, and to inaugurate a new heaven and new earth wherein dwells righteousness.

Memorable Quote:
"Like every other aspect of the NT teaching, the metaphysics of the NT are rooted in the same fundamental world-understanding as the Hebrew Scriptures - namely, the belief that the eternal, timeless, singular God created humanity male and female, as fundamentally good with authority and responsibility over creation. God is in control of the world and is personal. He engages with humanity graciously, even though there had been a breaking of this relationship because of sin. This world is bound in time, but God is eternal and will bring this current age to an end. He will re-establish His relationship with all creation in a new and everlasting age of goodness." JTP

Journaling Suggestion:
Read the New Testament as a philosophical book as a disciple of the Great Philosopher.

Memo for Meditation:
"Jesus performed many other signs in the presence of his disciples, which are not recorded in this book. But these are written that you may believe that Jesus is the Messiah, the Son of God, and that by believing you may have life in his name." John 20:30,31
"This is the disciple who testifies to these things and who wrote them down. We know that his testimony is true. Jesus did many other things as

well. If every one of them were written down, I suppose that even the whole world would not have room for the books that would be written." John 21:24,25

February 29 (intercalary/leap year day)

Motivational Idea: The proper use of philosophy

The Apostle Paul was familiar with the philosophers of his day and in Dr Luke's account (Acts 17:23-28) of his visit to Mars Hill, Athens, he records that Paul observed the objects of their worship and an altar, *"to the unknown god."* Paul then told them that he would proclaim to them, *"The God in whom we live and have our being; as even some of your own poets have said, 'We are indeed His offspring.'* Paul was referring to Creticia by Epimenides when he says, *"in whom we live and have our being."* He also quotes Aratus when he tells his audience that, *"We are His offspring."*

Paul, in using these philosophical sentiments, did now allow them to overtake the Scriptures and the theological claims it sets out as the revelation of God; he nevertheless employed them in subordination of his theological goal of presenting the Gospel of Christ. He didn't begin with Scripture as he would in the Jewish synagogues because of their familiarity with the Old Testament (Acts 17:2). Paul instead began with philosophical claims familiar to his pagan audience. We learn an important lesson from him that the abuse of philosophy should not disqualify its proper use. When Paul tells the Colossian church (2:8) *"Not to be taken captive by philosophy and empty deceit, according to human tradition,"* he is not condemning philosophy, rather he's warning them to look out for *bad* philosophies. They had been attacked by philosophical speculations that opposed the truth of Christ. We need good philosophy to refute bad philosophy. Paul was not anti-philosophy and for any well-meaning soul to argue against the use of philosophy is self-refuting because they will be using philosophical arguments in doing so.

Memorable Quote:

"For those who believe that we should excise all philosophy from theology do not realise that all of us use philosophical concepts and terms whether we realise it or not. He who believes he is free from

philosophy is the likely unwitting adherent to the philosophical teaching of a defunct philosopher or theologian. Rather than run from natural knowledge, or philosophy, we should seek God's wisdom wherever we find it. Subject to the magisterial authority of Scripture, true philosophy never conflicts with sacred theology." JTP

Journaling Suggestion:
Know good and true philosophy, and be able to refute bad philosophies.

Memo for Meditation:
"We are destroying sophisticated arguments and every exalted and proud thing that sets itself up against the [true] knowledge of God, and we are taking every thought and purpose captive to the obedience of Christ." 2 Corinthian 10:5.

THE PHYSICAL DIMENSION

March 1

Motivational Idea: Take a walk

The five-a-day for wellbeing includes exercise. Being physically active is not only great for your physical health and fitness – evidence also shows that it can improve your mental wellbeing as it causes chemical changes in your brain which can help to positively change your mood. Your self-esteem can improve. It can also help you set goals or challenges. These positives can be transferable and adapted in every area of your life, even at a subconscious level. Don't forget to set realistic goals and find the optimal level for you. Exercise to stimulate, not to annihilate! And when you're at it, don't forget those spiritual exercises too. The Bible often uses the metaphor of walking when it refers to our lives here on earth, and particularly in relation to the Christian life. Just as we have an end goal when it comes to a good walk, so we ought to have an end goal when it comes to our spiritual journey. Are we going in the right direction? Who are we walking with? What will we do when we face obstacles and difficulty? Is there any wise counsel to advise us? There are plenty of gurus on social media that tell us they have the answer.

Three thousand years ago, King David wrote what must be one of the most famous Psalms in the Bible, Psalm 23: *"The LORD is my shepherd; I have all that I need. He lets me rest in green meadows; he leads me beside peaceful streams. He renews my strength. He guides me along right paths, bringing honour to his name. Even when I walk through the darkest valley, I will not be afraid, for you are close beside me. Your rod and your staff protect and comfort me. You prepare a feast for me in the presence of my enemies. You honour me by anointing my head with oil. My cup overflows with blessings. Surely your goodness and unfailing love will pursue me, all the days of my life, and I will live in the house of the LORD forever."*

Walk with Jesus today and allow the wisdom of this Psalm to permeate every aspect of your life from this day on.

Memorable Quote:
"All truly great thoughts are conceived while walking." Friedrich Nietzsche

Journaling Suggestion:
Take a prayer walk and journal your thoughts.

Memo for Meditation:
"Exercise daily in God—no spiritual flabbiness, please! Workouts in the gymnasium are useful, but a disciplined life in God is far more so, making you fit both today and forever. You can count on this. Take it to heart." 1 Timothy 4:7,8.

March 2

Motivational Idea: Food for the body and food for the soul

Food for the body and food for the soul! We all have our favourite foods. When you have been out for a meal with friends, you will have experienced that convivial atmosphere and the good mood feeling when everyone has eaten well. Our bodies need good food, so eat well. That wisest of men said, *"So I decided there is nothing better than to enjoy food and drink and to find satisfaction in work. Then I realised that these pleasures are from the hand of God."* (Ecclesiastes 2:24). It is easy to forget that we also feed our minds every day too. You are what you think, so make sure that you feed your mind on that which is nourishing and wholesome, and not junk food. The mind matters and mental wellbeing is as important as physical wellbeing.

The memo for today reminds us of the best and most profitable food for the soul. In fact, it is absolutely essential for sustaining our inner life. And it was Jesus who said it in response to the evil one who would wish to fill us with seemingly tasty dainties that are but junk food at best and poisonous to humanity at worst. The Apostle Peter tells his readers to, *"Get rid of all evil behaviour. Be done with all deceit, hypocrisy, jealousy, and all unkind speech. Like newborn babies, you must crave pure spiritual milk so that you will grow into a full experience of salvation."* (1 Peter 2:1-3). We are to go on to maturity as we feed on God's word. Paul writing to the Corinthians told them: *"I had to feed you with milk, not with solid food, because you weren't ready for anything stronger. And you still aren't ready."* (1 Corinthians 3:2).

Are we on the road to spiritual maturity? Can we handle solid food, the meat of the word? The writer to the Hebrews says, *"You are like babies who need milk and cannot eat solid food. For someone who lives on milk is still an infant and doesn't know how to do what is right. Solid food is for those who are mature, who through training have the skill to recognize the difference between right and wrong."* (Hebrews 5:12-13). The author of Hebrews says that if all we have is milk, we are ignorant in the word of righteousness. In other words, the meat of the word isn't overly complicated theological teaching; it is righteousness, grace and truth, found in Jesus.

Memorable Quote:

"Happy were we then, for we had a good house, and good food, and good work." Richard Llewellan

Journaling Suggestion:

You are what you eat, so take good care of both body and soul.

Memo for Meditation:

"Bread alone will not satisfy, but true life is found in every word that constantly goes forth from God's mouth." Matthew 4:4.

March 3

Motivational Idea: The antidote to the poison that brings death

Five hundred years ago, the Swiss chemist Paracelsus set out the basic principle of toxicology: *"All things are poison and nothing is without poison; only the dose makes a thing not a poison."* This has been shortened to: *"The dose makes the poison."* In other words, any chemical can be toxic if too much is ingested or absorbed into the body. Six litres of water, 118 coffees and 13 shots of strong alcohol can potentially kill. Some regimes are extremely interested in toxicology, building up their stocks of poisons such as Novichok to kill their enemies. The poisoning of Sergei and Yulia Skripal in Salisbury, England, was a botched assassination attempt using the Novichok nerve agent. They were extremely fortunate to survive. (Alexander

Litvinenko was not so fortunate and succumbed to poisoning from polonium-210.)

A whole range of legitimate drugs have been designed to dispel pain and alleviate a range of health conditions, but these can also be used and abused to poison the system and cause death. In the mental health field, people who are ambivalent about attempting suicide are generally not aware that a relatively small amount of a common painkiller tablet could be fatal. The good news is that many poisons have been used for many positive purposes across the span of human existence, such as anti-venoms and medicines. The bad news is that we have all been affected by a poison that is universal and we will all eventually die. We have all been affected by original sin. The proof? Just visit the local cemetery and there you will find the evidence. The Bible says that, "*When Adam sinned, sin entered the world. Adam's sin brought death, so death spread to everyone, for everyone sinned.*" (Romans 5:12-19). Jesus, however, brought us the antidote in His sacrifice on the cross.

Memorable Quote:
'*For this is how God loved the world: He gave his one and only Son, so that everyone who believes in him will not perish but have eternal life.*" John 3:16.

Journaling Suggestion:
"*Today I have given you the choice between life and death, between blessings and curses. Now I call on heaven and earth to witness the choice you make. Oh, that you would choose life, so that you and your descendants might live!*" Deuteronomy 30:19.

Memo for Meditation:
"*For the sin of this one man, Adam, caused death to rule over many. But even greater is God's wonderful grace and his gift of righteousness, for all who receive it will live in triumph over sin and death through this one man, Jesus Christ.*" Roman 5:17.

March 4

Motivational Idea: A face that shines

'It's written all over your face'; 'Every face tells a story.' These are familiar phrases. The face can indeed tell a story. George Orwell wrote, *"At 50, everyone has the face he deserves."* These were apparently the last words the *Nineteen Eighty-Four* author penned in his personal diary. He died just over six months later, in 1950, at age 46. The fresh face of youth can indeed change over the years; the ageing process sets in, and depending on how we have lived, we may get the face we deserve. And yet in spite of ageing, and let's face it, fifty is young, people who have experienced tough lives, people who have lived with addictions of one kind or another, can change. We sometimes see before and after photos of people showing us what they looked like in the throes of their addiction, and then we see their appearance once they have kicked the habit. The transformation can be astounding; it's like looking at a different person. What story do our faces tell today? Perhaps we have truly 'lived-in' faces given the journey we have undertaken; perhaps it's even a miracle that we are here today. It has been said that there are no two faces the same on planet earth, and as for facial recognition, well, that is an amazing phenomenon! We recognise people, even a face we have not seen for a lifetime.

The Bible has a lot to say about faces. God knows us, every line and every furrowed brow. The prayer is heard in Scripture, *"Restore us, O God; Cause Your face to shine on us [with favour and approval], and we will be saved."* (Psalm 80:3,19). The word 'shine' (Hebrew *or*) means, 'to shed light' or 'illuminate'. God's light shines on us with His love, mercy, grace and salvation. May you feel the warmth of His light and favour shining upon you today.

Memorable Quote:
"God's face is a metaphor for his loving presence. When God's face shines, blessing and deliverance occur. When God shines His face upon us, His light infuses our hearts and minds with the knowledge that we are His precious children. His pure love radiates in and through us."

Journaling Suggestion:
"Make your face shine upon your servant; save me for your mercies' sake." Psalm 31:16

Memo for Meditation:
"The Lord bless you and keep you; the Lord make his face shine on you and be gracious to you; the Lord turn his face toward you and give you peace." Numbers 6:24-26

March 5

Motivational Idea: Face to face

Technology has transformed the world! Take virtual face-to-face meetings; we can talk with friends and family on the far side of the world, and see their faces. The workplace has undergone a revolution. Meetings can be held without having to travel anywhere. During the global Covid pandemic, the world went almost totally virtual, and in coming out of that time of isolation the virtual world of work has continued. However, people report that when they do get to actually meet face-to-face, seeing people, being with people is heart-warming and life-changing. As for family and loved ones, words cannot begin to express the joy of actually being together again, to look into the eyes of those we love, to see those smiles, to get those hugs, to feel that tender touch, be present again... you just can't beat being in the presence of the one you love!

One man stands out in history. He didn't have a mobile, nor did he have any technology; it was not a virtual world, it was a real world. One day he had an encounter that would change the course of his life. In fact, the encounter happened about 3,500 years ago. He was tending sheep in a dry desert. Life was hard; he had been a prince of Egypt but gave it all up. You can read all about him and his experience in Exodus, Chapter 3. He had an encounter with God. His name was Moses, and this is what the Bible says about him: *"The LORD would speak to Moses face to face, as one speaks to a friend."* (Exodus 33:11). Moses had an intimacy with God that we too can have through Christ today. God wants it! Do you?

Memorable Quote:
"Moses spent 40 years in Egypt learning to be something; he then spent 40 years of his life in the desert learning to be nothing; and from His encounter with God, he learned that God is everything."

Journaling Suggestion:
Intimacy with God.

Memo for Meditation:
"It was by faith that Moses, when he grew up, refused to be called the son of Pharaoh's daughter. He chose to share the oppression of God's people instead of enjoying the fleeting pleasures of sin. He thought it was better to suffer for the sake of Christ than to own the treasures of Egypt, for he was looking ahead to his great reward. It was by faith that Moses left the land of Egypt, not fearing the king's anger. He kept right on going because he kept his eyes on the one who is invisible. It was by faith that Moses commanded the people of Israel to keep the Passover and to sprinkle blood on the doorposts so that the angel of death would not kill their firstborn sons." Hebrews 11:24-28

March 6

Motivational Idea: God with a human face

The word 'bless' and its synonyms are found 600 times in the Old Testament and over 500 times in the New Testament. It means to be granted special favour by God. *"The blessing of the LORD makes rich, and He adds no sorrow with it"* (Proverbs 10:22). In all cases, the blessing serves as a guide and motivation to pursue a course of life within the blessing. The priestly blessing in Numbers 6:24-26 invites God to shine His face upon us. The context is a vow of separation to God, set apart for Him. Bless can mean to kneel, and in earlier times the recipient would kneel to receive the blessing. In Matthew 2, we find wise men kneeling before the Christ child. They looked into the face of the babe of Bethlehem and worshipped Him because they recognised His kingship. Herein is the mystery of the incarnation, that God became man. *"Veiled in flesh, the Godhead see, hail the incarnate deity. For you know the grace of our Lord Jesus Christ: Though he was rich, for your sake he became poor, so that by his poverty you might become rich."* 2 (Corinthian 8:9).

He has given us everything we need to be rich in pleasing Him, rich in glorifying Him, wealthy in magnifying His name. For Jesus to rescue us from sins's power, He died on the cross and defeated the devil. The prophet Isaiah gives us a vivid picture of the sufferings of Christ: *"But many were amazed when they saw him. His face was so disfigured he seemed hardly human, and from his appearance, one would scarcely know he was a man."* (Isaiah 52:14).

Check out Isaiah Chapter 53. In His first advent, He came to redeem His people and reign in our hearts. In His second advent, He comes to judge the world, and reign over the nations. *"Behold, he is coming with the clouds, and every eye will see him, even those who pierced him, and all tribes of the earth will wail on account of him. Even so. Amen."* (Revelation 1:7). Get ready, for all of us will see Him.

Memorable Quote:
"Though he was God, He did not think of equality with God as something to cling to. Instead, He gave up his divine privileges; He took the humble position of a slave and was born as a human being. When he appeared in human form, He humbled himself in obedience to God and died a criminal's death on a cross." Philippians 2:6-8.

Journaling Suggestion:
Seeking the face of God in His word and in prayer, and for all my days!

Memo for Mediation:
"Therefore, God elevated him to the place of highest honour and gave him the name above all other names, that at the name of Jesus every knee should bow, in heaven and on earth and under the earth, and every tongue declare that Jesus Christ is Lord, to the glory of God the Father." Philippians 2:9-11.

March 7

Motivational Idea: Tears in a bottle

There are three types of tears. *Basal tears* bathe our eyes. When we blink, we spread them evenly over the surface of our eyes to improve our vision and focus. They wash away dirt and germs to keep our eyes healthy and free of infection.

Reflex tears are the tears that our eyes produce when we chop onions. They wash away harmful irritants like smoke or particles. Our eyes make more of them than basal tears, and they contain substances, such as antibodies, to help fight germs.

Emotional tears are the ones that flow when we are feeling happy, sad, or overwhelmed with emotions. They contain additional proteins and hormones we won't find in other tears, such as prolactin, potassium, manganese and stress hormones. Emotional tears release stress and help calm the body down. Unlike basal tears, our bodies don't make them automatically. For emotional tears to kick in, the limbic system – the part of our brains that regulate emotions – sends a signal to the brain's message system to activate our lacrimal glands to produce tears. When we make a lot of them, they spill down our cheeks. 'Tears in a bottle' is not an exhibit in the Tate Gallery, although some artists may have already had the idea to collect them. It was the writer of Psalm 56 who penned the words, *"You have taken account of my wanderings. Put my tears in Your bottle—are they not in Your book?"* David was a prisoner of war and he was in deep trouble; his expression is a way of saying that God cares and God was with him to help him and save him. Whatever prison house you are in today, just know that God cares, He knows every tear you shed and He will rescue you. *"Weeping may endure for a night, but joy comes in the morning."* (Psalm 30:5).

There are three references in Scripture to the tears of Jesus (John 11:35; Luke 19:41; Hebrews 5:7-9). *"He was... a man of sorrows and acquainted with grief."* Isaiah 53:3. Jesus wept, identifying with our humanity. One day, He will wipe all our tears away for ever!

Memorable Quote:
Pope Leo the Great referred to the two natures of Jesus: *"In His humanity Jesus wept for Lazarus; in His divinity he raised him from the dead. The sorrow, sympathy, and compassion Jesus felt for all mankind. The rage He felt against the tyranny of death over mankind."*

Journaling Suggestion:
God knows your tears. Lord, thank you that you count all my tears and you are my help and my deliverer.

Memo for Meditation:
"And God shall wipe away all tears from their eyes; and there shall be no more death, neither sorrow, nor crying, neither shall there be any more pain: for the former things are passed away." Revelation 21.4.

March 8

Motivational Idea: Looking in the mirror

The giver is happier than the getter? Really! That is totally counter-intuitive today. Yet that is what Paul tells us. *"It is more blessed to give than receive."* (Acts 20.35). It's a quote from Jesus Himself, that the Apostles knew. Our role model is God Himself for He is a generous God. *"Every good and perfect gift is from above, coming down from the Father of the heavenly lights, who does not change like shifting shadows. He chose to give us birth through the word of truth, that we might be a kind of first fruits of all he created."* (James 1.17,18). *"He who did not spare his own Son, but gave him up for us all—how will he not also, along with him, graciously give us all things?"* (Romans 8.32). We say with Paul, *"Thanks be to God for his indescribable gift!"* (2 Corinthians 9.15).

When God gave us Jesus, He gave us everything! Everything we need is found in Him. The gift of salvation is found in Him. Our God is a good God, a giving God, a forgiving God and an unchanging God. We have been birthed in God through His word. *"So faith comes from hearing, and hearing through the word of Christ."* (Hebrews 11:6). *"And without faith it is impossible to please him, for whoever would draw near to God must believe that he exists and that he rewards those who seek him."* (Romans 10:17).

God has shown us in His word how to live. Let us Look in the mirror of His word today, and don't forget to put it into practice. Be blessed!

Memorable Quote:

"In God's economy you will be more blessed if you're a spiritual conduit rather than a spiritual cul-de-sac. God wants to work through you so that you will be a blessing to others. If you have the capacity to address a need (with your money, your time, or your encouragement), be used by God to give to and meet that need. God will return the favour." Tony Evans, *Bible Commentary*

Journaling Suggestion:

Look in God's mirror – the Bible is His mirror.

Memo for Meditation:

"Understand this, my dear brothers and sisters: You must all be quick to listen, slow to speak, and slow to get angry. Human anger does not produce the righteousness God desires. So get rid of all the filth and evil in your lives, and humbly accept the word God has planted in your hearts, for it has the power to save your souls. But don't just listen to God's word. You must do what it says. Otherwise, you are only fooling yourselves. For if you listen to the word and don't obey, it is like glancing at your face in a mirror. You see yourself, walk away, and forget what you look like. But if you look carefully into the perfect law that sets you free, and if you do what it says and don't forget what you heard, then God will bless you for doing it." James 1:19-25.

March 9

Motivational Idea: How's your walk?

Your walking style can reveal your personality type. Studies reveal that our walking styles, including stride and speed, can tell a lot of important traits about our personalities. Every one of us is unique in our own way and so is our walking style. One of the earliest studies into personality type by studying walking style was published in 1935 by German-born psychologist Werner Wolff. Since then, a number of studies into walking styles have been undertaken with some fascinating insights. The fast walker personality type reveals a highly diligent and outgoing kind of person. If you are a slow walker, then this can reveal that you are a cautious person. If you are a relaxed, strolling walker, then you love to live on your own terms in life, at your own pace. If you are the long quick-stride walker, then your walking personality type reveals you have a positive outlook, you are a competitive and fiery personality type that helps you to get things done. If you are the type of walker who drags their feet, then your walking personality type reveals that you are an anxious kind of person or you worry a lot.

The Bible refers to walking in a metaphorical sense. We have been created for a relationship with God and Jesus has made this possible. We ought to walk in the same way in which he walked (See 1 John 2.6). How are we walking today? Are we walking in the light? (See 1 John 1.7). Or in darkness? (See Proverbs 2.13).

Memorable Quote:

"The verb 'walk' in its literal sense of going along or moving about on foot at a moderate pace is found numerous times in the Gospels. However, this same verb is more often used throughout the Old Testament and the epistles of the New Testament in a metaphorical way. In this sense it means to follow a certain course of life or to conduct oneself in a certain way. Many times the verb translated 'walk' is present tense in the Greek of the New Testament, which means that the writer is referring to a continued mode of conduct or behaviour. In fact, the infinitive 'to walk' can be translated, in a Hebraistic way, 'to live'."
Baker's Evangelical Dictionary.

Journaling Suggestion:

God is the God of the journey, and not only the destination. My walk with God.

Memo for Meditation:

"You're blessed when you stay on course, walking steadily on the road revealed by GOD. You're blessed when you follow his directions, doing your best to find him. That's right—you don't go off on your own; you walk straight along the road he set. You, GOD, prescribed the right way to live; now you expect us to live it. Oh, that my steps might be steady, keeping to the course you set; Then I'd never have any regrets in comparing my life with your counsel." Psalm 119:1-7.

March 10

Motivational Idea: Trespassers will be prosecuted

The author and his faithful harrier hound enjoy walking in the fields at Ballydown, near Banbridge, Co Down in Northern Ireland. One day on a familiar walk, a new sign had been placed by the farmer on a post at the gate to the field. It read, *Keep out! Trespassers will be prosecuted.* There was no ambiguity here – you cannot enter this land! We didn't have permission to step onto the property without permission from the owner. An alternative route had to be taken, although there was the temptation to ignore the sign and carry on regardless; Barney was well up for it! The word 'trespass' means to transgress in some active manner, commit an aggressive offence, to sin, from Old French *trespasser*, to pass beyond or across, cross, traverse, infringe, violate. The Latin, *trans passus* means to pass through or enter unlawfully.

Jesus taught His disciples to pray: *"Forgive us our trespasses as we forgive those who trespass against us."* The important thing is that we all need God's forgiveness for we have transgressed against God. And having received His forgiveness, we are to forgive others. Some English versions use the word 'debts' instead of 'trespasses'. The word 'trespass' suggests that we have violated a rule or committed an infraction. The word 'debt' suggests we owe God something we cannot pay. Jesus paid the price on the cross when he bore our sins in His own body on the tree. "Forgive us our debts" suggests that we have done things that we should not have done, and left undone things we should have done. "Forgive us our trespasses" comes from the Book of Common Prayer, which is why many people use the word 'trespasses'. The Geneva Bible and the King James Bible used the word 'debts'. The truth of the Bible is that trespassers and debtors can be forgiven, and we are to be forgiving to those who have wronged us.

Memorable Quote:
"To forgive is the highest, most beautiful form of love. In return, you will receive untold peace and happiness." Robert Muller

Journaling Suggestion:
Journal on forgiveness.

Memo for Meditation:
"Our Father, who art in heaven, hallowed be thy name; thy kingdom come; thy will be done; on earth as it is in heaven. Give us this day our daily bread. And forgive us our trespasses, as we forgive those who trespass against us. And lead us not into temptation; but deliver us from evil. For thine is the kingdom, the power and the glory, for ever and ever. Amen." Matthew 6:9-13.

March 11

Motivational Idea: Restoration of a ruined house

When it comes to house renovations, the architect Antonia Marinucci, has some sound advice: *"I recommend tackling the most urgent needs* first: are there structural, roof, or foundation repairs that need to be made so that the home is safe to occupy? Addressing the biggest issues first gives a solid base for the rest of the work. You don't want to start cosmetic work if there are issues lurking beneath that will eventually need to be addressed!" Noted!

So, if you are contemplating an amazing and challenging project, be aware that the walls may be toxic, the roof will need to be carefully examined as it might not meet building regulations, the electrical wiring may be dangerous and out of date, the plumbing system will need attendance – it may have old galvanised pipes – and of course make sure you have a firm foundation. If this is not right, then the challenge of the 'fixer-upper' will be a total failure. Jesus came to restore us, He came to redeem us from our ruined condition because of sin. He does much more than undertake fixer-upper work, He makes us His new creation and, as the Master Builder, makes us into something beautiful (See 2 Corinthians 5.17). You are His Masterpiece! (See Ephesians 2.10), His dwelling house!

Memorable Quote:
"Imagine yourself as a living house. God comes in to rebuild that house. At first, perhaps, you can understand what He is doing. He is getting the drains right and stopping the leaks in the roof and so on; you knew that those jobs needed doing and so you are not surprised. But presently He starts knocking the house about in a way that hurts abominably and does not seem to make any sense. What on earth is He up to? The explanation is that He is building quite a different house from the one you thought of - throwing out a new wing here, putting on an extra floor there, running up towers, making courtyards. You thought you were being made into a decent little cottage: but He is building a palace. He intends to come and live in it Himself." C S Lewis, Mere Christianity.

Journaling Suggestion:
God lives in me so I can live in him and He can live through me, for His Glory!

Memo for Mediation:
"But Jesus deserves far more glory than Moses, just as a person who builds a house deserves more praise than the house itself. For every house has a builder, but the one who built everything is God Moses was

certainly faithful in God's house as a servant. His work was an illustration of the truths God would reveal later. But Christ, as the Son, is in charge of God's entire house. And we are God's house, if we keep our courage and remain confident in our hope in Christ." Hebrews 3:3-6.

March 12

Motivational Idea: Our lifetime home

The human body is perhaps the most complex composition ever to have existed. From a DNA perspective, all humans are more than 99 percent identical.

Here are some facts about the human body:

- There are 100,000 miles of blood vessels in the human body, laid end to end. An adult's blood vessels could circle Earth's equator four times!
- The fastest signals in our bodies are sent by larger myelinated axons found in neurons that transmit the sense of touch or perception from 179-268 miles an hour.
- The fastest-moving muscle in the human body is the orbicularis oculi, capable of contracting in less than 1/100th of a second. A blink typically can last 100-150 milliseconds. You blink more when talking and less when you are reading; this is why you get tired when reading. With the eye being the fastest muscle in the human body, when something happens quickly we often use the expression, *"In the blink of an eye!"*
- The human heart beats more than three billion times in an average lifespan.
- Every second, your body produces 25 million new cells. Put into context, this means that in 15 seconds, you will have produced more cells than there are people in the United States.
- Every new cell is reproduced from the template of our DNA. As we get older it is therefore not surprising that this DNA template gets worn away and errors occur.

Psalm 139 is worth a read and is referenced in our journal suggestion for today and the memo for meditation.

Memorable Quote:

"We are more than the chemicals that form our body. We are a special creation of God. Man is God's masterpiece—His workmanship, the crown of creation." The human body is a wonderful machine. The fact that any one of these devices exists is a complete demonstration that they are the work of an intelligent and skilful designer, God Himself. 'So God created man in His own image, in the image of God created He him, male and female created He them.'" Genesis 1:27.

Journaling Suggestion:

"Search me, O God, and know my heart; test me and know my anxious thoughts. Point out anything in me that offends you, and lead me along the path of everlasting life." Psalm 139:23-24.

Memo for Meditation:

"You made all the delicate, inner parts of my body and knit me together in my mother's womb. Thank you for making me so wonderfully complex! Your workmanship is marvellous—how well I know it. You watched me as I was being formed in utter seclusion, as I was woven together in the dark of the womb. You saw me before I was born. Every day of my life was recorded in your book. Every moment was laid out before a single day had passed." Psalm 139.13-16.

March 13

Motivational Idea: A new body

When Shane MacGowan, of *Fairytale of New York* fame, passed away on 30th November 2023, many of his other compositions came to the fore. One such song has the lyrics, *"If I should fall from grace with God/Where no doctor can relieve me/If I'm buried in the sod/But the angels won't receive me/Let me go, boys, let me go, boys/Let me go down in the mud, where the rivers all run dry."*

The meaning of the song has to do with his political outlook in relation to Ireland. For us, the important point here is the inevitability of death unless the second advent of Jesus takes place. But what about the body? We read in the Scriptures that *"Christ has been raised from the dead. He is the first of a great harvest of all who have died. So you see, just as death came into the world through a man, now the resurrection from the dead has begun through another man. Just as everyone dies because we all belong to Adam, everyone who belongs to Christ will be given new life. But there is an order to this resurrection: Christ was raised as the first of the harvest; then all who belong to Christ will be raised when he comes back."* (1 Corinthians 15:21-23).

Jesus' resurrection is the guarantee of ours. Then, in 2 Corinthians, Chapter 5, the Holy Spirit enlightens us concerning the immortality of those who are in Christ and this includes body, soul and spirit. Our redemption includes our bodies. We shall live with Him forever in our resurrection bodies. We need to ensure we are in Christ today and rejoice in Him and His plenteous redemption, which includes every aspect of our eternal wellbeing. And it's about the here and now, too. *"The Spirit of God, who raised Jesus from the dead, lives in you. And just as God raised Christ Jesus from the dead, he will give life to your mortal bodies by this same Spirit living within you."* (Romans 8:11). We have this life now.

Memorable Quote:
"Now may the God of peace make you holy in every way, and may your whole spirit and soul and body be kept blameless until our Lord Jesus Christ comes again." 1 Thessalonians 5:23.

Journaling Suggestion:
For me to live is Christ, and to die is gain.

Memo for Meditation:
"For we know that when this earthly tent we live in is taken down (that is, when we die and leave this earthly body), we will have a house in heaven, an eternal body made for us by God himself and not by human hands. We grow weary in our present bodies, and we long to put on our heavenly bodies like new clothing. For we will put on heavenly bodies; we will not be spirits without bodies. While we live in these earthly bodies, we groan and sigh, but it's not that we want to die and get rid of these bodies that clothe us. Rather, we want to put on our new bodies so that these dying bodies will be swallowed up by life. God himself has prepared us for this, and as a guarantee he has given us his Holy Spirit." 2 Corinthians 5:1-5.

March 14

Motivational Idea: Your amazing brain

It's a mass of wrinkly material weighing about three pounds and it controls everything you do. It all flows from the top of your head enabling you to think, learn, create and feel emotions. It controls every blink, breath and heartbeat. This fantastic control centre is your brain. Isaac Asimov said, *"The human brain is the most complex and orderly arrangement of matter in the universe".* Your brain contains about 100 billion microscopic cells called neurons – so many it would take you over 3,000 years to count them all. A piece of your brain tissue the size of a grain of sand contains 100,000 neurons and one billion synapses. There are 100,000 miles of blood vessels in your brain: compare this to the distance around the world at the equator which is 24,900 miles.

It might surprise you to know that your brain's storage capacity is considered virtually unlimited. Research suggests the human neuronal connections could add up to one quadrillion (1,000 trillion) connections. Over time, these neurons can combine, increasing storage capacity. Scientists and medical researchers have learned some incredible things about the brain. Yet they admit they still know very little since the brain is so complex. Various parts of the brain control specific things for our functioning. Take, for example, the cerebellum at the base of the brain, which controls balance and posture, heart and lungs, and the nerves and muscles that cause blood vessels to constrict or dilate. At the very bottom of the brain is the brainstem that serves as the motor and sensory pathway to the body and face.

Your amazing brain came about because God created you – you are not the product of chance. You are meant to *be* and to find your fulfilment in the God who enables you to think and use your brain.

Memorable Quote:

"The human brain is the most powerful, advanced, complex, information-processing system in the Universe. Anyone who says the human brain came about over millions of years by evolutionary processes is not using his brain! The brain is proof of God—an Almighty Mind that is infinite in power, knowledge, wisdom, and glory." David Miller, *The Brain Proof of God.*

Journaling Suggestion:
I believe that God made me and He made me to use my powers of intellect for His glory.

Memo for Meditation:
"Know that the Lord, He is God; It is He who has made us, and not we ourselves. Psalm 100:3
"I will praise You, for I am fearfully and wonderfully made; marvellous are Your works, and that my soul knows very well." Psalm 139:14

March 15

Motivational Idea: Renewing your mind

The mind, according to Scripture, is more than just your thoughts. It is a *"way of thinking, mind, attitude, as the sum total of the whole mental and moral state of being."* (William Arndt, et al., *A Greek-English Lexicon*). There are various words in both Hebrew and Greek translated as 'mind'. In the Old Testament, the word that is often translated 'mind' is the word for 'heart'. Sometimes it can refer to the physical organ, but mostly it refers to the inner being – the seat of the will and the emotions. In the New Testament, the word *kardia*, the Greek word for 'heart', is often translated 'mind' as well. In the Greek New Testament, *phroneo* is often translated 'mind' and most often refers to a person's understanding, views or opinions (Mark 8:33).

There are several other words that are often translated as 'mind'. One of the most important references is to *"Love the Lord your God with all your heart and with all your soul and with all your mind."* (Matthew 22:37). One of the dangers we face is imposing our ideas onto Scripture and in this instance we need to avoid imposing modern notions of mind, brain and intellect on the Scriptures of Truth. The Old and New Testaments had a much more integrated view of humanity and there was much less emphasis on the distinction between the material and the immaterial. When Jesus says you are to *"love the Lord with all your heart, soul, and mind"*, He is not highlighting various aspects of the personality; he is not differentiating between emotions and intellect; rather, He is saying that our love for God should be all-inclusive. The mind is simply one more way to identify the inner being – all that we are. In fact, in Matthew 22:37, Jesus uses the word *kardia* ('heart'), which in other contexts is translated 'mind'.

Memorable Quote:
"We look in vain in the Old Testament and New Testament for anything like scientific precision in the employment of terms which are meant to indicate mental operations." Biblically, the mind is simply the "inner being" or the sum total of all our mental, emotional, and spiritual faculties, without drawing fine distinctions between them." The International Standard Bible Encyclopedia

Journaling Suggestion:
Lord you have said, *"Give me your heart. May your eyes take delight in following my ways."* (Proverbs 23:26). Lord, I give to you my mind and heart and soul. Amen.

Memo for Meditation:
"Do not be conformed to this world, but be transformed by the renewal of your mind, that by testing you may discern what is the will of God, what is good and acceptable and perfect." Romans 12:1.

March 16

Motivational Idea: The value of your soul

At the beginning of God's creation, we are told, *"And the LORD God formed man from the dust of the ground, and breathed into his nostrils the breath of life; and man became a living soul."* (Genesis 2:7). The Hebrew word used for 'soul; is *nephesh*: a soul, a living being – life! Self! Personhood! Desire! Passion! Appetite! Emotion!

The Bible reveals that we are tripartite beings – spirit, soul and body – and it is the soul that gives us our personalities, self-awareness, rationality and natural feeling. George MacDonald said, *"You don't have a soul. You are a Soul."* Personhood requires a soul. The human soul is central to your personhood as a human being. The Bible frequently refers to people as 'souls'. Thus, you not only *have* a never-dying soul but you *are* a never-dying soul. It has been said that there are only two things that last: the word of God (Mark 13:31) and the human soul.

God's word is imperishable. The human soul is imperishable.

That thought should cause us to focus and should grab our attention. Every human being who has ever lived is a soul, and all of those souls are still in existence somewhere now. The question is, where? The souls that reject God's love are condemned to eternal loss in everlasting separation from God. (See Romans 6:23) – that's *hell*!! But the souls who acknowledge their own sinfulness and accept God's gracious gift of forgiveness through the sacrifice of Jesus will live forever with the Lord in the joy and pleasure of His presence – that's *heaven*! The soul, therefore, is the part of every human being that lasts on into eternity after the body experiences death. Genesis 35:18 describes the death of Rachel in childbirth. She named her son *"as her soul was departing."* From this we know that the soul is different from the body and that it continues to live after physical death. As for our physical bodies, the Bible tells us, *"For our dying bodies must be transformed into bodies that will never die; our mortal bodies must be transformed into immortal bodies."* (1 Corinthians 15:53). What value would you place on your soul? Jesus said, *"What good is it for someone to gain the whole world, yet forfeit their soul?"* (Mark 8.36).

Memorable Quote:
"The soul seeks God with its whole being. Because it is desperate to be whole, the soul is God-smitten and God-crazy and God-obsessed. My mind may be obsessed with idols; my will may be enslaved to habits; my body may be consumed with appetites. But my soul will never find rest until it rests in God." John Ortberg, *Soul Keeping.*

Journaling Suggestion:
Lord teaches me the value of my soul and to ensure my eternal destiny is with you!

Memo for Meditation:
"For you were going astray like sheep; but now have returned to the Shepherd and Overseer of your souls." 1 Peter 2:25.

March 17

Motivational Idea: The key is knowing your spirit

The Greek word for spirit is *pneuma* and roughly translated means to breathe. Our spirit is our God-given capacity for connection; we are enabled by our spirit to communicate with God Himself. How can we get to know the Lord Jesus more? How can we know Him in our daily lives? It is by our spirit communing with His Spirit. The spiritual nature of our humanity cannot be satisfied in any other way but by this communion and intimate relationship with Him. Knowing our spirit is the key to experiencing Christ, Paul said to Timothy, *"The Lord be with your spirit."* (2 Timothy 4:22). This means the Lord being in our spirit is something we can experience today and every day.

We can use the analogy of the radio to illustrate our spiritual capacity to commune with the living God. The radio needs to be turned on and tuned in to receive invisible radio waves. Our capacity to tune in to God is like the radio – our spirit needs to be tuned in, and, to continue the analogy, God is likened to the radio waves. It is only by our spirit that we can communicate with and know God, and He with us, who is Spirit. For this to happen we need to be born of the Spirit of God. (John 3:6). From the moment we believe in Jesus as our Saviour and Lord, His Spirit enters into our spirit and we are born again – reborn! We're born into the family of God and we receive His divine nature, His eternal life, in our spirit. We become the children of God. Our human spirit is the unique place for God's Spirit to enter into us to make us His children, and it is also the place from which He goes on to fill our entire being and to give us that joy, inexpressible and full of glory, which nothing in this world can offer or give us – *ever!* So, we need to be impressed with the importance of our spirit! What are we tuned into each day? We need to be turned on and tuned in to *Him*. This is where the Word of God comes into play; we need to sit down, and read and meditate on the Scriptures. As we hold the Bible in our hands, God communes with our Spirit and we speak to Him in prayer.

Memorable Quote:
"The first Spirit mentioned here is the divine Spirit, the Holy Spirit of God, and the second spirit is the human spirit, the regenerated spirit of man. Regeneration is accomplished in the human spirit by the Holy Spirit of God with God's life, the uncreated eternal life. Thus, to be regenerated is

to have the divine, eternal life (in addition to the human, natural life) as the new source and new element of a new person." Bible Recovery Version, John 3:6

Journaling Suggestion:
Lord, I yield my spirit to you alone and ask, please fill me with your Holy Spirit.

Memo for Mediation:
"God is Spirit, and those who worship Him must worship in spirit and truthfulness." John 4:24.

March 18

Motivational Idea: A clean bill of health

The phrase 'a clean bill of health' dates back to the 17th century and refers to the practice of a ship's crew being examined by a health official; if no infectious diseases were found in all those on board, the ship was given ;a clean bill of health'. The 'bill' was then presented before landing at port. The phrase has continued in its usage today and refers to the medical practitioner declaring that a patient is healthy, in good condition, and everything is in working order.

The opposite of the phrase denoting good health is 'a foul bill of health'. This was the certificate given to a ship's master at the time of leaving port, indicating that there was an epidemic at the place of departure. Spiritual health is now seen as an integral part of wellbeing. The psalmist in the memo for meditation today knew all was not well in his spiritual life and so he asked God to cleanse him and give him a clean bill of health. Do we have a clean bill of spiritual health today?

Memorable Quote:
"The Word, prayer and faith are the vitamins of the soul; and no one can live in health without them."

Journaling Suggestion:
Journal on how to protect and promote my spiritual health.

Memo for Meditation:

"Soak me in your laundry and I'll come out clean, scrub me and I'll have a snow-white life. Tune me into foot-tapping songs, set these once-broken bones to dancing. Don't look too close for blemishes, give me a clean bill of health. God, make a fresh start in me, shape a Genesis week from the chaos of my life. Don't throw me out with the trash, or fail to breathe holiness in me. Bring me back from grey exile, put a fresh wind in my sails! Give me a job teaching rebels your ways so the lost can find their way home. Commute my death sentence, God, my salvation God, and I'll sing anthems to your life-giving ways. Unbutton my lips, dear God; I'll let loose with your praise." Psalm 51:7-15.

March 19

Motivational Idea: Your amazing senses (1)

Aristotle (384-322 BC) is credited with being the first to number the senses in his work *De Anima*. We are all familiar with the big five: sight or vision, hearing or audition, smell or olfaction, taste or gustation, and touch. Neurologists today have come up with four more: thermoception which is the sense of heat (it is debated if cold is a separate sense), nociception which is the perception of pain, equilibrioception which is the perception of balance, proprioception which is the perception of body awareness. Close your eyes and touch your nose: that's proprioception in action. The important point is that we are all sensory creatures and that our human senses are a large part of who we are. Clare Francis, who writes eloquently on the subject, suggests, *"Because life in the 'developed' world is now so confined (Americans for instance spend an average of 95% of their lives indoors) our senses have little to do and consequently become either atrophied or over-sensitive, which in turn leads to many of the common ailments of today's existence, such as stress, anxiety and depression."* If our senses have shrivelled up in our claustrophobic existence, let's consciously exercise them again. The memo for today can make us take note of the wonders of creation around us and the wonder of you, too!

Memorable Quote:

"You made all the delicate, inner parts of my body and knit me together in my mother's womb. Thank you for making me so wonderfully complex!

Your workmanship is marvellous—how well I know it." Psalm 139:13,14

Journaling Suggestion:
Forget about indulging your senses and think more about exercising them, the way the Creator intended.

Memo for Meditation:
"God's glory is on tour in the skies, God-craft on exhibit across the horizon. Madame Day holds classes every morning, Professor Night lectures each evening. Their words aren't heard, their voices aren't recorded, But their silence fills the earth: unspoken truth is spoken everywhere. God makes a huge dome for the sun – a superdome! The morning sun's a new husband leaping from his honeymoon bed, the day-breaking sun an athlete racing to the tape. That's how God's Word vaults across the skies from sunrise to sunset, melting ice, scorching deserts, warming hearts to faith. The revelation of God is whole and pulls our lives together. The signposts of God are clear and point out the right road. The life-maps of God are right, showing the way to joy. The directions of God are plain and easy on the eye." Psalm 19:1-8

March 20

Motivational Idea: Your amazing senses (2)

God created us with amazing senses. These include sight, smell, hearing, taste and touch. God the great creator intricately designed each of our sense organs to transmit information to our brain. Our senses help us understand and notice what is going on in the world around us. We can and we need to connect with our creator God with all the senses we have, and this is an important aspect of our faith journey here on earth. The senses are referred to in the Bible in both physical and spiritual ways. For example, Jesus spoke to Thomas who wanted proof of Jesus' resurrection, and so Jesus invited him to touch His wounds. Then he said to Thomas, *"Put your finger here, and look at my hands. Put your hand into the wound in my side. Don't be faithless any longer. Believe!"* (John 20:27).

We also have many examples of Jesus touching the sick and healing them with His almighty power. In the spiritual sense, He touches lives today and can heal the body and the soul with His salvation power. Invite Him today to touch your life. We are exhorted by the Psalmist to *"Taste and see that the LORD is good. Oh, the joys of those who take refuge in him!"* (Psalm 34:8). Here is where real joy and authentic happiness are found. We are invited to examine the goodness of God for ourselves. Sometimes we take for granted the enjoyment, satisfaction, and joy that our senses bring. Imagine losing the sense of taste! It happened to the author during the covid pandemic. No taste! Glad to say it came back eventually. But imagine trying to interact in your world without your senses. There are many people who do just that. What if you couldn't speak or sing a song? Hear the birds singing, or reach out and hug a friend? Your world would be vastly different. Let us seek to increase our awareness today of our amazing senses.

Memorable Quote:
"If we touch others in kindness but our words sound only like abrasive noise, what does that say about how Jesus is working in our lives? I can bring the fragrance of the love of Jesus, but will it be cancelled out by a bitter flavour I leave in someone's mouth?"

Journaling Suggestion:
Let us joyfully and gratefully give thanks to God for our amazing senses.

Memo for Meditation:
"I tell you, love your enemies. Help and give without expecting a return. You'll never—I promise—regret it. Live out this God-created identity the way our Father lives toward us, generously and graciously, even when we're at our worst. Our Father is kind; you be kind. Luke 6.35, 36. Our lives are a Christ-like fragrance rising up to God. But this fragrance is perceived differently by those who are being saved and by those who are perishing." 2 Corinthians 2:15.

March 21

Motivational Idea: Your spiritual senses

God created us with amazing senses. He has weaved into our innermost being senses which are particular to the spiritual realm. Just as our physical senses of sight, smell, hearing, touch and taste help us to explore our physical world, our spiritual senses help us to learn about the spiritual world and, most especially, God Himself. *"God is spirit, and his worshippers must worship in the Spirit and in truth."* (John 4.24).

Our memorable quote from Origen below gives us an insight into the need for us to have spiritual insight and spiritual discernment. We need to develop our spiritual sight to see spiritual things, spiritual hearing to hear the voice of God, and our spiritual taste so we can enjoy spiritual food. It is truly awesome that God has gifted our souls with an array of senses for the singular purpose of perceiving Him more fully. God longs for us to know Him! This is not simply for the sake of knowledge, but as we come to know Him through the senses of our souls, our love and desire for God grows. *"As the deer longs for running streams, so my soul longs for you, O God. My soul thirsts for God, the living God."* (Psalm 42:1)

Our spiritual senses give a transcendent aspect to our nature and this enables us to perceive and process current events, not only through the reactions, emotions and judgments that our physical senses provoke, but by opening to something more: spiritual discernment. In a turbulent and disquieting world, we can seek and know calm and stillness as God invites us to rest in Him as we experience the unforced rhythms of grace.

Memorable Quote:
"In man, besides the bodily senses, there are five other senses which need to be exercised. Thus, the soul has a sense of sight to contemplate supernatural objects, a hearing capable of distinguishing voices that do not resound in the air, a taste to savour the living bread come down from heaven, a smell, leading Paul to speak of the perfume of Jesus." Origen

Journaling Suggestion:
Don't get too caught up with the world; no matter how pleasing or repulsive it may be to the senses, we must engage our spiritual senses as we love, serve and worship our glorious creator.

Memo for Meditation:
"Are you tired? Worn out? Burned out on religion? Come to me. Get away with me and you'll recover your life. I'll show you how to take a real rest. Walk with me and work with me—watch how I do it. Learn the unforced

rhythms of grace. I won't lay anything heavy or ill-fitting on you. Keep company with me and you'll learn to live freely and lightly." Matthew 11:28-30.

March 22

Motivational Idea: Don't forget to take your vitamin E

Vitamin E helps to maintain healthy skin; it is good for your eyes, and strengthens the body's natural defence against illness and infection. It's a must for protecting the immune system. Sources of Vitamin E include wheatgerm, nuts, seeds and plant oils such as olive oil.

Here are three Es to boost your spiritual immune system, give you clear vision and make you shine so that your family circle and the people you interact with will be attracted to your way of being and be inquisitive about your spiritual food.

The three Es are: exalt, exult, and extol. These three similar words all share the same prefix 'ex', which in this instance stands for 'high'. The words mean different things due to their root meanings.

The word 'exalt' comes from the Latin *altus* meaning high. Thus, to exalt someone is to view that person as high or superior. We need to exalt Jesus each day and recognize His Highness and that He is the Lord of all who reigns supreme on His heavenly throne.

The word 'exult' comes from the Latin root *salire* and means to show jubilation, to leap for joy. We are to rejoice in God. We are to jump for joy and to know Him and His love will have us rejoicing daily.

The word 'extol' comes from the Latin *extollō* and means to elevate or to raise high. We are to raise Jesus high and elevate Him and give Him the praise and honour due to Him. The three Es are biblical words and we need to keep these to the forefront of our minds on a daily basis in relation to God. This is the sure way to find our true selves and the secret of lasting happiness – it is found in our personal relationship with God. Exalt Jesus - give Him His rightful place. Exult in Jesus and jump for joy for all He is and what He has done for us. Extol Jesus and lift Him high.

Memorable Quote:
"Jumping for joy is the best exercise for the soul."

Journaling Suggestion:
Take the three spiritual Es today and every day for wellbeing and spiritual health.

Memo for Meditation:
*"**Exalt** the LORD our God, And worship at His footstool — He is holy."* Psalm 99:5
*"I shall **exult** and rejoice in your kindness, for you have seen my affliction, and you have known the affliction of my soul."* Psalm 31:7
*"I will **extol** You, O LORD, for You have lifted me up, And have not let my foes rejoice over me. O LORD my God, I cried out to You, And You healed me. O LORD,"* Psalm 30:1.

March 23

Motivational Idea: Do the lifting!

'The heavy lifting' is an informal idiom which refers to the most demanding part of an endeavour; work requiring the most effort, resources, or consideration. Life involves heavy lifting with responsibilities and pressures. Are you the one that does the donkey work in your set of circumstances? Perhaps it's the demands of family life, and you have to take the lead and do what needs to be done. Perhaps working life is the same, where you have so many things to juggle: meetings, budgetary reprofiling, staffing issues, targets, contractual obligations. Or perhaps you are at the coalface where you are dealing with the physical hard graft on the shopfloor. Whatever it is, you have a lot of heavy lifting to do. Then there is the emotional heavy lifting involved in some relationships and emotional attachments. It's not easy! In the midst of it all, here is something that we must give priority to; it's set out on the memo for today when we are exhorted to: *"Keep lifting all your praises to GOD! What we discover is that when we do this and on a daily basis, God does something for us, He is the lifter of our heads!"* (Psalm 3:3). *"He gives us strength and lightens our load. He lifts our heads from the depths of despondency and the overwhelming nature of it all. Go on doing the lifting - lifting up His Name in worship and praise. Jesus said, 'Take my yoke upon you for my yoke is easy and my burden is light.'"* (Matthew 28:11).

Memorable Quote:
"The one who lifts up my head! As a shield the Lord gives David complete protection from the enemy assaults. As his glory, the Lord gives him honour, dignity, and vindication in the place of shame, reproach and slander that were being heaped upon him. As the lifter of his head the Lord encourages and exalts him." The Believer's Bible Commentary on Psalm 3.

Journaling Suggestion:
Keep on lifting up the name of Jesus in worship and praise!

Memo for Meditation:
"Hallelujah! You who serve GOD, praise GOD! Just to speak, His name is praise! Just to remember GOD is a blessing— now and tomorrow and always. From east to west, from dawn to dusk, keep lifting all your praises to GOD!" Psalm 113:1-3.
"But you, LORD, are a shield around me, my glory, the One who lifts my head high." Psalm 3:3.

March 24

Motivational Idea: The chief pursuit

'Pursuits' is a great word. I for one readily connect it with the great outdoors having just returned from walking in the Lake District in England. Our smart watches and phones can even count our steps for us so we know how far we have walked. The word can also conjure up loads of concepts such as challenges, adventures, excitement, fresh air, as well as exercise and wellbeing. For the game enthusiasts, it may have different connotations; the game *Trivial Pursuits* comes to mind, and of course, as the name suggests, it's all about trivia. It's a board game in which winning is determined by a player's ability to answer general knowledge and popular culture questions. It was created in December 1979 in Montreal, Quebec, by Chris Haney and Scott Abbott. Ironically, Chris discovered that pieces of their Scrabble game were missing so they decided to create their own game. With the help of John Haney and Ed Werner, Chris and Scott completed their development of the game, which was released in 1982. People all over the world have spent many an evening in competitive spirits, seeking to answer a whole range of questions and become the King or Queen of *Trivial Pursuits.* In life, we engage in the serious business of the pursuit of happiness. In doing so, what are we pursuing and where are we pursuing it? The gateway to the Psalms begins with the word happiness. The Hebrew word originates from a word meaning 'to go straight', 'to go on', 'to advance'. And so the gateway to the Psalms tells us the secret of happiness and in the pursuit of God we find it. Advance in this pursuit above all else.

Memorable Quote:
"God cannot give us a happiness and a peace apart from Himself, because it is not there. There is no such thing." C S Lewis

Journaling Suggestion:
Don't chase butterflies, but take care of the garden so they'll come to you.

Memo for Meditation:
"Happy is the man who does not go in the company of sinners, or take his place in the way of evil-doers, or in the seat of those who do not give honour to the Lord. But whose delight is in the law of the Lord, and whose mind is on his law day and night. He will be like a tree planted by the rivers of water, which gives its fruit at the right time, whose leaves will ever be green; and he will do well in all his undertakings. The evil-doers are not so; but are like the dust from the grain, which the wind takes away For this cause there will be no mercy for sinners when they are judged, and the evil-doers will have no place among the upright, Because the Lord sees the way of the upright, but the end of the sinner is destruction." Psalm 1.

March 25

Motivational Idea: How's your appetite?

Appetite is our general desire to eat food. Our appetite can rise and fall due to a wide range of factors, sometimes causing us to eat less or more than our body needs. Have you ever been in a situation where your stomach rumbles or gurgles? It can be quite embarrassing, especially if you are in a meeting at a moment of complete silence. We are less likely to have a preference for what we want to eat when we are hungry. In contrast, our desire to eat may be influenced by specific factors which increase our appetite. These may include boredom, stress, or another heightened emotional state, seeing or smelling food that appeals to us, or even routine, habit, or a special occasion.

Our emotional state has a significant effect on our appetite. For some people, stress or grief may cause them to eat more food as a way of coping with how they feel, but for others, these emotions have the opposite effect. If a person has a low appetite due to an underlying medical condition, treating the condition may improve it. We need to eat, even if we don't have an appetite. We can obtain foods that look and smell appealing, be disciplined to eat at consistent times each day, plan meals the day before, and drink plenty of liquids.

Appetite is distinct from hunger, which is the body's biological response to a lack of food. A person can have an appetite even if their body is not showing signs of hunger, and vice versa. What about our spiritual appetite? As spiritual beings we have a God-shaped vacuum that only God can fill. When we try to fill it with success, money, position, power and possessions, or anything other than God, it's not going to be satisfying. God comes to us to make us aware of our spiritual needs. Our spiritual hunger can only be satisfied by God and feeding on his word. God enables us to exercise faith to make us aware of spiritual needs. We would never be aware of these spiritual needs unless God, by His Spirit, makes us aware. So, how's your spiritual appetite today?

Memorable Quote:
"To hunger is to be human, but to hunger for God is to feed on Him. Hunger and thirst after His righteousness and feed on Him in your heart. Taste and see that the Lord is good; it is He who will fill you to satisfaction." Joni Eareckson Tada

Journaling Suggestion:
Lord, increase my desire and hunger for you!

Memo for Meditation:
"For He satisfies the longing soul, and the hungry soul he fills with good things. Psalm 107.9. Jesus says, "I am the bread of life; whoever comes to me shall not hunger, and whoever believes in me shall never thirst." John 6:35

March 26

Motivational Idea: What's your poison?

'What's your poison?' is a question people sometimes use when going for a drink, with reference to the drink a person wants. It would seem that at some level, whether consciously or unconsciously, there is an awareness that alcohol is in reality a poison. *Alcohol. Think Again. What's your poison?* is a campaign to reduce harm from alcohol in Western Australia. Key messages are: our body converts alcohol to poison, and reduce your drinking to reduce the damage. The aim is to increase awareness about *how* alcohol causes harm to health. The campaign prompts people to reconsider the common phrase by showing that when a person drinks alcohol, the body converts it to acetaldehyde, a poison. It explains that every drink converts to more poison, increasing the damage, and increasing the risk of cancer. The message is stark – reduce drinking to reduce the damage. Around one in three adults (33%) who drink alcohol exceed the alcohol guideline. Nearly two out of three adults (63%) who drink above the guideline consider the amount they drink to be OK. Yet even drinking small amounts of alcohol increases the risk of developing all manner of health problems, and the liver takes the major hit.

The Bible has a lot to say about alcohol. For example, *"Wine is a mocker and beer a brawler; whoever is led astray by them is not wise."* (Proverbs 20:1). Yet John Calvin had a stipend of 250 gallons of wine per year written into his church contract. Martin Luther's wife was a famed brewer of beer, and the Guinness family created their renowned Irish stout as an act of worship. However, given the true nature of alcohol, we need wisdom; being under the influence is not a good thing. Freud said the superego was soluble in alcohol. As Christians, we need to be under the influence of the Holy Spirit and to avoid poison, whether it is in the form of an alcoholic drink or unhealthy things that poison the mind. We need to be holy and live under the discipline of the Holy Spirit.

Memorable Quote:
"Nothing is worth diminishing your health. Nothing is worth poisoning yourself into ill health and the stress, anxiety, and fear that accompanies."

Journaling Suggestion:
Being under the influence of the Holy Spirit.

Memo for Meditation:
"So be careful how you live. Don't live like fools, but like those who are wise. Make the most of every opportunity in these evil days. Don't act thoughtlessly, but understand what the Lord wants you to do. Don't be drunk with wine, because that will ruin your life. Instead, be filled with the Holy Spirit." Ephesians 5:15-18

March 27

Motivational Idea: Happy pills

David Herzberg's book, *Happy Pills in America: From Miltown to Prozac*, looks at the history of pharmaceuticals, the fascination with minor tranquillisers, and the advent of the mass-consumption of psychiatric drugs. Herzberg describes this as the *"commodification of 'happiness' as a medical product."* Patients commonly referred to the drug Prozac as 'the happy pill' or a 'magic cure'. It was initially thought of as a wonder drug to change one's mood or get rid of your struggles instantly. Prozac is one of a number of selective serotonin reuptake inhibitors (SSRIs). Today there are many mental health treatments available, including medication. The reality is there is not a one-time 'cure-all' treatment method for every condition or symptom. Talking to your doctor or mental health practitioner can be valuable in these cases, as not everyone responds to anti-depressants in the same way, and other treatments may be more suitable.

Today, social prescribing is on the increase. Social prescribing is an approach that connects people to activities, groups, and services to meet the practical, social and emotional needs that affect their health and wellbeing. Examples include volunteering, arts activities, group learning, gardening, befriending, cookery, healthy eating advice and a range of sports. It is a way of considering the whole person and moves away from a strictly medical model to a psychosocial model. GPs will sometimes prescribe self-help books and even gym membership.

Another element that is increasingly recognized as a vital component of wellbeing is spirituality. Spirituality can relieve the stress of everyday life. Research shows that spirituality can benefit both the mind and the body. Whether someone is coping with cancer or clinical depression, spiritual exercises help to increase acceptance, decrease negative emotions, find meaning, and deepen our relationships with others. Spirituality can help address issues such as poor self-esteem, low confidence, lack of self-control, and fear of daily tasks and challenges.

Memorable Quote:
"When you realise that God loves you and that He has a plan for your life, you can walk with your head held high — totally confident in who He created you to be." Joyce Meyer

Journaling Suggestion:
In all my struggles, the Lord is with me, and he gives me strength for each day!

Memo for Meditation:
"But You, O LORD, are a shield about me, My glory, and the One who lifts my head." Psalm 3:3

March 28

Motivational Idea: Laminin and biochemical evidence

Fazale Rana presents to audiences on the biochemical evidence for a Creator. He says, *"I'm determined to see people in all walks of life come to know the Creator as Lord and Savior."* Fazale does not agree with the notion of laminin and the cross postulated on social media. He wholeheartedly believes God did create and does sustain human life, but laminin's apparent cross-shape does not make the case. Portraying complex biomolecules in simplified ways is a common practice among biochemists. Yet the simplified cross-like shape of laminin and the role it plays in holding tissues together has prompted the claim that this biomolecule provides scientific support for passages such as

Colossians 1:15–17, and shows how God must have made and sustained humans. Fazale notes that the cross shape is a simple structure found throughout nature. So, it's probably not a good idea to attach too much significance to laminin's shape. The '†' configuration makes laminin ideally suited to connect proteins to each other and cells to the basal reticulum. This is undoubtedly the reason for its structure. Laminin is not the only molecule 'holding things together'. A number of other proteins are also indispensable components and none of these molecules are cross-shaped.

Memorable Quote:
"The structure and operation of biochemical systems provide some of the most potent support for a Creator's role in fabricating living systems. Instead of pointing to superficial features of biomolecules such as the "cross-shaped" architecture of laminin, there are many more substantive ways to use biochemistry to argue for the necessity of a Creator and for the value he places on human life. As a case in point, the salient characteristics of biochemical systems identically match those features we would recognize immediately as evidence for the work of a human design engineer. The close similarity between biochemical systems and the devices produced by human designers logically compels this conclusion: life's most fundamental processes and structures stem from the work of an intelligent, intentional Agent. When Christians invest the effort to construct a careful case for the Creator, sceptics and seekers find it difficult to deny the powerful evidence from biochemistry and other areas of science for God's existence." Fazale Rana

Journaling Suggestion:
God holds me together.

Memo for Mediation:
"He [Jesus, The Son of God] is before all things, and in him all things hold together." Colossians 1:17

117

March 29

Motivational Idea: The hairs on your head are numbered

The average person has about 100,000 hairs with a similar number of hair follicles which can help protect us from the elements, regulate our body temperature, and perceive sensations. People with blonde hair have about 150,000 hairs, those with red hair 90,000, those with brown hair have about 110,00, and those with black hair about 100,000. One particular study calculated hair density in 50 participants. They found that on average there were between 800 to 1,290 hairs per square inch (124 to 200 hairs per square centimetre).

Our hair follicles are small pouches in our skin out of which our hairs grow. The number of follicles more or less matches the number of hairs on our heads. On average, your hair grows about 6 inches in a year, that's about ½ inch per month. Male hair grows faster than female hair. You lose anywhere between 50 to 100 hairs each day, though depending on your hair care routine, you may shed even more.

As you age, your hair is more likely to turn grey or even white. In fact, after you turn 30, the likelihood of going grey increases by about 10 to 20 percent with each decade. Hair is actually stronger than you think. For example, one hair alone can withstand a strain of 3.5 ounces — almost ¼ pound. Water can affect some properties of your hair. For example, your hair can weigh 12 to 18 percent more when it's wet. Wet hair can also stretch 30 percent longer without damage. The hair on your head keeps your head warm and provides a little cushioning for your skull. My dad met an old station master when he started work on the railway in Antrim just after the Second World War. James had the most amazing head of hair for his age. One day, he said to Dad that from a lad he had massaged his hair for three minutes every morning. Dad began this practice faithfully every morning. He lived into his late 80s and had the finest head of white hair. Jesus' mention of hair in His teaching is a way of saying God is aware of and involved in the smallest detail of your life. It's also a way for Jesus to assure his followers that their lives are valuable.

Memorable Quote:

"Jesus declares that God our loving heavenly Father even knows the number of hairs on our heads. It means that God cares about the smallest

details of our lives. God is not only concerned with the big issues but with all the little things too."

Journaling Suggestion:

Praise God who made me, knows me, and always takes care of me.

Memo for Meditation:

"The very hairs on your head are all numbered." Matthew 10:30

March 30

Motivational Idea: He became human

The golden oldies, like the author (*Not!* Just a young 67 at the time of writing!), may well remember singing an old hymn, *Standing on the promises of God.* But have you ever wondered how many promises there are in the Bible? People have come up with a wide range of figures. The point we can miss, however, is that God is a faithful God and keeps His promises. Everet R Storms, a Canadian school teacher, decided to research all the Bible promises. He kept a record of these on his 27th reading of the Bible. It took a year and a half for Storms to compile his lists, including promises by God to man (7,487); one man to another (991); God the Father to God the Son (two); man to God (290); and several other combinations, including nine made by Satan. In all, Storms tallied 8,810 promises. That's a lot of promises.

Our memo for meditation for today gives us a promise that was written over 700 years before it was fulfilled. It's God's promise that the eternal God would become man in the person of Jesus Christ, that God would take into His eternal being our humanity and identify with us. The miracle and the marvel of the incarnation is described by the Apostle John: *"The Word became flesh and blood, and moved into the neighbourhood. We saw the glory with our own eyes, the one-of-a-kind glory, like Father, like Son, Generous inside and out, true from start to finish."* (John 1:14).

Isaiah tells us that the child was born but the Son was given. In Him we find salvation! Today, if you need guidance, He is the wonderful counsellor. Today, if you need empowerment and vitality for living, He is the Mighty God. Today, if you need comfort, He is the everlasting Father. If your memories of earthly fatherhood are upsetting and distressful because of the abuses you suffered, please know that our everlasting Father is the very antithesis of your earthly experiences and He comes today to comfort and heal you. If you need peace today, He is the Prince of Peace. He identified with our humanity so we could become the sons and daughters of God.

Memorable Quote:

"Jesus Christ became Incarnate for one purpose, to make a way back to God that man might stand before Him as He was created to do, the friend and lover of God Himself." Oswald Chambers

Journaling Suggestion:

Journal today on one of the precious promises of God, e.g. Hebrews 13:5.

Memo for Meditation:

"For unto us a child is born, unto us a son is given, and the government will be upon His shoulders. And He will be called Wonderful Counsellor, Mighty God, Everlasting Father, Prince of Peace." Isaiah 9:6.

March 31

Motivational Idea: Behold Him! (Be sure to see Him)

'Behold' is not a common word today. Try saying it some time. For example, *'Behold* my new coat!' You will get a reaction but they might think you're a bit weird. However, it is used in Scripture and it is used to grab our attention. It's used 1,298 times in the King James Version. But what does this word mean? It is taken from the old English word *bihalden*, meaning to thoroughly hold something (*bi-* 'thoroughly' and *haldan* 'to hold'). In the Old Testament, Hebrew 'behold' is a translation of *hinneh*, and is generally used to introduce something new or unexpected. It indicates that we need to pay close attention to what follows it. In the New Testament, the Greek word is *idou*, which holds the Hebrew meaning and also ties more to our verb 'to see'. Be sure to see! So why not just say 'Look!' or 'See!'? The simple answer is because those words alone don't convey the meaning of 'behold' in its entirety. 'To behold' is to do more than just glance or look at something. 'To behold' is to be totally captivated. When you behold something, you see it with your eyes, but you also hold your gaze on it in order to search and to understand. The word is an intense indicator, declaring, 'Stop, look and listen.'; 'Don't miss this." 'This is supremely important.'; or 'This changes everything.'. It alerts us to pay close attention to what comes next because it is so important!

Here are some powerful examples:

"Therefore the Lord himself will give you a sign. **Behold**, *the virgin shall conceive and bear a son, and shall call his name Immanuel."* Isaiah 7:14

*"**Behold**, I am doing a new thing; now it springs forth, do you not perceive it? I will make a way in the wilderness and rivers in the desert."* Isaiah 43:19

"And the angel said unto them, Fear not: for, **behold**, *I bring you good tidings of great joy, which shall be to all people.* Luke 2:10

*"**Behold**, the Lamb of God who takes away the sin of the world!"* John 1:29

*"And **behold**, I am with you always, to the end of the age."* Matthew 28:20

*"**Behold**, I stand at the door, and knock: if any man hear my voice, and open the door, I will come in to him, and will sup with him, and he with me."* Revelation 3:20

Memorable Quote:
"We probably won't start using the word behold in our everyday lives, but we can be intentional about beholding Him. In the busyness of this world, it can become so difficult to take the time to Behold Him. When we do, we allow Him to reframe what we see. Beholding Him in His Word allows us to understand His plan for restoration, and it reminds us that we can look forward to His promise for the renewal of all things. When we truly see and seek to understand, it can change everything!" Behold Him!

Journaling Suggestion:
Behold Him!

Memo for Meditation: *"And he who was seated on the throne said, 'Behold, I am making all things new.'"* Revelation 21:5

THE PSYCHOLOGICAL DIMENSION

April 1

Motivational Idea: Those critical voices silenced

Today we are focusing on the voices David heard when the seven-foot giant Goliath appeared before the armies of Israel. The battle lines were drawn and the Philistine champion did what he had been doing for forty days, morning and evening. His was **the voice of defiance!** His voice thundered, *"I defy Israel's troops this day! Give me a man so we can fight."*

Not only did David hear the voice of defiance that day, he also heard **the voice of despair.** *"When Saul and all the Israelites heard these words of the Philistine, they were upset and very afraid."* (1 Samuel 17:11). David ended up encouraging Saul and said, *"Don't let anyone be discouraged. Your servant will go and fight the Philistine."* (v32).

But the voice of Saul was also heard that day, it was **the voice of defeat**. *"You aren't able to go against this Philistine and fight him. You are just a boy! He has been a warrior from his youth."* (v33).

Another voice that David had to contend with that day was **the voice of disdain** – his very own brother's. *"Why have you come down here? To whom did you entrust those few sheep in the wilderness?"* (v28). In spite of all these critical and negative voices ringing in his ears, David went out to face the giant, and David's was **the voice of declaration**. Deal with those critical voices today the way David did! It's time to slay those giants!

Memorable Quote:

"I keep fighting voices in my mind that say I'm not enough/Every single lie that tells me I will never measure up/Am I more than just the sum of every high and every low Remind me once again just who I am, because I need to know/You say I am loved When I can't feel a thing/You say I am strong When I think I am weak/You say I am held When I am falling

short/When I don't belong/You say I am Yours/And I believe/I believe/What You say of me/I believe/The only thing that matters now is everything You think of me/In You I find my worth, in You I find my identity/Taking all I have and now I'm laying it at Your feet/You have every failure, God, and You'll have every victory/Oh, I believe/Yes, I believe/What You say of me/Oh, I believe." Lauren Daigle

Journaling Suggestion:

I declare the victory over all the negative voices in my life in the name of my God, Jesus Christ. *"But thanks be to God, who gives us the victory [as conquerors] through our Lord Jesus Christ."* 1 Corinthians 15:47. It's time to slay those giants!

Memo for Meditation:

"But David replied...I am coming against you in the name of the LORD of Heaven's Armies, the God of Israel's armies, whom you have defied!...This very day the LORD will deliver you into my hand...it is not by sword or spear that the LORD saves! For the battle is the LORD's, and he will deliver you into our hand." 1 Samuel 17:45-47

April 2

Motivational Idea: Usurping that critical inner voice

Psychalive (*Psychology for Everyday Life*) notes: *"The critical inner voice (CIV) is a well-integrated pattern of destructive thoughts toward ourselves and is the root of much of our self-destructive and maladaptive behaviour."*

The impact can be both debilitating and catastrophic for living a fulfilled life. A stream of destructive thoughts forms an 'anti-self' that discourages us from acting in our best interest. The CIV is an internal enemy that can greatly affect every aspect of our lives, including our self-esteem, confidence, relationships, and our accomplishments. These negative thoughts affect us by undermining our positive feelings about ourselves and others, and fostering self-criticism, inwardness, distrust, self-denial, addictions and a retreat from goal-directed activities.

As a left-hander, my inner voice is mostly, *You are stupid.* The CIV usually comes from early life experiences that are internalised and taken in as ways we think about ourselves. My 'stupid' voice comes mainly from a primary school teacher who seemed to think that left-handers should be summarily executed on the spot. I have internalised her incessant rants about my assumed stupidity.

In order to take power over such a destructive thought process, we must first become conscious of what our CIV is telling us so we can stop it from ruining our lives. To identify this, it is helpful to pay attention to when we suddenly slip into a bad mood or become upset. Often these negative shifts in emotion are a result of a CIV. Once we identify the thought process and pinpoint the negative actions it is advocating, we can take control over that inner voice by consciously deciding not to listen. Instead, we can take actions that are in our best interests. The CIV is not a conscience or a moral guide. What most distinguishes the inner voice from a conscience is its degrading, punishing quality. Its demeaning tone tends to increase our feelings of self-hatred instead of motivating us to change undesirable actions in a constructive manner.

Memorable Quote:
"As you emancipate yourself from your critical inner voice, you will be free to engage in your pursuit of satisfaction and meaning in life. You will feel at peace with yourself and close to those you love. You will enjoy a compassionate view of the world and an optimistic outlook on life."
Psychalive

Journaling Suggestion:
I see the CIV as a thief, a liar and a robber, and ask God to help me to overcome it!

Memo for Meditation:
"The thief comes only to steal and kill and destroy; I have come that they may have life, and have it to the full." John 10:10

April 3

Motivational Idea: The answer to the lying voices

The battle kicks off in your mind and those hate-filled, lying inner voices start up. *You're worthless. Nobody cares about you. This world would be so much better if you weren't even here.* Bonnie Paludan, who experienced the inner critics in all their intensity when dealing with postnatal depression, asks, *"Is this possible? Can we smash the inner critic and find true peace?"* Bonnie says 'yes' and from her own lived experience gives us three practical steps toward freedom we can take today.

Call the critic out. Call the demonic thoughts of worthlessness what they are: lies. Ask God to reveal the unhealthy thoughts, and start calling each one out. Say it out loud whenever you can. *"That is a lie. I will not believe this. This is not what God thinks of me."*

Bring the critic into the light. Tell someone what you're struggling with. The enemy wants you to stay in the dark. He tries to convince us that we don't need to tell anyone. Bring it into the light, whether it be with a trusted friend, your spouse, your partner, your pastor, your GP, or a professional counsellor. Get the full support you need – body, mind and spirit – to live your life to the fullest, the way God intends.

Replace the critic's lies with truth from the word of God. Lie: I'm a failure nobody cares about. **Truth:** *"For we are God's masterpiece. He has created us anew in Christ Jesus…"* (Ephesians 2:10) **Lie:** I'll never be able to change. **Truth:** *"… anyone who belongs to Christ has become a new person. The old life is gone; a new life has begun!"* (2 Corinthians 5:17) **Lie:** I will never be able to reach my full potential. **Truth:** *Now all glory to God, who is able, through his mighty power at work within us, to accomplish infinitely more than we might ask or think.* (Ephesians 3:20). **Lie:** I've done too many bad things for God to forgive me. **Truth:** *"But if we confess our sins to him, he is faithful and just to forgive us our sins and to cleanse us from all wickedness."* (1 John 1:9).

Memorable Quote:
"It's time to stand up against this epidemic in our minds, and start seeing it for what it is: lies. We must reject those inner demons in the name of Jesus. Through His power, and from His love and acceptance, we can begin to do the things that God has gifted us for and be the women (and men) of God we're meant to be." Bonnie Pauladan

Journaling Suggestion:
I'm of infinite worth! I am God's masterpiece! He loves me and I am His! Victory is mine in Jesus! I will live for Him and do the things He has gifted me to do!

Memo for Meditation:

"See how very much our Father loves us, for he calls us his children, and that is what we are! But the people who belong to this world don't recognize that we are God's children because they don't know him." 1 John 3:1

April 4

Motivational Idea: The voice of God

In this manic world and the incessant business of life, it is to our great detriment that we can miss out on one of the most astounding facts in the universe: God wants to speak to us! The Creator, the infinite, eternal and only true living God, wants to speak to us. God wants to talk to us but we may be too busy or too distracted with the many things we have to do, and the many responsibilities and actions we need to attend to, to be able to hear Him.

The secular world has recognised this incessant and unrelenting hamster-wheel lifestyle, and has given us things such as mindfulness and various other kinds of meditation. The Bible gives us the voice of God and the incredible truth of the up-close and personal God, revealed to us in Jesus Christ. For many, this is just incredulous and not worth a second thought, yet the fact is that God speaks and His voice can be heard by those who take the time to listen, by those who adopt a posture of listening.

Prayer is something the Bible tells us that we need to do, and do so frequently, but we often make the big mistake of thinking that prayer is all about talking 'to' God, or talking 'at' God, or talking 'with' God, but not 'listening to' God. Prayer, however, is a two-way process. We talk to God and He wants to talk to us. He has specific and particular things He wants to tell us. He wants to give us words of wisdom and wise counsel. He wants to give us direction and tell us about His plans for us, and what He wants us to do for Him. He wants to show us where we are getting it wrong and how to put it right. Have you heard the voice of God recently? Have you been in the posture of listening and heard Him speak to you?

In biblical days, people heard the audible voice of God. Today, God may not use an audible voice but He can speak to us in different ways and we shall explore these for the next day or so. In the meantime, reflect on how you can be in the posture of listening for the voice of God and hear Him speak to you in a way that is beyond doubt, the very voice of God speaking to you. This can be the norm and not the exception as we learn to cultivate the art of listening for the voice of the living God.

Memorable Quote:
"Listen to God in the silence of your heart and you will know His perfect plans for you." Psalm 37:4

Journaling Suggestion:
Lord, I want to be in the posture of listening so I can hear your voice. Speak, Lord, for your servant is listening.

Memo for Meditation:
"The LORD came and stood there, calling as at the other times, "Samuel! Samuel!" Then Samuel said, "Speak, for your servant is listening." 1 Samuel 3:10

April 5

Motivational Idea: The voice of God speaking to us today

The story of Samuel in the Old Testament has much to teach us about hearing the voice of God. We would have expected the audible message from God to have been given to the priest, Eli. He was an old priest, well experienced in the priestly ministry, yet God spoke his message to Samuel. Samuel was in the place of obedient posture for God to speak to him. We are reminded of the need for child-like faith. Eli was long in the tooth, and he had a lot on his mind, not least his rebellious sons. He was preoccupied with stuff and perhaps he was not in the right place for God to speak. It has been said that, *"Pursuing God is essential to hearing God."* (Brittany Yesudasan). God responds once we invite Him into our lives. He responds all the more as our desire for Him increases.

How can we demonstrate our desire for more of God? How can we pursue Him more every day? By reading and studying the Bible, and by spending unhurried time in prayer. We need fellowship with believers, and to meet regularly. These things help us to learn about His character and to learn to recognize His voice. He uses our knowledge of who He is and what He has done to help us respond to situations we face. We need to set aside everyday distractions to focus on God by centring our hearts on God so he has our complete attention. It's similar to relationships with other people. If we sit down to listen to a friend but check our text messages every few seconds, they will not feel we are listening to them, and we are less likely to hear them. How much more does God deserve our complete attention? We cannot expect to hear God's voice if we do not regularly focus our attention on Him as fully.

Memorable Quote:

"God's chain of command is based on faith, not on age or position. In finding faithful followers, God may use unexpected channels. Be prepared for the Lord to work at any place, at any time, and through anyone He chooses." Life Application Study Bible

Journaling Suggestion:

Lord, I want to be in the place of obedient posture before You so I can hear You speaking to me.

Memo for Meditation:

"You will seek Me and find Me when you seek Me with all your heart." Jeremiah 29:13

"Without faith it is impossible to please God, because anyone who comes to Him must believe that He exists and that He rewards those who earnestly seek Him." Hebrews 11:6

"I love those who love Me, and those who seek Me find Me." Proverbs 8:17

"The LORD looks down from heaven on all mankind to see if there are any who understand, any who seek God." Psalm 14:2

April 6

Motivational Idea: Dealing with distractions

God wants to make His voice known to us and He is not the author of confusion (see 1 Corinthians 14:33). His is the voice of clarity. So why do we live our lives wondering what God is saying? The problem is distractions that hinder us from hearing the voice of God. Life today is full of an abundance of things and people competing and clamouring for our attention. It's such a familiar pattern day in and day out we may not even recognize how they are coming between us and God.

Busyness is probably the most common distraction we face. Have a look at your schedule. Days start quickly, and we are racing from the off to one thing then another without pausing. No sooner has the day started but it whizzes on. We have every intention of reading and praying but we fall asleep at the end of the day, exhausted. We don't slow down long enough to hear God's voice.

Busyness can be exacerbated by apathy. We are so busy that we become apathetic to hearing the voice of God. If we feel apathetic toward God, we are unlikely to pay attention to the ways that God is speaking to us, and if we are not making time to pray or read the Bible, we are denying ourselves the opportunity to hear Him speak to us. A quick five minutes can be a salve to our conscience: a Bible verse, a brief hello to God, and off we go into the day. If we were to do the same with our other friendships and relationships, they wouldn't last long. Coldness, distance and indifference would set in and things would eventually break down. Has our fellowship with God broken down? Our behaviours and attitudes can also drown out the voice of God and lead us away from Him without us realising it. If we are not hearing His voice, then today is the day to take stock and fix it. Give time to God and be amazed at what happens. The combination of His Spirit within you and His living word, the Bible, in front of you is His plan for teaching you to recognize His voice. He will talk to you! He's waiting!

Memorable Quote:
"Choices can drown out God's voice. Your attitudes and habits can lead you away from Him without your realising it. Attitudes like jealousy, ingratitude, bitterness, cynicism or a critical nature do not reflect the message God is trying to send to us. The voice of God always says something that reflects His character. God is gracious, kind and patient, and He pursues peace and unity. The more space we give to attitudes that are opposed to God's qualities, the less we'll be willing to hear whatever He's trying to tell us." Brittany Yesudasan

Journaling Suggestion:
Journal on prioritising unhurried time with God.

Memo for Meditation:
"The LORD would speak to Moses face to face, as one speaks to a friend."
Exodus 33:11

April 7

Motivational Idea: The last word

Almighty God who inhabits eternity intensely desires a personal, intimate relationship with us! The psalmist wrote, *"What is man that You are mindful of him, And the son of man that You visit him?"* The Message Bible puts it this way, *"Why do you bother with us? Why take a second look our way?"* The psychology of Christianity presents us with the Triune God; God the Father, God the Son, and God the Holy Spirit. God is Three Persons, Blessed Trinity. God did something stupendous. *"For God sent not his Son into the world to condemn the world; but that the world through him might be saved. He that believes on Him is not condemned: but he that believes not is condemned already, because he hath not believed in the name of the only begotten Son of God."* (John 3:17, 18).

So God sent His Son, and in the Book of Hebrews we are told that in these last days, God spoke to us through His Son. This is His last and final word of God to humanity as a collective: 'Jesus!' *"Jesus is the answer for the world today, above Him there's no other, Jesus is the Way. If You Have Some Questions In The Corners Of Your Mind And Traces Of Discouragement And Peace You Cannot Find Reflections Of The Old Past, They Seem To Face You Everyday There's One Thing I Know For Sure That Jesus Is Away."* (Andrae Crouch).

Memorable Quote:

"The Lord Jesus is the greatest psychologist in the universe. He knows very intimately both the things that bless us and those which distress us. The Holy Spirit desires to come to us and to give us the mind of Christ. Therein we will walk a clear and healing pathway in our emotional and spiritual life. The Word of God contains great wisdom and insight into God's view of our own psychological well-being so that we can receive healing through God's divine instructions for life... and the wholeness prescribed by the Lord God Himself." Dr. David Jeffares

Journaling Suggestion:
Study the life of Jesus: His words of life, bringing joy and happiness.

Memo for Meditation:
"Long ago God spoke many times and in many ways to our ancestors through the prophets. And now in these final days, he has spoken to us through his Son. God promised everything to the Son as an inheritance, and through the Son he created the universe. The Son radiates God's own glory and expresses the very character of God, and he sustains everything by the mighty power of his command. When he had cleansed us from our sins, he sat down in the place of honour at the right hand of the majestic God in heaven. This shows that the Son is far greater than the angels, just as the name God gave him is greater than their names." Hebrews 1:1-4

April 8

Motivational Idea: The spirit of truth

Today we are thinking about the third person of the Trinity and the pneumatological experience associated with the confession *"I believe in the Holy Spirit."* Jesus promised us that after his ascension into heaven, He would send the Spirit to be our *paraclete* ('comforter', 'advisor', and 'helper') (cf. John 14:16, 26; 15:26; 16:7). We believe that the fulfilment of this promise occurred on the day of Pentecost (Acts 2). Early Christians confessed to experiencing an *"indwelling of the Holy Spirit"*, and, consequently, we believe that the Holy Spirit dwells *within* each believer.

The Holy Spirit fulfils His role within us as *paraclete*: guiding, empowering, revealing, prompting, assisting, convicting, helping, gifting, and transforming us on our spiritual journey. Theologically and psychologically, then, we experience our relationship with the Holy Spirit as one of a spiritual nature and an intimate partnership. Jesus explains in our memo for today that the person of the Holy Spirit guides us into all truth. We are not left in the dark; we are not left directionless in a world that has lost its way, we know the way, Jesus Himself, and the Spirit of Truth speaks to us and reveals more of Jesus to us and guides us in the way we should go. The thing is, are we sensitive to the voice of the Holy Spirit? We need both the anointing and the filling of the Holy Spirit.

The Scriptures tell us: *"Don't be drunk with wine, because that will ruin your life. Instead, be filled with the Holy Spirit, singing psalms and hymns and spiritual songs among yourselves, and making music to the Lord in your hearts. And give thanks for everything to God the Father in the name of our Lord Jesus Christ."* (Ephesians 5:18-20). A celestial joy and a heavenly happiness pervades our being when we are filled with the Spirit of God. Be filled with the Spirit!

Memorable Quote:
"Burn God's words into your heart, His thoughts into your mind and His ways into your actions; and you'll have a Spirit-filled life." Alisa Hope Wagner

Journaling Suggestion:
"Spirit of the Living God/Fall afresh on me/Spirit of the Living God/Fall afresh on me/Break me/melt me/mould me/fill me/Spirit of the Living God/Fall afresh on me." Daniel Iverson

Memo for Meditation:
"I have much more to say to you, more than you can now bear. But when He, the Spirit of truth, comes, He will guide you into all the truth. He will not speak on His own; He will speak only what He hears, and He will tell you what is yet to come. He will glorify Me because it is from Me that He will receive what He will make known to you. All that belongs to the Father is Mine. That is why I said the Spirit will receive from Me what He will make known to you." John 16:12-15

April 9

Motivational Idea: Psychology and the locus of control

The term 'locus of control' refers to the degree to which we believe we have control over life events. Locus of control is both internal and external. An internal locus of control puts *us* in control of events. We ask the question *"Why did this happen?"* and answer, *"I caused it."*

An external locus of control places the cause of the event outside of ourselves. So, factors outside of our control cause things to happen to us. Psychologists say that the two most common external loci of control are seen by most people as chance, or a powerful other. If people believe in chance and see this as the main locus of control in their life, they feel that events afflict them randomly, with no rhyme or reason. A powerful other locus of control, however, puts the control of events in the hands of the big bosses and those in authority. So how does all this relate to our relationship with God? If relying on a powerful other is generally seen as bad in the face of life's troubles, then what does this have to say about us leaning upon God? Is leaning on God, psychologically, a bad thing to do? Does it keep us passive? By contrast, an internal locus of control has been found to be, generally speaking, a good thing. But for Christians, isn't leaning upon yourself considered to be a bad thing, even a sin?

In short, we have a conflict between theology and psychology. In theology, an internal locus of control is seen as a bad idea and an external locus of control (i.e. God) is a good idea. In psychology, on the other hand, an internal locus of control is seen as a good idea but an external locus of control (powerful other) is seen as a bad idea. So how should we resolve this conflict?

Some people, in the face of trouble or illness, can effectively stick their head in the sand and wait on a miracle. We stop meeting God half-way and stop participating in our own rescue. God does not want us to sit passively and go into a learned helplessness mode; He gives us power to live the life He intended us to live. It's time to start moving. God does not want us to stay in our 'stuckness', He wants us to move on and into all the blessings He has waiting for us, if we would only say to our inertia, *"Be gone, I am moving on in the plan and purpose of God, with power He gives to me."* If it was good enough for Moses, it's good enough for you.

Memorable Quote:
"Do your best and let God do the rest." Proverbs 19:21

Journaling Suggestion:
Lord, help me to do my part, believing that You will do Your part.

Memo for Meditation:
"GOD said to Moses: 'Why cry out to me? Speak to the Israelites. Order them to get moving. Hold your staff high and stretch your hand out over the sea: Split the sea! The Israelites will walk through the sea on dry ground.'" Exodus 14:14-16

April 10

Motivational Idea: Personal responsibility

One day, a terrible flood came. Everyone evacuated the town except one man. *"Get out of town, the flood is rising!"* yelled his neighbours. The man responded calmly, *"Don't worry about me. God will save me."* The flood waters started filling the street. A neighbour drove by in a car and shouted, *"Get out, before the water closes the street!"* The man replied, *"Don't worry. God will save me."* The car drove away. The water filled the street and then flooded the man's first floor. He went upstairs and looked out his window at the rising flood waters. Some rescue workers came up to the window in a boat. *"Get out!,"* they yelled, *"You better get out of there before you drown!"* But the man waved them on. *"Don't worry. God will save me."* With that, the rescue workers left in their boat. Finally, the waters filled the house and the man was forced out onto his roof. A helicopter came by and yelled to the man, *"You better get out of there before you drown!"* The man refused to move and replied, *"Don't worry. God will save me."* With that, the helicopter flew away. Finally, the floods washed over the house and carried the man away. After struggling, he succumbed and drowned. When the man next opened his eyes, he noticed that he was in heaven. He saw God and asked, *"Oh God! Why didn't you save me from that horrible flood?"* God replied, *"I sent you a car, a boat, and a helicopter! What else do you want from me?"* In short, reliance upon God needs to be mutual and collaborative. People need to be actively engaged, struggling in facing the ups and downs of life, trusting God. Collaborating with God yields the best coping outcomes. So, despite a surface contradiction, there is a deeper agreement between psychology and theology on this issue. Basically, lean on God, trust in God, rely upon God. But when the car, boat or helicopter comes, get in! Personal responsibility is the key to resolving your conundrum.

Memorable Quote:

"Taking responsibility is the willingness to give an account for your actions—to willingly bear the burden of what you have, or have not, done. It is being willing to answer for your conduct and obligations. However, human nature can lead us to refuse to take responsibility for

our actions. In fact, when we're confronted with our mistakes, we'll often play the blame game and attempt to deflect our responsibility onto someone else." Isaac Khalil

Journaling Suggestion:
Lord, enable me to take personal responsibility for my life, trusting You in all I do.

Memo for Meditation:
"For we are each responsible for our own conduct." Galatians 6:5

April 11

Motivational Idea: Maslov's hierarchy of needs

Maslow is considered to be the father of humanistic psychology. Human beings are seen as being free to act and control their own destinies. Maslow's hierarchy of needs is one of the best-known theories of human motivation. His theory states that our actions are motivated by certain physiological and psychological needs that progress from basic to complex. It is only when we have the basics that we can pursue our quest for what he termed 'self-actualisation'. Maslov said that this concept, *"May be loosely described as the full use and exploitation of talents, capabilities, potentialities, etc. Such people seem to be fulfilling themselves and to be doing the best that they are capable of doing. They are people who have developed or are developing to the full stature of which they are capable."*

The Bible would certainly not refute our needs for physical provision, a sense of safety, a sense of love and belonging, or a sense of worth and respect from others. However, the 'growth need', as interpreted in secular psychology, is based on a denial of man's depravity and the false notion that mankind is basically good. Biblically, our deepest need is for a relationship with God, which comes only through salvation in Jesus Christ (see John 14:6.) Also, our spiritual needs for forgiveness and a relationship with our Creator are missing from Maslow's humanistic pyramid. Through Jesus' death and resurrection, we can have abundant life. It is in dying ourselves that we find life and who we really are, and our true purpose on earth. True self-actualization is found in Jesus Christ.

Memorable Quote:
"Life isn't always about finding yourself. More often than not, it's about discovering who God created you to be." David A R White

Journaling Suggestion:
True self-actualization is found in Jesus Christ.

Memo for Meditation:
"My old self has been crucified with Christ. It is no longer I who live, but Christ lives in me. So I live in this earthly body by trusting in the Son of God, who loved me and gave himself for me." Galatians 2:20, New Living Translation

---

April 12

Motivational Idea: The power of the plan

Psychological research has been shown to demonstrate that being committed to a specific plan frees up our cognition for our other pursuits. In addition to helping us be more successful with the specific goal we're actively working on, planning lets us get on with other things, too. Once a plan is made, we can stop thinking about that one goal and make room for others. Our minds are designed in such a way as to keep working on successful outcomes in our pre-conscious state. This is essential as we all juggle many goals throughout our days and lives.

Are you a planner or a procrastinator? Planners are those who form in advance an organised method for action, and procrastinators are those who intentionally put off tasks. If we have a tendency to acquiesce in a state of inertia, it's time to start redeeming the time. If you are a planner, what is the driving force behind your plans? The pursuit of happiness leads to many cunning plans. The question is, have we got the right plans? What influences us? Who is our role model? What self-help books are we delving into? Many of these can be useful. The writers of the Proverbs reminds us that, *"We humans keep brainstorming options and plans, but God's purpose prevails."* (Proverbs 19:21).

For many, God does not feature in their plans. Perhaps today is a wake-up call to us all to invite God to enable us to make the right plans and involve Him in all our decision making. That will prove to be the best decision and the best plan we will ever make. Our long-term plans need to be given over to Him and we need to ensure that we are following His plans as these bring true happiness, real joy and eternal outcomes.

Memorable Quote:
"Never commit your virtue or your happiness to the future. Happy work is best done by the man who takes his long-term plans somewhat lightly and works from moment unto the Lord." C S Lewis, *Learning in Wartime* and *The Weight of Glory.*

Journaling Suggestion:
Journal about inviting God to reveal His plans for my life and invite Him into all my decision making. I will follow Him wherever He leads.

Memo for Meditation:
"Look here, you who say, 'Today or tomorrow we are going to a certain town and will stay there a year. We will do business there and make a profit." How do you know what your life will be like tomorrow? Your life is like the morning fog—it's here a little while, then it's gone. What you ought to say is, "If the Lord wants us to, we will live and do this or that.' Otherwise you are boasting about your own pretentious plans, and all such boasting is evil." James 4:13-17

April 13

Motivational Idea: The secret of happiness

The famous preacher and evangelist, Billy Graham, in his book *Hope for Each Day* tells that King George V wrote on the flyleaf of the Bible of a friend: *"The secret of happiness is not to do what you like to do, but to learn to like what you have to do."* Focusing primarily on ourselves will stand in the way of seeking His kingdom. Egotism and an attitude of *"It's all about me"* hinders us. Let's be honest with ourselves and identify the obstacles that are preventing us from allowing the Lord to provide us with the happiness that we desire, and only He can provide.

Memorable Quote:

"Too many think of happiness as some sort of will-o'-the-wisp thing that is discovered by constant and relentless searching. It is not found in seeking. It is not an end in itself. Pots of gold are never found at the end of the rainbow, as we used to think when we were children; gold is mined from the ground or panned laboriously from a mountain stream. Jesus told His disciples, 'Seek first the Kingdom of God, and His righteousness, and all these things will be added unto you.' The 'things' He spoke of were the things that make us happy and secure - food, drink, clothes, shelter. He told us not to make these things the chief goal of our lives but to, 'Seek first the Kingdom of God,' and all these things would be automatically supplied. There, if we will take it, is the secret of happiness.'" Billy Graham

Journaling Suggestion:

Journal on what seeking first the Kingdom of God will look like for you. What obstacles do you need to get rid of? What is in effect standing in the way of your lasting happiness?

Memo for Meditation:

"Do not be anxious about your life, what you will eat or what you will drink, nor about your body, what you will put on. Is not life more than food, and the body more than clothing? Look at the birds of the air: they neither sow nor reap nor gather into barns, and yet your heavenly Father feeds them. Are you not of more value than they? And which of you by being anxious can add a single hour to his span of life? And why are you anxious about clothing? Consider the lilies of the field, how they grow: they neither toil nor spin, yet I tell you, even Solomon in all his glory was not arrayed like one of these. But if God so clothes the grass of the field, which today is alive and tomorrow is thrown into the oven, will he not much more clothe you, O you of little faith? Therefore do not be anxious, saying, 'What shall we eat?' or 'What shall we drink?' or 'What shall we wear?' For the Gentiles seek after all these things, and your heavenly Father knows that you need them all. But seek first the kingdom of God and his righteousness, and all these things will be added to you." Matthew 6:25-33

April 14

Motivational Idea: Call off the search

According to the triangular theory of love developed by psychologist Robert Sternberg, the three components of love are: intimacy, passion and commitment.

Intimacy encompasses feelings of attachment, closeness, connectedness and bondedness.

Passion encompasses drives connected to both limerence and sexual attraction. Limerence is having an uncontrollable desire for someone – an obsession that consumes the limerent person's thoughts, feelings, and behaviours, even when those feelings are not reciprocated. This can cause significant emotional distress, loss of energy and productivity.

Commitment encompasses, in the short term, the decision to remain with another, and in the long term, the shared achievements and plans made with that other person The song *Call Off the Search* by Katie Melua is a captivating piece that delves into the depths of love, longing, and the search for meaning in life. With her soulful voice and poignant lyrics, Melua takes the listener on an emotional journey that resonates deeply with many. Heidi Barrera comments, *"At its core,* Call Off the Search *is about finding that one person who completes you, who brings solace and understanding to your life. It explores the idea of searching for love and the profound impact it can have on one's existence. Melua's mesmerising vocals effortlessly convey the vulnerability and desire that come with seeking a deep connection."*

Memorable Quote:

"I won't spend my life, waiting for an angel to descend/Searching for a rainbow with an end/Now that I've found you/I'll call off the search/And I won't spend my life gazing at the stars up in the sky/Wondering if love will pass me by/Now that I've found you/I'll call off the search/Out on my own I would never have known/This world that I see today/And I've got a feeling/It won't fade away/And I won't end my days wishing that love would come along/Cause you are in my life where you belong/Now that I've found you/I'll call off the search/Now that I've found you/I'll call off the search/Now that I've found you/I'll call off the search." Katie Melua

Journaling Suggestion:

Have you called off the search? Do you have someone in your life? Are you alone? Don't give up your dreams! And if you have found the Messiah, the Christ (Anointed One), then you can call off the search in terms of chasing happiness and fulfilment on that higher level of being.

Memo for Meditation:

"On the next day Jesus wanted to set out for Galilee. He found Philip and said to him, 'Follow me.' (Now Philip was from Bethsaida, the town of Andrew and Peter.) Philip found Nathanael and told him, 'We have found the one Moses wrote about in the law, and the prophets also wrote about—Jesus of Nazareth, the son of Joseph.' Nathanael replied, 'Can anything good come out of Nazareth?' Philip replied, 'Come and see.'"
John 1:43-46

April 15

Motivational Idea: Commitment calls for investment

The social psychologist Caryl Rusbult suggests there are three major factors to be considered in relationship commitment: satisfaction level, comparison with other alternatives, and the level of investment. People will have a high level of satisfaction in relationships if they have more rewards (companionship, attention, emotional support) and fewer costs (arguments, time). People tend to be committed to relationships if, when asking themselves, *Is there a better alternative to satisfy my needs?* The answer is *'no'*. Alternatives can include staying on their own and not engaging in 'romantic' relationships at all, or finding a new partner.

However, for Rusbult, the most important factor that maintains commitment to a relationship is investment. Investment refers to the number of resources, both tangible, like money or possessions, and intangible, like happy memories, that people will lose if they leave relationships. The model proposes two types of investment: intrinsic and extrinsic.

Intrinsic investment comprises the things we put directly into the relationship, such as effort, money, possessions and self-disclosure.

Extrinsic investment refers to the things that are brought into our lives through relationships, such as children, friends and shared memories.

How are we doing in our relationship investments? When it comes to our relationship with God, are we investing in it the way we should? The reality is that God has invested everything in us! Romans 8:32 says, *"He who did not spare his own Son, but gave Him up for us all—how will He not also, along with him, graciously give us all things?"* That's God's investment in *you*! If you want to develop a committed personal relationship with God, and invest in this most important of all relationships, then give Him time each day by praying and reading his word consistently. Find out what He desires *from* you and *for* you; this is the road to the happiness and fulfilment you have yearned for so long, and the most important way to grow your relationship with Him because, practically, no relationship would thrive without intentional communication. And when you talk together, He will lead you and show you how to invest in the eternal. He wants the best for you and He has invested His all in you.

Memorable Quote:
"Invest time with God because it's an investment that lasts throughout eternity."

Journaling Suggestion:
Journal on God's investment in you and your investments in the bank of heaven.

Memo for Meditation:
"Do not lay up for yourselves treasures on earth, where moth and rust destroy and where thieves break in and steal, but lay up for yourselves treasures in heaven, where neither moth nor rust destroys and where thieves do not break in and steal. For where your treasure is, there your heart will be also." Matthew 6:19-21

April 16

Motivational Idea: Commitment principles

Psalm 15 sets out a range of commitment principles:

- Be genuine and just, walk with integrity and honesty.
- Restraining the tongue reflects the soul's condition.

- Speak from a heart of love.
- Don't slander or lie or give it house room.
- Work and live for righteousness and truth.
- Model the love of God to those in your world.
- Don't be evil or reproach others.
- Despise ungodliness.
- Honour those who fear the Lord.
- Don't take bribes or rewards.
- Allow the Holy Spirit to direct your life being immersed into the Holy Spirit.
- Keep your promises.

If you are committed to these principles, you will never be shaken. The memo for today employs the Message Bible. Eugene Peterson, in his own inimical style, kicks off with two intriguing questions to our Creator God: "GOD, who gets invited to dinner at your place? How do we get on your guest list?" It's about intimacy with God. Check out various translations. "Who may worship in your sanctuary, LORD? Who may enter your presence on your holy hill?" New Living Translation.

Memorable Quote"
"David meditates over the character of the person received into the presence of God."

Journaling Suggestion:
My commitment principles.

Memo for Meditation:
"GOD, who gets invited to dinner at your place? How do we get on your guest list? Walk straight, act right, tell the truth. Don't hurt your friend, don't blame your neighbour; despise the despicable. Keep your word even when it costs you, make an honest living, never take a bribe. You'll never get blacklisted if you live like this." Psalm 15, The Message

April 17

Motivational Idea: The psychologist and the baptism of the Holy Spirit

Dan trained as a clinical psychologist. Before that, he says that he had, *"... accepted Christ as Lord and Saviour as a seventeen-year-old. For the next five years, I struggled with my faith. Even though I prayed, studied scripture and attended church regularly, I often felt alone. Although my beliefs were strong, my heart and spirit seldom soared. For the most part, God was remote and – I assumed – busy running his Universe."*

It all changed when Dan experienced the baptism of the Holy Spirit. He was alone in an upper room of an old church when he asked Jesus to baptise him in the Holy Spirit. He sat expectantly in a little chair – the room was for teaching children's classes. He had a deep experience of the Holy Spirit and his heart leapt with love. His spirit soared. Several years later, he thought of training as a clinical psychologist, but would psychology be compatible with spirituality? Would training for a PhD lead him away from Christ?

Dan's academic studies and clinical experience actually strengthened his faith in God and gave him tools for understanding the baptism in the Holy Spirit. Dan says that the influence of the Holy Spirit in our personalities unifies the body, heart and mind. As a therapist, Dan advocates that growth towards a healthy personality requires the integration of the body, heart and mind. Jesus demonstrated this unity of the physical, emotional and mental in his commitment to do the will of the father.

Dan says he has observed how the Holy Spirit seeks to amalgamate a person's body, feelings and thoughts, so they can come to experience a Christ-like balance of personality. The baptism of the Holy Spirit facilitates the work of Christ in helping us to develop balanced personalities like His own. The baptism of the Holy Spirit brings a shift from 'God is out there' to 'the kingdom of God is within'. The God of the heavens becomes Jesus in the heart – an intimate friendship for the recipient. And, guess what? He isn't too busy running His Universe because you are His world, and the apple of His eye.

Memorable Quote:
"From a psychological point of view, the baptism in the Holy Spirit is a major way that God fills us with an awareness of his presence and facilitates even greater personality balance in our desire to be like Jesus. If we have served Christ through formal roles, we now feel the intimacy of his love for us. If we have made a god of religion, we now encounter the God of Abraham, Isaac and Jacob. And if we have mentioned the Holy Spirit only when reciting the Apostles' Creed, we now discover Him as a personal Comforter and Counsellor." Dr Dan Montgomery

Journaling Suggestion:
The baptism of the Holy Spirit.

Memo for Meditation:
"Keep me as the apple of the eye, hide me under the shadow of thy wings." Psalm 17:8
"Keep my commandments, and live; and my law as the apple of thine eye." Proverbs 7:2

April 18

Motivational Idea: I've got the power

In the late 1990s, Dr Martin Seligman (we met Martin on the 18th January) introduced us to Positive Psychology. His theory proposed three basic psychological needs: to feel positive emotion, engage in activities that give life meaning and purpose, and have positive relationships with others. Two other needs were subsequently added: finding meaning and fulfilment in what we do, and seeking and savouring achievements and accomplishments. Taken together, their pursuit leads to the development of personal wellbeing and the opportunity to flourish. This is the power of positive psychology. Good stuff! We can learn from this to be empowered in living the best life possible.

Did Snap! beat him to it? The early 90s were a defining era in the music industry, with an eruption of electronic dance music. One track that stood out from the pack *The Power* by Snap! which became a smash hit in 1990. At its core, *The Power* is a song about standing up for oneself and seizing control of one's destiny. *"I've got the power /*

Hey, yeah, heh, I've got the power." This refrain is repeated throughout the song, driving home the central message of individual strength and emotional resilience.

Reinhard Bonnke, the German Evangelist, is remembered as the man who changed the face of Christianity in Africa. He too spoke of power. His message of redemptive hope became important, particularly in African nations affected by drought, civil strife and other tragedies. Millions came to Christ as a result of his Holy Spirit-inspired ministry. The memorable quote from his pen is our feature today – this is the power you need to live for Christ today.

Memorable Quote:
"THOROUGHLY BATHED: The baptism of the Spirit is a complete immersion of your entire being– spirit, soul, body–into the Holy Spirit. It is not partial, symbolic or temporary. Every part of your being is dipped and thoroughly bathed in this precious Liquid Fire, permanently. It is not a one-time event, as in water baptism. It is an ongoing experience that changes your very nature and surroundings. SOME PEOPLE WANT ICE CREAM CHRISTIANITY, COLD BUT nice. They want their churches to be like museums. But the church is not a freeze box. It is the Father's house. The Holy Spirit warms us up for the Father's house." Reinhard Bonnke

Journaling Suggestion:
I seek the power of the Holy Spirit to live for Jesus in my generation. Be empowered.

Memo for Meditation:
"But you will receive power when the Holy Spirit comes on you; and you will be my witnesses in Jerusalem, and in all Judea and Samaria, and to the ends of the earth." Acts 1:8

April 19

Motivational Idea: The flourishing life or the fruitful life?

The question of what it means to flourish as a human has been around for aeons. Aristotle first coined the term and defined it as, *"The way we are supposed to be as human beings."* Flourishing implies the cultivation of virtue and good character in order for our souls to flourish — a state that transcends superficial happiness. Thanks to Dr Martin Seligman, the father of Positive Psychology, flourishing has seen a remarkable resurgence and is seen as the gold standard of human wellbeing.

Dr Dani Treweek notes that the Christian world has also adopted the notion of flourishing and is taken by many as a description of the "good Christian life". Yet should our focus be on a 'flourishing' life or a 'fruitful' life? Dani observes that, *"In the Old Testament, the concept of flourishing is a botanic metaphor. Those who live under God's rule will sprout and experience fresh, abundant growth. In that sense, 'flourish' may indeed seem to be an appropriate way to describe the 'good Christian life'. However, in the New Testament, the English concept of flourishing appears only in the book of Acts. Furthermore, it is always the preaching of the word or message of God that is described as flourishing within the early church (Acts 6:7, 12:24, 19:20). When writing about the abundant growth of individuals after the crucifixion and resurrection, it is the concept of "fruitfulness" that, well, flourishes!"*

Memorable Quote:
"The language of flourishing is popular today because it fits very comfortably within the individualistic secular culture we inhabit. In that culture, the concept of flourishing is not concerned with looking to God to bear fruit in our lives by his Spirit. Rather, it is concerned with looking deep within, as we go on a journey of self-discovery and self-realisation. It is not concerned with cultivating the type of other person-centred gospel fruit whose primary purpose is to glorify God and be a blessing to those around us. Rather, it is concerned with identifying what gives me a sense of fulfilment and so, as a matter of self-love, prioritising my "right" to reach my full potential. It is not concerned with conforming my otherwise distorted sense of self with my new identity in Christ. Rather, it is about defining my authentic self on my own terms, according to who I think I am, or perhaps who I'd like to be." Dani Treweek.

Journaling Suggestion:
Displaying the fruit of the Spirit in everyday life.

Memo for Meditation:
"But the fruit of the Spirit [the result of His presence within us] is love [unselfish concern for others], joy, [inner] peace, patience [not the ability

to wait, but how we act while waiting], kindness, goodness, faithfulness."
Galatians 5:22-23

April 20

Motivational Idea: RCA – root cause analysis

RCA (root cause analysis) is the process of discovering the root causes of problems in order to find solutions. Solving underlying issues rather than just treating ad hoc symptoms and putting out fires makes perfect sense.

Firstly, we need to discover the root cause of the problem. Secondly, understand it in order to fix it, and thirdly, apply what we learn to systematically prevent that problem in the future. One of the core principles that guide effective RCA is to *focus* on correcting and remedying root causes rather than just symptoms. Henry Thoreau captured one of the most persistent tendencies we humans have: we do not treat our problems at their roots. We treat *symptoms*, not diseases.

Whatever you are struggling with today, getting to the root of the matter will help you identify practical steps to solving the problem, like *"your very own crime mystery puzzle* (Anthony Sanni) *you are solving. Whatever the experience, it is always better to treat a cause instead of an effect. Remember that you will take care of many branches by cutting down just one root. And even though Root Work may be hard, it is worth it in the long run. Short cuts are short-lived. Get to the root, once and for all."*

Remember, too, that RCA can be equally as effective to find the root cause of our successes. If we find the cause of a success or an achievement, it's rarely a bad idea. This kind of analysis can help prioritise and pre-emptively protect key factors, and we might be able to translate success in one area to success in another area of our lives. In your RCA, use Scripture. Why not start with Psalm 1? It's called a 'wisdom Psalm' because we learn that happiness results from our choice to follow God's direction in life. In this Psalm, the writer sets forth two ways or two directions in life. One is the right way that leads to happiness, and the other is the wrong way that leads to misery – do your RCA.

Memorable Quote:
"There are a thousand hacking at the branches of evil to one who is striking at the root." Henry Thoreau

Journaling Suggestion:
Time for some RCA to move forward and be 'flourishingly fruitful'.

Memo for Meditation:
"Oh, the joys of those who do not follow the advice of the wicked, or stand around with sinners, or join in with mocker But they delight in the law of the LORD, meditating on it day and night. They are like trees planted along the riverbank, bearing fruit each season. Their leaves never wither, and they prosper in all they do. But not the wicked. They are like worthless chaff, scattered by the wind. They will be condemned at the time of judgement. Sinners will have no place among the godly. For the LORD watches over the path of the godly, but the path of the wicked leads to destruction." Psalm 1

April 21

Motivational Idea: The roots and fruits principle

The quality of the fruit of any tree depends on its roots. When the roots grow in deep, rich soil full of nutrients, the tree will be strong and healthy, and it will yield good fruit. The tree rooted in poor quality soil will have little nutrition for the branches and so the quality of its fruit will be poor. One of the main ways to cause a tree to produce good fruit is to attend to the roots. We need to attend to our root systems! We can only deal with our maladaptive and sinful behaviours by attacking the real causes (roots) in a biblical manner. We have to deal with the 'heart' of our problem. The root system is equal to the heart. We have to realise that we sin because we have focused our hearts on our wants, our perceived needs, our personal rights, our beliefs and desires. This results in a self-centred, idolatrous heart, which is revealed by our thoughts, words, and actions. *"Above all else, guard your heart, for everything you do flows from it."* (Proverbs 4:23).

We must give due diligence to attend to our hearts because whatever we allow to enter our hearts, if not examined and evaluated properly, will undoubtedly be expressed in our lives in terms of good fruit or bad fruit. If you want to change the fruits, you will first have to deal with the roots. If you want to change the visible, you must first change the invisible.

Jesus said, *"Make a tree good and its fruit will be good, or make a tree bad and its fruit will be bad, for a tree is recognized by its fruit. You brood of vipers, how can you who are evil say anything good? For the mouth speaks what the heart is full of. A good man brings good things out of the good stored up in him, and an evil man brings evil things out of the evil stored up in him. But I tell you that everyone will have to give account on the day of judgement for every empty word they have spoken. For by your words you will be acquitted, and by your words you will be condemned."* (Matthew 12:33-36).

Memorable Quote:

"It may surprise you that biblical counselling does not focus on the fruit of a specific sin most of the time. It is not profitable to simply pull the bad fruit off the tree, because new bad fruit will soon grow in its place. The sin you are committing is the result of the problem, not the problem itself. The way to deal with all sin biblically is to determine the source of the feelings—your beliefs, desires, and thoughts. The Bible says that the source to examine is your heart. Your heart focus must change from being "all about me" to glorifying God." Dr Julie Ganschow

Journaling Suggestion:

Examine your heart before God and attend to the roots to produce the fruits.

Memo for Meditation:

"Produce fruit in keeping with repentance." Matthew 3:8

April 22

Motivational Quote: The joy of curiosity

Angela Duckworth tells a story about Jane Goodall which illustrates the joy of curiosity and discovery. It all began with an egg. When Jane was 4 years old, she went to visit her grandmother at the family farm. One of her chores was to collect the hens' eggs. *"As the days passed, I became more and more puzzled,"* she recalls. *"Where on a chicken was there an opening big enough for an egg to come out?"* Without the internet, Jane decided to find out for herself. One afternoon, she crawled into an empty henhouse and, for hours and hours, hid in some straw, quietly waiting. More than seven decades later, Jane remembers what happened next as if it were yesterday: *"At last a hen came in, scratched about in the straw, and settled herself on her makeshift nest just in front of me. I must have kept very still or she would have been disturbed. Presently the hen half stood and I saw a round white object gradually protruding from the feathers between her legs. Suddenly with a plop, the egg landed on the straw. With clucks of pleasure the hen shook her feathers, nudged the egg with her beak, and left."* Jane's mother had been looking everywhere for her for hours and had even called the police, frantic with worry. Yet, Jane remembers, *"When mum, still searching, saw the excited little girl rushing toward the house, she did not scold me. She noticed my shining eyes and sat down to listen to the story of how a hen lays an egg: the wonder of that moment when the egg finally fell to the ground."* Duckworth notes that new research shows that it is not only curious *questions* but also interesting *answers* that further enhance learning and memory, particularly as children grow into adolescents. In other words, teenagers are smarter when they're tackling topics whose questions and answers fill them with wonder.

Memorable Quote:
"Do encourage curiosity at any age. Jane was 57 years old when she created Roots & Shoots, *which empowers young people to create positive change in their communities. This year, (2021), at 87, she published* The Book of Hope *and accepted the 2021 Templeton Prize saying, 'I am eternally thankful that my curiosity and desire to learn is as strong as it was when I was a child.' You're never too old, or too young, to puzzle over something you don't understand, to figure it out for yourself, and then, with shining eyes, to share your discovery with people you love".* Angela Duckworth

Journaling Suggestion:
The lesson for today is to rekindle my curiosity and the joy of discovery.

Memo for Meditation: *"An intelligent heart acquires knowledge, and the ear of the wise seeks knowledge."* Proverbs 18:12

April 23

Motivational Idea: More about curiosity

'Curiosity killed the cat' is a phrase commonly used to tell people to mind their own business and not to stick their noses in where noses have no business being. The saying can also be taken as a warning about the dangers of curiosity. Psychology defines curiosity as, 'The impulse or desire to investigate, observe, or gather information, particularly when the material is novel or interesting.'

Psychologists have compiled a large body of research on the benefits of curiosity and this has yielded several theories. Curiosity, rather than being seen as a single trait, can now be broken down into five distinct dimensions. Instead of asking, *"How curious are you?"* the question is, *"How are you curious?"* These dimensions are, firstly, the knowledge gap and the need to know which offers relief. People work relentlessly to solve problems. Secondly, joyous exploration, being consumed with awe and wonder. Thirdly, the need to observe others, what they think and what they are doing. Fourthly, stress tolerance with the 'novel' things of the world which can produce anxiety. Fifthly, thrill-seeking which involves risk-taking to acquire intense experiences; hence the 'danger warning' attached to this kind of curiosity.

Barnabas Piper suggests that for the believer curiosity ought to be a 'life enhancer'. When people of faith are curious, they grow in knowledge and their ability to rightly discern situations. Curiosity begets discernment! Curiosity isn't necessarily a dangerous trap; it's a thing God can use to make us wise and to be more discerning.

Memorable Quote:

"The evils of the world are a powerful gravitational pull for our sinful hearts. To say we're to be curious about the world denies none of this. Neither does it downplay the risks and dangers. Instead, proper curiosity about the world opens our eyes to the wiles of the world and provides the discernment we need to fight against them. Curiosity about God anchors us in God's strength as we learn more, seek more, and see more of him.

Curiosity drives us to seek out truth and discern right from wrong. Curiosity isn't a dangerous trap; it's the thing God uses to make us wise so we can avoid the traps of sin and live freely for him." Barnabas Piper

Journaling Suggestion:
Lord give me sanctified curiosity and the discernment it begets.

Memo for Mediation:
"Summing it all up, friends, I'd say you'll do best by filling your minds and meditating on things true, noble, reputable, authentic, compelling, gracious – the best, not the worst; the beautiful, not the ugly; things to praise, not things to curse." Philippians 4:8

April 24

Motivational Idea: Consequences

THREE THINGS:

Primary Priority

The main priority in my life – the big overarching priority. What is my big priority? What is the big goal now? I refer to the wisdom of C S Lewis (an analogy): health is very important, but the moment you make health (the primary priority) your obsession (goal obsession), you start becoming fearful and imagining there is something wrong with you. You actually become more unhealthy. You are only likely to enjoy good health if you just get on with your life and do what needs to be done. Work so you can buy good food, have time for relaxation and breaks (holidays), have fun, exercise, fresh air. Buy the things you need and want. Basically, enjoy your life and love yourself. We will never get healthy if health is our big obsession. We must learn to want the other things more and get on with doing them to be healthy! Am I obsessing on my big priority to the point where I can't obtain it and feel helpless?

Personal Responsibility

I need to take personal responsibility for my big priority and I need to do what needs to be done to fulfil that big priority. It's my responsibility! So, what do I need to do?

Consequences

Every decision has a consequence. If I don't make the right decisions, then the law of unintentional consequences kicks in. What are the pleasing consequences that I want to enjoy which will be determined by my actions? What are the painful consequences that I don't want to experience as a result of my inaction or wrong actions? The journey begins with naming the big priority, accepting personal responsibility, and then just doing what needs to be done that will lead to those pleasing consequences. It also means taking personal responsibility for painful consequences if I make the wrong decisions or as a direct result of my indecision, procrastination and inaction.

Memorable Quote:

"Health is a great blessing, but the moment you make health one of your main, direct objects you start becoming a crank and imagining there is something wrong with you. You are only likely to get health provided you want other things more—food, games, work, fun, open air. In the same way, we shall never save civilization as long as civilization is our main object. We must learn to want something else even more." C S Lewis

Journaling Suggestion:

Journal about the big priority for my life, taking personal responsibility and making the right decisions to achieve pleasing consequences.

Memo for Meditation:

"Each one should test their own actions. Then they can take pride in themselves alone, without comparing themselves to someone else, for each one should carry their own load." Galatians 6:5

April 25

Motivational Idea: Goal obsession

Goal obsession has been described as the ultimate flaw that demolishes success. In our pursuit of happiness, setting ambitious goals has long been viewed as a key driver of achievement. However, danger lurks beneath and we need to take cognizance of a hidden pitfall. As our aspirations grow, there exists a delicate line that separates our healthy ambitions from the potential dangers of goal obsession. One could be misled into thinking that being obsessed with goals is the rocket fuel of exceptional outcomes. Goal obsession, however, is a state in which we become excessively fixated on achieving a specific goal, often to the detriment of our overall wellbeing and our lasting happiness. It has the potential to lead us down a tunnel-vision path, overlooking the broader context and long-term consequences.

While ambition and determination are essential traits of success, an unhealthy obsession with what we want can cause us to lose sight of the bigger picture, neglecting other important aspects of our lives. We need to learn how to strike a balance between relentless pursuit and healthy ambitions. The reality is that our ambitions can become toxic.

The Bible is clear that we shouldn't make selfish ambition our life's goal. All that time and effort we spend trying to rise up the success ladder, chasing that elusive happiness we think goes with it, to the detriment of ourselves and, sadly, those around us, in our quest to reach the top. But is there such a thing as godly ambition? God says yes! The Bible tells us that God's highest vision and noblest ambition for us is to become like Christ. Paul explains this process in our memo for today.

Memorable Quote:
"Goal obsession can be seen as the force at play when we get so wrapped up in achieving our goals that we do it at the expense of our divine calling and the larger mission." Adapted by the author

Journaling Suggestion:
Today I bring my ambitions to the cross and ask the Lord to sanctify my goals.

Memo for Meditation:
"...I consider everything a loss because of the surpassing worth of knowing Christ Jesus my Lord...that I may gain Christ and be found in him, not having a righteousness of my own that comes from the law, but that which is through faith in Christ—the righteousness that comes from God on the basis of faith... I do not consider myself yet to have taken hold of it. But one thing I do: Forgetting what is behind and straining toward what is ahead, I press on toward the goal to win the prize for which God has called me heavenward in Christ Jesus." Philippians 3:7-15

April 26

Motivational Idea: The pursuit of goals without the obsession

Goal setting is an effective way to increase our motivation and help us to create the changes we want to see. It's a good way to focus our attention on the things that are important. It allows us to create a vision of how we would like our life to be. When we have a goal, we tend to increase the amount of time and effort we spend on an activity, and develop effective strategies to achieve that goal. We need to set SMART goals, i.e. Specific, Measurable, Achievable, Relevant and Time-Bound goals. Defining these parameters helps ensure that your objectives are attainable within a certain time frame. We need to set realistic goals which are achievable. So far so good!

The problem arises, however, when we begin to obsess over our goals. Perhaps your goal is to get your to-do list done each day, and heaven help the person who gets in the way of your list. We become obsessed which, in point of fact, is detrimental to achieving our goal and can result in missing the mark we had set for ourselves.

Barb Raveling gives some ideas about how to stop the obsessing from her own personal experience. Firstly, find out what makes you obsessed. "Why are we struggling? Why so heavy-laden?" Chances are, the reason we're so heavy-hearted (and obsessed) is because we're making the goal a lot more important than God wants us to make it. The next question we need to ask is, "What happened that triggered the obsession?" Once you discover what triggered the obsession, go ahead with the next step (for tomorrow). We need to keep in mind in all our goal setting what God's ultimate goal is for our lives, and then all our other goals will be in subservience to His glorious goal for us.

Memorable Quote:
"God's ultimate goal for your life on earth is not comfort, but character development. He wants you to grow up spiritually and become like Christ." Rick Warren

Journaling Suggestion:
Lord help me to understand why I am obsessed and what triggers it.

Memo for Meditation:

"Are you tired? Worn out? Burned out on religion? Come to me. Get away with me and you'll recover your life. I'll show you how to take a real rest. Walk with me and work with me—watch how I do it. Learn the unforced rhythms of grace. I won't lay anything heavy or ill-fitting on you. Keep company with me and you'll learn to live freely and lightly." Matthew 11:28-30

April 27

Motivational Idea: Taking the obsessional goal to the expert

Setting goals is an important step in the recovery journey with mental health problems. Common disorders like depression or anxiety can make it hard to function. Setting goals can be used as part of cognitive behaviour therapy (CBT) to start the process of getting well and rebuilding a meaningful life. Once you discover what triggered the obsession, you can then go ahead with the next step. For believers, the next step is to go to Jesus whenever you find yourself obsessing.

If you are not a believer, try praying. Why do we need to come to Jesus? Because He is the only one who can help us let go of the obsession. Counsellors can help but only the Wonderful Counsellor can take it away. We tend to cry out to the Lord, "Jesus, fix this! Help me reach my goal." Yet He tells us to rest! Rest in Him! Rest does not mean doing nothing and just waiting for a miracle. Learning to rest in Him means we can then take the next step and continue pursuing our goals, but do it with God.

We don't need to stop pursuing our goals because we were making them too important. God may want us to *keep* pursuing our goals, but to do it *with* Him. Jesus tells us to learn from Him. Then He goes on to give us that beautiful image (Matthew 11:28-30) of the two of us pulling the wagon together, side by side. He's the head oxen. We're His trainee. We're not sitting in the back of the wagon, watching Him do all the work. We're walking *with* Him. That's not always easy, but it's a whole lot easier than trying to pull the wagon all by ourselves! As we walk with Him, we'll have to keep remembering to keep in step with Him.

Memorable Quote:
"There's nothing wrong with those requests. But when they come in the middle of a goal-induced frenzy, they're often asked with impure motives–we want our goals more than we want God. So what we really need to do is forget the requests, come to God, and just rest in Him. Remember who He is. Remember what's important. Remember how much we love Him. And just rest. It's an incredible blessing to be able to rest in Him. Forget the world. Forget our goals. Forget our problems. Just soak in His love. Jesus says He'll give us rest. He doesn't say He'll give us a perfect life, a perfect relationship, or a perfect body. But rest is far better than any of those things." Barb Raveling

Journaling Suggestion:
Lord teach me the art of resting in You.

Memo for Meditation:
"Then, because so many people were coming and going that they did not even have a chance to eat, He (Jesus) said to them, "Come with me by yourselves to a quiet place and get some rest." Mark 6:31

April 28

Motivational Idea: Carrying a burden He doesn't want you to carry

So often when we pursue our goals, we take on burdens God doesn't want us to carry. We somehow let those goals get so intertwined with our identity that if we fail at the goal, we feel like we're also failures at life. Satan loves this, but it isn't true. We're not defined by what we do, but by who we are in Christ. And in Christ, we're God's children. Beautifully and wonderfully made. Greatly loved. Valuable. And that's whether we reach the goal or not. His burden is light: walk with Him. *Our* burden is incredibly heavy: be successful! Don't disappoint anyone! Be the best! Earn respect! Don't make anyone mad! Don't fail!

Those burdens weigh us down because they're self-focused goals. And when we try to fill ourselves up with all of those things, we never get enough to satisfy us. We'd be far better off if we let go of our burdens and focused on Him: loving Him, enjoying Him, and learning from Him. God can use the goal-pursuing process for our growth and also for the good of ourselves and others. But don't let the tyranny of the 'ought' wreck us in our walk with God. That 'ought' tyranny may be an integral part of us that has been embedded from our early years. You got eight A stars and one B, and you were asked what happened to you to get a B. God can change that horrible legacy from the past, and the harsh super-ego that pulls you down every time.

Ask God for the goals He has for your life then pray that your mind and heart and will is shaped into alignment with His will, and then do it. You will not be disappointed! As we walk the path He has for us and as we learn the unforced rhythms of grace, we are living in the light of the Lord and the joy of the Lord is our strength.

Memorable Quote:
"God wants to produce in us what we don't have in ourselves. And the way it happens is through abiding. We can truly abide with God when our heart, our life, and our relationship with Jesus is our first priority."
Chip Ingram

Journaling Suggestion:
Journal on the mind and heart and will, shaped into alignment with His will.

Memo for Meditation:
"I am the true vine, and My Father is the vinedresser. Every branch in Me that does not bear fruit, He takes away; and every branch that bears fruit, He prunes it so that it may bear more fruit. Abide in Me, and I in you. As the branch cannot bear fruit of itself unless it abides in the vine, so neither can you unless you abide in Me. I am the vine, you are the branches; he who abides in Me and I in him, he bears much fruit, for apart from Me you can do nothing." John 15:1-3, 4-5

April 29

Motivational Idea: Master your day, and you will master your life

"You won't be able to master your life tomorrow, in a week, a month, or even a year from now. You have to do it today, right now. Master your day, and you will master your life."

Many people are either living in the past or living in the future. This 'stuckness' usually involves past regrets and/or future fears, to the extent that living in the here and now is well nigh impossible. 'Presentism' is now being used in the workplace to describe people who are at work but not as productive as they could or should be; they are not functioning well or to the best of their ability. Can the same word be applied to your life? Are you suffering from 'presentism'? Your life is just aimless, without zest and totally devoid of bliss in a belligerent world.

It's time to deal with this inertia and malevolent paralysis. So, what can we do? The quotation comes from Recovery in the Pines, an organisation in Arizona which offers a Christian, 12-step based extended care, drug and alcohol program focusing on long-term, successful recovery. There is learning here for us all.

Basically, there are four steps we need to take:
1. Know what you're aiming at and why.
2. Create a plan.
3. Get into massive action ... of small steps.
4. Rinse and repeat.

Determine what actions are top priority for you to master the day... and ultimately your life. Think about the best version of yourself and identify the top 5/10 characteristics you wish to master mentally, emotionally, physically, spiritually and socially, followed by SMART goals. Craft powerful 'whys?' + a negative one. Create a daily plan to work on your best version of you. Break up the actions into micro habits (2-5+ minute actions) and activities (30-60 minute events) that strengthen your best version in doses.

Memorable Quote:
"Massive right action is required to learn a new habit or skill and build a competency at it. Get into a habit of a massive amount of consistent, small steps. Pause and reflect at the end of the day. Identify ways you can learn to increase the frequency, duration, complexity, efficiency, and effectiveness of your micro habits and activities. Keep getting after it, diligently, daily ... and you will become unconsciously competent in whatever you're aiming at to master your life." Recovery in The Pines

Journaling Suggestion:
Journal on the small steps you need to take today.

Memo for Meditation:
"Let me hear in the morning of your steadfast love, for in you I trust. Make me know the way I should go (point out the road I must travel), for to you I lift up my soul." Psalm 143:8

April 30

Motivational Idea: The art of self-mastery

Gregory Dicklow talks about, *"the profound and transformative art of self-mastery."* It makes perfect sense since self-mastery is transformative and has such potential that we need to engage in this skilful art. Gregory gives us six biblical pillars for our 'self' project: self-control, facing weakness, discipline, humility, wisdom, and love. On the face of it, this all sounds somewhat familiar and indeed a bit simplistic. However, when we take a deep dive into these, we discover these are the seeds of destiny, the antecedents of a mighty harvest.

The first pillar is self-control. *"Better to be slow to anger than to be a mighty warrior, and one who controls his temper is better than one who captures a city."* (Proverbs 16:32). The second pillar is facing our weakness. We need to acknowledge and take ownership of our weakness. Only when we have done so can we take the next step. Weakness is not failure, rather it qualifies us for power. Name it, don't shame it! Then ask God for His power (2 Corinthians 12:8-10). See your weakness as but a stepping stone into the unlimited power and strength of God. The third pillar is discipline. This is self-government. *"To learn, you must love discipline; it is stupid to hate correction."* (Proverbs 12:1). The fourth pillar is humility. Be humble! Be aware that God is good and anything you have or ever will have comes from Him. It all belongs to Him; we are the custodians of His gracious favour and blessings. It does not mean that you think less of yourself, but rather that you think of yourself less. The fifth pillar is the pursuit of wisdom. Wisdom and understanding are the cornerstones of self-mastery. Gain knowledge and learn wisdom to apply that knowledge. Wisdom is the ability to apply that knowledge. Knowing what to do when we don't know what to do. The sixth pillar is love. Love never fails. Love people – make a difference for good in their lives. Aim for maximum positive impact. This is the chief goal in the work of self-mastery.

Memorable Quote: *"Your life of self-mastery has the potential to make a massive positive impact on the people in your world, and the people in their world for generations to come. Grow those seeds that will reap a bountiful harvest for time and eternity. Build those pillars."* Author

Journaling Suggestion: Journal on sowing good seeds and building the pillars of self-mastery.

Memo for Meditation: *"If any of you lacks wisdom, you should ask God, who gives generously to all without finding fault, and it will be given to you."* James 1:5

THE EMOTIONAL DIMENSION

May 1

Motivational Idea: Handling our emotional life

How are you managing your emotions? There are loads of theories about emotions. Some would even suggest we have no free will, we are just destined to follow what's written into our genes and these dictate our behaviours. Sometimes we look back and think, *'Why on earth did I ever do that?'* Was it our emotional rollercoaster that pushed us in a particular direction? *'It wasn't me, it was my emotions!'* This is referred to as emotional dysregulation, and depending on its severity can disrupt your life, social relationships, career and more.

Emotional *regulation* on the other hand is the ability to better control our emotional state. Some people are afraid to feel, and seem to think that emotions are the black sheep of our makeup – not at all! We were made to experience emotions, but we need to know how to handle them. Emotions are a normal part of everyday life. We feel frustrated when we're stuck in traffic. We feel sad when we miss our loved ones. We can get angry when someone lets us down or does something to hurt us. We need emotional regulation, the ability to effectively exert control over our emotions. Some people are better at regulating their emotions than others; they are high in emotional intelligence and are aware of both their internal experiences and the feelings of others. While it may seem like they're just 'naturally calm', these people experience negative feelings too. They've just developed coping strategies that allow them to self-regulate difficult emotions. The good news is that emotional self-regulation isn't a static trait. Skills can be learned and improved over time. Learning how to manage negative experiences can benefit your mental and physical health.

To start us off on our month's journey into our emotional life, here are five emotion regulation skills that can help us regulate our emotions:

1. Create space.
2. Notice what you feel.
3. Name what you feel.
4. Accept the emotion.
5. Practice mindfulness.
We will be considering these skills over the next two days.

Memorable Quote:
"Mindfulness helps us "live in the moment" by paying attention to what is inside us. Use your senses to notice what is happening around you in nonjudgmental ways. These skills can help you stay calm and avoid engaging in negative thought patterns when you are in the midst of emotional pain." Bethany Klynn

Journaling Suggestion:
Journal on naming my emotions today and becoming aware of them.

Memo for Meditation:
"But don't let the passion of your emotions lead you to sin! Don't let anger control you or be fuel for revenge, not for even a day. Don't give the slanderous accuser, the Devil, an opportunity to manipulate you!" Ephesians 4:26.

May 2

Motivational Idea: Emotional regulation – skills to master

Let's elaborate today on mastering three of those skills:
1. Create space: Our emotions happen fast. Bethany Klynn says, *"We don't think 'now I will be angry' — we are just suddenly clenched-jawed and furious. So the number one skill in regulating difficult emotions, the gift we can give ourselves, is to pause. Take a breath. Slow down the moment between trigger and response."* Create that safe space.
2. Noticing what you feel: This is an equally important skill and its awareness about *how* you are feeling. Dr Judson Brewer in his book *Unwinding Anxiety* recommends becoming more curious about our physical reactions. You need to 'tune-in' to yourself and become aware of the parts of your body where you are noticing sensations. Upset

stomach? Racing heart? Neck or head tension? Physical symptoms can be communicating what we are experiencing emotionally. Being curious about what is happening to you physically can also distract your focus and allow some of the intensity of the emotion to ease.

3. Naming what you feel: After noticing what you feel, the ability to name it can help you take control of what is happening. Ask yourself: What would I call the emotions I'm feeling? Is it anger, sadness, disappointment, or resentment? What else is it? One strong emotion that often hides beneath others is fear. We can feel more than one emotion at a time, so don't hesitate to identify multiple emotions you might be feeling. Then dig a little deeper. If you feel fear, what are you afraid of? If you feel anger, what are you angry about or toward? Being able to name your emotions will help you get one step closer to being able to manage your emotions and articulate your feelings to yourself and others.

Memorable Quote:
"We think of anxiety as everything from mild unease to full-blown panic. But it's also what drives the addictive behaviours and bad habits we use to cope (e.g. stress eating, procrastination, doom scrolling and social media). Plus, anxiety lives in a part of the brain that resists rational thought. So we get stuck in anxiety habit loops that we can't think our way out of or use willpower to overcome. We can learn to map our brains to discover our triggers, defuse them with the simple but powerful practice of curiosity, and to train our brains using mindfulness and other practices that have been proven to work."

Journaling Suggestion:
Journal on how you will pause, create a safe space and develop a healthy curiosity about becoming aware of your emotions.

Memo for Meditation:
"O my people, trust in him at all times. Pour out your heart to him, for God is our refuge." Interlude Psalm 62:8.

May 3

Motivational Idea: Emotional regulation – skills to master (2)

4. Accepting the emotion: We need to recognise that emotions are a normal part of how we respond to situations. Rather than beating yourself up for feeling angry or scared, recognise that your emotional reactions are valid. Perhaps you need to practise self-compassion and give yourself grace. God certainly gives grace and He knows and loves us! He made us with emotions, and emotions when handled correctly can lead to good outcomes, and not the maladaptive behaviours and the cul-de-sac addictions of the past.

5. Practising mindfulness: Mindfulness helps us to *'live in the moment'*, and we do this by paying attention to what is going on inside of us. Use your senses to notice what is happening around you in non-judgmental ways. These skills can help you stay calm and avoid engaging in negative thought patterns when you are in the midst of emotional pain. It is in these ways we can learn to control emotions that in the past have caused us to do and say things we lived to regret.

When our emotions feel overwhelming, our self-talk tends to become negative: *"I messed up again."* If you treat yourself with compassion, you can replace negative talk with positive comments. Try encouraging yourself by saying, *"I always try so hard."* This shift can help mitigate the emotions we're feeling. Once you work at mastering these techniques, you are in a place of empowerment. Weaknesses become strengths as we manage our emotions for our good and His glory.

Memorable Quote:
"If you tend to respond to feelings of anger by lashing out at people, you likely notice the negative impact it is having on your relationships. You might also notice that it doesn't feel good. Or, it feels good at the moment, but the consequences are painful. Next time you feel anger or fear, recognize that you get to choose how you want to respond. That recognition is powerful. Rather than lashing out, can you try a different response? Is it possible for you to tell someone that you're feeling angry rather than speaking harshly to them?" Bethany Klynn

Journaling Suggestion:
It's time to get to grips with managing my emotions with the Lord's help.

Memo for Meditation:

"A gentle answer turns away wrath, but a harsh word stirs up anger. The tongue of the wise commends knowledge, but the mouth of the fool gushes folly. The eyes of the LORD are everywhere, keeping watch on the wicked and the good. The tongue that brings healing is a tree of life, but a deceitful tongue crushes the spirit." Proverbs 15:1-4

May 4

Motivational Idea: Finding our validation, identity and worth

Coupled with humanity's quest for happiness is the great pursuit of finding our identity. Yet chasing validation in temporary sources will give us a fleeting measure of satisfaction. Our perceptions, beliefs and emotions all play a part in the chase and are often trigger actions. For followers of Jesus, we have an eternal identity gifted to us by God Himself. We have been reconciled to God with a new identity defined by Christ's righteousness (see 2 Corinthians 5:11-21). Christ has sacrificially given us a new identity and purpose. We find our worth in Him. In humanity's desire for validation, we have a longing to belong, to fit in, to be authentic, and to realise those dreams and aspirations; so many are rudderless in restless seas of emotions that pull and push this way and that. Yet when we realise the true reality, who we are, or can be, in Christ, we are a new creation, and this changes everything! Yes, our emotions are still there but we have both an anchor and a captain to enable us to realise our potential for living in the reality of our eternal identity, and He can guide us constantly in all our ways, accompany us in all our days and empower us in all our struggles. Our feelings come and go but this is our assurance in a world of doubt and fear. This is the bedrock upon which we can build our lives and manage our emotions. When we hand it all over to the Lord and surrender to Him, this is transformative, this is life-changing. Our mind, will and emotions are infused with the Holy Spirit. We can sing with joyous emotion our memorable quote today in the form of a breathtaking hymn.

Memorable Quotation:

"O Christ, in Thee my soul hath found, And found in Thee alone, The peace, the joy I sought so long, The bliss till now unknown. [Refrain] Now

none but Christ can satisfy, None other name for me, There's love, and life, and lasting joy, Lord Jesus, found in Thee. I sighed for rest and happiness, I yearned for them, not Thee; But while I passed my Saviour by, His love laid hold on me. [Refrain] I tried the broken cisterns, Lord, But ah! The waters failed, E'en as I stooped to drink they'd fled, And mocked me as I wailed. [Refrain] The pleasures lost I sadly mourned, But never wept for Thee, Till grace the sightless eyes received, Thy loveliness to see. [Refrain]" Frances Bevan

Journaling Suggestion:

These lines came to my mind this morning: *"O the bliss til now unknown. Bliss in a belligerent world. It's only found in Jesus . Bliss – perfect joy, lasting happiness here and now and then eternal bliss."* Author

Memo for Meditation:

"This means that anyone who belongs to Christ has become a new person. The old life is gone; a new life has begun!" 2 Corinthians 5:17

May 5

Motivational Idea: We need a perfect role model

What if we had a counsellor who was also the perfect role model, who walks the walk and talks the talk, and who travels with us on our journey day in and day out? We do! That person is God Himself, the One who created us and knows us better than we know ourselves, the God Man, Jesus, has the know-how to steer us through what can be the minefield of our emotions.

Bill Gaultiere says, *"To become like Jesus we need to befriend His emotions. It's important to appreciate that Jesus is a feeler who experiences and expresses deep and vivid emotions about many things in life."* As we grow in our relationship with Jesus, we get to know Him and we learn from Him. Jesus, The Lord from heaven, the perfect man on earth with deep emotions. That's good news for those of us who have difficulty expressing emotions. We get into a relationship with Jesus, the only one who is sinlessly perfect, and He teaches us how to handle our emotions as we walk with Him.

Jesus always expressed His emotions in love. He never did anything or said anything, or expressed deep emotion without extravagant love in His heart. Gaultiere, noting how Jesus demonstrates the full range of human emotions, identified 39 different emotions that Jesus experienced. That's a lot of emotions! He then grouped these feelings into eleven core emotions: *anxiety, anger, shame, sadness, pain, surprise, hope, faith, love, joy and peace.* Each offers us a mirror to help us to verbalise our emotions.

Memorable Quote:
"Jesus is a 'feeler'. You may disagree with us. Most Christian leaders today seem to. Early in my life and ministry, I discounted my emotions and stayed in my thinking. But the truth is that Jesus felt all the struggles that we do, including temptations to sin, so He empathises with us to help us grow in emotional wholeness and holiness." Hebrews 4:15
"If we admire and bond with Jesus the Feeler then it will help us put more value on the emotions that we and other people have. It will encourage us to convey more emotion in our relating, praying, leading, preaching, and teaching. It will help us to clothe ourselves with the compassion, kindness, humility, gentleness, and patience of Christ." Colossians 3:12/Bill Gaultiere

Journaling Suggestion:
Journal about walking with Jesus today, and every day, and learn all about dealing with emotions from Him, my perfect role model.

Memo for Meditation:
"For a child is born to us, a son is given to us. The government will rest on his shoulders. And he will be called: Wonderful Counsellor, Mighty God, Everlasting Father, Prince of Peace." Isaiah 9:6

May 6

Motivational Idea: Handling anxiety

Anxiety is usually a natural response to pressure, feeling afraid or threatened, which can show up in how we feel physically, mentally and in how we behave. Anxiety is often described as a feeling of fear or unease, and it's something everyone experiences at times. It's a perfectly natural reaction to some situations. One of the advantages of our media age is that we can access lots of information about coping strategies. Ironically, the deluge of information we are bombarded with every nanosecond can give us anxiety. Watch out for 'doomscrolling'. This is when you actively seek out saddening or negative material to read or scroll through on social media.

There are many self-care tips you can build into your daily routine, and doing them regularly can make a big difference. For example, 'Make time for worries'. If anxiety or worry is taking over your day, try setting a daily 'worry time' to acknowledge your anxieties and fears, and pray about them. Doing this at a set time every day can help you to focus on other things. Preparing to go to the cross, Jesus prayed with such great anxiety that he sweat drops of blood (see Luke 22:44). Jesus experienced hematohidrosis, a rare condition in which a human being sweats blood, while praying in the garden of Gethsemane before his crucifixion. Dr Luke writes, *"And being in anguish he prayed more earnestly and his sweat was like drops of blood falling to the ground."* It is in relationship with Him that He can empathise with us, sustain us and help us in our human trials and weaknesses.

Memorable Quote:
"People think that faith is about religion when in reality it's not, it's about relationship! A personal relationship with God. This is mind-blowing! The eternal God who inhabits eternity is so infinitely transcendent yet immanent that He can have a unique personal relationship with the one who invites Him to do so, He is gracious enough to have a relationship with me, a one to one, uniquely mine, unworthy as am - and you too! Keep company with Him. Walk in extravagant love and learn from Him. He is the only one who can truly change you! Ask Jesus to help you today. Ask Him again tomorrow and every day for the rest of your life." Author

Journaling Suggestion:
Journal about your anxieties, and talk to God about them.

Memo for Mediation:
"One day Jesus told his disciples a story to show that they should always pray and never give up." Luke 18:1

May 7

Motivational Idea: Dealing with anger

Anger has been described as, 'an emotional state that varies in intensity from mild irritation to intense fury and rage.' It is accompanied by physiological and biological changes in heart rate, blood pressure, levels of energy, hormones, adrenaline, and noradrenaline. The instinctive way to express anger is to respond aggressively. Anger can inspire powerful, often aggressive behaviours. Anger itself, however, is not sin; how we *use* it determines whether it is sinful or not. Legitimate righteous anger toward sin or injustice can be productive. Jesus displayed righteous anger with the Pharisees who opposed Him healing the man with a deformed hand on the Sabbath (see Mark 3:5) and most notably when He cleaned out His Father's house, the temple (see John 2:13–16). But, more often than not, for us, anger becomes sinful because our own selfish interests and pride motivate it. Someone or something offends us, and we lash out. We end up saying and doing things that we ought not. Anger rooted in our own sinfulness is dangerous and destructive to others and to ourselves. We need to learn to control anger before it controls us! The goal of anger management is to reduce both the emotional feelings and the physiological arousal that anger causes. We can learn to control our reactions. For example, psychologists refer to 'cognitive restructuring'. This means changing the way we think. We should remind ourselves that getting angry is not going to fix anything, that it won't make us feel better and may actually make us feel worse. It is important nevertheless to acknowledge our anger and what's caused it. Then deal with it in a constructive manner, and remember – don't go to bed angry! It's an important command to obey for our own good.

Memorable Quote:

"We've all felt the furnace of wrath rising in us like molten mercury in a thermometer. Different sparks light the fire for each of us: disappointment, failure, disagreement, stress, betrayal, finances, exhaustion, and more. Whatever it is on any given day, anger can leave us lying in bed, contemplating another one-night stand against someone (or everyone). Then the ten words come to mind we've tried hard not to

memorise: "Do not let the sun go down on your anger" (Ephesians 4:26). With that strange and familiar chorus ringing in our ears, we may begin to loosen our grip on our wrath and consider how to move toward (the source of our anger) and reconcile." Marshall Segal

Journaling Suggestion:
I'm asking God to help me control my anger and how to use it constructively.

Memo for Meditation:
"In your anger do not sin. Do not let the sun go down while you are still angry, and do not give the devil a foothold." Ephesians 4:26.

May 8

Motivational Idea: Expressed and unexpressed anger

There are three main approaches that people use when dealing with angry feelings: *expressing, suppressing, and calming.*

Expressing your angry feelings in an assertive – not aggressive – manner is the healthiest way to express anger. To do this, you have to learn how to make clear what your needs are, and how to get them met without hurting others. Being assertive doesn't mean being pushy or demanding; it means being respectful of yourself and others.

One of the ways to enable ourselves to get to a point of clarity to appropriately express our feelings is to use a technique which has been called 'code red'. When that feeling of anger starts to rise, identify on a scale of 0-10 where the anger level is (don't use 7 as this is a sit on the fence number). If it's a score of 8 or above it's a code red. Danger! Risk of explosion! This is the signal to stop and think since immediate reaction at this point will usually be counterproductive and not serve a useful purpose. This technique will give you time to acknowledge your anger, the level it is at and weigh up the situation and begin to assess the optimal response and best actions. Try it and see and find out how to make it work for you.

Suppressing happens when you hold in your anger, stop thinking about it, and focus on something else. The danger in this type of response is that if it isn't allowed outward expression, your anger can turn inward, leading to hypertension and even depression. Better to acknowledge it and express it, but using your code red technique.

Calming means not just controlling your outward behaviour, but also controlling your internal responses, taking steps to lower your heart rate, calm yourself down, and let the feelings subside.

Memorable Quote:
Suppression *"can lead to pathological expressions of anger, such as passive-aggressive behaviour (getting back at people indirectly, without telling them why, rather than confronting them head-on) or a personality that seems perpetually cynical and hostile. People who are constantly putting others down, criticising everything, and making cynical comments haven't learned how to constructively express their anger."* American Psychological Association

Journaling Suggestion:
Code red trial today to see if it works – happier when in control!

Memo for Meditation:
"A soft and gentle and thoughtful answer turns away wrath, but harsh and painful and careless words stir up anger." Proverbs 15:1

May 9

Motivational Idea: It's OK to feel sad

We all feel sad sometimes, just like we can feel joyful, angry, proud, and plenty of other emotions. No one wants to feel sad. As one of the negative emotions, we associate it with a reduction in confidence, self-esteem, and general life satisfaction. Yet sadness, like happiness, plays a part in the fulfilled life. We can't be on the crest of the wave all the time. Disappointments come into our lives and we feel sadness. But this can be a blessing in disguise as it can slow us down and enable us to reflect on our lives and what's important.

Being sad doesn't mean we are not coping with the situation we find ourselves in. Rather, it can help us come to terms with that situation and move on. Sadness is an important emotion that can help us to adapt, accept, focus, persevere and grow. Recognising our own sadness, and understanding that it is okay to feel sad, is a sign of a stable sense of wellbeing. However, we need to be aware that holding on to our sadness can lead to a downward spiral. We need to deal with our sadness appropriately. Sadness will normally ease with time. We need to allow ourselves to feel it! Then acknowledge it, and any other negative emotions that accompany it, and accept it.

Emotions ebb and flow, and we can move through sadness to a more positive emotion. We need to focus on our life's purpose. We can also do things we would normally enjoy. Jesus felt sadness. From the Mount of Olives, He looked down on Jerusalem and wept with sadness because the people rejected God's offer of peace (see Luke 19:41). He also felt grief (see Mark 3:5), gave deep sighs (see Mark 8:12), felt deep distress (see Matthew 26:37), crushing grief (see Mark 14:34), and shed tears (see John 11:35,43). How did Jesus handle sadness? Our memo today tells us what He did. It was the primary purpose of His perfectly fulfilled life that brought joy to His heart in the midst of deep sadness.

Memorable Quote:
"Sadness is but a wall between two gardens. The walls we build around us to keep sadness out also keeps out the joy." Kahlil Gibran

Journaling Suggestion:
Journal about acknowledging your sadness but pressing on in the joy of your primary purpose!

Memo for Meditation:
"Looking away from all that will distract us and] focusing our eyes on Jesus, who is the Author and Perfecter of faith [the first incentive for our belief and the One who brings our faith to maturity], who for the joy [of accomplishing the goal] set before Him endured the cross, disregarding the shame, and sat down at the right hand of the throne of God [revealing His deity, His authority, and the completion of His work]." Hebrews 12:2, AMP

May 10

Motivational Idea: Experiencing joy

Dr Pamela King, Associate Professor of Applied Developmental Science and an ordained Presbyterian Minister, conducted an in-depth study on the meaning and depth of joy. In reviewing philosophical, theological and psychological approaches, Dr King's work has identified three areas that deeply inform joy:

1. Growing in authenticity and living more into one's strengths
2. Growing in depth of relationships and contributing to others, and
3. Living more aligned with one's ethical and spiritual ideals.

"I hypothesise that the more one is able to live a strength-based life, reciprocate relationships with others, and live with moral coherency, the more joy one will experience in life. This suggests that joy is not just an individual pursuit, but one that deeply involves our connections with others. We can discover and experience joy in a variety of ways—doing those things we love to do, growing in intimacy or providing for others, and clarifying and coherently pursuing our values. When these domains of the self, others, and values overlap, that is perhaps when we experience the most joy."

Joy is a core human experience. Joy is more complex than a feeling or an emotion. It is something one can practise, cultivate, or make a habit. Consequently, joy is most fully understood as a virtue that involves our thoughts, feelings, and actions in response to what matters most in our lives. Thus, joy is an enduring, deep delight in what holds the most significance. Sustained joy can be experienced by cultivating it, and connection with others is one of the key factors in a joy-filled life.

Memorable Quote:

"Joy is really complex! This work helped me realise how joy and sorrow are deeply connected. Both are a response to those things that matter most. Joy is our delight when we experience, celebrate, and anticipate the manifestation of those things we hold with the most significance—like a birth or graduation. Sorrow is our response to the violation, destruction, or deterioration of such sacred things. ..This complexity also informs how

we can experience joy and sorrow at the same time, how true joy that is tied to our potential to grow as an individual and relate and give to others, and how our values can endure in the face of loss and suffering. The trick is to stay connected to those things that deeply matter in the face of adversity and loss." Dr Pamela King

Journaling Suggestion:
Journal on cultivating joy in your life.

Memo for Meditation:
"The king rejoices in your strength, LORD. How great is his joy in the victories you give! Surely you have granted him unending blessings and made him glad with the joy of your presence." Psalm 21:1,7

May 11

Motivational Idea: Other worldly joy

The Bible refers to happiness, sometimes interchanging it with the word joy. For instance, it refers to food (see Ecclesiastes 9:7), pleasures from God (see Psalm 16:11), and those that keep the law resulting in happiness (see Proverbs 29:18 and Psalm 144:15).

God's heart desires for us to enjoy these blessings, but also to acknowledge that He is their source (James 1:17). The Bible, however, defines joy very differently from the cultural view of happiness. Joy comes from God's presence (see Psalm 16:11), His strength (see Nehemiah 8:10), deliverance (see Psalm 71:23), and through trial (see James 1:2). This is so countercultural! A comparison of worldly happiness and biblical joy helps us to understand that we should pursue a joy that is everlasting instead of just chasing a happiness that is fleeting. Happiness is based on circumstances, biblical joy is ours, despite our circumstances. Happiness is 'us' focused, joy is God focused. Happiness is in reaction to accomplishments, achievements and material gain; joy is from a place of gratitude, praise and confidence. Happiness is a feeling (remember, feelings are fleeting), joy is a state of being. Happiness is looking to earthly things, joy is viewing things from a heavenly perspective. Happiness is hope in 'it' (it being the thing you think will bring you happiness), joy is full of God's eternal hope. Choose joy!

Memorable Quote:

"In C S Lewis' autobiography, Surprised by Joy, he tells of experiencing an other-worldly joy — a specific Joy that defies our modern understanding. This idea of Joy is not a satisfied desire but an unsatisfied desire — a deep longing for God, a hungry pursuit of God's heart that never ends and is more satisfying than any earthly happiness. Lewis recalls three seemingly trivial and disconnected events with a common thread: he experienced a sudden, piercing pang of longing — a bittersweet ache and yearning for something far-off, other-worldly, and unnamed during each event. He would later recognize these sudden aches of longing: a deep spiritual hunger for God — not just for an intellectual knowledge of God, but for a real relationship with Him. These deep longings in Lewis' life — these stabs of Joy — worked as flashing sign-markers pointing him down the path toward Christ." YouVersion

Journaling Suggestion:

Journal on pursuing joy compared to chasing fleeting happiness.

Memo for Meditation:

"Though you have not seen him, you love him; and even though you do not see him now, you believe in him and are filled with an inexpressible and glorious joy." 1 Peter 1:8

"You reveal the path of life to me; in Your presence is abundant joy; in Your right hand are eternal pleasures." Psalm 16:11

May 12

Motivational Idea: True love

Ancient Greek society understood eight different concepts of love, and each had its own particular word.

Eros is about sexual passion; Philia, deep friendship; Ludus is playful love; Pragma, long-standing love; Philautia is love of the self; Storge, family love; Mania is obsessive love' and Agape stands out as different from the other types of love. Britannica gives a synopsis. *"Agape, in the New Testament, (is) the fatherly love of God for humans, as well as the human reciprocal love for God. In Scripture, the transcendent agape love is the highest form of love and is contrasted with eros, or erotic love, and philia, or brotherly love."* John 3:16 is the Gospel (Good News) of God's Agape in a nutshell.

God so loved the world! Here is the superlative, infinite, eternal love of God displayed in sending His 'only one of a kind' unique son for your redemption and mine. We are called upon to believe in Him, and in doing so we have eternal life. There are two categories of people in the world: those who trust Him and have eternal life, and those who don't, who will perish. Such is His love for us that in believing He gives us the right to become children of God, even to those that trust in His Name (John 1:12). So, we become the King's kids. God is our heavenly Father – we are part of His family. O how He loves us and we reciprocate that love in loving Him back! We also learn to love our fellow human beings. God's very nature is love itself: *"God is love."* (1 John 4:8). God does not merely love; He *is* love. Everything God does flows from His love. Love like Him!

Memorable Quote:
"Agape love is always shown by what it does. God's love is displayed most clearly at the cross. "God, being rich in mercy, because of the great love with which he loved us, even when we were dead in our trespasses, made us alive together with Christ—by grace you have been saved." Ephesians 2:4-5
"We did not deserve such a sacrifice, but God demonstrates his own love for us in this: While we were still sinners, Christ died for us." Romans 5:8
"God's agape love is unmerited, gracious, and constantly seeking the benefit of the ones He loves. The Bible says we are the undeserving recipients of His lavish agape love." 1 John 3:1 – Bible: Got Questions

Journaling Suggestion:
Journal as a King's kid! I love Him because He first loved me. My identity is in Jesus and it's all because of His agape love for me! I'm the King's kid and God is my Father.

Memo for Meditation:
"For this is the way God loved the world: He gave His one and only Son, so that everyone who believes in Him will not perish but have eternal life." John 3:16.

"But to all who have received Him—those who believe in his name, He has given the right to become God's children." John 1:12

May 13

Motivational Idea: The healing can begin

The power of the pause cannot be underestimated but is often missing from our lives. What blessings we sorely miss! Our memo today invites us to intentionally stop and consider something that has the power to heal our damaged emotions. Here is something that is so vital to our wellbeing and our flourishing in our languishing world. It's not something that the manic chaotic world will give a first glance, not a second, never mind a prolonged gaze. We need to fix our attention on the profound depths of God's love that surpasses human understanding. It sounds simple and in one sense it is; God's love is so simple that a child can grasp this truth. But it is also profoundly deep to think that the Creator of the universe loves you and loves me, and wants a personal intimate relationship with us where we experience His love every day!

Once we start to truly meditate on the love of God, and with the aid of the Holy Spirit, begin to plumb its depths, embracing its reality, our emotions will experience new heights of feeling and expression, reaching their zenith in wonder, worship and praise. It is in the personal experience of this unconditional love of God that your healing can begin. Those feelings that have lain dormant – those emotions that have been in a state of paralysis – frozen in a state of suspended animation because of deep hurts, painful traumas and the abuses of those who said they loved you but caused you to activate (unconsciously) emotional numbing and the shut-down of your emotional life – all can be healed in the sunshine's blaze of the love for God.

Allow the healing rays of His love to heal you and to make you whole again. Give God your emotions. Your identity is in Him, the King's kid!

Memorable Quote:

"Long my imprisoned spirit lay/Fast bound in sin and nature's night;/Thine eye diffused a quickening ray,/I woke, the dungeon flamed with light;/My chains fell off, my heart was free,/I rose, went forth, and

followed Thee./My chains fell off, my heart was free,/I rose, went forth, and followed Thee." Charles Wesley

Journaling Suggestion:

Heal me, Lord, and I will be healed; save me and I will be saved, for You are the one I praise.

Memo for Meditation:

"See [Look, Behold] what great love the Father has lavished *on us, that we should be called* children *of God! And that is what we are! The reason the world does not know us is that it did not know him."* 1 John 3:1.

"This is how God showed his love among us: He sent his one and only Son into the world that we might live *through him. This is love: not that we loved God, but that he loved us and sent his Son as an atoning sacrifice for our sins. Dear friends, since God so loved us, we also ought to love one another. No one has ever seen God; but if we love one another, God lives in us and his love is made* complete *in us."* 1 John 4:9-12

May 14

Motivational Idea: Weaponizing love for our healing

Jude gives us a powerful revelation that will enable us to keep on track as we continue to grow and develop in our faith and experience the healing that God has for us. The short, one-chapter book is written against the backdrop of a languishing world that is alien to our welfare and will play havoc with our wellbeing and our damaged emotions if we are not on our guard. The divine instruction is set out in our mediation for today.

We need to *'keep ourselves in the love of God.'* The Greek word is rendered in various ways in the translations: *keep, guard, observe, watch, mediate,* and in the NET, *remain.* Eugene Peterson in the *Message Bible Paraphrase* renders it, *'staying right at the centre of God's love.'* This should not be misinterpreted as being able to lose the love of God in some way. No! God's love is unconditional and unchanging. He loves you! It does mean, however, we need to keep our hearts and minds fixed on God's love, the source of our wellbeing and the means of our healing from sin, and the damage that goes with it.

We need to be aware of His love and immerse our souls in it.

When those feelings of emptiness and dis-ease sweep over us, when those feelings of self-loathing and self-deprecation come out to play, we need to shine the effulgent and effervescent light of God's love on these dark forces that lurk in those dungeon hidden places. Rather than become trapped in the prison-house of bondage to these damaged emotions, let's learn to vaporise them in the light of His love. Darkness cannot stand against the light! We need to learn to remain in and meditate upon the love of God.

The thought *'I hate myself,'* and the cluster of powerful negative emotions that accompany such thought patterns, can be swept away when we weaponize the love of God in our lives. Bring it all to the place where God's love for us was most fully and wonderfully displayed – bring it all to the cross! *"By His wounds we are healed."* (Isaiah 53:5).

Memorable Quote:
"God's love extends everywhere, and nothing can separate us from it. But we can deny ourselves the benefits of God's love. People who don't keep themselves in the love of God end up living as if they are on the dark side of the moon. The sun is always out there, always shining, but they are never in a position to receive its light or warmth. An example of this is the Prodigal Son of Luke 15, who was always loved by the father, but for a time he did not benefit from it." Enduring Word

Journaling Suggestion:
Journal about learning to live and dwell and occupy yourself with God's love, and weaponize it for healing.

Memo for Meditation:
"But you, dear friends, carefully build yourselves up in this most holy faith by praying in the Holy Spirit, staying right at the centre of God's love, keeping your arms open and outstretched, ready for the mercy of our Master, Jesus Christ. This is the unending life, the real life!" Jude 1:21, 22

May 15

Motivational Idea: Meditation for healing

Reading Well is a UK national books-on-prescription programme that helps people to understand and manage their wellbeing using *'quality endorsed reading'*. Recommended books can be 'prescribed' by GPs and other allied professionals. God has been doing this for millenniums. Take for example Joshua (1300 BCe) who was given *'quality endorsed reading'* by God Himself. God told Joshua to *"meditate"* on his book of instruction, day and night. Biblical meditation is pondering the words of Scripture with a receptive heart, trusting the Holy Spirit to work in us through those words. Pondering is more than reading or studying. The Hebrew word for meditate (*hâgâh*) implies something more than silent reflection. It means 'to whisper or murmur', a use that may point to the fact that reading was usually done aloud in biblical times. Another Hebrew word for meditation in the Old Testament is *siyach*: *"Oh how I love your law! I meditate on it all day long."* (Psalm 119:97) David Saxton writes, *"Siyach means to lovingly rehearse or go over in one's mind; but in contrast to hâgâh, siyach can be either spoken out loud or said silently in one's heart."*

In the Old Testament, meditation involved repeated vocalisation of God's truth, rehearsal of it in the mind, and focused thought. In the New Testament, the word meditate is not used as often but rather the words 'think' or 'consider' are used to convey the idea of pondering or reflecting. In Philippians 4:8, the Apostle Paul lists things we should 'think' about. He uses a form of the word *logizomai*, a Greek word found forty times in the New Testament that means 'think [about], consider, ponder, let one's mind dwell on.' Biblical meditation therefore involves our minds. By focused thought upon God's truth, we reflect upon the meaning and our souls are fed, our hearts warmed and our needs met.

Memorable Quote:

"Meditating on God's words is an ancient practice —one that's long been a vital component of a vibrant relationship with God. We would be wise to embrace this God-given discipline. Biblical meditation is distinct from other forms of meditation because the focus of our "pondering" is Scripture. Our goal is not to empty our minds but to be nourished by

focusing on God's words. This is for our wellbeing and in the context of the emotional dimension, for our healing." Adapted by author

Journaling Suggestion:

Journal on giving priority to the ancient and beautiful art of biblical meditation.

Memo for Meditation:

"And don't for a minute let this Book of The Revelation be out of mind. Ponder and meditate on it day and night, making sure you practise everything written in it. Then you'll get where you're going; then you'll succeed." Joshua 1:8, MSG

May 16

Motivational Idea: An analysis unlike any other

Freud attempted to set up his 'secular church' in the psychoanalytic framework centred on the therapeutic encounter: the 'confessional box' of therapy. The patient on the couch tells the therapist whatever comes to mind: thoughts, dreams, free associations and so forth. The 'manifest' content will be carefully considered by the analyst who will give insights and interpretations about what has been expressed in terms of the 'latent' content – the deep unconscious stuff coming to the surface. The purpose is to enable the patient to be aware of conflict and unresolved issues, and then, with the knowledge they have obtained, make the right decisions and enhance their wellbeing.

As someone who is trained in psychotherapy, I am not denigrating the talking therapies since most therapists have integrity and do sincerely wish to help their patients. We have to be careful, however, because we are putting a measure of faith and trust in a flawed human being in the form of a therapeutic alliance. Counselling and psychotherapy have their place for those who need it, and for those who avail of this type of service, one needs to ensure that the therapist is appropriately trained and knows what they are doing. In Psalm 139, the psalmist does something that we all can learn from. Here is biblical therapy, and the therapeutic alliance is between the writer and his Creator. David asks God, indeed he *invites* God to search him. *"Search me, God, and know my heart; test me and know my anxious thoughts."* God already knows everything about him, but David does not know everything about himself so he invites God to examine him thoroughly and for God to reveal to him what he needs to know. The outcome is enlightenment and our sense of awareness becomes heightened as God reveals things to us – things we need to deal with, sins we need to confess, decisions we need to make and aspects of our lives we need to work on. It is in this therapeutic encounter with our Creator that our emotions can be healed as we let go of past hurts and learn forgiveness. Our relationship with God is enriched, our lives are more purposeful and fulfilled as we continue on our onward journey as He leads us along the path of everlasting life.

Memorable Quote:
"We can't be healed from the things we hide. Honesty before God is the only way we can grow. We cannot grow by trying to hide our secrets or guard our thoughts from God. The good, the bad and the ugly need to be exposed by His analysis for our wellbeing and flourishing to progress."

Journaling Suggestion:
Journal about time with the greatest therapist, Jesus, the wounded healer.

Memo for Meditation:
"GOD, investigate my life; get all the facts firsthand. I'm an open book to you; even from a distance, you know what I'm thinking. Investigate my life, O God, find out everything about me; Cross-examine and test me, get a clear picture of what I'm about. See for yourself whether I've done anything wrong— then guide me on the road to eternal life." Psalm 139:1, 23-24

May 17

Motivational Idea: The secrets that you keep

It's no secret that you're keeping a secret right now. Researchers have identified 36 common secrets ranging from infidelity to addiction to financial woes. Secrets don't have to be extreme and may include such things as job dissatisfaction, political views or pursuing an unusual hobby. We may harbour secrets of traumatic experiences. The average person has about 12 secrets. Some secrets are harmful because they evoke shame, but others can be empowering.

Here's a fourfold distinction to help us categorise our secrets. Galvin, Braithwaite & Bylund (2015) came up with four types: sweet, essential, toxic and dangerous secrets. Sweet secrets are those that protect fun surprises and they are time-limited. Essential secrets tend to foster closeness and are mostly related to relationships and families. Toxic secrets are labelled as poisonous. Dangerous secrets involve physical or emotional danger to self or others.

Our purpose on this page is to consider our wellbeing. Keeping certain secrets can often be harmful in the long-run, both physically and psychologically. According to psychologists Michael Slepian and Alex Koch, *"it's not the withholding that hurts us; instead, it's the ruminating that harms us."* Maggie Tipton says, *"Secrets can make you sick."*

Today is a day for simply considering our secrets and how we would categorise them: sweet, essential, toxic or dangerous, but not necessarily to take action unless we or others are in danger. We need to be aware of concealing any poisonous or dangerous secrets that are psychologically damaging because we have no opportunity to talk about them and we feel shame, we are reluctant to share them, often for good reason. Where is the first place we can confidently bring them today? Bring them to the secret place with God.

"He who dwells in the secret place of the Most High Shall abide under the shadow of the Almighty. I will say of the LORD, 'He is my refuge and my fortress; My God, in Him I will trust.'" (Psalm 91:1,2). This secret place is a good place to unburden – a place of safety and security!

Memorable Quote:
"We all have secrets – parts of ourselves or our past that we keep hidden. At first, a secret may feel like a form of protection, but ultimately the anxiety, fear, shame, regret and guilt take a toll on our body and mind. Secrets come in many forms such as trauma, unhealthy behaviour or even negative beliefs about oneself. It's easy to internalise them without realising how harmful they are to our health. The emotional, mental, physical and spiritual impact of secrets are well documented." Maggie Tipton

Journaling Suggestion:
Journal about your secrets. Are these taking a toll on your potential to flourish?

Memo for Meditation:
"Would not God discover this? For He knows the secrets of the heart."
Psalm 44:21

May 18

Motivational Idea: Dealing with harmful secrets

Secrets come in many forms. Some are healthy, but some are toxic. What do we do with toxic secrets? Who can we trust? We know that we can trust God and as we open ourselves up to Him, we experience true freedom in Christ. We can let go of the past, and we can know that congruence and freedom which the guilt of secrecy has kept us in bondage for years. The counsellor Teri Claassen says *"Secret keepers feel like they walk around wearing a mask to protect others from seeing who they really are. They fear the vulnerability of someone finding out who they really are underneath."* Teri goes on to say that, *"Toxic secrets can "haunt" you and cause emotional havoc. They can become poisonous and bleed dysfunction into your relationships and your moods without you even realising it."*

What are some examples of toxic secrets? One common secret is secret emotions. We can hide our emotions from others and this can result in us having to live with internal turmoil. Keeping our emotions a secret will cause us to carry our pain alone. On the other hand, sharing our emotions will keep us real and open up doors to emotional intimacy in relationships. Counsellors such as Teri encounter a whole range of secrets with people who have the courage to deal with them. Secrets can range from health concerns, addictions, legal issues, affairs, to past and current abuse.

If we take the issue of abuse, one of the first steps of healing this horrible wound is to share the secret with a trusted person and or support system/group/organisation. If you are dealing with current abuse and someone is hurting you emotionally, verbally, sexually or physically, you might be thinking you will make things worse for yourself, and possibly for others. Yet if you do not voice your pain, the

185

perpetrator could inflict abuse on someone else down the road. Sharing this secret could save someone else's life, including your own. (Teri's advice is, *"If you are in an abusive relationship, please seek professional help to consult on a safe way to disclose the abuse and get help."*)

Memorable Quote:
"I'm not saying you need to share every detail of your life with everyone you meet. There are boundaries to keep in mind and you need to make sure you are revealing secrets to people you feel emotionally safe with. Remember, toxic secrets have more power when they are kept. The more you keep them, the more alone you will feel. Break free from your toxic secrets by opening up and starting to process them. What scares you about sharing toxic secrets with those you love and trust?" Author

Journaling Suggestion:
Time to deal with the secrets that are hurting me and keeping me in bondage.

Memo for Meditation:
"There is a time for everything, and a season for every activity under the heavens: a time to be silent and a time to speak." Ecclesiastes 3:1,7b

---

May 19

Motivational Idea: Handling hate

Hate is an overused word today. It has become diluted and so the power of the word is gone because we apply it to everything in our life. *'I hate it when that happens. I hate the way that makes me feel.'* It sort of rolls off the tongue. Yet the word hate is a very powerful word, with a very powerful meaning. To hate something is to detest it and, in some cases, to want to destroy it. It is the exact opposite of love. It can become an all-consuming passion akin to rage. Hate can be destructive both to the person who hates and the person being hated. Hate is driven by anger and often is accompanied by fear. Merriam-Webster defines the noun hate as *"intense hostility and aversion usually deriving from fear, anger or sense of injury."*

Hate when used in its most virulent form likely has its roots in anger and in a belief that someone has hurt us. The fourth century B.C.

Greek philosopher Diogenes Laertius wrote that hate is one of the irrational urges that threatens to destroy mankind. He defined hate as *"a growing or lasting desire or craving that it should go ill with somebody."* In relation to our emotional dimension, we can say that hate is a negative emotion that can have severe consequences for both the individual and society as a whole. It can lead to physical health problems, such as high blood pressure and increased stress levels. It can also lead to social problems, such as discrimination and violence. Just look at the world today – a hate-filled world! So, how do we let go of our anger and bitterness? It's not always easy to let go of negative emotions, but here are some ideas to help us in our healing processes. It's important to remember that hate is a choice. We can choose to let go of our anger and move on, or we can choose to hold onto it and allow it to consume us. If you're struggling to let go of hate, you're not alone. It's normal to feel anger and resentment towards someone who has hurt you. This might seem like an impossible task, but forgiveness is a crucial part of letting go of anger. Forgiveness doesn't mean we forget what happened or condone the person's actions. It simply means that we're willing to let go of the anger and resentment that we feel. If you're struggling to let go of self-hatred, practise self-compassion. Be kind and understanding towards yourself, Forgiveness is a process, and it might take time to let go of all the anger and resentment. But it's important to keep working on it.

Memorable Quote:
"Hate cannot drive out hate. Only love can do that." Martin Luther King Jr.

Journaling Suggestion:
Journal about any hatred you may have and how you are going to deal with it.

Memo for Meditation:
"Be kind and compassionate to one another, forgiving each other, just as in Christ God forgave you." Ephesians 4:32

May 20

Motivational Idea: Healthy hate

Solomon says there is a time to love and a time to hate. This could be seen as rather perplexing at first glance since we are encouraged in the Bible, rather, *commanded*, to love and not to hate. The reality is there is no contradiction whatsoever because hatred of certain things in our fallen world is the legitimate response to evil from a genuine heart of love for justice and equality. Thus, our hatred of sin arises out of our love for God. It does not legitimise our hating our brother because we have been wronged. We are to love our brother. *"Whoever says he is in the light and hates his brother is still in darkness. Whoever loves his brother abides in the light, and in him there is no cause for stumbling."* (1 John 2:9–10). We are to love our enemies. *"You have heard that it has been said, You shall love your neighbour, and hate your enemy. "But I say unto you, Love your enemies, bless them that curse you, do good to them that hate you, and pray for them which despitefully use you, and persecute you."* (Matthew 5:43–44).

Jesus tells us that if we hate someone in our heart, it is the same in God's sight as if we murdered them (see Matthew 5:21-22). The Bible tells us that God hates evil, and counsels us to *"hate evil"* and *"love good"*. *"Hate evil and love what is good; turn your courts into true halls of justice. Perhaps even yet the LORD God of Heaven's Armies will have mercy on the remnant of his people."* (Amos 5:15).

In our fallen world, as it hastens to the end of time and the final judgement, the antithesis is the case. *"What sorrow for those who say that evil is good and good is evil, that dark is light and light is dark, that bitter is sweet and sweet is bitter."* (Isaiah 5:20). We are commanded to love good and hate evil! *"You who love the LORD, hate evil!"* (Psalm 97:10). *"All who fear the LORD will hate evil. Therefore, I hate pride and arrogance, corruption and perverse speech."* (Proverbs 8:13).

Fearing the Lord means to be in reverent awe of His holiness, to give Him complete reverence and to honour Him as the God of great glory, majesty, purity and power. Only as we truly fear the Lord will we be freed from all destructive and satanic fears. By fearing God, we can avoid being trapped by the natural pull toward going our own sinful way, defying God and giving in to the inviting ways of immoral behaviour which God hates. Healthy hate is hating what He hates.

Memorable Quote:

"'A time to love and a time to hate' covers the full range of human affections and emotions. Our capacity to both love and hate is part of being created in God's image. Therefore, sometimes hatred and anger are manifestations of the fullness and intensity of our love." Got Questions

Journaling Suggestion:

Lord, I want to love and fear You and hate what You hate.

Memo for Meditation:

"A time to love and a time to hate, a time for war and a time for peace." Ecclesiastes 3:8

May 21

Motivational Idea: Connecting the disconnect

Does God's glory and honour feature in our everyday lives? We can read about it and sing about it but more often than not it can be divorced from the reality of the hustle and bustle of our busy lives and all those many responsibilities that take up our every waking moment. Is God's honour and glory expressed and exhibited in our thoughts, ideas, emotions, behaviours and our actions and reactions? What about our negative thoughts and emotions, those days of grumpiness and irritability when we can fly off the handle in the blink of an eye? Those days when we feel we have one nerve left and that person who annoys us is playing it like a rock guitarist? The honour, glory and praise of God can be conspicuously absent.

This is not said to shame you; our human condition is such that we are all flawed, and fail miserably a lot of the time. But we need to deal with the great disconnect! We are in a relationship with God through faith in Jesus our Saviour, Lord and Master and His merits, not ours. So how do we do it? We can't do it on our own strength. We need to go to the deeper well to drink in and see His glory. We become like the people we spend time with, influenced by the company we keep. We need to get before the Lord and know Him and it is in the knowing that we flourish. Those mundane tasks take on new meaning – everything we do can bring honour and glory to God. We can make dinner for His glory. We can take that friend to their hospital appointment. Everything becomes sanctified to the extent that everything we do glorifies and honours God, every part of our being is given over to Him in praise and worship. We become a living sacrifice which is our spiritual act of worship. *"I cannot imagine how religious persons can live satisfied without the practice of the presence of GOD. For my part I keep myself retired with Him in the depth of centre of my soul as much as I can.."* Brother Lawrence.

Memorable Quote:
"We ought not to be weary of doing little things for the love of God, who regards not the greatness of the work, but the love with which it is performed." Brother Lawrence

Journaling Suggestion:
A prayer: "God I want to honour You with every thought, idea, feeling, intention and action. So today I give You permission to change me. Let my whole life be one that honours You and brings You glory. A life lived in Your power – the power of the Holy Spirit. In Jesus' name, Amen."

Memo for Meditation:
"You are worthy, our Lord and God, to receive glory, honour and power, since you created all things and because of your will they existed and were created." Revelation 4:11
"To Him who is able to do far more than we ask, think or imagine, to Him be all glory, honour and praise." Ephesians 3:20, 21

May 22

Motivational Idea: Feel the fear and do it anyway

Fear is ingrained in us. We are all afraid of something; our natural response to life events is very often fear. We may fear the burden of personal responsibilities, sickness or even death. We may fear being alone or even the fear of living itself. We can be afraid to take the next step, to embrace the opportunity before us and to walk through the open door to the next chapter of our lives. If you could choose someone to give you a good pep talk, who would you choose? Joshua was okay when he played second fiddle to Moses, but he was out of his comfort zone. The great leader of Israel was dead, Joshua had to step up, and he was very afraid. Estimates of the number of people he had to lead range from the low hundreds of thousands to 1.5 million. We know Joshua was afraid because he was told three times not to be. But there were good reasons why he should move forward in spite of fear. He got the pep talk of all pep talks – from God, the Lord God, Creator of the universe spoke to him and gave him a solid promise that He would be with him. Moses had left the stage but the undying One would be with Joshua. God didn't ask Joshua how he was feeling, He already knew. Nor did He beat about the bush, rather, he was commanded to be strong and of good courage – be brave!

The Hebrew word *tzivviticha* is translated as a command, order, instruction, charge. Joshua's was commissioned by God and so he went forward in humble obedience. He took the book of life, God's manual for living, for guidance, instruction and reassurance. Courage is not the absence of fear but it is choosing to no longer let it dominate. The word God gave to Joshua stands true today for you right now. We, too, are commissioned to go forward and do what God put us here to do, and our heavenly Joshua. Jesus is at our side every step of the way.

Memorable Quote:
"No matter what God is calling you to do, fear may always be there. Courage is not the absence of it but a stage of mind where you actually do not let fear dominate you." Adapted by author

Journaling Suggestion:
I will trust in God, and His sovereignty, and move forward in His plan for my life with courage.

Memo for Meditation:
"Be strong and courageous, for you are the one who will lead these people to possess all the land I swore to their ancestors I would give them. Be strong and very courageous. Be careful to obey all the instructions Moses gave you. Do not deviate from them, turning either to the right or to the left. Then you will be successful in everything you do. Study this Book of Instruction continually. Meditate on it day and night so you will be sure to obey everything written in it. Only then will you prosper and succeed in all you do. This is my command—be strong and

courageous! Do not be afraid or discouraged. For the LORD *your God is with you wherever you go."* Joshua 1:6-9

May 23

Motivational Idea: Peace and quiet

"All I want is a bit of peace and quiet!" Sound familiar? We all want it but how do we get it in a world of warmongering, and when we struggle with interpersonal and intrapersonal conflict? Across all cultures, and throughout all human time, we share the same six basic emotions – sadness, anger, fear, joy, love and peace. Today we delve into that elusive peace we seek.

Peace of mind is a much sought-after commodity. Attempts to finding an inner calm include accepting what we can't control, forgiving ourselves and others, focusing on the here and now, journaling our thoughts and emotions, and connecting with nature. These are things we can do to get some peace. Yet the Bible talks about a peace that exceeds anything we can understand. In the Old Testament, the primary Hebrew word for 'peace' is *shalom,* and refers to relationships between people, nations and God Himself. For example, *"I listen carefully to what God the* LORD *is saying, for he speaks peace to his faithful people. But let them not return to their foolish ways."* Psalm 85.8.

Peace is seen to be interpersonal in nature, both manward and Godward. We need a right relationship with God first and foremost. *"Therefore, since we have been made right in God's sight by faith, we have peace with God because of what Jesus Christ our Lord has done for us."* (Romans 5.1). The Bible teaches that ultimately peace is a gift from God and we can experience this intra-personally – within ourselves. This was Jesus' promise to His disciples and to us today. *"I am leaving you with a gift — peace of mind and heart. And the peace I give is a gift the world cannot give. So don't be troubled or afraid."* (John 14.27).

In the New Testament, the primary Greek word for 'peace' is *eirene*; it refers to rest and tranquillity. The world will continue to have wars and interpersonal conflicts and intrapersonal turmoil, but if we tune into the God of peace, we will find a peace that transcends everything. *"Once His peace rules in our hearts, we are able to share that peace with others; we become publishers of peace."* (Isaiah 52:7). *"Peace*

is the emotion of faith. It is an emotion, not of the head, but of the heart."
(Mechanics of Faith).

Memorable Quote:
"The beginning of anxiety is the end of faith, and the beginning of true faith is the end of anxiety." George Mueller

Journaling Suggestion:
Since peace is found in the God of peace, I am going to seek Him today and every day.

Memo for Meditation:
"Don't worry about anything; instead, pray about everything. Tell God what you need, and thank him for all he has done. Then you will experience God's peace, which exceeds anything we can understand. His peace will guard your hearts and minds as you live in Christ Jesus."
Philippians 4:6, 7

May 24

Motivational idea: The clean heart is a happy heart

Jesus spoke about the pure heart in the Sermon on the Mount. So, what did He mean by *"pure in heart"?* He prefixed the phrase with the word 'blessed.' The Greek word is *makarioi* and means 'happy'. Ask any parent what they want for their children and the most common answer would be 'to be happy.' This is also the universal goal of mankind. The problem is we seek it in the wrong places. Contrary to what the enemy would like us to believe, God our Father has our best interests at heart and He wants His children to be happy. The word used by Jesus does not just mean a fluffy feeling, rather it needs to be understood as a person enjoying a special privilege of some kind, to be in a desirable place or position that we recognise as a good reason for happy feelings. It can also be translated as 'privileged' or 'fortunate'. The Ancient Greeks described their gods as *makarios*, living in Mount Olympus and enjoying the riches and carefree living in their position of divine power. Everything was theirs. We can see how this would equate to most people's idea of happiness in terms of possessions.

Jesus declares that true happiness is found in the pursuit of God and knowing Him. God, the true God is the *makarious* God (see 1 Timothy 6:15), who blesses us with every spiritual blessing in Christ and who provides for all our needs in this life. Once we grasp that lasting happiness is found in God, then we'll keep our hearts pure and clean as we get to know Him better. The word 'clean' is the Greek word *katharos*, and in this context it means free from corrupt desire, sin and guilt; free from that which is false, insincere and counterfeit. It's being free in God from the taint and corruption of the world's culture and hedonism; it's living the kingdom life in the power of the Holy Spirit (see Galatians chapter 5).

Memorable Quote:
"All men seek happiness. This is without exception. Whatever different means they employ, they all tend to this end. The cause of some going to war, and of others avoiding it, is the same desire in both, attended with different views. The will never takes the least step but to this object. This is the motive of every action of every man, even of those who hang themselves." Blaise Pascal

Journaling Suggestion:
The road to true happiness is the pursuit of God, getting to know Him and knowing Him better.

Memo for Meditation:
"Create in me a clean heart, O God, and renew a right spirit within me. Cast me not away from your presence, and take not your Holy Spirit from me. Restore to me the joy of your salvation, and uphold me with a willing spirit." Psalm 51:10-12

May 25

Motivational idea: Emotions – the language of the heart

Emotions are the language of the heart. You probably won't say to the one you love, *"I love you with all my blood pump,"* rather you would say, *"I love you with all my heart!"* The classic red love heart will be your emoji of choice used as an expression of your love and romantic feelings. You won't use a brain emoji because it's the language of the heart – but why? The Ancient Egyptians noticed that the veins and arteries, as well as many nerves, radiate outwards from the heart, and concluded that it was central to both reason and emotion. Later, the Ancient Greeks moved responsibility for rational thought to the brain, but passion has always remained associated with the heart. The adrenaline surge from any strong emotion has a powerful effect on our heart rate, so naturally we feel the pangs of love and attraction in our chest first.

The ancient Israelite writers of the Bible knew that the heart was an organ in the chest that sustains life. But the heart was seen not only as the generator of physical life but the seat of the emotions too. So then, in the Bible, the heart is the centre of all parts of human existence as in the well-known Proverb, *"Guard your heart because from it flows your whole life."* (4.23). The Bible says a great deal about the heart, using the term 830 times, but only rarely does Scripture mention the heart as a sustainer of physical life; instead it is more often used to define what is in a person's personality and also to express human emotion.

The memo for today is worthy of our meditation. When was the last time you had a good 'heart to heart' with your friend, God? It's a wonderful thing to talk honestly about our feelings, be candid, be intimate in that close-up and personal interaction – to open your heart. The lesson is clear from the quill of the sweet psalmist of Israel today, *"Pour out your heart to Him."*

Memorable Quote:
"The idea is, that the heart becomes tender and soft, so that its feelings and desires flow out as water, and all its emotions, all its wishes, its sorrows, its troubles, are poured out before God. All that is in our hearts may be made known to God. There is not a desire which he cannot gratify; not a trouble in which he cannot relieve us; not a danger in which he cannot defend us. And, in like manner there is not a spiritual want in which he will not feel a deep interest, nor a danger to our souls from which he will not be ready to deliver us. Much more freely than to any earthly parent - to a father, or even to a mother - may we make mention of all our troubles, little or great." Barnes' Notes on the Bible

Journaling Suggestion:
Journal about opening your heart to the Lord.

Memo for Meditation:

"O my people, trust in him at all times. Pour out your heart to him, for God is our refuge." Interlude Psalm 62:8

May 26

Motivational Idea: And it's good for your heart!

What does science have to say about prayer, spirituality, and health? A lot, actually! Research that's looked extensively at the mental and emotional health effects of prayer has revealed a variety of positive outcomes. For example, the Journal of Religious Health study (2023) found that offering up worshipful thanks can calm anxiety and reduce depression. Findings from other studies refer to lowering of stress, improving heart health and having a deep sense of connectedness. This should not surprise us since prayer is about a personal relationship with our Creator God, made possible through Jesus who is the only way to the Father (see John 14.6).

Let's listen to a man praying at a time of deep trouble. Psalm 55 expresses the extreme anguish of David's heart. *"My heart pounds in my chest. The terror of death assaults me. Fear and trembling overwhelm me, and I can't stop shaking."* (v4,5). One can almost feel the deep tides of emotion surging over him. One of his most trusted advisors, Ahithophel, had deflected to the other side. His name means, 'brother of ruin or folly.' David's first impulse is to fly away. *"Oh, that I had wings like a dove; then I would fly away and rest! I would fly far away to the quiet of the wilderness. [Interlude] How quickly I would escape—far from this wild storm of hatred."* (v6-8).

Yet in all his emotional turmoil, David is assured of the help he needs to be sustained. The golden peak is reached and is our memo for meditation today. The Hebrew *shalak* means 'to throw, fling, cast down'; give that burden to God and be nourished and sustained for the journey today! *"He who once bore the burden of our sins and sorrows requests that we should now and ever permit Him to bear the burden of our care."* Bishop Horne.

Memorable Quote:

"My troubled soul, why so weighed down?/You weren't meant to bear this heavy load/So cast all your burdens upon the Lord/'Cause Jesus

cares, He cares for you/Jesus cares, He cares for you/And all your worrying won't help you make it through/So cast all your burdens upon the Lord/And trust again in the promise of His love/And I will praise the mighty name of Jesus/Praise the Lord, the lifter of my head/Praise the Rock of my salvation/All my days are in His faithful hands/My anxious heart, why so upset?/In troubled times how you so easily forget/To cast all your burdens upon the Lord/'Cause Jesus cares, He cares for you/Jesus cares, He cares for you etc." Robert Critchley

Journaling Suggestion:
I will cast my burden upon my Lord, the one who sustains me and the lifter of my head.

Memo for Meditation:
"Give your burdens to the LORD, and He will take care of you. He will not permit the godly to slip and fall." Psalm 55:22

May 27

Motivational Idea: Inarticulate speech of the heart

Wikipedia notes that *Inarticulate Speech of the Heart* was the fourteenth studio album by Northern Irish singer-songwriter Van Morrison, released in 1983. Morrison said he arrived at the title from a Shavian (George Bernard Shaw) saying: *"That idea of communicating with as little articulation as possible, at the same time being emotionally articulate."*

Back in 1983, Dave Fricke of the *Rolling Stone* gave a powerful explanation: *"More than just an album title,* Inarticulate Speech of the Heart *is an evocative, breathtaking description of the humble act of prayer. It captures in a simple phrase that desperate expression of pain and need, as well as the floundering over words inadequate to communicate one's joy over a new love or a gorgeous country sunrise. 'I'm a soul in wonder, I'm a soul in wonder,' Van Morrison repeats over and over in the vocal version of his new LP's title song, at once a helpless confession and a celebratory declaration."*

What Van the Man captured in the profundity of this concept is found in scripture; prayer is not only about words, sometimes we can't articulate our thoughts and feelings in the place of prayer. The great

197

Apostle Paul, with all his astounding intellect, in-depth knowledge, literary expressiveness, and experience of the spiritual life, tells us in Romans chapter 8 that the Spirit comes to us and helps us in our weakness. We do not know what prayer to offer or how to offer it as we should, but the Spirit Himself knows our need and at the right time intercedes on our behalf with sighs and groanings too deep for words.

Memorable Quote:
"Inarticulate speech, inarticulate speech of the heart/ Inarticulate speech, inarticulate speech of the heart/ Inarticulate speech, inarticulate speech of the heart/ Inarticulate speech, inarticulate speech of the heart/I'm a soul in wonder(ahahah)/I'm a soul in wonder(ahahah)/I'm a soul in wonder(ahahah)/I'm a soul in wonder (ahahah)/Inarticulate speech, inarticulate speech of the heart/Inarticulate speech, inarticulate speech of the heart/" Van Morrison

Journaling Suggestion:
My prayers don't always have to be with words but rather the inarticulate speech of my heart, which only God can hear and understand, as the Holy Spirit intercedes on my behalf.

Memo for Meditation:
"Meanwhile, the moment we get tired in the waiting, God's Spirit is right alongside helping us along. If we don't know how or what to pray, it doesn't matter. He does our praying in and for us, making prayer out of our wordless sighs, our aching groans. He knows us far better than we know ourselves, knows our pregnant condition, and keeps us present before God. That's why we can be so sure that every detail in our lives of love for God is worked into something good." Romans 8:26-28

May 28

Motivational Idea: Unfailing transformative love

How do you begin your day? The psalmist David's desire for each morning was to hear of God's unfailing love. The spectrum of subjects and moods contained in the psalms are astounding. As to the backdrop of Psalm 143, it could be from the time before David was recognized as king, living as a fugitive from King Saul, or it could be from David's time as king, particularly when his son Absalom led a rebellion against him. In this crisis, David knew that he must cry out to God and that God must hear him, or he would be lost. He requests an audience with God and this is something we can request and obtain because of God's unfailing love. If we could only grasp the extent of God's love for us, its depth, its oceanic, how that will transform us each day and positively impact everything in our day.

We find penitence in v2. We are all undeserving penitents. Verse 3 is about an acute crisis – he is being pursued relentlessly. What's pursuing you today? Remember His grace and mercy follows you in spite of the enemy. Verse 4 is all about desperation. He can't take much more. Verse 5 is reminiscence. He remembers God's past deliverances. Verse 6 expresses fervency – his sincerity – his hands pleadingly spread out to God. Verse 7 is about urgency. Lord, hurray to my rescue! Verse 8 is the plea to be greeted with the unfailing love of God in the morning. Verse 9 is about deliverance, verse 10 an appeal for instruction, verse 11 a plea for preservation, and verse 12 retribution on those who are evil.

As we experience His unfailing love, may we be transformed and go the way He wants us to go. Do what pleases Him as He teaches us. Listen for His voice today and hear Him speak to YOU of how much He loves you. And do it again tomorrow and the day after, and keep going; rather, the reality of His love will keep you, and keep you going on.

Memorable Quote:
"God's love is meteoric, his loyalty astronomic, His purpose titanic, his verdicts oceanic. Yet in his largeness nothing gets lost; Not a man, not a mouse, slips through the cracks. How exquisite your love, O God! How eager we are to run under your wings, To eat our fill at the banquet you spread as you fill our tankards with Eden spring water. You're a fountain of cascading light, and you open our eyes to light. Psalm 36.5-7." The Psalmist

Journaling Suggestion:
Journal a love letter to God. Cause me to hear Your loyal love in the morning and know the way in which I should walk, for I lift up my soul to You (verse 8).

Memo for Meditation:
"Let me hear of your unfailing love each morning, for I am trusting you. Show me where to walk, for I give myself to you. Rescue me from my enemies, LORD ; I run to you to hide me. Teach me to do your will, for you are my God. May your gracious Spirit lead me forward on a firm footing."
Psalm 143:8-10

May 29

Motivational Idea: The answer to guilt

When Jesus was facing an illegal trial, Peter was waiting nervously in the courtyard of the high priest. As he warmed himself at the fire, he was petrified with fear of being recognised, and when asked if he knew Jesus, he vehemently denied his Lord and Master three times. Such was his guilt that he broke down in bitter tears (see Mark 14:72). He decided to take himself off the scene and go back to his old job as a fisherman. Peter must have thought he was finished – he had blown it big time, and so, overwhelmed with guilt and shame, the old life beckoned and off he went.

After a fruitless night of fishing, Peter was invited to have breakfast on the seashore, prepared by none other than the risen Lord. That must have been extremely uncomfortable for Peter as he sat at the fire that morning. When they had finished eating, Jesus spoke to Peter and asked him three questions which John records in John 21:14-18. When they had finished eating, Jesus said to Simon Peter, *"Simon son of John, do you love me more than these?"* Peter answered, *"Yes, Lord, you know that I love you."* Jesus' purpose was to offer Peter a way back from the prison-house of guilt and shame, to forgive him, reinstate him, and recommission him again. Jesus was not finished with him, nor was Peter finished; quite the contrary.

Notice that Jesus called him by the name he used when Peter was first called. This was a clear statement to Peter that he was being called again. But did he love Jesus more than the old life? Yes, he did and he answered, *"Yes!"* The question was asked again and again and each time Peter said, *"Yes,"* he felt hurt, but Jesus was dealing with his threefold denial. Peter was fully restored and, as they say, the rest is history. His failure was a thing of the past and he fulfilled the role that he had been chosen to fulfil with power and passion and set the world ablaze for God.

There is a beautiful phrase in John 21:4. *"Jesus stood on the shore..."* At first Peter and the other men did not recognise Jesus, but there He stood, and He was there to bring Peter and the rest back to their first love. What about you today? What prison-house are you in? Is it failure? Is it guilt? Is it shame? Or is it fear, anxiety, depression, addiction? Whatever it is, Jesus stands on the shore of hope and calls you to come back to Himself. He will restore you and prepare you for the purpose you were put on earth to fulfil. Can you hear him say, *"Do you love me more than these?"*

Memorable Quote:
"Success is not final, failure is not fatal: it is the courage to continue that counts." Winston S. Churchill

Journaling Suggestion:
Journal acknowledging your failures and guilt, and write a love letter to Jesus. *"Yes Lord, you know I love you!"*

Memo for Meditation:
"Though you have not seen him, you love him; and even though you do not see him now, you believe in him and are filled with an inexpressible and glorious joy." 1 Peter 1:8

May 30

Motivational Idea: Do you love me?

Jesus doesn't give up on those who have failed, even if some churches have a tendency to shoot their wounded, metaphorically speaking of course! If you have been written off, don't fall for the devil's trap, even if its so-called Christians are inadvertently doing his bidding.

Peter stands out as a beacon of hope for all who have failed, and who hasn't in some way or another? When Jesus asked Peter, *"Do you love me more than these?"* He used the Greek word *agapas* for love, which is the greatest form of love; He used the same word for the second question, and then *phileo* for the last question, which is the love between friends. Peter had used the word *phileo* each time in his answer when stating his love for Jesus.

Whether Jesus was meeting Peter at his level of understanding of love or not, the focus was on Peter's reinstatement. It is important to know that Jesus meets us at our level of understanding. Another angle on this story could be that Peter may not have felt he could use the word *agapas* but was more comfortable with the word *phileo*. What we do find is that when Peter wrote his first letter, he used the word *agapas*.*"Though you have not seen him, you love him; and even though you do not see him now, you believe in him and are filled with an inexpressible and glorious joy."* (1 Peter 1:8).

Peter's renewal and restoration led to a rekindling of his love for Jesus, a fervent, passionate love that led him back to his calling and mission, and he became a dealer in hope for all who fail. John, who witnessed Peter's restoration, wrote, *"We love Him because He first loved us."* (1 John 4:19). The compelling, unquenchable, incomparable, infinite love of Jesus caused Peter to reciprocate that love. Once we have grasped something of the sacrificial love of Jesus, the wonder of His Calvary cross, we too will want to love and serve Him all our days, doing what He has called us to do at this time in history. Our time!

Memorable Quote:
"Morning, I see You in the sunrise every morning/It's like a picture that You've painted for me/A love letter in the sky/Story, I could've had a really different story/But You came down from heaven to restore me/Forever saved my life/(Refrain) Nobody loves me like You love me, Jesus/I stand in awe of Your amazing ways/I worship You as long as I am breathing/God, You are faithful and true/Nobody loves me like You/Mountains, You're breaking down the weight of all my mountains/Even when it feels like I'm surrounded/You never leave my side, oh oh oh. Refrain. Etc." Chris Tomlin

Journaling Suggestion:
I love you Lord because You first loved me. I want to love You more Jesus.

Memo for Meditation:
"Love the Lord your God with all your heart and with all your soul and with all your mind." Matthew 22:37

May 31

Motivational Idea: Give me your heart

In 1976, Elton John and Kiki Dee sang one of the most famous duets of all time, *Don't Go Breaking My Heart*. The truth is, many famous celebrities have opened up about their personal heartbreaks. Katy Perry has talked about her suicidal ideation when dealing with a break-up. Katy also took her divorce from comedian Russell Brand in 2011 very hard. (Russell has since become a Christian and he is overjoyed about it. He talks about it a lot on social media and how he has given his heart to the Lord.) Katy later revealed that she made a conscious choice to deal with the break-up in a positive way and to not self-destruct. *"There are two ways you can go: You can either nurture yourself or go destructive."* She added, *"I have gone down the destructive path before, and that didn't work for me. You dig deep beyond those scars and find that soft tissue again, and you massage and nurture it and bring it to life, little by little, through serving yourself well. I did it through hikes and vitamins and therapy and prayer and good friends."*

Tasha Layton, who performed backing vocals for Katy Perry, was given the opportunity to become a mega pop star in her own right. She turned her back on stardom, deciding, having already given her heart to Jesus Christ, to pursue a gospel music ministry. Life was tough for her, too; she wrote the song *Never*. You can be sure of this, when you give your heart to the Lord, He will take care of it! He holds you together on the true path to live the authentic life you were made for, and long for!

Memorable Quote:

"NEVER! When this broken world is breaking me down/When my tears and knees both fall to the ground/When my questions make me doubt You more than ever/You remind me that Your answer is always never/Refrain/Never forgotten, never forsaken/Never abandoned/Not for a second/I am safe in Your hands/Always and forever/You're never not working/My heart is the proof/There's not a broken too broken for You/Will there ever come a day when You're not holding me together?/You say never (oh-oh, oh-oh)/Every single time I look back I see/There's never been a promise You didn't keep/You don't waste the

wounds, You use them for the better/When it comes to You, Your answer is always, never/You never let me down/No, You never let me down/When did You ever let me down?/Never, no, never/You never let me down/No, You never let me down/When did You ever let me down? Never/refrain etc." Tasha Layton

Journaling Suggestion:
Lord, I give You my heart.

Memo for Meditation:
"O my son, give me your heart. May your eyes take delight in following my ways." Proverbs 23:26

THE SPIRITUAL DIMENSION

June 1

Motivational Idea: The great awakening!

This month we are considering the Spiritual Dimension with reference to a wide range of views on spiritual and human spirituality. We kick off the month with 'the great awakening' because we have the capacity to know God and be in a right relationship with Him. We fill the void with everything and anything to try and experience the spiritual. Some try to find it in a beautiful sunset, others try to find it in mindfulness and meditation. Some seek to find it in the worship of a person or an object. However, without God we are spiritually dead but diabolically alive – the walking dead. Spiritually dead to God. Our understanding of this condition is heightened when we meet the living Lord of Glory, Jesus Christ. To enjoy the fullness and wholeness and completeness of our true spirituality, we need to be made alive to the experience of God. It is God who makes us alive to Himself.

Our memo for meditation today sets out the reality of the human condition, but also gives us the solution, and how we are raised from spiritual death to spiritual life – the great awakening! Oh, yes, and about being spiritually healthy? That's the motivational idea for tomorrow! Get life, and then get health!

Memorable Quote:
"To be spiritually dead is to be diabolically alive." R C Sproul

Journaling Suggestion:
God , I pray for spiritual life and spiritual health. In Jesus' name, Amen.

Memo for Meditation:
"Once you were dead because of your disobedience and your many sins. You used to live in sin, just like the rest of the world, obeying the devil— the commander of the powers in the unseen world. He is the spirit at

work in the hearts of those who refuse to obey God. All of us used to live that way, following the passionate desires and inclinations of our sinful nature. By our very nature we were subject to God's anger, just like everyone else. But God is so rich in mercy, and he loved us so much that even though we were dead because of our sins, he gave us life when he raised Christ from the dead. (It is only by God's grace that you have been saved!) For he raised us from the dead along with Christ and seated us with him in the heavenly realms because we are united with Christ Jesus. So God can point to us in all future ages as examples of the incredible wealth of his grace and kindness toward us, as shown in all he has done for us who are united with Christ Jesus. God saved you by his grace when you believed. And you can't take credit for this; it is a gift from God." Ephesians 2:1-8

June 2

Motivational Idea: Spiritual health

Spirituality has been defined as, 'that which affects the human spirit or soul as opposed to material or physical things.' When we come to 'spiritual wellness', we discover a wide range of definitions, and these are reflective of the particular worldview in vogue. 'Connecting to your inner and outer worlds to support you in living your values and purpose' is a very general subjective approach to cover all conceivable views. A delve into the secular world of 'spiritual health' will yield some good fruit and food for thought. For example, a typical checklist for signs of spiritual wellness will include such things as developing a purpose in life, taking time to reflect on the meaning of events in life, having the ability to spend reflective time alone, being able to practise forgiveness and compassion in life, and having a clear sense of right and wrong and acting accordingly. This is good and has a lot to teach us. Then we will find material that gives us questions to consider which will help us gauge our spiritual health. For example, do you allow yourself time alone? Do you pray? Or reach out to a higher power? Do you think about the meaning of life? Do you take walks in nature? Appreciate the transformation of each season? Do you pause to remind yourself that life isn't all about you? Do you put down your phone to just *be*? Do you practise activities that allow you to slow down? If we put these things into practice, we would be doing well! Thanks to the University of New Hampshire for these great ideas!

When we come to the biblical worldview, we find that there's more. Romans chapter 12 is a good place to start to consider our spiritual health with some more questions. Am I increasing my love of God? (v.9, 11, 12). Am I increasing in my hatred of sin? (v.9). Am I increasing in holy living? (v.9). Am I increasing in my love of others? (v.10,14-18). Am I increasing in the fruits of God's Spirit? (v.12, 21). Am I increasing in generosity to God & others? (v.13,21). Am I increasing in forgiveness? (v.18-20). You can see there's quite an overlap, the difference being knowing God. Let's not confuse spirituality with religion. Biblical spirituality is about a personal relationship with God, and it all flows from Him – the spiritual life, spiritual vitality and spiritual health – the abundant life with divine purposefulness.

Memorable Quote:
"Spiritual wellness may not be something that you think much of, yet its impact on your life is unavoidable. The basis of spirituality is discovering a sense of meaningfulness in your life and coming to know that you have a purpose to fulfil." University of New Hampshire

Journaling Suggestion:
Journal time to think of my divine purpose on earth!

Memo for Meditation:
"Practise these things, immerse yourself in them, so that all may see your progress." 1 Timothy 4:15

June 3

Motivational Idea: Spiritual barometers

Those that follow their chosen belief system need some kind of spiritual barometer to gauge how well they are doing and how much they are progressing. Take for example the Divine Life Society (DLS), a Hindu spiritual organisation founded in India in 1936. Swami Sivananda Saraswati, its founder, came up with what he described as, *"An infallible barometer to find out the degree of your spiritual progress. How would you feel if, for example, your clean hands or best clothes are stained? You stumble down or commit a blunder and are laughed at? You suffer from illness or pain? You do not succeed in your efforts? You do not get a thing that you want, or find that something you possess is missing? You are kept waiting for a long time by some other person? You are insulted or abused for no reason? Others fail in their duties towards yo?. You suffer a loss or bereavement?"* Swami says, *"If none of these can disturb your peace of mind and you are indifferent to them, you have won the struggle and achieved 50% self control. God sends trials and troubles to strengthen your character: Greet them and test yourself."*

The key is said to be Yoga! *"Yoga kills all sorts of pain, misery and tribulation. It gives you freedom from the round of births and deaths, with its concomitant evils of disease, old age, etc., and bestows upon you all the Divine Powers and final liberation through super-intuitional knowledge."* But is this the truth? Christian meditation is very different from Eastern meditation. Followers of Jesus Christ are not to sit in the lotus pose in an altered state of consciousness seeking the "god within." The Bible teaches that when Christians meditate, our minds are to be fully engaged. We are never to go into a trance state.

For the Christian believer, our life has a barometer attached to it. By looking at this barometer, we can tell a lot about our spiritual life. It can be quickly determined if we are stagnating or thriving, about to dry up or blossom. Want to know what it is? Your involvement in the Word of God. Christianity is about a personal relationship with the Creator God made possible through Jesus, the Son of God. The Bible is the ultimate barometer of the spiritual life and spiritual wellbeing. Get into the Word of God – it's for real! All other brief systems, from which we can learn, are but a stab in the dark and humankind's way of trying desperately to fill the unfillable void. *"Only Jesus can do that, since He alone is the way, the truth and the life."* (John 14:6.)

Memorable Quote:
"Let the words of my mouth and the meditation of my heart be acceptable in your sight, O LORD, my strength and my redeemer." Psalm 19:14

Journaling Suggestion:
Journal about spending more time in God's Word and how you can grow deeper in your relationship with the Creator of the universe.

Memo for Meditation:
"Study this Book of Instruction continually. Meditate on it day and night so you will be sure to obey everything written in it. Only then will you prosper and succeed in all you do." Joshua 1:8

June 4

Motivational Idea: Spiritual barometers (2)

You can tell a lot about your spiritual life from your time in the Word of God. Leonard Ravenhill said, *"Sinning will keep you from praying, and praying will keep you from sinning."* The same is true about Scripture. *"The Bible will keep you from sin, or sin will keep you from the Bible."* The quote is attributed to D.L. Moody. But apparently John Bunyan, who lived centuries before Moody, is reported to have written something similar in the cover of his Bible: *"Either this book will keep you from sin, or sin will keep you from this book."*

Before you dive into God's Word, take a moment to ask the Holy Spirit to illuminate your mind and to reveal truth to you. As you read, stop to ponder what God has spoken through the words on the page. Always consider the context. In Charles Spurgeon's sermon *"Pray Without Ceasing,"* he says there are four important questions to be asked: *"What do these words imply? Secondly, what do they actually mean? Thirdly, how shall we obey them? And, fourthly, why should WE especially obey them?"* So, what does your barometer say about your spiritual life today? How has your time in Scripture been? Has it been dull and lifeless, or is it full of life and insight as the Spirit reveals truth to you and uses it to change your life? What if we could be in the Word like a sponge in water? Spending time thinking, pondering, and praying over our meditations? If we are to know happiness and the true path to the joyful life, the secret barometer of this true spiritual life is the BIBLE!

Memorable Quote:
"The Word grounds you upon a Rock (Jesus) and your life is able to be built strong and solid. There is no substitute for being in the Word! If all your spiritual nourishment comes from attending classes, listening to sermons, and reading devotionals (while they all can be good), it is not more than mere milk or regurgitated food from someone else. You need

to be in the Word yourself! Everything else is secondhand". The Deeper Digest

Journaling Suggestion:
Journal on the work of the Holy Spirit as you meditate on God's word.

Memo for Meditation:
"Oh, the joys of those who do not follow the advice of the wicked, or stand around with sinners, or join in with mockers. But they delight in the law of the LORD, meditating on it day and night. They are like trees planted along the riverbank, bearing fruit each season. Their leaves never wither, and they prosper in all they do. But not the wicked! They are like worthless chaff, scattered by the wind. They will be condemned at the time of judgement. Sinners will have no place among the godly. For the LORD watches over the path of the godly, but the path of the wicked leads to destruction." Psalm 1

June 5

Motivational Idea: Heed the barometer

Captain Oldrey had responsibility for the good ship *Hyacinth*, working for the Barbadoes. These were in the days before radio. On deck, he breathed in the fresh air and relished the finest of weather on a beautiful calm evening, one of the very best he had ever witnessed in that climate. The atmosphere on the horizon had been perfectly clear, and not a cloud obscured the sky. There was not the least probability of change from anything his experienced eye had seen. It was going to be a calm night for sailing. His tiredness drew him below deck to his quarters to retire for the evening. As he was relaxing on his sofa, he happened to glance at the barometer and noticed that mercury was falling. (Today we are digital, then it was mercury.) He rubbed his eyes, and thinking he had misread it, looked again but this time more intently. Sure enough, the mercury was falling. He got up and had another good look – the mercury was falling with a perceptible motion. Again, he went up on deck and observed the beautiful calm evening – it was a perfect evening to be at sea. *"That barometer must be playing up",* he thought to himself. So, he descended again to his cabin and this time he gave the instrument a shake but the fall in reading was now rapid. It was nothing short of remarkable – he had never seen the like of it before! He was now convinced that in spite of what he had observed above deck, this barometer was warning him to get ready and prepare. He called his first lieutenant and master and told them what he had seen from the barometer. The officers protested. *"All is calm,"* they said. Captain Oldrey overruled his well-meaning officers and crew and told them to prepare – they *must* get ready! They must prepare for a mighty storm! And so reluctantly they prepared. An hour or two passed – nothing. Then suddenly they all had proof of the biometric warning – the storm struck and reached its peak almost at once. The wind blew as furiously as it could and the storm was as violent as it could be. Needless to say, because of the wise captain, the ship and all aboard were saved, and lived to tell the story of the night they would have been lost but for the barometer and the wise captain who heeded the warning. The Bible also gives warning of the storm of God's wrath and judgement that is coming on the world. But the Captain of our salvation, Jesus Christ, is the only one who can save us! Trust Him! Be safe in Him!

Memorable Quote:
"For he says, "In the time of my favour I heard you, and in the day of salvation I helped you." I tell you, now is the time of God's favour, now is the day of salvation." 2 Corinthians 6:2

Journaling Suggestion:
Get ready to be ready! How can we prepare?

Memo for Meditation:
"Where is this 'coming' he promised?" See 2 Peter, chapter 3. Read the whole chapter for context.

June 6

Motivational Idea: Physical and spiritual analogies

Remember Maslow and his five levels of need, the first being physiological needs? For Maslow, these most basic human survival needs include food and water, sufficient rest, clothing and shelter, overall health, and reproduction. Maslow states that these basic physiological needs must be addressed before humans move on to the next levels of fulfilment.

In John 6, Jesus spoke with a group of religious people and He explained to them what is required to sustain spiritual life. Unless you eat and drink physical food and water, you will no longer have physical life. Likewise, unless you, spiritually speaking, eat and drink the flesh and blood of the Son of Man, Jesus, you will have no spiritual life. Jesus uses an analogy of spiritual rather than literal significance. Trusting in His sacrificial death on the cross is necessary for eternal (spiritual) life. The eating of His flesh and drinking of His blood metaphorically symbolise the need for accepting Jesus' crosswork. Our spiritual life is then maintained by feeding on the Bread of Life (John 6.35). C S Lewis, in his book *Mere Christianity*, differentiates biological life, which he refers to as *"Bios"*, and spiritual life, which he calls *"Zoe"*. He defines *Zoe* as *"The Spiritual life which is in God from all eternity, and which made the whole natural universe."* He uses the metaphor of humans possessing only *"Bios"* as statues.

Memorable Quote:
"A man who changed from having Bios to having Zoe would have gone through as big a change as a statue which changed from being a carved stone to being a real man. And that is just precisely what Christianity is about. This world is a great sculptor's shop. We are the statues and there is a rumour going round the shop that some of us are some day going to come to life." ... *"The whole offer which Christianity makes is this: that we can, if we let God have His way, come to share in the life of Christ. If we do, we shall then be sharing a life which was begotten, not made, which always has existed and always will exist."* C S Lewis

Journaling Suggestion:
Journal on leaning in and feeding on the Bread of Life – Jesus the True Bread from Heaven.

Memo for Meditation:
"Jesus said to them, "Very truly I tell you, unless you eat the flesh of the Son of Man and drink his blood, you have no life in you. Whoever eats my flesh and drinks my blood has eternal life, and I will raise them up at the last day. For my flesh is real food and my blood is real drink. Whoever

eats my flesh and drinks my blood remains in me, and I in them. Just as the living Father sent me and I live because of the Father, so the one who feeds on me will live because of me. This is the bread that came down from heaven. Your ancestors ate manna and died, but whoever feeds on this bread will live forever." John 6:53-58

June 7

Motivational Idea: Vital steps to spiritual growth

(1) By the book

Any desktop research will yield loads of personal spiritual journeys which challenge us to see if we are ready to take *our* spiritual journey to the next level. Various steps are then suggested to help us to continue onwards and upwards, experiencing spiritual growth. The following is a distillation of steps for us to seriously consider.

Firstly, prioritise God's Word. We need to set aside time for the reading and studying of the Bible. In this way, we get to know God more intimately and understand His character and will for our lives. The Bible is a living book and it's God's way of communicating with us today. It is through this spiritual activity that we can examine our hearts and minds as we invite God to show us those areas of our lives that need attention. We are transformed when we encounter God as we invite Him to change us and make us what He wants us to be.

Secondly, practise prayer. Jesus taught us how to pray – the disciples' prayer, *"Our Father."* It gives us a pattern to enable us to pray. But we need to understand that we need to be ourselves; it's not about long, wearisome dull prayers with pious platitudes and insincere rhetoric. It's about being honest with God. It's amazing when we take the elements of the Lord's Prayer, as it is commonly called, and reflect on these:

1. A personal relationship with God – *"Our Father."*
2. Faith – *"who is in heaven."*
3. Worship – *"May your Name be honoured."*
4. Expectation – *"May your Kingdom come."*
5. Submission – *"May your will be done on earth as it is in heaven."*
6. Petition – *"Give us today our daily bread."*

7. Confession – *"And forgive us our debts."*
8. Compassion – *"As we ourselves have forgiven our debtors."*
9. Dependence – *"And do not lead us into temptation, but deliver us from the evil one."*
10. Acknowledgement – *"For yours in the Kingdom and the power and the glory for ever and ever, Amen."*

It's simple! Get reading and get praying! More steps tomorrow, fellow travellers.

Memorable Quote:
"The Bible is the greatest of all books; to study it is the noblest of all pursuits; to understand it, the highest of all goals." Charles C. Ryrie

Journaling Suggestion:
Lord, teach me to pray and how to study your Word. Amen.

Memo for Meditation:
"So pray this way: Our Father in heaven, may your name be honoured, may your kingdom come, may your will be done on earth as it is in heaven. Give us today our daily bread and forgive us our debts, as we ourselves have forgiven our debtors. And do not lead us into temptation, but deliver us from the evil one. {For yours is the Kingdom and the power and the glory, forever and ever, Amen." Mathew 6:6-13.

June 8

Motivational Idea: Vital steps to spiritual growth

(2) Coals of fire

Johnny and I walked home from church every Sunday. He lived ten doors up from me. Our walk took a good forty minutes. Many an in-depth conversation took place. Johnny was much older than me and had many golden nuggets of wisdom to impart, particularly about the spiritual life. On one occasion, he began to talk about a piece of coal – it didn't make sense at first. We had open coal fires in those days and the coal bucket wasn't too far away from the fireplace. We had coal houses and the coalman would deliver bags of coal every week. Our central heating system was an open fire and the chimney heat – that was it! It was not unusual to scrape the frost off the inside of the bedroom window on a wintery morning. No radiators in those days. Johnny began his talk – he liked to talk and I learned to listen. It went something like this, as I recall over fifty years later. *"Isn't it lovely to sit at the open fire as the flames grow bigger and brighter, and you feel the lovely warmth spread throughout the room?"* Johnny continued, *"Have you ever seen a live burning coal fall out of the fire onto the hearth?"* "Yes," I replied. *"And have you ever let it sit there burning bright to see what would happen?"* *"Yes, when mother was not around."* *"And so tell me, and what happened?"* *"Well, it burned for a short while but then the flame started to peter out and it stopped burning."* *"Then what did you do?"* *"Well, I would put it back in the fire and it would start to burn again".* *"Exactly,"* said Johnny. Then came one of Johnny's nuggets. *"Now here's the lesson you need to learn and never forget. You can't make it on your own. You need fellowship, you need to meet regularly with fellow believers. Get to church on Sunday even when you don't feel like it. The fire glows when we are together. The fire goes out when you go it alone."* It's a lesson I will never forget. We need fellowship and support!

Memorable Quote:

"Engage in fellowship and worship – as a Christian, it's important to engage in fellowship and worship with other believers. This can involve attending church, Bible studies, or small group meetings where you can share your faith journey with others and receive support and encouragement. Through worship, you can express your gratitude and love for God and deepen your connection with Him". Adapted

Journaling Suggestion:

Journal on the concept of fellowship and the need for other believers so you can glow and grow with them in Christ.

Memo for Meditation:

"And let us hold unwaveringly to the hope that we confess, for the one who made the promise is trustworthy. And let us take thought of how to spur one another on to love and good works, not abandoning our own meetings, as some are in the habit of doing, but encouraging each other, and even more so because you see the day drawing near." Hebrews 10:23-26

June 9
Motivational Idea: Vital steps to spiritual growth
(3) At your service

In today's memo, we find the word 'grow' mentioned three times. First, we're called to grow like Christ. Second, we're told that serving in our own special calling allows other individuals to grow. Third, we're called to grow collectively in community. Each one of these indicates a life of service.

One of the vital steps to spiritual growth is service. We are called to serve others with compassion and kindness. This is an essential aspect of Christian spirituality. As we follow Christ's example, we are called to use our gifts and talents to serve others in our community, church or family. By showing love and kindness to others, we can reflect God's love and make a positive impact in the world. C T Studd said, *"If Jesus Christ be God and died for me, then no sacrifice can be too great for me to make for Him."* An all-England cricket star who lived from 1862-1931, Studd had the world at his feet, so to speak, but he gave up, and why? He left behind a professional career as a cricket player to become a missionary to China, India and Africa. At the age of 25, he gave away a great family fortune to support the mission work of men of God such as George Mueller and Hudson Taylor. Every one of us needs a continual reminder about our foremost purpose as believers and followers of Jesus Christ. Our foremost purpose is to know God and serve Him, fulfilling the purpose for which He put us on this earth. Find your purpose and find your happiness and joy unspeakable. This is the flourishing life! What are you being called to give up?

Memorable Quote:
"How could I spend the best years of my life in living for the honours of this world, when thousands of souls are perishing every day?" "Some want to live within the sound of church or chapel bell; I want to run a rescue shop within a yard of hell." "Let us not glide through this world and then slip quietly into heaven, without having blown the trumpet loud and long for our Redeemer, Jesus Christ. Let us see to it that the devil will hold a thanksgiving service in hell, when he gets the news of our departure from the field of battle." C T Studd

Journaling Suggestion:
At your service Lord! Here am I, send me.

Memo for Meditation:
"So Christ Himself gave the apostles, the prophets, the evangelists, the pastors and teachers, to equip his people for works of service, so that the body of Christ may be built up until we all reach unity in the faith and in the knowledge of the Son of God and become mature, attaining to the whole measure of the fullness of Christ...speaking the truth in love, we will grow to become in every respect the mature body of him who is the head, that is, Christ. From him the whole body, joined and held together by every supporting ligament, grows and builds itself up in love, as each part does its work." Ephesians 4:10-16

June 10

Motivational Idea: Coming back to life

We have a whole month to look forward to the musical dimension, so here is a Pink Floyd Song to whet the appetite: *Coming Back to Life.* It begins with a period of suffering and isolation, feeling *"burned and broken"* and *"hurt and helpless".* A sense of abandonment during a time of need. The imagery of watching life pass by from a window underscores a feeling of detachment and passivity.

"The song then shifts to a metaphorical resurrection, with the speaker 'coming back to life.' This transition is marked by a 'heavenly ride through our silence', which could symbolise a journey of self-discovery or a spiritual awakening. The 'seeds of life and seeds of change' suggest that even during the darkest times, there is potential for growth and transformation. The repeated reference to the 'shining sun' serves as a powerful symbol of hope and the promise of a new beginning." Lyric Layers.

Coming Back to Life can be interpreted as a narrative of overcoming adversity and finding strength within oneself. Our memo for today is about the biblical truth of spiritual resurrection. Throughout music there is this continuous cry for redemption – the soul's unrealised desire for God's intervention bringing us to life spiritually. Have you been resurrected spiritually?

Memorable Quote:
"Where were you/When I was burned and broken?/While the days slipped by from my window, watching/And where were you/When I was hurt and I was helpless?/'Cause the things you say/And the things you do surround me/While you were hanging yourself on someone else's words/Dying to believe in what you heard/I was staring straight into the shining sun/Lost in thought and lost in time/While the seeds of life/And the seeds of change were planted/Outside, the rain fell dark and slow/While I pondered on this dangerous but irresistible pastime/Chorus/I took a heavenly ride through our silence/I knew the moment had arrived for killing the past/And coming back to life." Dave Gilmore

Journaling Suggestion:
Journal on walking in the newness of life in Christ. See Romans 6:4.

Memo for Meditation:
"As for you, you were dead in your transgressions and sins, in which you used to live when you followed the ways of this world and of the ruler of the kingdom of the air, the spirit who is now at work in those who are disobedient. All of us also lived among them at one time, gratifying the cravings of our flesh and following its desires and thoughts. Like the rest, we were by nature deserving of wrath. But because of his great love for us, God, who is rich in mercy, made us alive with Christ even when we were dead in transgressions—it is by grace you have been saved. And God raised us up with Christ and seated us with him in the heavenly realms in Christ Jesus." Ephesians 2:1-6

June 11

Motivational Idea: Leaving Lo-Debar for the king's table

When David was King of Israel, he kept his covenant promise and showed great kindness to Jonathan's son, Mephibosheth, who was living in a place called Lo-Debar, which means 'no pasture' – a barren place, where there is nothing and no prospect of anything. Then out of the blue Mephibosheth, whose name means 'beloved', was brought to Jerusalem to a position of great honour at the king's table. Everything he had lost was fully restored and his future was secure as long as the king reigned. Mephibosheth is a picture of the person who is away from the King of kings and Lord of lords, without the abundant life Jesus offers, in a barren place. But the invitation is given to us to dwell no longer in sin's misery but come to the table of the King and receive what He has to give. By grace we are objects of divine favour. He seeks to lavish His grace upon us and restore all to us that was lost in the fall. We are elevated to a place in the family of God and made joint heirs with Christ our King, who keeps His promises and will meet our every need both now and forever. *"He brought me to His banqueting house, and His banner over me was love."* (Song of Solomon 2:4).

Memorable Quote:
"We are all Mephibosheths! Beloved. From Lo-Debar, the place of no pasture, helpless and hopeless. But the grace of God that brings salvation is offered to us and we are invited to the King's table, with all restored! Awesome grace and mercy! Our response – at your service, Lord!" Author

Journaling Suggestion:
Journal on being a child of the King. *"He prepares a table before me in the presence of my enemies; He anoints my head with oil; my cup overflows."* Psalm 23:5

Memo for Meditation:
"So King David had him brought from the house of Makir son of Ammiel in Lo Debar. When Mephibosheth son of Jonathan, the son of Saul, came to David, he bowed low with his face toward the ground. David said, "Mephibosheth?" He replied, "Yes, at your service." David said to him, "Don't be afraid, because I will certainly extend kindness to you for the sake of Jonathan, your father. I will give back to you all the land that belonged to your grandfather Saul, and you will be a regular guest at my table." Then Mephibosheth bowed and said, "Of what importance am I, your servant, that you show regard for a dead dog like me?" Then the king summoned Ziba, Saul's attendant, and said to him, "Everything that belonged to Saul and to his entire house I hereby give to your master's grandson. You will cultivate the land for him—you and your sons and your servants. You will bring its produce and it will be food for your master's grandson to eat. But Mephibosheth, your master's grandson, will be a regular guest at my table." 2 Samuel 9

June 12

Motivational Idea: True friends bring real happiness

True friends bring real happiness! True friends are those who accept us for who we are, warts and all. True friends genuinely want us to succeed and flourish in life. True friends are encouragers and desire that we achieve our goals. True friends will stay the course with us in every circumstance and season. True friends are reliable, dependable and completely trustworthy. True friends will be honest with us and tell us the truth even if it's not what we want to hear. True friends will make the time for us and prioritise us even in the midst of a hectic schedule. True friends will never be too busy to be there for us.

Research has shown that 36% of people reported having between three and five close friends. Forty-nine per cent reported having three or fewer closest friends. Make sure you choose your friends carefully. Who's your best friend? Who sees you as their best and truest friend? Is there a friend that we really need but haven't met yet? In the Gospel of John chapter 15, Jesus describes Himself as the true vine. Jesus goes on to say, *"You are my friends if you do what I command. I no longer call you slaves, because a master doesn't confide in his slaves. Now you are my friends, since I have told you everything the Father told me. You didn't choose me. I chose you. I appointed you to go and produce lasting fruit, so that the Father will give you whatever you ask for, using my name. This is my command: Love each other."*

Those that follow Jesus and obey Him are described as His friends. Are we His friends? Do we know Him? To be in a relationship with Jesus means that we have been chosen and appointed to go and be productive in serving Him. We have been chosen for a purpose. We have one primary purpose on earth – to serve Jesus. Yes, we have lots of responsibilities to family and friends, but the overarching purpose on earth is to know Jesus as our Saviour, Lord and friend, and to bring glory to Him. As we travel the path of life – the path He has chosen for us, and life, the abundant life He as our good shepherd has called us to – we have a friend that sticks closer than a brother. *Carpe diem* – pluck the day, seize the day, for Jesus, today and every day!

Memorable Quote:

"Friendship is the only cement that will ever hold the world together."
Woodrow T Wilson

Journaling Suggestion:
Make stronger friendships by being a true friend, and know the truest friend: Jesus.

Memo for Meditation:
"The man of too many friends [chosen indiscriminately] will be broken in pieces and come to ruin, But there is a [true, loving] friend who [is reliable and] sticks closer than a brother." Proverbs 18:24

June 13

Motivational Idea: Watch out for the false flags

The term 'false flag' was first used in the 16th century and referred to an orchestrated deception describing a stratagem in naval warfare where a vessel flew the flag of a neutral or enemy country in order to hide its true identity. Pirates used it to deceive other ships into allowing them to move closer before attacking them.

Our focus today is on spiritual false flags. The reality is we are in a spiritual battle. This is made explicit from the beginning when Satan deceived our first parents, leading to the fall of mankind. He is described as the one who has deceived the whole world (see Revelation 12:9.)

Paul warned the Corinthians about false apostles. *"They are deceitful workers who disguise themselves as apostles of Christ. But I am not surprised! Even Satan disguises himself as an angel of light."* (2 Corinthians 11:13,14). Here is the dark side of our kaleidoscopic explorations. You have an enemy who not only wants you to live an unfulfilled life and miss your God-given purpose, he wants to destroy you. The Bible warns us about false teaching. *"Now the Holy Spirit tells us clearly that in the last times some will turn away from the true faith; they will follow deceptive spirits and teachings that come from demons."* (1 Timothy 4:1).

Satan is a master manipulator and that is why the doctrines of demons are so effective. We can identify the doctrines of demons by immersing ourselves in the truth – read and study the Bible. Know what God says on any given subject, then any deviation from that teaching will prepare us for the false flags of deception. When we are in tune with God's Word, aberrations from that keynote will ring hollow and off-key. So, take note! We need to be alert to the enemy's false flags and not swallow everything we hear. (See Ephesians 6:18-20.)

Memorable Quote:
"How are the doctrines of demons promulgated? They are delivered through human instructors: "Such teachings come through hypocritical liars, whose consciences have been seared as with a hot iron." 1 Timothy 4:2
These false teachers are hypocritical; that is, their lives do not evidence the holiness they seemingly espouse. They are liars; that is, they deal in falsehood and knowingly lead others into apostasy. And they are beyond the reach of conscience; that is, they have found a way, in their own minds, to justify their lies. These false teachers may be personable, charming, and persuasive, but they do not receive their message from the Holy Spirit; rather, they spout the suggestions of evil spirits, whose work it is to lead people astray." Got Questions – Your Questions, Biblical Answers

Journaling Suggestion:
Journal on developing the spirit of discernment!

Memo for Meditation:
"Dear friends, do not believe every spirit, but test the spirits to determine if they are from God, because many false prophets have gone out into the world." 1 John 4:1

June 14

Motivational Idea: The false flags phenomenon

The false flag phenomenon (FFP) is everywhere in our conspiracy theory world. FFP refers to operations conducted by a country (or individual[s]) designed to deceive the public in such a way that the operations appear as though they are being carried out by another country or entity. As stated yesterday, the phrase is derived from the military concept of flying false colours or flags of a country other than one's own. For example, numerous sources have purported that the events related to 9/11 were false flag operations. Again, today we consider the spiritual analogy of the false flag phenomenon. The Bible speaks of false flags, or deceptions, by false prophets that will be used against believers in the days before Christ's second coming (see Matthew 24:11). Furthermore, the risk is that the very elect may be deceived (see verse 24).

The enemy is very subtle. How can we avoid being deceived by the spiritual false flags contrived by Satan and his agents? How can we ensure our insulation from FFP? We do need to be alert and take the necessary steps to prevent us falling prey to FFP and clever deceptions. We need to know what the truth is in all matters. Jesus prayed to the Father for His disciples of all generations, and that includes us. *"Sanctify them by the truth, your word is truth"* (John 17:17). Note the word 'sanctify' – it's loaded with significance. It means that when we sincerely pursue truth, we open ourselves to be consecrated, holy, separated, set apart from the world and brought into the sacred sphere of God's providence, order and control.

The study of God's Word is more than learning or relearning truth; it allows us to be drawn into an intimate relationship with the Father, Son, and Holy Spirit. Remember that one of the pieces of armour we need to put on every day is the belt of truth! (See Ephesians 6:14.) It's the truth that holds everything together. John tells us, *"Jesus then said to the Jews who had believed in him, 'If you continue in my word, you are truly my disciples, and you will know the truth, and the truth will make you free.'"* (John 8:31,32).

Memorable Quote:
"Precious Bible! What a treasure/Does the Word of God afford!/All I want for life or pleasure,/Food and Medicine, shield and sword;/Let the world account me poor—/Christ and this, I need no more." John Newton

Journaling Suggestion:
Journal on giving priority to the Word of God with a daily reading plan to know the truth.

Memo for Meditation:
"Every scripture is inspired by God and useful for teaching, for reproof (censure), for correction, and for training in righteousness, that the person dedicated to God may be capable and equipped for every good work." 2 Timothy 3:16,17

June 15

Motivational Idea: Get your armour on – truth

Happiness and the fulfilled life is not about a life free of trouble and adversity; on the contrary, we are engaged in a spiritual battle every day. The enemy, Satan, is the thief which Jesus talked about, who comes to steal, kill and destroy. The reality of our engagement in spiritual warfare is not meant to frighten us but rather to embolden us. And we are emboldened because Jesus stands with us on the battlefield and He has come to give us life – life to the full.

"The thief's purpose is to steal and kill and destroy. My purpose is to give them a rich and satisfying life." (John 10:10). Any soldier worth their salt needs to prepare for war, and that means wearing suitable attire. And so it is for us" we need to get our armour on, not only emboldened but equipped for the fight! The Apostle Paul was well acquainted with Roman soldiers and he observed their armour. This led him, under the inspiration of the Holy Spirit, to use six items of Roman armour to illustrate our spiritual armour. God's armour is readily available to us but we must be intentional in dressing ourselves for battle every day. We are going to find that we are to be equipped with five defensive items of armour, and one offensive item.

The first defensive item is 'the belt of truth'. The Roman belt Paul observed was a broad leather belt which was tied around the waist. The Roman soldier would tuck his garments into the belt to give him freedom and swiftness of movement in close combat. It also meant he was less likely to trip up as he stood on the battlefield. The devil is the father of lies, and these manifest in different forms and in various guises, including world religions. As the Roman soldier held his armour with the belt around his waist, so for us the truth is our integrity. We get our truth from God, our knowledge and belief of the truth. God's truth is the only way to encounter Satan's schemes. Girding ourselves with the belt of truth relates to our readiness for battle, it gives us freedom to do the right. God's truth frees us to act with integrity. God's truth will deliver us from error and will give us the spirit of discernment to know a lie exquisitely dressed up as truth.

Memorable Quote:
"The entirety of your word is truth, and all Your righteous judgments endure forever." Psalm 119:160

Journaling Suggestion:
Be battle-ready! Get the armour on.

Memo for Meditation:
"Stand your ground, putting on the belt of truth and the body armour of God's righteousness. For shoes, put on the peace that comes from the Good News so that you will be fully prepared. In addition to all of these, hold up the shield of faith to stop the fiery arrows of the devil." Ephesians 6:14-18

June 16

Motivational Idea: Get your armour on – righteousness

Paul the prisoner saw the Roman soldiers dressed in their armour. He observed the breastplate. It was made of bronze or chain mail. This was a necessary piece of equipment for protecting vital organs, namely the heart. No soldier would enter the battlefield without it; to do so would be almost certain death. We need to remember that while God wants us to live the abundant fulfilled life, we have an enemy called Satan, who, along with his evil forces, really hates us as much as he, and they, hate Christ.

It is imperative that we intentionally put on our spiritual armour every day and this includes *'the Breastplate of Righteousness.'* (Ephesians 6:14). This is Christ's righteousness imputed to us through His crosswork. We stand against the forces of darkness protected by His righteousness. The fiery darts will come but we have Jehovah-*tsidkenu* (the Lord our righteousness) standing with us and we can declare to the enemy: *"He made Christ who knew no sin to [judicially] be sin on our behalf, so that in Him we would become the righteousness of God [that is, we would be made acceptable to Him and placed in a right relationship with Him by His gracious lovingkindness]."* (2 Corinthians 5:21. AMP).

We are protected from sin and Satan's deceptions by Jesus' righteousness. Our sins are gone and we don't have to listen to the lies of the enemy – the accuser (see Revelation 12:10-12). We are called to live righteously and to follow after holiness. Jesus' righteousness leads us in the path of sanctification. *"But now you must be holy in everything you do, just as God who chose you is holy."* (1 Peter 1:15).

Memorable Quote:
"Heavenly Father, no one is righteous, not one. But you have given us the gift of righteousness to follow the path you have set before us, and to avoid the snares of temptation and sin set up by the devil. Help me to pursue you today. Whenever I encounter temptation, help me to find a way out (1 Corinthians 10:13). Steer me away from situations or places which may tempt me more to sin, and when I am tempted, remind me of your goodness and that you are the way of life. No matter what these temptations may promise, they cannot promise me eternal life, joy, or love, which comes from you alone. Arm me with the breastplate of righteousness today, so I may be ready when Satan unleashes heavy torrents of blows on the battlefield. Amen." Crosswalk

Journaling Suggestion:
Journal on how you can use the breastplate of righteousness.

Memo for Meditation:
"For the grace of God that brings salvation has appeared to all people , teaching us that, denying ungodliness and worldly lusts, we should live soberly, righteously, and godly in the present age, looking for the blessed hope and glorious appearing of our great God and Saviour Jesus Christ." Titus 2.11-13

June 17

Motivational Idea: Get your armour on – peace

Elvis sang about his blue suede shoes in 1956 as he danced; Jimmy Nail sang about his crocodile shoes in 1994 as he walked; Paolo Nutini sang about his new shoes in 2006 which made him feel good. Paul didn't produce a song about shoes but he did write about 'Gospel shoes'. *"And having strapped on your feet the preparation of the gospel of peace."* (Ephesians 6:15). Shoes are the third item of attire for the Christian soldier.

The Gospel is our sure foundation and we are to walk being worthy of it and bear testimony in regard to it. The word *gospel* is translated from the Greek word *euangelion*, and it means 'good news' or 'good tidings'. We have good news to share. We have a message of hope for the world and it's the Gospel of peace. We need to spread the message everywhere we go. Let's get our shoes on and present the Gospel of peace in everything we do and say. *"The maid who sweeps her kitchen is doing the will of God just as much as the monk who prays – not because she may sing a Christian hymn as she sweeps but because God loves clean floors. The Christian shoemaker does his Christian duty not by putting little crosses on the shoes, but by making good shoes, because God is interested in good craftsmanship."* This quote has been attributed to Martin Luther. It's a good quote although experts on Luther say it's not his. However, the historians tell us that our memorable quote for today is 100% Luther's.

Memorable Quote:

"The prince should think: Christ has served me and made everything to follow him; therefore, I should also serve my neighbour, protect him and everything that belongs to him. That is why God has given me this office, and I have it that I might serve him. That would be a good prince and ruler. When a prince sees his neighbour oppressed, he should think: That concerns me! I must protect and shield my neighbour. ... The same is true for shoemaker, tailor, scribe, or reader. If he is a Christian tailor, he will say: I make these clothes because God has bidden me do so, so that I can earn a living, so that I can help and serve my neighbour. When a Christian does not serve the other, God is not present; that is not Christian living." Martin Luther

Journaling Suggestion:
Get the Gospel shoes on!

Memo for Meditation:
"How beautiful on the mountain are the feet of the messenger who brings good news, the good news of peace and salvation, the news that the God of Israel reigns! The watchmen shout and sing with joy, for before their very eyes they see the Lord returning to Jerusalem. Let the ruins of Jerusalem break into joyful song, for the Lord has comforted his people. He has redeemed Jerusalem. The Lord has demonstrated his holy power

before the eyes of all the nations. All the ends of the earth will see the victory of our God." Isaiah 52:7-10

June 18

Motivational Idea: Get your armour on – faith

"In addition to all this, take up the shield of faith, with which you can extinguish all the flaming arrows of the evil one." (Ephesians 6:16). Don't forget your shield today. The Roman soldier's shield that Paul observed was called a *scutum*, and was such a sizable object that it would cover the warrior, affording great protection in battle. It was mainly a defensive weapon but could also be used to push opponents away. Soldiers could also form a phalanx and position their shields to form what was called a *testudo*; this was like a tortoise shell and especially useful when arrows were being fired from city walls. The shields were often made of wood and covered in hide, and, when wet, could extinguish the flaming fiery arrows that were raining down on them. This was Paul's inspiration to teach the Lord's army about the shield of faith. Take the shield of faith today and stand firm!

Memorable Quote:

"Hebrews 11:1 says, "Without faith it is impossible to please God." Satan's attacks can sometimes cause us to doubt God. Faith prompts us to believe God. We give in to temptation when we believe what it has to offer is better than what God has promised. Faith reminds us that, though fulfilment of God's promise may not be readily visible to us, God is true to His Word. When Satan attempts to plague us with doubt or entice us with instant gratification, faith recognizes the deceptiveness of his tactics and quickly extinguishes the arrows. When Satan accuses us, faith chooses to believe that Jesus has redeemed us and that there is no more condemnation" Romans 8:1, 34; Revelation 12:10–12, Got Questions

Journaling Suggestion:

Journal on carrying the shield of faith.

Memo for Meditation:

"Faith shows the reality of what we hope for; it is the evidence of things we cannot see. Through their faith, the people in days of old earned a

good reputation. By faith we understand that the entire universe was formed at God's command, that what we now see did not come from anything that can be seen. And it is impossible to please God without faith. Anyone who wants to come to him must believe that God exists and that he rewards those who sincerely seek him. It was by faith that Abraham obeyed when God called him to leave home and go to another land that God would give him as his inheritance. He went without knowing where he was going. And even when he reached the land God promised him, he lived there by faith—for he was like a foreigner, living in tents. And so did Isaac and Jacob, who inherited the same promise. Abraham was confidently looking forward to a city with eternal foundations, a city designed and built by God." Hebrews 11:1-3, 6, 9-10

June 19

Motivational Idea: Get your armour on – salvation

The helmet of salvation is arguably the Christian's most important piece of spiritual armour. To understand this vital equipment, we need to understand the purpose of the helmet used by Roman soldiers in the days when Paul was writing the inspired letters to the early church. War history online gives us a great description: *"The Roman helmet was called a galea, and it had two purposes: protection and identification. The helmets usually came with cheek guards and were thicker in places most likely to be hit. Helmets worn by legionaries and centurions had crests made of plumes of horse hair which were usually dyed red. With the distinct nature of their helmets, it was easy to identify these men in the midst of a battle."*

The back of the helmet had an elongated bill to protect the neck from sword strikes. On the front of the helmet was another rim located about three inches above the first to protect the forehead. As believers, Satan seeks to attack our minds. If he and his demonic forces can influence the way we think, then they will influence the way we act. One of the key strategies of the enemy is to sow the seeds of doubt, seeking to get us to doubt God and His Word. Doubt can lead to discouragement and discouragement to despair, but the helmet of salvation is our protection. We need to put it on each day. Why the helmet of 'salvation'? In 1 Thessalonians 5:8, Paul describes this piece of armour more fully as the *"helmet of the hope of salvation."* The helmet is our sure hope of salvation. This firm promise of the salvation of God provides the basis for our secure hope amid life's trials and difficulties. The helmet of salvation also identifies us with Jesus, our victorious King.

Some ancient historians believed that the helmet worn by the Roman soldiers had a psychological function to it. Polybius said that the helmets were adorned with a 'circle of feathers' which served to make a soldier appear twice as tall as he actually was. As believers, we stand tall, not in our own strength but in the strength of our Lord and Master, *Yahweh Tsebaoth*, which literally means 'Lord of Armies,' 'Lord of Soldiers', or 'Lord of War'.

Memorable Quote:
"You can make the argument that the rest of the armour of God it will not work without the helmet of salvation. Without salvation, you can't even put on the rest of the armour. Those other pieces are rendered useless until the moment of salvation. Your salvation is the thing that identifies you as belonging to Christ and that activates the armour." Clarence L Haynes

Journaling Suggestion:
Journal on the helmet of salvation and how it protects us.

Memo for Meditation:
"But let us who live in the light be clear headed, protected by the armour of faith and love, and wearing as our helmet the confidence of our salvation." 1 Thessalonians 5:8

June 20

Motivational Idea: Get your armour on – the word

Few weapons in world history have had such great tactical importance as the Roman *gladius*. It literally was the sword that conquered the world. When first examining the *gladius*, it is difficult to see how such a small weapon, just 18 inches long, was capable of being so effective. However, its ingenious design and its correct usage and implementation made it unparalleled in victorious warfare. It was very sharp on both edges, with a diamond tip for effective penetration; a most feared and effective weapon. This lethal close combat weapon inflicted more damage than larger swords and was easier for a soldier to handle in battle. The soldier was trained to stab at the enemy in a very fast back and forth motion. This was most effective as it meant a much faster rate of attack, probably as much as four stabs per second, as opposed to the one slice every two seconds if the *gladius* was used in a swinging motion.

History records battles where the enemy was torn to shreds with this masterful stunningly sharp sword. The Roman soldier was never off-balance because he could wield his sword in any direction. Paul the Apostle was well used to Roman soldiers and their regalia. In fact, his letter to the Ephesians was written from prison, possibly in Rome. He was well acquainted with the *gladius* and when he compares the Bible, the Word of God, to a Roman *gladius,* he is comparing the power and strength of the Bible to the most powerful fighting weapon of his day. The Ephesians, the first recipients of his letter, would have understood exactly what Paul was getting at; the Word of God is more powerful, more active and sharper than any two-edged sword and able to penetrate into the deepest inner parts of mankind. It's the Christian soldier's *gladius* against the arch enemy of our souls. Let us take up the sword of the Spirit, spend time in it, know it, use it, and experience how alive and active it is in our lives and in our daily battles. Let us rely on and trust in His Word. *"There is a battle going on – keep your eyes open and your sword sharp."*

Memorable Quote:
"The Word of God is like a lion. You don't have to defend a lion. All you have to do is let the lion loose, and the lion will defend itself." C H Spurgeon

Journaling Suggestion:
Today, I pick up the sword of the Spirit and will spend time with my sword so I can know how to skilfully use it in spiritual warfare and every battle.

Memo for Meditation:
"For the word of God is living and active and full of power [making it operative, energising, and effective]. It is sharper than any two-edged sword, penetrating as far as the division of the soul and spirit [the

completeness of a person], and of both joints and marrow [the deepest parts of our nature], exposing and judging the very thoughts and intentions of the heart." Hebrews 4:12

June 21

Motivational Idea: Know your enemy!

Christian warfare is spiritual warfare, and this conflict is with the devil and his crafty scheming to take us away from Jesus Christ and the fulfilled life He made us to enjoy. Our struggle is not against flesh and blood but against satanic powers, against the rulers of the darkness of this world – spiritual forces of evil in the heavens. The Holy Spirit inspired Paul to write the Letter to the Ephesians (see chapter 6, 12-18), giving a divine revelation concerning the powers of darkness. The Scriptures plainly teach that there is a vast dominion of darkness over which Satan is the head, and that as the god of this present evil age he rules over this world and a large army of evil spirits in the heavenlies. Are we indifferent? Time to wake up and get the armour on and use the sword of the Spirit. The best way to understand how to deal with our arch enemy's stratagems is to follow the example of Jesus. Our memo for meditation today is dedicated to Jesus's response to Satan's wiles or strategies.

Memorable Quote:
"These wicked spirits are against the masterpiece of God. Those who are in Christ and lay hold in the power of His Spirit of the great and ever blessed truths revealed in this epistle, who know the hope of His calling, who rejoice in God and the glory to come, who walk worthy of the calling, come face to face with these powers of darkness. The wiles of the devil, not his power, we are exhorted to stand against. His wiles are all aimed at getting us away from the enjoyment of the fellowship into which God has called us, the fellowship of His Son Jesus Christ our Lord." A C Gaebelein

Journaling Suggestion:
I am in a spiritual battle and my victory is in Jesus and His crosswork.

Memo for Meditation:

"Then Jesus was led by the Spirit into the wilderness to be tempted by the devil. After fasting forty days and forty nights, he was hungry. The tempter came to him and said, "If you are the Son of God, tell these stones to become bread." Jesus answered, "It is written: 'Man shall not live on bread alone, but on every word that comes from the mouth of God.'" Then the devil took him to the holy city and had him stand on the highest point of the temple. "If you are the Son of God," he said, "throw yourself down. For it is written: " 'He will command his angels concerning you, and they will lift you up in their hands, so that you will not strike your foot against a stone.'" Jesus answered him, "It is also written: 'Do not put the Lord your God to the test.'" Again, the devil took him to a very high mountain and showed him all the kingdoms of the world and their splendour. "All this I will give you," he said, "if you will bow down and worship me." Jesus said to him, "Away from me, Satan! For it is written: 'Worship the Lord your God, and serve him only.'" Then the devil left him, and angels came and attended him." Matthew 4:1-12

June 22

Motivational Idea: Who's in the driving seat?

In our hunt for happiness, who's in the driving seat? Most people have been in the driving seat for most of their lives. It begs the question: how's it going? Too many cul-de-sacs, too many wrong turns, and getting more lost in the busy roads of life? It's the most counterintuitive thing to take our hands off the steering wheel and to invite someone else to take over the driving seat. That's what our memo for the day tells us, and it's the words of Jesus Himself. It's another way of saying, make Him Lord of your life and let Him lead and guide you in the direction you should go.

It isn't natural to even consider disregarding our own interests for the interests of others and yet many people do the most amazing things and live a life of self-sacrifice – and do so with their hands still on the steering wheel. How much more can be accomplished if you invite Him to be Lord of your life?

Jesus said, *"Very truly I tell you, whoever believes in me will do the works I have been doing, and they will do even greater things than these,* because I am going to the Father." You will never know what Jesus can do with your life if you never hand it over to Him. Jesus calls you to give up your self-interests and put His interests first. He has a plan for you but you need to hand over the keys of your life to Him first. Be ready to be amazed and find happiness on the journey. It's the most amazing adventure you could ever take!

Francis Xavier once said, *"Tell the students to give up their small ambitions and come eastward and preach the gospel of Christ."* C T Studd said, *"If Jesus Christ be God and died for me, then no sacrifice can be too great for me to make for Him."* Corrie ten Boom said, *"Never be afraid to trust an unknown future to a known God."* C S Lewis said, *"To have Faith in Christ means, of course, trying to do all that He says. There would be no sense in saying you trusted a person if you would not take his advice. Thus if you have really handed yourself over to Him, it must follow that you are trying to obey Him."*

Memorable Quote:
"When you put God first in everything you do you'll be amazed at what happens in your life. With Him in the driver's seat of your life, under His control, you will never be out of control." Anon

Journaling Suggestion:
Journal on asking God to take control of your life and asking Him to guide you in everything you do.

Memo for Meditation:
"Calling the crowd to join his disciples, He [Jesus] said, "Anyone who intends to come with me has to let me lead. You're not in the driver's seat; I am. Don't run from suffering; embrace it. Follow me and I'll show you how. Self-help is no help at all. Self-sacrifice is the way, my way, to saving yourself, your true self. What good would it do to get everything you want and lose you, the real you? What could you ever trade your soul for?" Mark 8:34-37

June 23

Motivational Idea: The joy of forgiveness

The Pharisees taught that forgiveness was to be exercised three times. It was three strikes and you're out. Jesus taught differently; given the extravagance of His love, one would expect His forgiveness to be nothing short of extravagant (see Matthew 18:21,22). And it is! The Psalmist David wrote, *"He is the one who forgives all your sins,"* and then he goes on to elaborate, *"As far as the eastern horizon is from the west, so he removes the guilt of our rebellious actions from us."*

Wesley could not contain his rapturous joy when penning the words, *"Ransomed, healed, restored, forgiven, who like me His praise should sing."* We know forgiveness since we are the recipients of God's abounding grace and mercy, but we also know that even though this is our personal experience we can find it difficult to forgive those who have hurt us. We can be well acquainted with some of the lovely quotes on forgiveness but in the school of hard knows and hurtful blows, we just can't find it in ourselves to forgive, and this is exacerbated when the perpetrator may not even acknowledge the grievous wrong done to us, never mind actually intentionally seeking our forgiveness – how downright despicable and infuriating! Yet Jesus teaches us to forgive generously and continuously. Forgiveness is offering mercy and compassion to those who have hurt us. With our Lord's help we can learn to forgive and then that quote which seemed so remote yesterday comes alive. *"It's not an easy journey, to get to a place where you forgive people. But it is such a powerful place because it frees you."* (Tyler Perry). Alan Paton says, *"When a deep injury is done to us, we never recover until we forgive."*

In the traumatic clutches of hurt, when we forgive, we are free to enjoy post-traumatic growth. We tend to think of traumas as high up on the Richter scale, but then there are the lesser traumas which build up and can be just as debilitating in the long run. It's time to put that hurt where it belongs – to be swallowed up in the sea of God's mercy and grace as we bring it to Him, tell Him how difficult we find it to forgive, and then, in faith before God, acknowledge that we now forgive them. *"Holding on to hurt will hurt you, but letting go will free and heal you."* (The author). Let it go!

Memorable Quote:

"Forgiveness is not an occasional act; it is a permanent attitude." M L King, Jr.

Journaling Suggestion:

Today, by God's grace and mercy, I forgive all those who have hurt me; now to walk in freedom.

Memo for Meditation:

"I tell you, love your enemies. Help and give without expecting a return. You'll never—I promise—regret it. Live out this God-created identity the way our Father lives toward us, generously and graciously, even when we're at our worst. Our Father is kind; you be kind." Luke 6:35,36

June 24

Motivational Idea: Joy overflowing

In John 15.11, Jesus said, *"I have told you these things so that you will be filled with my joy. Yes, your joy will overflow!"* The question is, what things? The phrase is also translated, *"That your joy may be complete."* At first glance, it may seem rather strange. Jesus was on His way to the cross and these were his last discourses with his troubled, anxious and fearful disciples, so how could their joy be complete? One writer on biblical hermeneutics seeks to answer this: *"Loving the Lord Jesus and believing in him, results in joy unspeakable and full of glory. That is the experience of those who follow the commands of Jesus: to believe in his name and to love one another. Being justified (through faith) they receive the indwelling of the Person of the Holy Spirit. His Divine Presence is holiness and thus the indwelt know true joy, within."*

We can take great encouragement from the disciples because the penny didn't drop immediately. When we follow the disciples' journey leading up to the crucifixion and then in the initial post-resurrection recordings of their activities, we find an unhappy, joyless group of forlorn men and women for whom the world was dark and without a future. Yet this all changed when they realised the true significance of the death of Christ and his glorious resurrection. When they grasped the revelation of redemption and restoration found in Jesus, they were changed men and women, revolutionised by the power of divine love. They realised they had been crucified with Christ and had been raised to newness of life. Life took on a new meaning and purpose. Thus, they grasped this teaching of Jesus for his followers of all generations that only when His divine joy is placed in us that our joy is complete. This is a joy that is placed in us by the Holy Spirit as we love and follow Jesus. The force of Jesus' remark is that the greatest and most complete joy only has its source in the divine joy placed in us by the Holy Spirit and the outworking of that joy is experienced in obeying the commands of Jesus out of love for Him.

Memorable Quote:
"The reason why some people do not have joy is that they are looking for it in the wrong place. If you are a Christian walking in the Spirit, you are to have conspicuous, conscious, continual, contagious joy—the joy of the Lord. Most of the people you meet are not concerned about going to Heaven or Hell—they want to know how to hack it on Monday. If you "rejoice with joy inexpressible and full of glory" (see 1 Peter 1:8), you will make a difference." Adrian Rogers

Journaling Suggestion:
Joy is not based in me, it is placed in me by God Himself – complete joy complete!

Memo for Meditation:
"May the God of hope fill you with all joy and peace in believing, so that by the power of the Holy Spirit you may abound in hope." Romans 15:13

June 25

Motivational Idea: Complete joy

There is joy found in a loving relationship! It's quite unlike anything else in the world. To love and to be loved. It has inspired countless songs, books and films. The joy of relationships takes us to a level of living that is arguably unparalleled. Jesus, in John 15:11, spoke to the disciples of a joy that would remain in them, an in-dwelling dynamic joy for which God created us. The Father and Son paradigm of love is the basis for such abiding joy. It is in an inter-relationship with Jesus that we find this complete joy. His love for us, our love for Him and for others. Being a disciple of Jesus is not some bleak, barren, unproductive existence, with a shallow, maudlin joy. On the contrary, true joy is found in following Jesus and fulfilling the purpose for which He put us on this earth. There is a joy in service for the King of kings which can only be experienced as we live in His grace and follow the path He has for us to follow. If our lives are joyless, we need to return to the real joy giver, Jesus Himself, and make Him the apple of our eye. You are the apple of His eye and he wants you to experience this abiding joy in an intimate relationship with Him.

Jesus is our role model. Because of the joy awaiting him, he endured the cross, disregarding its shame. Now he is seated in the place of honour beside God's throne (see Hebrews 12:2). Today He imparts this joy to us as we fix our eyes on Jesus, the champion who initiates and perfects our faith. Bryan Head Welch, the rock star of Korn fame who took to drugs and then found Jesus, or rather, Jesus found him, said, *"The crazy thing is I had an experience with something from another dimension. And it wasn't the religion — going to church and being a good boy — it was, like, I felt something come into my house, and I can't explain it to this day. But I believe that it was Christ doing something in me. So that was real – that was very real."*

Memorable Quote:
"King David's two year hiatus from God resulted in the loss of joy. But after being restored to a right relationship with God, he found his joy again, full, complete and abiding." See Psalm 51/author

Journaling Suggestion:
Guard intimacy with God and keep close to Him, inviting Him into every aspect of the day.

Memo for Meditation:
"Restore to me the joy of your salvation, and make me willing to obey you." Psalm 51:12
"I know the LORD is always with me. I will not be shaken, for he is right beside me. No wonder my heart is glad, and I rejoice. My body rests in safety." Psalm 16:8,9

June 26

Motivational Idea: The joy of building a wall

"The joy of the LORD is your strength." (Nehemiah 8:10b). We do well to understand that this is a powerful declaration that has deep spiritual significance for us in the journey of life with all its twists and turns. It reminds us of the incredible source of strength and empowerment that comes from having a personal relationship with God. The context of this verse is when Ezra the scribe brought the Book of the Law to the people after the walls of Jerusalem were rebuilt. The people had been in exile and were deeply moved by the reading of the Law. However, instead of being sorrowful and overwhelmed by their failures, Nehemiah encouraged them to rejoice in the Lord's goodness and faithfulness.

God is the God of joy and joyfulness and He wants us to experience this amidst the trials and challenges of life. Yes, we need to feel sorry and be remorseful for our failures and confess our sins to Him, but He does not want us to spend the rest of our lives in the doldrums with our metaphorical dust and ashes, acting as if we are agents of the local undertaker. That's where Satan wants to keep us and rob us of the joy of the Lord. Don't let him. Here is the sword of the Spirit – remember the armour! Use the sword! The joy of the Lord is your strength! We can find strength not in our own efforts, but in the joy that comes from our relationship with God. It is His joy that empowers us to face difficulties, overcome obstacles, and persevere in our faith.

Memorable Quote:
"When we experience the joy of the Lord, it brings a shift in our perspective. It enables us to view life's challenges through a spiritual lens, focusing on God's faithfulness and promises rather than being overwhelmed by our circumstances. This renewed perspective infuses us with strength, as we realise that our joy is not contingent on what we face but on who walks beside us."

Journaling Suggestion:
The joy of the Lord is my strength!

Memo for Meditation:
"Then Nehemiah the governor, Ezra the priest and scribe, and the Levites who were interpreting for the people said to them, "Don't mourn or weep

on such a day as this! For today is a sacred day before the LORD your God." For the people had all been weeping as they listened to the words of the Law. And Nehemiah continued, "Go and celebrate with a feast of rich foods and sweet drinks, and share gifts of food with people who have nothing prepared. This is a sacred day before our Lord. Don't be dejected and sad, for the joy of the LORD is your strength!" And the Levites, too, quieted the people, telling them, "Hush! Don't weep! For this is a sacred day." So the people went away to eat and drink at a festive meal, to share gifts of food, and to celebrate with great joy because they had heard God's words and understood them." Nehemiah 8:9-12

June 27

Motivational Idea: Joy abundant

We all want to be happy but don't get sidetracked with the happiness fix – instead, get joy! Is this easier said than done? The reality is we overcomplicate it when it's really simple. The first step to obtaining it is to get life. It was T S Eliot who said, *"Where is the Life we have lost in living? Where is the wisdom we have lost in knowledge? Where is the Knowledge we have lost in information?"* Jesus said, *"I came that they may have life and have it abundantly."* This is the starting point to finding abounding joy because the life that Jesus gives us is more abundantly richer and fuller than anything we could dream of. It's eternal life and it begins the moment you trust Christ. *"It begins immediately. Life in Christ is lived on a higher plane because of His overflowing forgiveness, love and guidance. Have you taken Christ's offer of life?"* (Application Bibles notes). If we have failed, failure is not final. That's the devil's lie. Remember King David when he confessed his sin in Psalm 51:12: *"Restore to me the joy of your salvation, and make me willing to obey you."* And the secret of this abundant joy is found in the path of obedience. That's the simplicity of salvation. Adrian Rogers says, *"Jesus does not have halfway joy."* The Book of Hebrews says, *"God, Your God, has anointed You with the oil of gladness more than Your companions."* (Hebrews 1:9; Psalm 45:7).

Nobody has joy like Jesus. The word 'gladness' in the last quote is translated as 'exceeding joy' in Jude 1:24. It literally means leaping and dancing. You may have already found out that you cannot live the Christian life without joy, and if you have met some joyless Christians, then they are the ones with the problem, not you. Jesus does not call people to be miserable; there is more than enough of that toxicity in our world. Jesus gives full-on, abiding joy. Ask Him for His brand of joy!

Memorable Quote:
"You will not win people to Jesus if you go around looking like an advance agent for the undertaker. "Don't you want to be a Christian so you can be as miserable as I am?" They will say, "No, thank you; I have enough problems." Adrian Rogers

Journaling Suggestion:
Restore to me the joy of your salvation!

Memo for Meditation:
"The thief comes only to steal and kill and destroy. I came that they may have life and have it abundantly. I am the good shepherd. The good shepherd lays down his life for the sheep. I am the good shepherd. I know my own and my own know me, My sheep hear my voice, and I know them, and they follow me. I give them eternal life, and they will never perish, and no one will snatch them out of my hand. My Father, who has given them to me, is greater than all, and no one is able to snatch them out of the Father's hand. I and the Father are one." John 10:10,11,14, 27-30

June 28

Motivational Idea: Joy abounding

The joy of the Lord is *abundant.* Abounding, abundant – what's the difference? They can be used as synonyms but they can also be used slightly differently. 'Abounding' speaks of the *quality* of the joy. Abundant speaks of *how much* joy there is.

Joy is one of the great themes of the Bible. From the very first Book, we find that God's plan for mankind has been to bring us joy and peace. Throughout the Bible, we see stories of joy in response to God's blessings and celebration of His promises. In the Old Testament, the Israelites rejoiced and sang songs of joy when they escaped from the Egyptians and made their way to the Promised Land. Joy is a constant theme in the song book of Israel – the Psalms. For example, the psalmist in 118:15 says, *"Songs of joy and victory are sung in the camp of the godly. The strong right arm of the LORD has done glorious things!"* The voice of rejoicing and salvation is in the tents of the righteous: Having received God's wonderful rescue, God's people give voice to their joy. It would be wrong for those who have received so much to be silent about it. The right hand of the Lord does valiantly. Repeatedly (for emphasis), the singer praises the right hand of God, recognizing it as the hand of skill and strength. God will not use lesser measures to rescue His people.

In the New Testament, Jesus brings joy to those who follow Him, and encourages others to do the same. The Apostle Paul also speaks of joy in his letters, urging believers to be joyful even in difficult circumstances. The Bible teaches us that joy is God's gift from God to us, and that it is something to be celebrated and shared with others. Bible verses about joy can help us in every season, and we are reminded of the calm joyfulness that is ours through faith in God. Joy is rooted in who God is. It is not fleeting or based on circumstances. Worldly possessions, accomplishments, even the people in our lives, are blessings that make us happy and fuel joyfulness. However, the Bible teaches that the source of all joy is Jesus. God's plan from the beginning, the Word made flesh to dwell among us, is rock solid, allowing us to navigate difficult situations without happiness while sustaining our joy.

Memorable Quote:
"Only in God is there fullness of joy!"

Journaling Suggestion:
Lord help me to learn to fuel the joyfulness that You give to me.

Memo for Meditation:
"I pray that God, the source of hope, will fill you completely with joy and peace because you trust in him. Then you will overflow with confident hope through the power of the Holy Spirit." Romans 15:13

June 29

Motivational Idea: Joy abiding

Jesus said, *"These things I have spoken to you, that my joy may be in you, and that your joy may be full."* (John 15:11). To understand what Jesus is saying, we need to take cognizance of *"these things"*. When we take the verse in its context, we find that Jesus has been speaking about the vine and our need to abide in Him. *"Abide in me, and I in you."* (John 15:4). This joy can only be experienced when we abide in Him. And how do we abide in Jesus? Each day of our lives we need to be in the place of fellowship so we can guard our personal relationship with Jesus, so our lives are characterised by faith, trust, prayer and obedience. This abiding in Jesus gives us abiding joy.

Jesus also said, *"If you abide in me, and my words abide in you, ask whatever you wish, and it will be done for you."* (John 15:7). We need to be people of 'the Book' – the Bible! We need to be in the Word daily so that the words of Jesus abide in us. Do we have any idea how powerful His words are? They yield the purest joy! And Jesus tells us to ask Him and He will answer us. This is not a wish-list but rather praying in tune with the Spirit as we humbly ask Him and wait for Him to answer.

The prophet Jeremiah tells us about the joy he found. *"Your words were found, and I ate them, And your words became to me a joy and the delight of my heart, For I am called by your name, O LORD, God of heaven's armies."* (Jeremiah 15:16). The Psalmist wrote, *"Your statutes are my heritage forever; they are the joy of my heart."* (Psalm 119:111).

We can know perpetual joy as we walk in obedience to Jesus. Jesus is the vine and we are the branches. A branch has one concern: to stay connected with the vine. Our one overarching goal in life is to be totally, completely surrendered to Jesus Christ. Everything else is a subset of our main desire to surrender to Jesus Christ. What we find is, if our relationship with Jesus is right, then we will bring this pure joy into everything: our relationships, our workplace, and our everyday living. We will be joyous!

Memorable Quote:

"When you surrender, you must depend. What can a branch do without a vine? Nothing! It's a twig. Jesus said, 'Without me you can do nothing.' Nothing counts until you are dependent upon Christ."

Journaling Suggestion:

"The purest joy in the world is joy in Christ Jesus." Robert Murray McCheyne

Memo for Meditation:

"If you keep My commandments, you will abide in My love, just as I have kept My Father's commandments and abide in His love." John 15:10

June 30

Motivational Idea: The secret of memorisation

We conclude the month of June in the spiritual dimension by considering the secret of memorisation. The author was exercised when we considered the sword as part of our armour. Years ago, memorisation of scripture was a regular thing for many but fell into disrepair, so to speak. And so, the memo for meditation today became the memory verses for one week for the author. The verses were written out and placed in my wallet. One memorable moment comes to mind. Standing peeling spuds (potatoes) for my elderly mother was a daily task; mother's mantra was: *"You have to have potatoes for dinner or it's not a dinner."* The thought came to mind, *"Here we go again, more spuds to peel and..."* It was on the tip of the tongue: *"I detest peeling potatoes,"* perhaps even the word *"hate"*? Then the memory verses came to me in a flash. *"Always rejoice, constantly pray, in everything give thanks. For this is God's will for you in Christ Jesus. Do not extinguish the Spirit."* (1 Thessalonians 5:16-19). It brought a smile to my face, and I was indeed rebuked: rejoice, pray, give thanks – don't quench the Spirit. The sword came to the rescue – a rescue from a negative frame of mind and a bad attitude that could have spiralled out of control.

This is what is written on the back of the card in my wallet: the 8Rs for Readiness in Battle:

1. Read it.
2. Record it.
3. Retain it!
4. Remember it.
5. Raise it (as was done in the peeling potatoes session to challenge a negative attitude)
6. Reflect on it.

7. Review it.
8. Repeat it.

"Your mind will take the shape of what you frequently hold in thought, for the human spirit is coloured by such impressions." Marcus Aurelius.

Memorable Quote:
"Here is a simple method to get started. When you are impressed with a verse then, write it out on a piece of paper, card, or notebook and carry it with you. Repeat the first part of the verse over and over until you can say it without looking then add the second part repeating the two together until you can say the whole verse without looking. Repeat the whole verse a number of times as you go through your day praying it to the Lord to get it firmly fixed in your memory. Keep the paper, card or notebook with you and add more while reviewing the verses aloud at least once a week. So let us grow in God's Word by hiding it in our heart and memory (Psalm 119:11) *and applying it in obedience to the Lord in our life.* (Psalm 119:9). *Start to develop the mind of Christ and begin to quote Scripture like He did* (Matthew 4:1-10; et al) *in the circumstances of life you are faced with."* Adapted

Journaling Suggestion:
Making memorisation a must!

Memo for Meditation:
"Always rejoice, constantly pray, in everything give thanks. For this is God's will for you in Christ Jesus. Do not extinguish the Spirit." 1 Thessalonians 5:16-19

THE RELATIONAL DIMENSION

July 1

Motivational Idea: You can't feel better if you are bitter

Bitterness can feel worse than anger because we are left feeling helpless. It's referred to as 'embitterment' in the psychology world, and saps all the joy out of our lives. It's a robber that steals away the goodness from our lives. It paints our blue skies black and holds us in bondage. Embitterment hurts us far more than the person who originally hurt us. It destroys peace and poisons every fibre of our souls. Bitterness also affects the people around us; our embitterment spills onto everyone around us, and our negativity can cause others to avoid us. Bitterness can lead to damaged relationships. We may even feel bitter toward God for a loss we have experienced. It's human nature to blame God for things that He could have made turn out in a different way.

Our bitterness toward God could be creating big problems in our spiritual lives. But how do we fix our bitterness? Firstly, we must admit that we feel bitter; we need to face it, in order to leave it behind. Most importantly, talk to God about it and hand it over to Him. We also need to forgive those who have hurt us. The person or persons who have wronged us don't need to apologise or make amends to us, and we don't need to go to their door to ask for it. They may not live there anymore, but they are living rent free in our heads – we are paying the ginormous rent!

Forgiveness will work its healing power. Forgiveness is an act of the will. It doesn't require us to make contact with our offender. It is simply an act of faith between us and God. Let us decide to let go of it and to live joyfully today, having dealt with it before God. You will feel much better if you are not bitter. Phan Thi Kim Phuc, known as the napalm girl, whose photograph became a symbol of the horrors of the Vietnam war, said, *"For years I bore the crippling weight of anger, bitterness and resentment toward those who caused my suffering. Yet as*

I look back over a spiritual journey that has spanned more than three decades, I realise the same bombs that caused so much pain and suffering also brought me to a place of great healing. Those bombs led me to Jesus Christ."

Memorable Quote:
"Bitterness clouds the mind and poisons the soul." Allene vanOirschot

Journaling Suggestion:
Acknowledge the embitterment; give it to God; let it go and live joyfully.

Memo for Meditation:
"Get rid of all bitterness, rage and anger, brawling and slander, along with every form of malice." Ephesians 4:31
"See to it that no one falls short of the grace of God and that no bitter root grows up to cause trouble and defile many." Hebrews 12:15

July 2

Motivational Idea: Words are powerful

"Words kill, words give life, they're either poison or fruit—you choose." (Proverbs 18:21). *"Their tongue would cut steel."* That's not a nice observation about people and it may be true, but there may be some projection going on. Have I a tongue that would cut steel? But we get it, we have all been on the receiving end of a fiery tongue and suffered because of it. And none of us get off the hook because we know that we too have used the power of the tongue to do damage to another.

The world of psychological research has found that if we are the recipient of a negative comment, then it can take four positive comments or affirmations to undo the damage of the negative comment and help to restore our self-esteem. It has been said that there are three things that once they go forth cannot be recalled: the spent arrow, the spoken word, and the lost opportunity. We have the power on our lips today to take the opportunity to give that word of encouragement to another. Let us refrain from firing the poisoned arrows and use words that bring happiness to others in our interactions today. Poison or good fruit? You choose, and don't forget to observe how you speak to yourself. In 1 Samuel 30:6, we find that David was greatly distressed because the people were talking about stoning him. Did he retaliate? No, absolutely not. We are told that he encouraged himself in the Lord. Now, there's a lesson!

Memorable Quote:
"Words have a magical power. They can either bring the greatest happiness or the deepest despair." Sigmond Freud

Journaling Suggestion:
"May the words of my mouth and the meditation of my heart be pleasing to you, O LORD, my rock and my redeemer." Psalm 19:14

Memo for Meditation:
"Likewise, the tongue is a small part of the body, but it makes great boasts. Consider what a great forest is set on fire by a small spark. The tongue also is a fire, a world of evil among the parts of the body. It corrupts the whole body, sets the whole course of one's life on fire, and is itself set on fire by hell. All kinds of animals, birds, reptiles and sea creatures are being tamed and have been tamed by mankind, but no human being can tame the tongue. It is a restless evil, full of deadly poison. With the tongue we praise our Lord and Father, and with it we curse human beings, who have been made in God's likeness. Out of the same mouth comes praise and cursing. My brothers and sisters, this should not be. Can both fresh water and salt water flow from the same spring? My brothers and sisters, can a fig tree bear olives, or a grapevine bear figs? Neither can a salt spring produce fresh water." James 3:5-12

July 3

Motivational Idea: The designer's greatest delight

The joy of being a successful designer must rank amongst one of the greatest joys on earth. To design something from nothing, make it, and then see it fulfil its function and reach its full potential must give the designer tremendous satisfaction and a deep sense of personal fulfilment. The Bible declares God to be creation's amazing architect, and the designer of the human race. The history of the human race begins in the book of Genesis, with a perfect environment and perfect people. Our first parents brought great joy and delight to the Designer, for not only was He their maker but He was their God, and they enjoyed perfect, uninterrupted intimate fellowship with Him; they were functioning as designed and were fulfilling their potential and the purpose for which God made them. It was a world of complete happiness and perfect joy, a far cry from today, and the purpose for which the human race made. What happened? This can be explained by way of an analogy; today there are fears about AI – artificial intelligence – and how AI could potentially try and take control of the future and our destiny. Real fears abound. This is what happened in Genesis, but it wasn't AI, it was HI – human intelligence – supposedly.

Humankind began to think that we knew better than our Designer, we rejected His wisdom and His perfect plan. Just look at the world today. We have made a total mess of it. But the Designer has made a way back in the plan of redemption through Jesus and His crosswork. It's time to return to God and in bringing joy to our Designer, we will find the greatest joy and happiness on earth by being in a right relationship with God, and realising our potential and the purpose for which we were designed and made. The Designer's manual for living is on the shelf – it's time to give the Bible its proper place in our lives again, if we have not done so already.

Memorable Quote:
"The Son of God became a man to enable men and women to become the sons and daughters of God." Adapted from C S Lewis

Journaling Suggestion:
"Come close to God and He will come close to you." James 4:8

Memo for Meditation:
"Jesus said, 'The first in importance is, 'Listen, Israel: The Lord your God is one; so love the Lord God with all your passion and prayer and intelligence and energy.' And here is the second: 'Love others as well as you love yourself.' There is no other commandment that ranks with these." Mark 12:30

July 4

Motivational Idea: Relational happiness

People who have one or more close friendships appear to be happier. In close friendships, we have the blessing of being able to share our feelings without the fear of being judged. This kind of close interpersonal relationship has been shown to play a major role in the relief of stress and depression. That close friend will listen to us in a careful and empathic manner; they will respond with words of honesty and in encouraging ways. This is referred to by the experts as 'Active-Constructive Responding' and has been proven to be very effective in cultivating positive emotions and deepening relationships. It can be said that our journey to happiness is one we make with companions.

Two of the pioneers of positive psychology, Ed Diener and Martin Seligman, said, *"People with 'strong ties to friends and family and commitment to spending time with them' have the highest levels of wellbeing."* (Diener & Seligman, 2002). At the University of Illinois, a survey on the personal happiness of the 10% of students with the highest scores recorded was conducted. They found that the most salient characteristics shared by students who were very happy and showed the fewest signs of depression were *"their strong ties to friends and family and commitment to spending time with them."* (The New Wallis, 2005).

Human relationships are essential to human happiness and no one is an island, even though we may like to think so. The ultimate relationship and greatest friendship is the one we can have with God and yields the greatest measures of authentic happiness and a joy that cannot be fully expressed or extinguished. It is in a personal relationship with God that we find ultimate happens and real joy. We can trust Him and we need to spend time with Him to get to know Him better and to be on His wavelength. Jesus told His disciples that he no longer called them servants but friends, if they did what He commanded. How is our friendship with God today?

Memorable Quote:

"Trust is an indispensable element of a happy life. A suspicious, distrustful soul is like one walking in a fog, chilling, perplexing, distorting. One of a trustful nature who has no one to trust is like a lonely traveller, hungry and homeless." Donald Maurice Spence-Jones

Journaling Suggestion:
Today I will determine to build my friendship with God and get to know Him better.

Memo for Meditation:
"But let all who take refuge in you rejoice; let them ever sing for joy." Psalm 5.11
"The Lord is my strength and my shield; in him my heart trusts, and I am helped; my heart exults, and with my song I give thanks to him." Psalm 28.7
"For our heart is glad in him, because we trust in his holy name." Psalm 33.21

July 5

Motivational Idea: Living in God reality

We don't have to look too far for things that stress us out. It can be difficult to relax and, ironically, we can get stressed out by trying to relax. There is even a word for this relaxation-induced anxiety –it's called 'stresslaxing'. According to the Urban Dictionary, stresslaxing is defined as *"being so stressed that relaxing makes you more stressed because you're not working on what's making you stressed."*

We are offered all kinds of tools to counteract this post-modern phenomenon, some with £ or $ signs attached to encourage us to sign up to the latest flavour of the month. However, there are genuine people who really care and seek to help us to reduce our stress levels. The Bible has a unique angle on our stress-filled lives. God has our best interests at heart and He wants us to be able to relax; that's right, you heard correctly, God is interested in your stressors and stress levels. Jesus in the manifesto of the Kingdom of God gives us divine insights into how to truly relax. The secret is our personal relationship with God and, in knowing Him, we get to know how He works – He instructs us in His manual for living. Read it!

Our memo for today tells us to live in 'God reality'. Now, this is foreign to the natural world of mankind. Paul sheds light on this when writing to the Ephesians where he refers to spiritual wisdom and revelation, and their growing knowledge of God since *"the eyes of their hearts have been enlightened"* so that they can know the hope of God's calling, the wealth of His glorious inheritance and the incomparable greatness of His power toward those who believe.

Let's look with enlightened spiritual eyes and hear with spiritual ears, and learn what in our relationship with God true relaxation really is.

Memorable Quote:
"Seeking God needs to be our first priority not our last resort."

Journaling Suggestion:
Steep your life in God-reality and live in Him, developing your relationship with Him.

Memo for Meditation:
"If God gives such attention to the appearance of wildflowers - most of which are never even seen - don't you think he'll attend to you, take pride in you, and do his best for you? What I'm trying to do here is to get you to relax, to not be so preoccupied with getting, so you can respond to God's giving. People who don't know God and the way he works fuss over these things, but you know both God and how he works. Steep your life in God-reality, God-initiative, God-provisions. Don't worry about missing out. You'll find all your everyday human concerns will be met. Give your entire attention to what God is doing right now, and don't get worked up about what may or may not happen tomorrow. God will help you deal with whatever hard things come up when the time comes." Matthew 6:30-34

July 6

Motivational Idea: Living a God identity

The freedom that comes to us in the Kingdom of God enables us to experience happiness and joy expressed in loving, giving and authentic living. This means even loving our enemies. That's a tall order, but we are to love as God loves and that means unconditionally. Who are the enemies you are dealing with at this time? Only with a God-identity can we love them, but we have our heavenly Father's DNA and we can do all things through Christ who enables us. We are enabled, and indeed emboldened, to love unconditionally, give generously, and live fully and authentically. This is the salvation life promised from the days of the Old Testament prophets.

The Messiah has come and dealt with the sin problem, conquered death, rose again from the dead, and will return again. We can live this resurrection life because we are made alive in Christ. We can live a life of generosity and graciousness because this is the way God treats us, even at our worst.

C S Lewis said, *"To be a Christian means to forgive the inexcusable because God has forgiven the inexcusable in you."* So don't forget to be compassionate and kind. We have experienced divine mercy and we too are to be merciful, which means without judgement. We only cause ourselves grief and unhappiness when we live in judgmental ways – it tears us up inside as we obsess about judging. We can choose which way we live – the God-identity way or alternatively the self-identity way. The latter will cause regrets, if not immediately but eventually as we get older. On the other hand, God gives us a promise: if we live the God-identity way, we will have no regrets.

Memorable Quote:
"To the degree that we embrace the truth that our identity is not rooted in our success, power, or popularity, but in God's infinite love, to that degree can we let go of our need to judge." Henri J M. Nouwen

Journaling Suggestion:
"I will endeavour to, Do all the good I can, By all the means I can, In all the ways I can, In all the places I can, At all the times I can, To all the people I can, As long as ever I can." Adapted from John Wesley

Memo for Meditation:
"I tell you, love your enemies. Help and give without expecting a return. You'll never—I promise—regret it. Live out this God-created identity the way our Father lives toward us, generously and graciously, even when we're at our worst. Our Father is kind; you be kind." Luke 6.35-36

July 7

Motivational Idea: If you could have one superpower, what would it be?

An applicant for a school principal post was interviewed by a number of panels over two days. On the second day, it was the turn of the pupils' panel. One of the questions put to the candidate was, *"If you could have one superpower what would it be?"* The candidate thought for a moment and then answered, *"If I could have one superpower, it would be kindness, so everyone in the world would make kindness a priority in all their relationships and dealings with others."* The candidate was successful and became the principal of that academy. (He happens to be my older son.)

Can you imagine what this would do in a world of hatred, bigotry, racism, xenophobia, and all the hate-filled phobias that poison and pollute our world? Think of all the horrid stuff that goes on between individuals, in families, political parties, in nations, organisations and religions. It would change everything! You don't have to compromise your belief system or your principles to be kind. The world needs more of the milk of human kindness. This expression comes from the English playwright William Shakespeare in his play *Macbeth*, Act 1 Scene 5, in the year 1605. Lady Macbeth is contemplating her husband's character and his ambition. She expresses concern that he may not be ruthless enough to seize power and suggests that he should be more deceitful and less compassionate. She tells her husband, *"Yet doe I feare thy Nature, It is too full o' th' Milke of humane kindnesse."* Lady Macbeth was not sure if her husband would be able to act as ruthlessly as he might have to as king. He was too filled with the milk of human kindness, and, as an attribute, that might hinder Macbeth's ruthless ambition.

The phrase 'the milk of human kindness' has survived down the centuries and today we use it in contexts where individuals want to emphasise the caring and empathetic qualities of a person. *"What wisdom can you find that is greater than kindness?" "Tenderness and kindness are not signs of weakness and despair, but manifestations of strength and resolution." "Wherever there is a human in need, there is an opportunity for kindness and to make a difference." "No act of kindness is too small."* (Jean Jacques Rousseau).

Start the kindness resolution!

Memorable Quote:
"Human history is not the battle of good struggling to overcome evil. It is a battle fought by a great evil struggling to crush a small kernel of human kindness." Vasily Grossman

Journaling Suggestion:
Being kind is a strength, not a weakness, it's revolutionary and has world-changing potential!

Memo for Meditation:
"Love is patient and kind; love does not envy or boast; it is not arrogant or rude. It does not insist on its own way; it is not irritable or resentful; it does not rejoice at wrongdoing, but rejoices with the truth. Love bears all things, believes all things, hopes all things, endures all things." 1 Corinthians 13.4-7

July 8

Motivational Idea: My heart is fixed

The common usage of the word 'fixed' is the idea of repairing or restoring something. The word that is used here, however, in our meditation for today means 'steadfast'. The backdrop to this song is concerned with a murder bid on the life of David as he fled from Saul and hid in a cave. This was a most dangerous and perilous situation. David was being haunted like a wild animal; Saul and his forces were closing in. In vivid language, he describes himself as being amongst lions (see Psalm 57.4). His precarious predicament caused him to do what was second nature to him – because of his relationship with God, he looked up and cried out to Him (see Psalm 57.1). Rather than relying on his own devices and ingenuity for deliverance, he was fully trusting in God (see Psalm 57.3). Listen to his confidence: *"He sends orders from heaven and saves me, he humiliates those who kick me around. God delivers generous love, he makes good on his word."* His heart is fixed – steadfast! (see Psalm 57.7). His heart is steadfast in the Lord, and in that confidence, he desires to worship and praise the Lord.

David's confidence in God is so rock solid that in this dire situation he does not respond with fear and trembling, but confidence and praise. Hopefully we will never find ourselves in a place where we are being hunted down. However, we do face trials and adversity in our lives. Wouldn't it be great if we could respond like David did? May our walk with the Lord be so strong that we can fully trust in God for deliverance, and that we praise Him as He guides us through life's storms. Don't let the storms become your focus but rather let the God of heavens' armies be your focus as you face the storm. You may have heard the quote from the warrior, *"Fate whispers to the warrior, 'You cannot withstand the storm.' The warrior whispers back, 'I am the storm.'"* In other words, it's the calm of having inner strength. For the Christian, this calmness and strength comes from God.

Memorable Quote:
"And the Christian life is simply the process of bringing my sense of self, my Identity with a capital "I," the ego, my swirling internal world of fretful panicky-ness arising out of that gospel deficit, into alignment with the more fundamental truth. The gospel is the invitation to let the heart of Christ calm us into joy, for we've already been discovered, included, brought in. We can bring our up-and-down moral performance into subjection to the settled fixedness of what Jesus feels about us." Dane C Ortlund

Journaling Suggestion:
Fix your heart on God! Stay fixed!

Memo for Meditation:
"My heart is fixed, O God, my heart is fixed; I will sing and give praise. Awake, my glory! Awake, lute and harp! I will awaken the dawn. I will praise You, O Lord, among the peoples; I will sing to You among the nations. For Your mercy reaches unto the heavens, And Your truth unto the clouds." Psalm 57:7-10

July 9

Motivational Idea: I've got the power

As humans, we possess an innate desire for connection and we seek out friendships and relationships in the hope that they will be healthy and satisfying. One of the big conversations today is around empowerment relationships. This is one of the key features of a healthy relationship; building and maintaining such a relationship can sometimes be challenging. You will find all kinds of advice in any Google search for the decisive elements of empowerment. The experts in this field tell us that, *"Empowerment means being aware of who we are, confident in what we want, and communicating this respectfully. It is the middle ground between passivity and control. Empowerment is important as it helps us build autonomous, strong and compassionate relationships."* (Veretis).

Building empowered relationships requires a number of factors, which include setting healthy boundaries, communicating assertively, and being aware of each other's strengths. The antithesis of empowerment is disempowerment. Too many relationships fall into this category, where one person wants it all their own way and puts the other person down. Why people stay in such relationships is a topic for another day in our kaleidoscopic explorations. Ways of empowering your nearest and dearest include leading by example and acknowledging the skills they have that you might not be so proficient in. Use active listening to empower them as they express their point of view. Affirm their abilities and strengths, and demonstrate empathy. Seek to grow spiritually, mentally, emotionally and physically together.

Don't forget your relationship with God! Be aware that your relationship with God is one of empowerment. The reality is, His divine power has given us everything we need. Embrace who you are in Christ. Live life to the full in His power. Apply this life-giving truth to your life today and move from victimhood into victory, from the dark end of the street to the bright side of the road. It is as we know Him – we are empowered.

Memorable Quote:
"His divine power has given us everything we need for a godly life through our knowledge of him who called us by his own glory and goodness." 2 Peter 1:3, NRSV

Journaling Suggestion:
Living the fulfilled life empowered by God Himself. He empowers me! I've got the power!

Memo for Mediation:
"By his divine power, God has given us everything we need for living a godly life. We have received all of this by coming to know him, the one who called us to himself by means of his marvellous glory and excellence. And because of his glory and excellence, he has given us great and precious promises." 2 Peter 1:3,4

July 10

Motivational Idea: Who are you?

If you are living in a world of what Robin Sharma calls *"energy vampires and dream stealers,"* then it's time to get real. Some people will drain you and leave you feeling wrecked and miserable. Your sense of self will be ghostly to say the least, and you'll inhabit a mere existence and lead an unfulfilled life. Robin says we need to surround ourselves with people who fuel our joy. He asks the question, *"Who in your circle do you need to let go of who irritate, frustrate and exhaust you?"* It may not be that easy when it's family but you do need to consciously develop a safe distance, psychologically at least, from them. Jesus did not pull any punches, *"Let the dead bury the dead, but you go and proclaim the kingdom of God."* (Luke 9:59–60).This was Jesus' response to a disciple who wanted to spend time at home before committing himself to the Lord. Jesus said, *"Follow me."* The disciple was not prepared to let go of that which was familiar, and it probably involved waiting until his father's eventual death to gain wealth of some kind in terms of inheritance.

The reality is, the rich life does not depend on riches but on inner wealth. Who are you? This is who God says you are. Are you ready for this? It's mind-blowing and a life-changer when you grasp it. You are God the Father's beloved child. (see 1 John 3.1-2). You are chosen by God. (see 1 Peter 2.9), chosen from before the creation of the world. You are so valuable. (see 1 Peter 1.18-19) and so very precious. You are God's friend. (John 15.14-15). You are His ambassador. (see 2 Corinthian 5.20). As you go into your day, know who you are – you are an ambassador of the Kingdom of God. Don't forget you have been forgiven. (see 1 John 2.12). Remember you have a definite purpose in this world. (see Romans 8.28). You are redeemed. (see Ephesians 1.7).

You are made in God's image. (Genesis 1.27), born to be creative and know mastery in your God-given craft.

Do you remember as a child having that existential moment when you looked in the mirror for ages and thought, *"This is me, but who am I?"* As you look into the mirror of God's Word today, this is who you are, and we have only just scratched the surface!

Memorable Quote:
"Grab your Bible, open it up and discover who God declares you to be. Let it be a springboard to relish who He proclaims you to be. Then let His Words and truth settle into your heart, reminding you that you were so intricately made with love and called to a greater purpose, setting your sights beyond this world and embracing eternity." 2 Corinthians 4:18, adapted

Journaling Suggestion:
It's time to shine in my God-given identity and live out my divinely ordained purpose!

Memo for Meditation:
"This means that anyone who belongs to Christ has become a new person (a new creation). The old life is gone; a new life has begun!" 2 Corinthians 5:17

July 11

Motivational Idea: Are you receiving me?

Healthy relationships mean good communication. Any initial research will yield ideas as to how to communicate. It's important! *"We all have a strong need for connectivity and belonging. This is why positive social interactions increase our subjective wellbeing and provide greater life satisfaction."* (Lyubomirsky, 2008).

In terms of social interactions, research by Fredrickson & Joiner, 2002, stated, *"Relationships enhance happiness because spending time with friends or colleagues builds positive emotions—a key component of happiness."*

We tend to think of communication in terms of talking, and there are all sorts of elaborate models that you can study. A basic communication model involves a sender, a receiver, and a (verbal or nonverbal) message which is encoded by the sender and decoded by the receiver. It includes feedback, the response of the receiver to the message, as well as anything that can disrupt communication. Yet one of the most important communication skills is listening. Deep, positive relationships can only be developed by listening to each other. Scott Peck said, *"You cannot truly listen to anyone and do anything else at the same time."* In the counselling and psychotherapeutic world, we talk about 'active listening', which is so much more than not talking. It is an art that requires a genuine interest in the other person, a curiosity rather than an anticipative mind. Active listening is concerned with nonverbal involvement (show your attention), paying attention to your vis-à-vis, not your own thoughts, being non-judgmental, and tolerating silence. In my early days studying psychotherapy, I came across the five levels of listening: ignoring, pretend listening, selective listening, attentive listening and empathetic or active listening. Worth checking these out to brush up on your communication skills.

In the spiritual sphere, don't forget your communication with God. Prayer is just a fancy word for talking 'with' God. It's about listening and responding, as well as talking about our needs. It's also worship. Prioritise the habit of prayer. Make it a regular part of your daily life. Prayer is the conduit to our source of power, God Himself. The prayer house is the power house. Here, we are energised and sustained and refuelled.

Memorable Quote:
"Prayer is first of all listening to God. It's openness. God is always speaking; He's always doing something." Henri J M Nouwen

Journaling Suggestion:
Open my ears, Lord, and teach me to listen.

Memo for Meditation:
"Be still, and know that I am God;" Psalm 56:10
"Come to me with your ears wide open. Listen, and you will find life. I will make an everlasting covenant with you. I will give you all the unfailing love I promised to David." Isaiah 55:3

July 12

Motivational Idea: You've got great potential

A mother was reading stories to her little one about great Bible heroes. The little girl was enthralled when she heard of Moses, Joshua, Gideon, Easter and Deborah. One day the child said, *"You know what, Mum? God was a lot more exciting back then."* But God hasn't changed one iota since the days of those great heroes. He is still producing heroes, ordinary people from different backgrounds, people to whom the world may not give a second thought, but nevertheless people who, in God's eyes, are heroes. The words of the little girl should challenge us to consider again the greatness of God who sees potential in the most unlikely of people – even us!

Learn the lesson from the life of Gideon. We remember him as a mighty warrior leader of Israel who won a massive victory over a Midianite army despite his 300 men being vastly outnumbered. But he did not start off as a mighty leader. We meet him in Judges chapter 6 where he is harvesting wheat and hiding it from the feared Midianites. God steps in and the rest is history. He wants to do for you what He did for Gideon, to imbue you with His power so you can fulfil the purpose for which He put you here, to be the best that you can possibly be for Him. You are the apple of His eye and He so wants you to succeed. Isn't it time we started to get excited because Gideon's God is our God too? Listen! Ask for confirmation! Obey, and just do what He says! Just do it, you mighty warrior!

Memorable Quote:
"Mighty hero, the Lord is with you!" God

Journaling Suggestion:
God help me to see me as You see me!

Memo for Meditation:
"Then the angel of the Lord came and sat beneath the great tree at Ophrah, which belonged to Joash of the clan of Abiezer. Gideon, son of Joash, was threshing wheat at the bottom of a winepress to hide the grain from the Midianites. The angel of the Lord appeared to him and

said, "Mighty hero, the Lord is with you!" "Sir," Gideon replied, "if the Lord is with us, why has all this happened to us? And where are all the miracles our ancestors told us about? Didn't they say, 'The Lord brought us up out of Egypt'? But now the Lord has abandoned us and handed us over to the Midianites." Then the Lord turned to him and said, "Go with the strength you have, and rescue Israel from the Midianites. I am sending you!" "But Lord," Gideon replied, "how can I rescue Israel? My clan is the weakest in the whole tribe of Manasseh, and I am the least in my entire family!" The Lord said to him, "I will be with you. And you will destroy the Midianites as if you were fighting against one man." Gideon replied, "If you are truly going to help me, show me a sign to prove that it is really the Lord speaking to me." Judges 6:11-17

July 13

Motivational Idea: Friends sharpen friends

Dwight Lyman Moody was born the sixth child of Edwin and Betsy Holton Moody in Northfield, Massachusetts, on 5th February 1837. His schooling came to an end at fifth grade, and he rapidly grew tired of life on the family farm. He left home at age 17 to seek employment in Boston. His uncle reluctantly employed him as a shoe sales assistant, the one condition being he would attend church. At church in 1855, Moody accepted Jesus Christ as his Lord and Saviour and devoted his life to serving Him. The following year brought Moody to Chicago with dreams of making his fortune in the shoe business. As he achieved success in selling shoes, Moody grew interested in providing a Sunday School class for Chicago's children and the local Young Men's Christian Association. He went on to become a global evangelist – from shoe seller to soul winner! Perhaps the line most frequently attributed to Dwight L Moody is the famous quotation: *"The world has yet to see what God can do with a man (or woman) fully consecrated to him. By God's help, I aim to be that man."* These words actually originated from Henry Varley, a British revivalist who had befriended the young American in Dublin. He recalled that in 1873 Moody asked him to recount words they had spoken in private conversation a year earlier, just before Moody's return to the United States. Varley records that during the afternoon of the day of conference Moody asked if he would join him for a private conversation. Moody asked if he remembered what he had said a year before. Varley could not, so Moody reminded him. *"Don't you remember saying, 'Moody, the world has yet to see what God will do with a man fully consecrated to him?'"* *"Not the actual sentence,"* Varley replied. Varley recorded Moody's response: *"Ah," said M. Moody, "those were the words sent to my soul, through you, from the Living God. As I crossed the wide Atlantic, the boards of the deck of the vessel were engraved with them, and when I reached Chicago, the very paving stones seemed marked with 'Moody, the world has yet to see what God will do with a man fully consecrated to him.' Under the power of those words I have come back to England, and I felt that I must not let more time pass until I let you know how God had used your words to my inmost soul."*

Friends sharpen one another! Choose your friends carefully.

Memorable Quote:
"Our greatest fear should not be of failure, but succeeding at something that doesn't really matter."
D L Moody

Journaling Suggestion:
Make sure to succeed at what you were called to succeed at.

Memo for Meditation:
"As iron sharpens iron, so a friend sharpens a friend." Proverbs 27:17

July 14

Motivational Idea: Beyond meditation – contemplation

The human soul hungers for the fulfilled life. The challenge to us all is to seek it in a personal relationship with God which is possible only though The Way, Jesus. When we seek His forgiveness and embrace Him and the love He has for us, we enter into this personal relationship. But even for some who have taken this step, they have not found the level of fulfilment that they had hoped – they live in quiet disappointment. The reality is we have to work at this relationship on a daily basis. Donning the Sunday suit or the Sunday jeans is not enough. We need to read the Bible, meditate, pray. What we have read and meditated upon will help us grow in our relationship with the Almighty.

However, there is a fourth element we need to grasp, and this is where many have missed out on the fulfilled life that God has for them. It's the lost art of contemplation. The contemplative life is the fulfilled life. A life characterised by contemplation is the key to the mastery of the fulfilled life. We live in an age of constant distraction, hence the pressing need to cultivate the contemplative lifestyle. You don't need to shut yourself away in a monastery or a convent to embrace the contemplative life; it is possible to embrace it without relinquishing your responsibilities. The pursuit of this spiritual discipline will draw us into a more intimate and vibrant walk with God. The fulfilled life will begin to unfold and blossom before us.

Over the next several days we are going to take our kaleidoscopic approach to exploring the realms of contemplation. But what is the difference between meditation and contemplation, given that these concepts are used in different ways and indeed sometimes used interchangeably? Meditation is the active use of the mind to engage with God through reading and praying of Scripture, an actual and intentional reflection. Contemplation is, on the other hand, our loving and attentiveness and grateful gazing upon God. It's the experiential and savouring of God – beyond words, embracing Him in the intimacy of silence enthralled with the beauty of God. It's an intentional focus on God. In contemplation, He opens His Spirit to our inner spirit. Oneness!

Memorable Quote:
"The ultimate goal of the fulfilled life can only be realised upon the awareness and cultivation of the contemplative life." Author

Journaling Suggestion:
Time to embrace the contemplative life.

Memo for Meditation:
"I pray for you constantly, asking God, the glorious Father of our Lord Jesus Christ, to give you spiritual wisdom and insight so that you might grow in your knowledge of God. I pray that your hearts will be flooded with light so that you can understand the confident hope he has given to those he called—his holy people who are his rich and glorious inheritance." Ephesians 1.15-18

July 15

Motivational Idea: The art of contemplation

In a world of distraction, how can we develop a more contemplative lifestyle? We need to set aside times of solitude from the world so we can engage in the contemplation of God. Our contemplation must arise from a sound theological framework, but that does not mean we are not open to new aspects of spiritual experiences that we have not yet developed. The well-quoted text comes to mind: *"Taste and see that the LORD is good. Oh, the joys of those who take refuge in him!"* (Psalm 34.8). Matthew Henry said, *"This tasting and seeing His goodness involves discovery as well as enjoyment."*

We must know more than know *about* Him – we must *know* Him. Yet in the Christian world, we can be influenced to be more concerned with the 'condiments'. Some are more concerned with their flavourings and, according to them, theirs are the best. You must be a Baptist, or you must be a Calvinist, or you must belong to our group and see it the way *we* see it. We can be so concerned with flavourings that we don't really get to taste because the taste is tainted with our preconceived notions and our interpretations.

We don't need to worry about the condiments – the Baptist relish, the Calvinist Dijon mustard or the Pentecostal mayonnaise; we just need to get on with tasting and seeing that God is good. However, to experience the benefits of contemplation we need to be firmly rooted in the Scriptures. Get into the Word of God. Remember the four keys to finding our true fulfilment in God: read the Scriptures, meditate on what you read, pray Scripture and develop the art of contemplation. The contemplation life is the steady gaze of the soul upon God who loves us. We need to be open to His self-revelation. We experience Him in the here and now, up close and personal, not remotely or in a text book. Allow God to be real to you. Allow Him to be Himself, not who we perceive Him to be. With biblical knowledge, we can move beyond our preconceived notions to the experience of God that is generated in us by His Holy Spirit. We gaze upon Him, knowing Him more and more!

Memorable Quote:

"The contemplation life is the steady gaze of the soul upon God who loves us. We need to be open to His self-revelation." Author

Journaling Suggestion:
Read the Scriptures daily, meditate, pray Scripture and develop the art of contemplation.

Memo for Meditation:
"Are you tired? Worn out? Burned out on religion? Come to me. Get away with me and you'll recover your life. I'll show you how to take a real rest. Walk with me and work with me—watch how I do it. Learn the unforced rhythms of grace. I won't lay anything heavy or ill-fitting on you. Keep company with me and you'll learn to live freely and lightly." Matthew 11.28-30

July 16

Motivational Idea: Contemplation and 'the absolute'

In our desire to develop a contemplative lifestyle, we need to be aware of distortions that will take us away from 'the absolute'. We will come back to 'the absolute' in a moment. All world religions and indeed secular spirituality offer a plethora of techniques to anyone who is earnest about the contemplative discipline. The popularity of practices that offer calm to body and mind, and release from mental dis-ease, can take you into the eastern religious practices of Hinduism, Buddhism, and New Age Transcendental Meditation. These systems claim to connect their followers to the transcendent in transformative ways through contemplation. But be warned, for there is no scriptural basis for these claims since what they offer does not lead us to the truth of the absolute – the true God Himself and the only means of intimacy with Him in a personal relationship through Jesus Christ as revealed in His Word. The transcendental approach, rather than being the contemplation of the true God, puts the focus on the self and self-sufficiency of the self, the attraction being the offer of physical and psychological benefits, when first and foremost our focus must be on God, His sufficiency and our dependence upon Him. Why settle for imitations and distortions? Remember the motto from yesterday? *"Read the Scriptures, meditate, pray Scripture and develop the art of contemplation."*

Take, for example, one verse of Scripture, *"Jesus Christ is the same yesterday and today and forever."* What a text for contemplation on 'the absolute'! In an ever-changing, fast-paced constantly shifting world, He is the God who does not change – the constant in the chaos. Take the title 'Trinity'. For God is Trinity, Father, Son and Holy Spirit. The Trinity is not Father, Son and the Holy Bible, but it is the Spirit who through the truth of the word reveals God Himself to us, God in three persons, blessed Trinity. It is Jesus made flesh who makes God accessible to us and opened up the way of access to God. Jesus declared, *"I and the Father are one."* (John 10.30). Anyone who sees Him sees the Father. (John 15.9). To contemplate 'the absolute' is to be enraptured with the God who is immutable, the immovable rock where we can fully plant our faith. In a shifting, unstable world in a state of constant flux and shifting sands, we can know 'the absolute' and the immutable. Here is the solid ground for biblical contemplation, not the fake and the false.

Memorable Quote:
"Biblical contemplation is not the emptying of the mind but rather the filling of the inner spirit with the absoluteness of the immutable God of eternity who loves us with an unquenchable love." Author

Journaling Suggestion:
Embrace the absoluteness and the immutability of God in the contemplative discipline.

Memo for Mediation:
"I am the LORD, and I do not change." Malachi 3:6

July 17

Motivational Idea: 'Something lives in every hue'

Connection with God flourishes as we develop a balanced contemplative lifestyle. We need to get away from the notion that contemplation is monks chanting in some far away monastery. We can develop a contemplative discipline even in the business of life and know calm in the chaos.

Contemplative spirituality opens the door to an acute awareness of the presence of God, right here, right now. God transcendent yet immanent. Not a God who is remote and far off, but here with us. It's the name given to Jesus: *"Immanuel, God with us."* (Matthew 1:22-23). Not one who sits in judgement but who lavishes us with His love. He has set a day in which He will judge the world, but today is the day of grace, and contemplative spirituality is the way to intimacy with God. We are invited by God into a truly spiritual filled world. It is what writers on the subject call the 'intimate immediacy of God'. To be in the presence of God continuously. *"I cannot imagine how religious persons can live satisfied without the practice of the presence of GOD. For my part I keep myself retired with Him in the depth of centre of my soul as much as I can; and while I am so with Him I fear nothing; but the least turning from Him is insupportable."* (Brother Lawrence).

It is the contemplative discipline that opens our innermost being to His personhood. In a world of many techniques, 'centring' is used to give us peace within the chaos that might be surrounding us. It's about being 'in check' with what's going on. Individuals who are centred are typically calm and peaceful. 'Grounding' is a term used in conjunction with the energy fields around us. Being grounded means that we're content with who we are. We're sure of ourselves and have confidence in the decisions we make.

These techniques can be helpful and the author has been in seminars where these have been used effectively with a secular audience. But contemplative spirituality takes us further and deeper since our true centring is in God and our true grounding is in Him. We live in the spiritual realm and we see things differently. We get a God perspective on life and we begin to discover that everywhere is filled with the sacred, with the divine, with God Himself, who is wholly present and whose being and nature is reflected in all of His creation. Creation has God's DNA all over it.

Memorable Quote:
"Heaven above is softer blue/Earth around is sweeter green/Something lives in every hue/Christless eyes have never seen/Birds with gladder songs o'erflow/Flow'rs with deeper beauties shine/Since I know, as now I know/I am His, and He is mine." Wade Robinson

Journaling Suggestion:
God open my eyes so as I walk through this world, I experience intimate immediacy with You.

Memo for Meditation:
"Draw near to God and He will draw near to you." James 4:8

July 18

Motivational Idea: Seeing the light

Jesus is, *"The true light that gives light to everyone coming into the world."* (John 1:9). That light has been diminished by sin and darkness. *"This is the verdict: Light has come into the world, but people loved darkness instead of light because their deeds were evil."* (John 3:19). Hence the multiplicity of belief systems that take humanity away from the True Light.

When we say God's DNA is everywhere in creation, we do not mean pantheism. God is separate from His creation, and is transcendent. Pantheists reject the personhood of God, believing that God and the universe are the same. *"God is all, and all is God."* Christians, however, see all finite things as being dependent on one supreme reality, God Himself.

The Aurora Borealis has been visible in many locations across the world in recent days: the result of massive geomagnetic storms prompted by eruptions on the solar surface. Our sun hangs in the universe about 93 million miles away from where we are. It has storms on its surface that are caused by its magnetic fields twisting as the sun rotates on its axis. These storms have created disturbances to Earth's magnetic fields, creating dazzling displays of lights. Scientists rave about it but you won't hear them on MSM giving God the glory. King David wrote, *"The heavens proclaim the glory of God. The skies display his craftsmanship."* Even though the auroras seem like colourful, dancing lights to us, they are really a testament to God's glory and powerful mind. You can't define God with mathematics or science, although these cry out to us and give evidence of God the Creator, but He can only be known by experience. In our desire for deeper contemplative spirituality, we seek a more intimate relationship with the personhood of God, the God of wonders!

Memorable Quote:
"I looked, and I saw a windstorm coming out of the north–an immense cloud with flashing lightning and surrounded by brilliant light." Ezekiel 1:4

Journaling Suggestion:
Walking in the light of God today!

Memo for Meditation:
"The Life-Light was the real thing: Every person entering Life He brings into Light. He was in the world, the world was there through Him, and yet the world didn't even notice. He came to his own people, but they didn't want Him. But whoever did want Him, who believed he was who He claimed and would do what He said, He made to be their true selves, their child-of-God selves. These are the God-begotten, not blood-begotten, not flesh-begotten, not sex-begotten." John 1:9-13

July 19

Motivational Idea: From incessant doing to intentional being

Some of those engaged in the study of contemplative spirituality quote the French philosopher, Pierre Teilhard de Chardin: *"We are not human beings having a spiritual experience. We are spiritual beings having a human experience."* It initially sounds smart and appealing. Those who take the view that we are spiritual beings having a human experience believe that we are immortal and eternal beings on a never-ending journey. Such postulations point up a salient point made some days ago that we need a firm foundation upon which to base our contemplative spirituality. This is where God's Word comes in to enable us to engage in a 'check in', and when we do so, we discover we are human beings who are dead in sin with no spiritual life whatsoever. *"And you He made alive, who were dead in trespasses and sins,"* writes the Apostle Paul in Ephesians chapter 2.

We are human beings who need a spiritual awakening so we can possess eternal life through Jesus and enjoy the spiritual life that He gives us. And we then need to grow and to go deeper with God. To live in a world where we in tune with God is not only possible but also vital. This is the fulfilled life.

Here are some more ideas to consider to help us in the art of spiritual contemplation: 'Silence, Solitude, Stillness and Solidarity.' Regard these as the stepping stones to deepen your relationship with God. In the human struggles we face and in the supernatural battles we are engaged in, we need to live in close communion with God. The psalmist in Psalm 23 talked about his cup overflowing – brimming over with all good things, blessings! Yet all too often our cup is brimming over with fears and anxieties. We need to get alone with God. 'Less incessant doing and more intentional being.' Get into the silence. Silence: read, meditate and pray. Solitude: the place of retreat and withdrawal. Stillness: taking time to rest and relax in God's presence to be rejuvenated. Solidarity: then re-enter that busy world we inhabit with God embused power to be active in for good. Spread the good news of the Gospel and seek justice for the marginalised and the downtrodden. We don't withdraw permanently but rather we withdraw to be renewed and restored and then enter the fray with power. He gives this power to the faint. (see Isaiah 40:29-31).

Memorable Quote:
"Be still and know that I am God." God

Journaling Suggestion:
The thunder of silence in the solitude and stillness.

Memo for Meditation:
"And he said to them, 'Come away by yourselves to a desolate place and rest a while.' For many were coming and going, and they had no leisure even to eat." Mark 6:31

July 20

Motivational Idea: Following in their footsteps

The Scriptures are replete with believers' contemplative prayers and their exhortations for us to personally experience God. We can learn much from their contemplative prayers. For example, in the Old Testament we read of the psalmists *"gazing on the beauty of the Lord"* (Psalm 27:4). In the New Testament, we read of the Apostle Paul praying that the *"eyes of our hearts would be enlightened"* (Ephesians 1:16-19).

Believers throughout Church history, moved by the Spirit, have pursued greater intimacy with God through contemplation. St Augustine wrote of his pursuit of God, *"O Beauty, ever ancient, ever new,*

I sought you outside and I had you within." Jonathan Edwards, one of the most brilliant theologians and pastors in American history, wrote *"My manner has commonly been to walk for divine contemplation and prayer. Recently, I had a view of the glory of the Son of God... of his full, pure, sweet grace and love, with an excellency great enough to swallow up all thought and conception, which continued about an hour and kept me in tears."*

We find both in Scripture and throughout Church history that biblical contemplation and prayer is the practice of attentive beholding – a gazing on the object of our delight that assumes and builds on rational convictions about Christ, but goes beyond them in terms of the experience they generate. We behold in order to become. *"This personal knowledge of God cannot be attained by human effort or spiritual activities on their own, but is always grounded in the regenerating and ongoing illuminating and animating ministry of the indwelling Holy Spirit, who connects us back to God."* (John Coe, quoted in FBC). Let us then take unhurried time to practise opening our hearts to discern and experience the Spirit's work in us. God wants to move us from mere head knowledge to the personal experience of the indwelling Spirit. He wants to take what Christ has made available to us on the basis of His finished work on the cross and make it a reality in our lives.

Memorable Quote:
"We can conclude that the practice of contemplative spirituality is grounded in the work of Christ to reconcile our sinful nature to Him. It values both the intellectual precepts of our faith, and the self-revelation of God to us, in order to love and strengthen us. It does not encourage us to 'empty our minds,' but rather to empty our hearts of unnecessary distractions to open our spirit to the work of the Holy Spirit. It is not solely dependent on an engineered spiritual discipline, but is the work of the Spirit of God, who initiates His presence, resulting in greater intimacy and maturity." Adapted

Journaling Suggestion:
Lord, teach me the lived experience of true contemplative spirituality. Amen.

Memo for Meditation:
"Filled with all the fullness of God." Ephesians 3:19

July 21

Motivational Idea: From scarcity to abundance (1)

We have already thought of ways in which to cultivate a deeper contemplative spirituality. 'Silence, Solitude, Stillness and Solidarity' can be used as tools to mount the summit of greater God awareness. Becoming accustomed to living in the presence of God will impact every part of our life and the 'solidarity' element is the outworking of our relationship with our heavenly Father. Take for example the generosity of God. How do we know He is generous? The short answer is, He gave us His one and only Son. A short answer, but to plumb its depths, not all the printing presses in existence, past or present, could publish enough volumes to explain it – that would take eternity.

We have a tendency to store up to give us security for the future and, in one sense, it is wise 'to save for a rainy day'. But human nature has a tendency to over-indulge in the habit of 'muchness', and if we are not careful, we will lead an impoverished life with no real depth to our relationships because we have hoarded for ourselves. This is the skin-flint mentality which Freud referred to as the 'anal-retentive personality type.' We live in relational poverty because we put ourselves first. To live in the presence of God will mean a paradigm shift from the prison-house of scarcity to building what Tim Macey of the Bible Project has called 'an abundance mindset'.

This Christ-like mindset moves us from scarcity to abundance. We tend to think of giving in monetary terms, but that is only a part of it. We have so much more to give. One of the most precious commodities we can give to anyone is our time. Do we live freely so we can give off our unhurried time to others? It's much easier to Netflix than to network. But what is the right thing to do? Do the right thing, not necessarily the easy thing. Dwell no longer in the dungeon of the impoverished spirit but live in the freedom of the generous spirit, and prosper. A generous lifestyle is not limited to the wealthy. Yet those who are truly wealthy are generous in spirit and reflect the very nature and character of almighty God.

Memorable Quote:
"Trust that God has packed creation with enough resources and people that can be used by God to provide for me, even if I don't store it up for myself. The way to join that divine economy of support is through generosity."

Journaling Suggestion:
Lord, create in me a self-awareness of anything I am holding back and which stops me from living freely and generously in You.

Memo for Meditation:
"One person gives freely, yet gains even more; another withholds unduly, but comes to poverty. A generous person will prosper; whoever refreshes others will be refreshed." Proverbs 11:14,25
"Freely you have received; freely give." Matthew 10:8

July 22

Motivational Idea: From scarcity to abundance (2)

We worry if we will have enough. Gisle Sorli, a financial planner who works with some of the wealthiest people in the world says, *"Paradoxically, this 'scarcity mindset' often increases as wealth increases. Families with massive resources start placing their trust in the provision, not the provider."* Gisle refers to a couple in their 80s, worth over $20 million. After spending time with them planning for their future, Gisle thought it was all sorted but suddenly the woman of the couple blurted out, *"What if I get a chronic illness?"* She was worried about running out of money, a prime example of scarcity with no abundance.

The French philosopher, Jean-Paul Sartre, in his book *The Critique of Dialectical Reason*, observes that scarcity is the overriding rule of life. Reflecting on the philosophy of Marx, Aristotle, Plato and Kant, he concludes that the fundamental issue of human existence is scarcity when you examine it from a purely physical realm. As Christians, we're not looking at life from a purely physical realm, we are to live in the spiritual realm which impacts on the physical realm. Gisle says, *"It is important to remind ourselves over and over how God has provided in the past."*

The miracle of the feeding of the five thousand is a great lesson for us to learn. Matthew records that the disciples viewed life through the lens of scarcity: *"We only have five loaves and two fish."* (Matthew 14:13-21). If we do what the disciples did that day, we will view life through the lens of scarcity; we will always be fearful and anxious. We could say that the disciples should have exercised faith and believed that Jesus was able to meet the needs of every person that day, but that would be hypocritical because we tend to be like the disciples and our faith can be severely lacking when faced with future uncertainty. So how do we live the abundant life Jesus promises? We need to focus on God, the God of abundance, who promises to always meet our every need.

Memorable Quote:
"We are human. We fail to remember what God has done and therefore what he is capable of doing presently. It is important to remind ourselves over and over how God has provided in the past. That could be why 'remember' is one of the overarching themes of Scripture, occurring some 269 times because God knows how easily we forget. Our definition and understanding of whatever 'scarcity' and 'abundance' means is shaped by remembering who God is, what God cares about, and how God does things. And that shapes our trust and confidence." Gisle Sorli

Journaling Suggestion:
Lord, enable me to live with an abundance mindset and leave behind the old scarcity mindset.

Memo for Meditation:
"And God is able to bless you abundantly, so that in all things at all times, having all that you need, you will abound in every good work." 2 Corinthians 9:8

July 23

Motivational Idea: From scarcity to abundance (3)

Do we view our lives through the lens of scarcity? Are we afraid we will not have enough time or resources? Will we have enough money to provide for our families? This is the scarcity mindset and it's common to every class and creed, and even for those who have more than enough financial resources it is still a common outlook. How do we square this scarcity paradigm with the words of Jesus when he referred to Himself as the Good Shepherd? He has emphatically said that as far as His sheep are concerned, He came to give us life – life more abundantly (see John 10.10, KJV). The NLT renders the text, *"The thief's purpose is to steal and kill and destroy. My purpose is to give them a rich and satisfying life."*

We know that the thief is the enemy of our souls and our wellbeing – Satan himself. He does not want us to live a happy, fulfilled life, rather he wants to destroy us, and one of the tools in his toolbox is the scarcity mindset. If he can get us to take our eyes off the Good Shepherd, he will not rob us of our eternal security, but he will have succeeded in robbing us of the blessed life we can enjoy here on earth with an abundant mindset. When we think of our Shepherd, we are reminded of the words of the psalmist David in the best known Psalm in the bible: *"The Lord is my shepherd, I shall not want."* (Psalm 23:1. KJV). *"The LORD is my shepherd, I lack nothing."* NIV. *"The LORD is my shepherd; I have all that I need".* (NLT). *"The LORD is my Shepherd [to feed, to guide and to shield me], I shall not want."* (AMP).

When we fix our eyes on Jesus and realise that He is the God of infinite resources, then we can enjoy the abundance He has for us. We need to turn our eyes upon Jesus. Our scarcity becomes abundance when we hand all over to Him and allow Him to take control. David's testimony was, *"Once I was young, and now I am old. Yet I have never seen the godly abandoned or their children begging for bread."* (Psalm 37:25). If we set our minds on things that are above, the attitude of our hearts and the perspective of our gaze will be totally different– we will live in abundance. We will enjoy our lives differently than other people. We will be fearless, with an abundant mindset focused on our Creator and provider, our shield and our defender.

Memorable Quote:
"We serve the king of Kings who has abundance at his disposal." Author

Journaling Suggestion:
Look to the LORD and his strength; seek his face always.

Memo for Meditation:
"GOD, my shepherd! I don't need a thing. You have bedded me down in lush meadows, you find me quiet pools to drink from. True to your word, you let me catch my breath and send me in the right direction." Psalm 23:1-2

July 24

Motivational Idea: Moving from scarcity to abundance (4)

In I Kings 17:7-16, we find the Prophet Elijah who encounters the widow of Zarephath. She is about to run out of food, but because she submitted to Elijah's request to feed him, her small amount of flour and olive oil never ran out. She went from scarcity to abundance because she put God first. The key message from the God of the Bible is: *"Put the resources in my hand and see what I can do with it."* We can transition to this place of insight, and scarcity becomes abundance. The disciples transitioned to this insight. So should we! This is not advocating the prosperity Gospel – 'Trust God and get rich quick.' This is about living the abundant life where we have enough and we live in the realm of the Kingdom of God where all the glorious riches of grace are ours in Christ Jesus. If you haven't yet tapped into this spiritual dimension, if it's foreign to you, then why not ask God to reveal it to you? This is not some modern day gnostic cultish idea; it's open to the whosoever will may come. *"The Spirit and the Bride say, "Come. And let the one who hears say, 'Come.' And let the one who is thirsty come; let the one who desires take the water of life without price."* (Revelation 22:17).

Memorable Quote:
"Pride must die in you, or nothing of heaven can live in you. Here is the path to the higher life: down, lower down! Just as water always seeks and fills the lowest place, so the moment God finds men (and women) abased and empty, His glory and power flow in to exalt and to bless." Andrew Murray

Journaling Suggestion:
Pursuing the path to the higher life.

Memo for Meditation:

"Hey there! All who are thirsty, come to the water! Are you penniless? Come anyway—buy and eat! Come, buy your drinks, buy wine and milk. Buy without money—everything's free! Why do you spend your money on junk food, your hard-earned cash on cotton candy? Listen to me, listen well: Eat only the best, fill yourself with only the finest. Pay attention, come close now, listen carefully to my life-giving, life-nourishing words. I'm making a lasting covenant commitment with you, the same that I made with David: sure, solid, enduring love. I set him up as a witness to the nations, made him a prince and leader of the nations, And now I'm doing it to you: You'll summon nations you've never heard of, and nations who've never heard of you will come running to you Because of me, your GOD, because The Holy of Israel has honoured you." Seek GOD while he's here to be found, pray to him while he's close at hand. Let the wicked abandon their way of life and the evil their way of thinking. Let them come back to GOD, who is merciful, come back to our God, who is lavish with forgiveness." Isaiah 55:1-7

July 25

Motivational Idea: The true meaning of abundance

We are serving the King of Kings who has abundance at his disposal. After the feeding of the five thousand, there are twelve baskets full of food leftover. The leftovers of the abundance of the kingdom are far greater than the scarcity the world offers. Oftentimes abundance is confused with having all our material desires met. In Scripture, abundance is God's sufficiency. Being close to Jesus, giving him what we have, and trusting him to provide for what we need is the way to go. His abundance is sufficient, enough.

This truth of abundance is difficult to apply to daily life. We do worry about our daily bread, especially in a cost of living crisis. Will we have enough money for the future? Will it be heat or eat? We pray, *"Give us our daily bread."* We must take our needs to God and ask Him to meet our needs. He has promised to do so. But we also need to intentionally think about our spiritual wellbeing. We need to focus on staying close to Jesus, listening to Him, and obeying what He tells us to do.

There are many lessons from Scripture to teach us about living in the abundant sufficiency of what God has for us. This is one of the reasons we need to read the Bible. The Apostle Paul reminds us, *"For everything that was written in the past was written to teach us, so that through the endurance taught in the Scriptures and the encouragement they provide we might have hope."* (Romans 15.4). Remember Elijah in 1 Kings 17? Elijah told King Ahab that the Lord was sending a drought. God led Elijah to a dry land called Cherith, east of the Jordan (see 1 Kings 17:3). He tells Elijah that he will drink from the brook and ravens will give him food (see 1 Kings 17:4). Elijah boldly and confidently obeyed the voice of God in an unknown circumstance. So many times we find ourselves anxious about the unknowns of this earthly journey. However, the story of the ravens feeding Elijah gives us great hope that our God is omniscient, and He is in control. Our God sees things that we do not see from our narrow point of view. Our God loves us more than we will ever know this side of Heaven. May we have the courage like Elijah to follow the Lord's leading and trust His purposes.

Memorable Quote:
"The sooner I learn to forget myself in the desire that He may be glorified, the richer will be the blessing that prayer will bring to myself. No one ever loses by what he sacrifices to the Father." Andrew Murray

Journaling Suggestion:
Jesus, I want to believe more in abundance! Help me with my unbelief.

Memo for Meditation:
"For we live by faith, not by sight." 2 Corinthians 5:7
"Trust in the Lord with all your heart and lean not on your own understanding; in all your ways submit to him, and he will make your paths straight." Proverbs 3:5-6

July 26

Motivational Idea: Honesty connects us to abundance

Relationships require honesty; if there is a lack of honesty, they will eventually break down, even if they teeter on for a time. Relationship with God requires honesty; God is honest with us and He expects us to be honest with Him. God is able to handle our deepest emotions and complaints. This is where the lament Psalms come into play. Lament is a major theme in the Bible, and particularly in the book of Psalms. The Psalms of lament express every aspect of human frailty and our daily struggles. They comprise the largest category of Psalms, making up about one third of the entire Psalter. These are prayers that lay out a troubling situation to the Lord and make a request for His help. Be encouraged today because these timeless, inspired writings are recorded for us so that we, too, can be totally honest with God. Don't sit in the pretence of a spiritual cocoon detached from reality! God wants us to tell Him exactly how we feel, and the lament is a way of expressing our vulnerability to Him. Psalm 42 is a case in point; it's a song about the writer's current state of hopelessness. The Psalm exudes deep sorrow and grief which is part of the tapestry of life. Furthermore, a meditation upon the Psalm shows that the writer is not even sure why he is so downcast and he does not understand why he has experienced so many curveballs. But he does something that we need to do; he goes to God and lays it all bare, expressing the deepest parts of his soul.

Now here is a lesson which may well be the most important thing that is said in this book on happiness and the fulfilled life: one of the purposes of the lament song/Psalm/prayer is to make a connection between the seeming hopelessness of life with the hope God gives. The lament acts like a bridge between the here and now and the timeless eternal hope of our everlasting God. We find the psalmist having made this connection; speaking to himself, he speaks to his own soul and encourages himself to continue to hope in God. He moves from hopelessness to hope, and to the abundance of God's promises for his life yet to be fulfilled. Not least, God is with him and is the constant in a world of chaos. From scarcity to abundance with the connexity of lament.

Memorable Quote:
"One of the main purposes of the lament song is to make a connection between the seeming hopelessness of life with the hope God gives. The progression is negativity, honesty, connexity and then positivity. Record, recount, remember, rest, rejoice. Move to songs of praise despite current circumstances." Author

Journaling Suggestion:
Take cognizance of the purpose of lament.

Memo for Meditation:

"Why are you cast down, O my soul, and why are you disquieted within me? Hope in God, for I shall again praise him, my help and my God." Psalm 42:11

July 27

Motivational Idea: The promises that you keep

The Scriptures are filled with the promises of God. The writer of *GotQuestions* says, *"In each promise, God pledges that something will (or will not) be done or given or come to pass. These are not flippant, casual promises such as we often make; these promises of God are rock-solid, unequivocal commitments made by God Himself. Because God is faithful, the recipients of the divine promises can have full assurance that what God has pledged will indeed be realised."* (Numbers 23:19).

The 19th century British preacher, Charles Spurgeon, said, *"All the purposes of man have been defeated, but not the purposes of God. He is a promise-keeping God, and every one of his people shall prove it to be so."* No purpose of God can be stopped; that is immensely wonderful news. God has proven Himself to be faithful throughout all of history. He has honoured His promises and kept His covenants even when we have broken ours. He consoles us when our plans go awry and He fills us with joy by knowing that His plans will never be stopped.

The great news of God's love for us sinful, broken people means happy and fulfilled lives; eternal destinies are changed forever as we hope in His promises. As followers of Jesus, united to Him by faith, God's promises are ours. *"For all the promises of God find their Yes in him. That is why it is through him that we utter our Amen to God for his glory."* (2 Corinthians 1:20). All God's promises are 'yes' in Christ, from the temporal promises of meeting our needs on a daily basis, to the eternal promises of glory in heaven, and every promise in between. God keeps all His promises, these promises are ours, and His plans will never be thwarted. So be encouraged today in your relationship with God, He will not fail you or let you down. What He has promised, He will deliver, and we await that final glorious promise when Jesus will return and He will make all things new.

Memorable Quote:
"The Bible is the story of a sovereign, loving, and promise-keeping God. God is reigning even when everything is a chaotic mess. God is loving even when life is painful and cruel. And God will keep His promises even when it seems impossible. God's promise to give Abraham and Sarah a son could not be stopped by old age. God's promise to deliver His people from slavery could not be stopped by a stubborn Pharaoh or his army. God's promise to send a messiah could not be stopped by murderous King Herod. These are a few of the many wonderful and seemingly impossible promises God has made." Noah S Crane

Journaling Suggestion:
Standing on the promises I shall not fail.

Memo for Meditation:
"You will keep in perfect peace those whose minds are steadfast, because they trust in you." Isaiah 26:3

July 28

Motivational Idea: They're all dead but one!

The founder of Taoism, Laozi Tzu, died in 286 BC. Siddhartha Gautama, commonly referred to as the Buddha, the founder of Buddhism, died in 483 BC. Muhammad, founder of Islam, died in 632 AD. And we could name a whole host of others who left the stage of history in a casket, as dead as dead could be. But there is one who stands out from the crowd, and His name is Jesus. Notice the dividing line of history. Christ's birth changed the entire course of history. We even separate history according to Jesus' birth (BC to AD)!

Jesus changed the world by entering history as the God-man, and He can change our lives as well. Jesus was born and lived, and then He died in the year 33 AD. But that was not the end; He rose bodily from the dead. Through His resurrection, He conquered death and the evil supernatural powers that oppose God. We have been rescued from the dominion of darkness. Forgiven in Christ, we have a new life in God's Kingdom. We can enjoy a personal intimate relationship with God through His beloved son. Jesus specifically made a way for us to have a personal relationship with Him. We can be free from our old ways. We have victory in the risen living Jesus. And the Spirit of God dwells within us, guiding us toward what God has planned for us as we walk in close communion with Him.

Memorable Quote:
"We live and die; Christ died and lived!" John Scott

Journaling Suggestion:
"For to me to live is Christ and to die is gain." Philippians 1:21

Memo for Meditation:
"God rescued us from dead-end alleys and dark dungeons. He's set us up in the kingdom of the Son he loves so much, the Son who got us out of the pit we were in, got rid of the sins we were doomed to keep repeating. We look at this Son and see the God who cannot be seen. We look at this Son and see God's original purpose in everything created. For everything, absolutely everything, above and below, visible and invisible, rank after rank after rank of angels—everything got started in him and finds its purpose in him. He was there before any of it came into existence and holds it all together right up to this moment. And when it comes to the church, he organises and holds it together, like a head does a body. He was supreme in the beginning and—leading the resurrection parade—he is supreme in the end. From beginning to end he's there, towering far above everything, everyone. So spacious is he, so expansive, that everything of God finds its proper place in him without crowding. Not only that, but all the broken and dislocated pieces of the universe—people and things, animals and atoms—get properly fixed and fit together in vibrant harmonies, all because of his death, his blood that poured down from the cross." Colossians 2:13-20

July 29

Motivational Idea: That's the spirit

Before Jesus left the disciples, He gave a promise to them and to us. Dr Luke records the conversation for us. *"So when the apostles were with Jesus, they kept asking him, 'Lord, has the time come for you to free Israel and restore our kingdom?' He replied, 'The Father alone has the authority to set those dates and times, and they are not for you to know. But you will receive power when the Holy Spirit comes upon you. And you will be my witnesses, telling people about me everywhere—in Jerusalem, throughout Judea, in Samaria, and to the ends of the earth.'"* (Acts 1:6-8).

In the Christian faith, the Holy Spirit is seen as the third person of the Holy Trinity, along with God the Father and God the Son, Jesus Christ. The Holy Trinity is the Christian understanding of the nature of God as three distinct persons in one divine essence. God in three persons, blessed Trinity. The Holy Spirit is God, the third Person of the Holy Trinity, who eternally 'proceeds' from the Father (John 15:26). The Holy Spirit is co-equal with the Father and the Son. The word 'Spirit' commonly translates the Greek New Testament word *pneuma*. Jesus did not leave us alone; He promised The Holy Spirit to each believer. The Holy Spirit indwells us and we are His temple (see 1 Corinthians 3:16). The Holy Spirit is our 'Counsellor' and 'Helper' (*paraclete* in Greek, guiding us in the way of the truth.) The 'Fruit of the Spirit' (the result of His work) is love, joy, peace, patience, kindness, goodness, faithfulness, gentleness and self-control (see Galatians 5:22). He, the person of the Holy Spirit, enables us to have an intimate relationship with God.

As we develop in our relationship with God, The Holy Spirit empowers us to live the way we were intended to live, to enjoy the happiness God intended us to have and the fulfilled life that is part of His plan for us. The Holy Spirit equips us with spiritual gifts to fulfil our purpose on earth and enables us to live according to God's will. Lean into the Holy Spirit and learn to listen to what He has to say.

Memorable Quote:
"Many people feel so pressured by the expectations of others that it causes them to be frustrated, miserable and confused about what they should do. But there is a way to live a simple, joy-filled, peaceful life, and the key is learning how to be led by the Holy Spirit, not the traditions or expectations of man." Joyce Meyer

Journaling Suggestion:
Holy Spirit, speak to me, lead me into all Truth, and empower me for Kingdom service.

Memo for Meditation:
"But the Helper, the Holy Spirit, whom the Father will send in my name, he will teach you all things and bring to your remembrance all that I have said to you." John 14:26

July 30

Motivational Idea: Why did He leave?

Why did Jesus leave? He came to earth and after thirty three and a half years He left. It does not seem to make sense at first, but Jesus explains the rationale behind it. John Piper says that Christ's physical absence from us is better for us than His physical presence in the world in this period of history, from the time of His ascension to heaven to the day of His return, the second advent. It does cause us to consider, as Pastor John puts it, *"What is God doing in the world, and why does he do it the way he does it?"* We would not understand unless He had told us; that's why we need to meditate on the Scriptures for it is the Scriptures that give us the answers.

Before His death, Jesus told the disciples the reason He was going away. *"Nevertheless, I tell you the truth: it is to your advantage that I go away, for if I do not go away, the Helper will not come to you."* Now we should ask, "Well, why not?" And let's watch what he says. *"But if I go, I will send him to you."* Now, here is what he's going to do: *"And when he comes, he will convict the world concerning sin and righteousness and judgement."* Then he unpacks what he means by those three things: *"Concerning sin, because they do not believe in me; concerning righteousness, because I go to the Father, and you will see me no longer; concerning judgement, because the ruler of this world is judged."* (John 16:7–11).

Jesus tells us that God's plan of redemption, whereby we can enter into a relationship with Him, involved the birth, life, death, resurrection and ascension of Jesus. Our memo for today contains the follow-on verses. John Piper says that John 16:14 is the most important sentence about the work of the Holy Spirit in the Bible: *"He will glorify me."* Specifically, the Holy Spirit glorifies Christ's resurrection glory and his achievements over sin and Satan on the cross. *"That's the peak, the apex of the glory of Christ in the gospel."* The Holy Spirit is here and He opens up to us the glories and wonder of the victor Jesus.

Memorable Quote:

"Couldn't the Spirit have come in full power while Christ was on the earth?" He could not have come in full Christ-exalting, gospel-applying, new-covenant-fulfilling, deepest sin-convicting, Satan-defeating power. All of those aspects of the power of the Holy Spirit's ministry are based on the death, the resurrection, and the triumphant ascension of Jesus to God's right hand as king." John Piper

Journaling Suggestion:

Spirit of God my teacher be, showing the things of Christ to me.

Memo for Meditation:

"Jesus said, 'I still have many things to say to you, but you cannot bear them now. When the Spirit of truth comes, he will guide you into all the truth, For he will not speak on his own authority, but whatever he hears he will speak, and he will declare to you the things that are to come. He will glorify me.'" John 16:12–14

July 31

Motivational Idea: The greatest influencer

Influence is a powerful force that can shape the course of history, culture and society. Throughout the ages, there have been individuals whose impact has transcended their lifetimes, leaving a lasting legacy on the world.

Here are some famous names of people throughout history who have shaped the world:

Galileo Galilei (1564-1642) **Cosmos**: his pioneering work in the early 17th century ignited a profound transformation in our comprehension of the cosmos.

Mary Wollstonecraft (1759-1797) **Advocacy**: she left her mark on women's rights advocacy.

Mahatma Gandhi (1869-1948) **Truth**: stands as an enduring symbol of non-violent resistance and civil disobedience. His philosophy of Satyagraha, which emphasised the power of truth and moral force, has left an indelible mark on the pages of history.

Albert Einstein (1879-1955) **Creation**: the renowned physicist reshaped our understanding of the universe with his theory of relativity.

Rosa Parks (1913-2005) **Equality**: the mother of the Civil Rights Movement, she played a pivotal role in the fight against racial segregation in the United States.

Nelson Mandela (1918-2013) **Justice**: his unwavering commitment to reconciliation and justice in a deeply divided nation played a critical role in ending apartheid and establishing a democratic South Africa. Mandela's legacy of forgiveness and leadership in the face of adversity serves as an inspiration for those working towards peace and justice worldwide.

Steve Jobs (1955-2011) **Communication**: the co-founder of Apple Inc. was a visionary entrepreneur and inventor. His groundbreaking products, such as the iPhone, Macintosh and iPod, revolutionised the way we communicate, work and entertain ourselves.

Malala Yousafzai (1997-present) **Rights**: is a Pakistani education activist who, at a young age, defied the Taliban's ban on girls' education and became a global advocate for girls' rights to education.

We can learn from great influencers, but the greatest influencer in our lives should be the Holy Spirit, who influences influencers (look at the words in bold), enables our access to God and our intimacy in our relationship with God, pointing us to Jesus, alive and supreme over all.

Memorable Quote:
"The major determinant of the Spirit's influence is how much of us we let Him consume, meaning how much of our lives we allow Him to control."

Journaling Suggestion:
I need to be under the influence of the greatest influencer – the Holy Spirit

Memo for Meditation:
"Do not get drunk on wine, which leads to debauchery. Instead, be filled with the Spirit." Ephesians 5:15-20

THE ATTITUDINAL DIMENSION

August 1

Motivational idea: Rose-coloured glasses

The phrase 'seeing the world through rose-coloured glasses' means that a person has a positive attitude and has an outlook of super optimism. The origins of the phrase are unclear but what we do know is that in the 1700's 'rose' and 'rosy' meant to be optimistic about outcomes. Samuel Pepys (1633-1703), a 17th-century member of the British parliament and diarist, didn't wear rose-coloured spectacles, rather he used green-lensed glasses made by spectacle maker John Turlington to alleviate sore eyes in the winter of 1666 which he believed was caused from working by candlelight. This fits with the colour theory that tinted-glass lenses can be used as a therapeutic device to treat many ailments. Having a positive attitude has been shown to benefit wellbeing. We look forward to the future with optimism. People with a positive attitude tend to work harder and are more cooperative, simply because they believe in good outcomes.

The opposite is the case for the person with a negative attitude; they are pessimistic about the future and make negative and unstable decisions that in turn badly affect the outcomes of their lives. Tali Sharot, writing about the effects of optimism on the brain, says, *"Anticipating something wonderful seems to activate the same neural systems as experiencing it."* The Bible says much about negative and positive attitudes. Elizabeth Peale Allen says, *"Philippians 4:8 provides a foolproof strategy to keep your thoughts positive and God-centred: 'From now on, brothers and sisters, if anything is excellent and if anything is admirable, focus your thoughts on these things: all that is true, all that is holy, all that is just, all that is pure, all that is lovely, and all that is worthy of praise.' Sure, negative thinking is powerful. But it can't begin to stand up to the faith-filled joy and hope God wants to give you. Read your Bible. Claim its promises. Let its truths trample negative thoughts. Think positive!"*

Memorable Quote:
"An attitude is like a pair of glasses that each of us wears. Just like glasses can be tinted to make the world look darker or brighter, our attitudes colour the way we see things around us. Imagine going through life with rainbow-coloured glasses that make everything seem exciting! Or think about wearing grey-tinted glasses that turn everything dull and boring. That's what attitudes do—they shape how we feel, act, and even how others see us." Practical Psychology

Journaling Suggestion:
Ac-cent-tchu-ate the positive, e-lim-i-nate the negative.

Memo for Meditation:
"Finally, brothers and sisters, whatever is true, whatever is noble, whatever is right, whatever is pure, whatever is lovely, whatever is admirable—if anything is excellent or praiseworthy—think about such things." Philippians 4:8

August 2

Motivational Idea: Identify determines attitude

We choose our attitude from our feelings and beliefs about ourselves. Our identity determines the value we place on ourselves and others. Darla Colinet names two potential value extremes. One is that we think we are less than others, undeserving of anything good, and if we do experience something good, bad things are waiting round the corner to destroy it. *"Our false identity is formed from comparing ourselves to others and painful devaluing experiences that have skewed our self perception."* We live in a constant self-fix-it mode and our false identity causes us to live in a state of desperation with a negative attitude to life. The second extreme is the belief that we are better than everyone else. *"We become arrogant, entitled, a bully, a mean person, narcissistic, and abusive. Living in this mindset and identity is at the centre of the devil and man's fall. The fall of both comes from the sin of pride."*

We think the universe revolves around us. Darla says that one of the greatest revelations in her life was when she realised that her true identity was in Christ. We need to do the same; our Christ identity is not affected by who we believed ourselves to be in the past. The best way to get and keep a positive attitude is to realise that we are rooted in Christ, and to allow the Spirit of God to shape us. Identify the lies, shift perspective and declare what is true in your Christ identity.

Memorable Quote:
"If you proclaim to be Christ's disciple, but you are living in this devaluing false identity, you haven't learned and accepted who you are, a miracle created by the hands of God himself. Although you have received Salvation, you will not instantly know who you are in Christ as a new creation. You will need to grow your relationship by studying God's word and Christ's life to know who you are in Christ." Darla Colinet

Journaling Suggestion:
Time to get rid of the false narrative, I tell myself.

Memo for Meditation:
"Those who think they can do it on their own end up obsessed with measuring their own moral muscle but never get around to exercising it in real life. Those who trust God's action in them find that God's Spirit is in them—living and breathing God! Obsession with self in these matters is a dead end; attention to God leads us out into the open, into a spacious, free life. Focusing on the self is the opposite of focusing on God. Anyone completely absorbed in self ignores God, ends up thinking more about self than God. That person ignores who God is and what he is doing. And God isn't pleased at being ignored." Romans 8:5-8

August 3

Motivational Idea: 'Make yourself happy'

Clarke University sits on a bluff in a quiet residential area overlooking the city of Dubuque, Iowa (population 58,000), and the Mississippi River. Their website contains a wonderful section on 'Developing a Positive Attitude', with an interesting subtext, 'Make Yourself Happy'. Remember as a child being reprimanded by a parent? *"You are just making yourself miserable and everyone else along with you."* We can't recall being told, *"Make yourself happy."* It's a novel idea but Clarke adds weight to the concept by reminding us: *"Your mind is a powerful thing. If you allow yourself to keep a positive state of mind, your attitude will follow."*

Prospective students are then given some ideas as to how to develop positive attitudes and behaviours. First up is, 'Listen to your internal dialogue.' Become aware of your self-talk. More often than not our thoughts about ourselves can be negative in nature, so when faced with a negative thought, turn it around to make it into a positive thought.

Secondly, 'Interact within positive environments and with positive people.' Do things with people who reinforce you in a positive way. Go places that have special meaning and positive memories or associations. Seek out positive people. Be aware of negative people and the toxicity they bring with them. Seek out positive role models that will boost you and reinforce the positive in life.

Thirdly, 'Volunteer.' Do something that will help others. This will give you a sense of fulfilment and make you feel happy inside. Look up the five-a-day for mental wellbeing.

Fourthly, 'Get pleasure out of the simple things in life.' Laughter is one of the most powerful mood enhancers. Allow yourself to laugh.

Fifthly, 'Permit yourself to be loved.' Everyone deserves to be loved. Everyone is loved. One of Clarke University's core values is freedom. *"As a community seeking to live authentic lives, we invite all to be open to God's love and to be true to their best selves."* Perhaps it's time to stop making ourselves miserable and start making ourselves happy by starting to utilise some of the suggested ideas as to how to develop positive attitudes and behaviours.

Memorable Quote:
"If you think you are beaten, you are; If you think you dare not, you don't; If you want to win but think you can't; It's almost a cinch you won't. If you think you'll lose, you're lost; For out of the world we find Success begins with a person's will; It's all in a state of mind. Life's battles don't always go To the stronger and faster human, But sooner or later the people who win Are the ones who think they can." Walter D Windle

Journaling Suggestion:
I can make myself happy or sad. Today I choose happiness!

Memo for Meditation:
"I know that there is nothing better for people than to be happy and to do good while they live." Ecclesiastes 3:12

August 4

Motivational Idea: Why do attitudes matter?

An attitude isn't just a random thought that pops into our heads; rather, it's a mental habit. We need to view our attitude as a habit. It's the way we think or feel about all manner of things. Attitudes matter because they have implications for every aspect of our lives. Our attitudes are both about the big things and the small things; they can range from what we think about science and faith, to our attitudes about red or brown sauce. Attitudes have been described as magnets, drawing us to the positive or the negative. Our attitude impacts our relationships with others. If we have a positive attitude about certain people, we are likely to be drawn towards them. If we have a negative attitude about them, we'll probably avoid them.

Do we see the best in others or the worst? Are people drawn to us because of our attitude or are they crossing the street when they see us because we have a critical, judgmental attitude and therefore they avoid us like the plague? Another reason our attitudes matter is because they influence and shape not only the way we relate to others but every aspect of our behaviours. How do we feel about work? How do we feel about helping others? What about our personal responsibilities? Our citizenship and our civic responsibility? Are we good Samaritans or modern-day pharisees?

Understanding our attitudes helps us to understand ourselves, and that's where we can begin to consider personal growth, developing and improving ourselves. The good news is we can change our mental habits from the negative to the positive. It's a choice, and with God's help we can.

Memorable Quote:

"Attitudes can either add a sparkle or a cloud to your personal happiness. Imagine waking up every day feeling that the world is full of possibilities. Sounds great, doesn't it? But if you wake up thinking everything is

terrible, you're setting yourself up for a day that's likely to be, well, not so great." Practical Psychology

Journaling Suggestion:
Mental note: attitude is a mental habit that I have developed and can be changed.

Memo for Meditation:
"A man was going down from Jerusalem to Jericho, when he was attacked by robbers. They stripped him of his clothes, beat him and went away, leaving him half dead. A priest happened to be going down the same road, and when he saw the man, he passed by on the other side. So too, a Levite, when he came to the place and saw him, passed by on the other side. But a Samaritan, as he travelled, came where the man was; and when he saw him, he took pity on him. He went to him and bandaged his wounds, pouring on oil and wine. Then he put the man on his own donkey, brought him to an inn and took care of him. The next day he took out two denarii and gave them to the innkeeper. 'Look after him,' he said, 'and when I return, I will reimburse you for any extra expense you may have.' "Which of these three do you think was a neighbour to the man who fell into the hands of robbers?" The expert in the law replied, "The one who had mercy on him." Jesus told him, "Go and do likewise." Luke 10.25-37

August 5

Motivational Idea: The origins of attitudes

Our attitudes didn't just happen. They came from somewhere, but where did they come from? How were they formed? It's important for us to seek to understand how they came about as this will help us to see not only the force they are in terms of our behaviours and actions, but how we can modify them if they lead us into toxic relationships and maladaptive coping strategies.

We need to look back to our early and informative years. This is where the powerful mindsets we have today came to life. Early life experiences have most likely shaped our attitudes, and even our personality. Our environment will have played a part in our development and our outlook on life. Bad experiences can lead to negative attitudes. A harsh, deprivation approach by our parents/carers will have had a negative impact, whereas a caring, loving and embracing approach will have helped to form positive attitudes. By observing others, and especially role models and those we looked up to, will have not only caused us to copy their actions but also to adapt their attitudes. As we grow up, we make friends and our peers can have a big impact on the attitudinal dimension. To fit in and to be part of the crowd, we will adopt similar attitudes to them. Don't underestimate the power of peer pressure. We now live in a social media world of overexposure to all kinds of things and all kinds of people. Then there is the type of films we watch, the content on line, and the music we listen to. This all impacts our attitudes. The lessons for today are to be aware of how powerful attitudes are, where they may have come from, and what is shaping them today. Self-mastery and self-awareness means we can get to choose the attitude we're going to have every single day.

Memorable Quote:
"Your attitude, not your aptitude, will determine your altitude. People may hear your words, but they feel your attitude. You cannot (always) control what happens to you, but you can control your attitude toward what happens to you, and in that, you will be mastering change rather than allowing it to master you." Zig Ziglar

Journaling Suggestion:
I don't have to stay in the straightjacket of attitudes formed from the multiplicity of negative and toxic influences on my life. I can break free with God's help and influence.

Memo for Meditation:
"Do nothing out of selfish ambition or vain conceit. Rather, in humility value others above yourselves, not looking to your own interests but each of you to the interests of the others. In your relationships with one another, have the same attitude as Christ Jesus. Who, being in very nature God, did not consider equality with God something to be used to his own advantage; rather, he made himself nothing by taking the very nature of a servant, being made in human likeness."
See Philippians 2:3-11

August 6

Motivational Idea: It's a recipe but what are the ingredients?

Think of your attitude as a recipe with different ingredients. A positive attitude will have certain ingredients, as will a negative one. If we see our attitude as having certain ingredients, then just like recipes can be changed so we can change the ingredients.

Practical Psychology gives us four ingredients we find in the positive attitude. Firstly, we find 'Optimism'. Optimists see challenges through the lens of opportunity rather than an insurmountable obstacle mentality. Research shows that optimistic students get better results, and optimistic athletes perform better. Optimists tend to live longer and are happier.

Secondly, we have the ingredient of 'Gratitude' – the attitude of gratitude. The grateful person will be thankful for what they have, not catastrophize about what they don't have. Dr Robert Emmons, a leading expert on gratitude, says that this attitude can make you happier and even improve your physical health.

Thirdly, we have the ingredient of 'Enthusiasm'. The person with a positive attitude gets excited about what they are doing. The psychologist Mihaly Csikszentmihalyi talks about the 'flow state' to explain that when you're enthusiastic, you're more likely to be 'in the zone' or in a state of flow. This means you'll perform better and enjoy what you're doing a whole lot more. Thomas A Edison said, *"I never did a day's work in my life. It was all fun."*

Fourthly, 'Open-mindedness'. The Practical Psychology people refer to the work of psychologist Carol Dweck who says this aligns with a 'growth mindset' – *"the belief that abilities and intelligence can be developed through hard work and dedication."* Open-minded people are like explorers, always looking for new things to learn and new ways to grow. They're more likely to take on challenges, seek out new experiences, and even change their minds when presented with new information.

Memorable Quote:

"Open-mindedness opens doors to opportunities and helps you get along with people who think differently than you do." Practical Psychology

Journaling Suggestion:
"Resolve to keep happy, and your joy and you shall form an invincible host against difficulties." Helen Keller. That's my resolve today, going forward.

Memo for Meditation:
"I'm glad in God, far happier than you would ever guess - happy that you're again showing such strong concern for me. Not that you ever quit praying and thinking about me. You just had no chance to show it. Actually, I don't have a sense of needing anything personally. I've learned by now to be quite content whatever my circumstances. I'm just as happy with little as with much, with much as with little. I've found the recipe for being happy whether full or hungry, hands full or hands empty. Whatever I have, wherever I am, I can make it through anything in the One who makes me who I am. I don't mean that your help didn't mean a lot to me - it did. It was a beautiful thing that you came alongside me in my troubles." Philippians 4:10-14

August 7

Motivational Idea: Different recipe, different ingredients

Today we turn to the ingredients that pertain to the negative attitude. The guys from Practical Psychology have identified four elements.

Firstly, 'Pessimism' raises its ugly head. This is 'the glass is half empty' viewpoint. Dr Martin Seligman observes that pessimists are more likely to suffer from stress and poor health compared to optimists. Pessimists often feel helpless and may give up more easily when faced with challenges. Having an awareness of this way of thinking helps us to challenge this mindset, and our goal is to identify these negative thought-patterns and replace them with more positive and realistic ones.

Second up is 'Cynicism.' *"If something seems too good to be true, it probably is."* That's a classic cynical thought. Ralph Waldo Emerson said, *"A cynic can chill and dishearten with a single word."* Cynicism is arguably the most toxic of the negative attitude ingredients. Cynicism can lead to social isolation because you don't trust anyone and you are always sceptical. Being aware of our cynicism can help us to change and look for the good instead of the bad.

Thirdly, we find 'Apathy' lurking in the negative mindset. Apathy is about having a lack of interest or concern, a decreased desire to take action, engage with others, or find meaning in life. Then fourthly we have 'Negativity' itself. Negativity is like that cloud that follows you around, raining on your parade. It's a general attitude of expecting the worst and finding faults in everything. Research has shown that a constant negative attitude can create a 'negativity spiral', making it hard to experience positive emotions. Being aware of this spiral, we can then start to challenge it with positive affirmations, being able to build positive experiences into our life to balance out the negative ones. The good news is these, too, are ingredients and we can change them. The life manual as set out in our memo for today gives us the key. Be like a healthy tree, not a dead one!

Memorable Quote:
"What is a cynic? A man who knows the price of everything and the value of nothing." Oscar Wilde

Journaling Suggestion:
Time to hound out all that negative stuff and be free to a positive influence in the world!

Memo for Meditation:
"Oh, the joys of those who do not follow the advice of the wicked, or stand around with sinners, or join in with mockers. But they delight in the law of the LORD, meditating on it day and night. They are like trees planted along the riverbank, bearing fruit each season. Their leaves never wither, and they prosper in all they do. But not the wicked! They are like worthless chaff, scattered by the wind. They will be condemned at the time of judgement. Sinners will have no place among the godly. For the LORD watches over the path of the godly, but the path of the wicked leads to destruction." Psalm 1

August 8

Motivational Idea: The mindset of mixed attitudes

Having considered the positive and negative nature of attitudes, we now turn our attention to 'mixed' attitudes. The person whose mindset tends to be of the mixed attitudes variety has a number of ingredients, the first being, 'Scepticism'. Sceptics don't believe things easily and look for conclusive evidence. It's your detective stance. In many ways, healthy scepticism is a good thing as it can save us from falling for scams and believing fake news. On the other hand, we need to carefully manage our scepticism as it can tip the other way so that we are devoid of any trust and our minds are closed to new experiences and adventures. *"Scepticism, in moderation, can be your friend, helping you navigate the world thoughtfully. But taken to an extreme, it can limit your experiences and keep you stuck in a mental rut."* (Practical Psychology)

The second element that usually exists in the mixed attitude mindset is 'Ambivalence'. We find ourselves with conflicting attitudes about something or someone, and we find decision-making tough: 'Should I stay or should I go?' We are on the fence and not sure which way to jump! Our decision-making becomes complicated, but there is a positive side to ambivalence – we can weigh up options and not rush into unwise and regrettable decisions.

A third element that we can name is 'Curiosity'. This can be a very positive experience as we have a desire to know how things work, a healthy thirst to learn and to explore new territory. The Practical Psychology guys refer to Dr Todd Kashdan, who has researched curiosity extensively. He argues that curiosity can increase our wellbeing and add richness to our lives. But, again, like scepticism, we need balance as, too much curiosity can lead to risk and danger.

Our fourth element is 'Realism'. This is about seeking the truth without pretence. A realistic attitude can prepare us for challenges and even improve performance. One of the key words for today is balance and this pertains to realism too. Too much of it and we end up with a negative view of the world, and see only the unfairness and injustice of it all. We need to see the whole tapestry of life.

Memorable Quote:
"We need healthy realism; think of it as the salt cellar on your dinner table; a pinch of salt will add some flavour to your dinner, but too much and you will ruin it." Adapted by author

Journaling Suggestion:
Balance and moderation in the mindset of mixed attitudes.

Memo for Meditation:
"Cynics look high and low for wisdom - and never find it; the open-minded find it right on their doorstep! Escape quickly from the company of fools; they're a waste of your time, a waste of your words. The wisdom of the wise keeps life on track; the foolishness of fools lands them in the ditch. The stupid ridicule right and wrong, but a moral life is a favoured life." Proverbs 14:6-9

August 9

Motivational Idea: Ways to change your attitudes

If you have ever undertaken a time of reflection, you may have stumbled across some attitudes that you are not proud of. The author has had this experience and found unjustified criticism and negativity towards some people. So how can we change our attitudes?

Firstly, we need 'Self-awareness'. Times of self-reflection will help to cultivate and heighten our self-awareness. Our internal monitor will kick in when that negative attitude goes into action, and we will get a prompt to remind us to exchange it for the positive. It works and our interventions will help us to change. *"Self-awareness is the cornerstone of emotional intelligence and can really help you understand your attitudes."* (Dr Daniel Goleman).

Secondly, 'Journaling'. Keep a journal of your thoughts. Write down at the end of your day three good things about your day. Aaron Beck, the father of CBT, did this with depressed patients, and in three months their attitudes had dramatically changed. Focusing on positive things every day caused a shift in the negative mindset, produced positivity and a more positive outlook on life.

Thirdly, 'Goal-setting'. What do you want to achieve? Set realistic goals and write them down. Set SMART goals: 'specific, measurable, achievable and timely/time bound'.

Fourthly, 'Support network'. We were never meant to plough a lonely furrow – we need community, we need each other. Not necessarily a whole crew to man your ship on the sea of life, but a few true reliable friends who are there for us, through thick and thin.

Fifthly, the experts recommend 'Meditation'. The reason we have a memo for meditation each day is to remind us that we need to meditate on Scripture because it is unlike any other book in the world; it is inspired by God and He speaks to us through it. He enables us to reflect. He can help us in our journal writing as well as setting good goals for our lives in the context of His will as He desires us to be happy and lead a fulfilled life. He is our greatest support and we need to meditate not only on His woes but also upon Him.

Memorable Quote:
"The most important thing you'll ever wear is your attitude." Jeff Moore

Journaling Suggestion:
Today I will begin to record three positive things about my day and do this consistently for weeks.

Mem for Meditation:
"But that's no life for you. You learned Christ! My assumption is that you have paid careful attention to him, been well instructed in the truth precisely as we have it in Jesus. Since, then, we do not have the excuse of ignorance, everything—and I do mean everything—connected with that old way of life has to go. It's rotten through and through. Get rid of it! And then take on an entirely new way of life—a God-fashioned life, a life renewed from the inside and working itself into your conduct as God accurately reproduces His character in you." Ephesians 4:22-24

August 10

Motivational Idea: Attitudes to watch out for – arrogance

'Arrogance' is overbearing pride or haughtiness; a sense of one's own importance that shows itself in a proud and insulting way. You see this behaviour exhibited in a person when they feel that they are more important than other people, are rude and don't consider others; unfeeling! Arrogance comes from the Latin *arrogans* which means not only to be overbearing and proud but also insolent and offensive to others. We find it in 1300 from the old French *arrogance* which is defined as 'a manifest feeling of superiority of one's worth or importance, combined with contempt of others'.

But why are people arrogant? Are *we* arrogant? Are we *perceived* as arrogant? What might be the root causes? The root cause of arrogance will vary depending on the arrogant person. For some, it could be a sense of insecurity, for others a sense of superiority. Low self-esteem may be a key factor for some or the fear of competition for others. Arrogance may come from a lack of self-awareness as some arrogant people cannot see their weaknesses and exaggerate their strengths. Arrogance for some people could be a case of masking up their fears. This can often be seen as a form of overcompensation that can create serious issues for every aspect of life, not least relationships.

The arrogant individual may be lacking or not well aware of certain abilities which creates a sense of superiority just to make up for their perceived flaws. Arrogance becomes their defence mechanism which allows them to hide how they really feel inside and so they display their greater superiority, totally disregarding the feelings or opinions of others. It is a negative trait and it can be horrible to be on the receiving end of such behaviour. In our own self reflections, as we seek to grow in self-awareness, we may find that we, too, have our own bitter flavour of arrogance lurking, which we need to deal with. The root approach will help us. As we learn about the roots and shoots of arrogance in ourselves, we can begin to deal with it and be aware of the arrogant people we meet and what makes them tick, tick, tick! But remember that confidence isn't arrogance.

Memorable Quote:
"Keeping your ego within the bounds of humility. Many of us have to keep our egos in check. Your ego is both a valuable asset and a potential major liability that can bring your life to ruin. To make sure you keep it as a valuable asset, you need to keep it within the bounds of humility. Then it allows for high performance, healthy confidence, and an elevated level of gravitas. On the other hand, ego without humility becomes pride and turns from superpower to kryptonite."

Journaling Suggestion:
Keeping my ego within the bounds of humility!

Memo for Meditation:
"I thank you God that I am not as others are." Check out Luke 18:9-14

August 11

Motivational Idea: Attitudes to watch out for – defeatist

The person with a defeatist attitude lives in the land of negativity. This is the type of person who gives up even before trying. The defeatist will seek to drag you down, and their toxicity and negativity will impact everyone around them. We want to live in a world of hope and optimism but the defeatist is the opposite of the optimist. A defeatist will be convinced that they are going to fail, and are not surprised when they do.

Defeatism is like a form of paralysis. If you are unfortunate enough to have such a person in your circle, they will spread despair and bring you down with them. The advice is *"When you find a defeatist, run away as this attitude can be quite contagious."* At this point we are probably asking ourselves, 'Am I defeatist?' If we have these tendencies, we need to renew our minds and get rid of this debilitating mindset. The defeatist will always find a million different ways to fail. We need to take stock, and if we find that people in our world exhibit this kind of behaviour, we need to consider how to either challenge this, reduce contact with them, or remove ourselves altogether.

It's difficult when it is a family member and this has been their way of being all their life. To disconnect psychologically is possible and we need to learn to disregard their toxic defeatism. We need to surround ourselves with people who look for a million ways to succeed rather than the opposite.

Remember that defeatists come up with problems, not solutions. Defeatists are experts in defeatism techniques but will use the defence mechanism of projection and blame others – they may blame *you*. When you take the initiative and come up with solutions, you may well hear the well-worn defeatist phrase, *'We tried it before and it didn't* work.' Choose to change the language, *'We will win.' 'We will get it done.' 'We are on the winning side.'*

Be aware that the defeatist attitude is a self-limiting behaviour and toxic for anyone, any team or group that wants to achieve something big or challenge the norm. If defeatism is dragging you down, remember the road may be hard but it's worthwhile. The experts tell us to learn to reroute our self-talk; challenge it as well as facing head on those notions of failure by identifying which emotions are holding us back. And don't forget to celebrate the small wins, too. Remember, you are a winner!

Memorable Quote:
"I'm not going to take this defeatist attitude and listen to all this crap any more from all these people who have nothing except doomsday to predict." Carroll Shelby

Journaling Suggestion:
Root out defeatism and get on with my life's purpose undaunted.

Memo for Meditation:
"This is the day of the LORD's victory; let us be happy, let us celebrate! Save us, LORD, save us! Give us success, O LORD! May God bless the one who comes in the name of the LORD!" See Psalm 118: 24-29, the Psalm of Victory

---

August 12

Motivation Idea: Attitudes to watch out for – unbelief

Victor Meldrew, played by Richard Wilson in the British television sitcom, *One Foot in the Grave*, had a catchphrase that once heard is hard to forget: *"I don't believe it!"* When faced with a difficulty or an unexpected problem, Victor, with his usual melodrama, declares with the greatest of emphasis, *"I don't believe it!"* He would exhibit a state of disbelief in relation to the scenario he would find himself immersed in. His long-suffering wife, Margaret, played by Annette Crosbie, would then seek to calm him down. We can laugh at the shenanigans of the main character but we can probably identify with him in so many ways. We too can find ourselves in a state of disbelief when life turns up some unexpected surprises.

On a serious note, the term 'unbelief' is usually related to matters of faith and belief in God. The Bible has much to say about unbelief and it comes with a health warning. In Hebrews, the warning is given to believers. It's a contradiction in terms but believers can sometimes be unbelieving believers. Here is the warning: *"Take care, brothers and sisters, that there not be in any one of you a wicked, unbelieving heart [which refuses to trust and rely on the Lord, a heart] that turns away from the living God."* The context concerns Israel and the lesson is not to repeat the mistakes that they made. Israel lost faith in God. They gave in to fear, and that led to disobedience and stubbornness. They did not 'hold fast' and they missed out on God's blessing. This is one of the toxic attitudes we need to avoid. Let's not trivialise unbelief. It's a massive thing and has massive implications for us in life. 'Unbelieving believers' will not lose their salvation but will lose out on God's best and His purpose for us in this life. This is in contrast to what we could call the 'unbelieving unbelievers' who reject God and refuse his gift of salvation. This is described in what is the best known verse of the Bible, John 3:16: *"For God so [greatly] loved and dearly prized the world, that He [even] gave His [One and] only begotten Son, so that whoever believes and trusts in Him [as Saviour] shall not perish, but have eternal life."*

Do you believe it?

Memorable Quote:
"No man is excluded from calling upon God, the gate of salvation is set open unto all men: neither is there any other thing which keepeth us back from entering in, save only our own unbelief."
John Calvin

Journaling Suggestion:
"Lord, I believe but help my unbelief." Luke 9:23-25

Memo for Meditation:
"But as many as received him, to them gave He power to become the sons and daughters of God, even to them that believe on His name." John 1:12

August 13

Motivational Idea: Attitudes to watch out for – selfishness

Selfishness can be defined as the trait that leads people to frequently act in their own interests without any regard for how their actions could impact others. Selfish people also have, *"The tendency to act excessively or solely in a manner that benefits oneself, even if others are disadvantaged."* Des Marais has come up with a number of signs to look out for which selfish people exhibit in their behaviours. These include having no regard for how their behaviour impacts others; consistently acting in their own self-interests instead of meeting the needs of others; having no empathy for the suffering of other people; showing no remorse when they've hurt other people; using manipulation tactics to get what they want; always asking for favours but never repaying them; being unkind, or showing a kindness that comes with a price; using others to get what they want; not giving back to others, feeling entitled to always getting what they want, even if it means that others will be pushed down.

Some people will, however, hold tenaciously to the 'entitlement' position. You have perhaps heard people say things like, 'take all you can get,' or 'it's a cruel world and it's every man/woman for themselves.' Self-centred people tend to be overly focused on themselves; the Merriam-Webster dictionary defines 'self-centred' as 'preoccupied with oneself and one's affairs'.

The reality is that all of us behave in selfish or self-centred ways sometimes; it's one of the flaws in our human and fallen nature. It's not a pretty picture but the motivational idea today is for us not only to be on the lookout for people like this and be on our guard, but also to undertake some self-reflection and see if any of these behaviours belong to us. If that is the case, we need to change. But why do we need to change? Simply put, because it's the right thing to do. Check out the memo and learn from our role model who came to save us from ourselves!

Memorable Quote:

"Don't look out only for your own interests, but take an interest in others, too." Philippians 2:4

Journaling Suggestion:
Selflessness, not selfishness!

Memo for Meditation:
"If you've gotten anything at all out of following Christ, if his love has made any difference in your life, if being in a community of the Spirit means anything to you, if you have a heart, if you care—then do me a favour: Agree with each other, love each other, be deep-spirited friends. Don't push your way to the front; don't sweet-talk your way to the top. Put yourself aside, and help others get ahead. Don't be obsessed with getting your own advantage. Forget yourselves long enough to lend a helping hand." Philippians 2:1-4

August 14

Motivational Idea: Attitudes to watch out for – foolishness

When you find a book that mentions the fool seventy-two times, then one would think that it would be worth more than a quick look. When that book was written by the wisest man who ever lived, apart from Jesus, we would do well to understand what is written. Furthermore, when it's written under the inspiration of God the Holy Spirit then we have to take it seriously. Proverbs tell us that the fool does not learn from their mistakes but keeps repeating them. (see Proverbs 26:11).

We all make mistakes but hopefully we are transient fools and not chronic ones. Fools usually like to talk and are full of words even when they don't understand the subject – they have an opinion on everything. (see Proverbs 12:23). They have no interest in understanding. (see Proverbs 18:2,6,7). It's all about them and their opinion. Fools hate wisdom and discipline. (see Proverbs 22:15). They are good at relinquishing responsibility and are not interested in self-improvement and self-development. (see Proverbs 1:7). They are usually given to having a quick temper. (see Proverbs 29:11). Fools don't like change and are dismissive of new ideas. (see Proverbs 27:17). Fools are good at misrepresentation and misquote others to put themselves in a good light. Some fools also argue that there is no God. (see Proverbs 28:26).

Foolishness is about attitude and behaviour. One writer says that intelligent fools with gifts and talents are dangerous and their selfish ambition will amount to throwing anyone who gets in their way under a bus. Fools will do anything for their own benefit. For some fools, ethics are negotiable and it doesn't matter who gets in the way of their reckless and destructive behaviour. They are harsh and angry, and engage in self-protection and self-comfort to extremes. They are also quick to quarrel – a hothead who feels secure in their folly. Fools have control issues. Fools spend a lot of time trying to get a greater level of control to do what they want: "If only so-and-so would do such-and-such, then my life would be a lot better." "If only she would realise that what she's doing is wrong and listen to my advice, then I wouldn't worry so much."

Don't be a fool – it does not become you and you certainly won't find a happy and fulfilled life in folly!

Memorable Quote:
"Why, thou sayst well. I do now remember a saying: "The fool doth think he is wise, but the wise man knows himself to be a fool." Shakespeare, *As You Like It*, Act V, Scene 1, page 2

Journaling Suggestion:
"A wise man learns more from a fool than a fool learns from a wise man."

Memo for Meditation:
"It is better to heed the rebuke of a wise person than to listen to the song of fools." Ecclesiastes 7:5
"The way of fools seems right to them but the wise listen to advice." Proverbs 12:15

August 15

Motivational Idea: Attitudes to watch out for – stupidity (1)

One of Todd Murat's *Toddcast* presentations is called *Stupid People – 10 Facts Bonhoeffer's Theory*. He recalls that the young German pastor and philosopher Dietrich Bonhoeffer saw the darkest times of German history first-hand. He witnessed mobs of previously civilised people throw stones at and break the windows of innocent shop owners. Further, he saw the humiliation of children and women in public.

Bonhoeffer spoke out publicly against the atrocities. Years later, still trying to stop the senseless acts, he came home one evening to be met by two men who took him off to prison. While there, Bonhoeffer reflected on how Germany, a country of poets and thinkers, was turning into a society of cowards, thieves and criminals, and how even smart people could be stupid in what they did. He concluded the cause of the problem was not malice but stupidity.

Facts challenging stupid people's prejudgments are simply not believed. When faced with the truth, stupid people see facts as inconsequential or incidental. The cycle continues with the stupid person being self-satisfied and, being a weak person who is easily triggered, goes on the attack pointlessly and dangerously. Dietrich Bonhoeffer died participating in a plot against Adolf Hitler on 9th April 9 1945. This happened at the Flossenbürg concentration camp just 14 days before US soldiers rode in and liberated the camp. After years of doing what he believed was right – Dietrich Bonhoeffer's life ended and his legacy was cemented in history.

Bonhoeffer theorised that stupid people are far more dangerous than evil people. Why? Simply because we can fight bad people, but with stupid ones, we are powerless — all reason falls on deaf ears. Bonhoeffer's theory warns free societies of what can happen when certain (nonsensical) people acquire too much power. They cannot be trusted to be honest because to them everything is purely subjective. Objectivity and truth go together, but from a personal viewpoint, there is no objective input. It's one-sided.

Memorable Quote:
"The problem with stupid people, which makes them dangerous, is that they do not listen. Anything outside their self-imposed limited view is not of interest to these people. Truth is absent from their thinking, and they have no desire to find a reason or expand their minds. They are too busy echoing talking points to justify their position. They fight for all the wrong reasons and gaslight everyone who attempts to challenge their views. Even when presented with verifiable evidence to the contrary."
Todd Murat

Journaling Suggestion:
Don't be stupid!

Memo for Meditation:
"Whoever loves discipline loves knowledge, but whoever hates correction is stupid." Proverbs 12:1

August 16

Motivational Idea: Attitudes to watch out for – stupidity (2)

There is an internet adage that goes like this: *"Debating an idiot is like trying to play chess with a pigeon — it knocks the pieces over, messes on the board, and flies back to its flock to claim victory."* It's funny and clever. When we encounter stupidity, most of the time we laugh it off, but it can be deeply depressing and worrying. Stupidity has its dark side. For theologian and philosopher Dietrich Bonhoeffer, the stupid person is often more dangerous than the evil individual. You can fight the evil person, you can protest, raise awareness and challenge evil. Stupidity, however, is different and can be hard to weed out. That's why it's a dangerous weapon: evil people may find it hard to take power, not always unfortunately, but they need stupid people to do their work. Like sheep in a field, a stupid person can be guided, steered and manipulated to do any number of things. Evil is a puppet master, and it loves nothing so much as the mindless puppets who enable it — be they in the general public or inside the corridors of power.

Dietrich Bonhoeffer's 10 facts about stupid people are as follows:

1. Stupid people often do not listen to anything outside their personal viewpoint.
2. Truth means nothing to the stupid person, instead they argue a false position.
3. Evil is moral, not intellectual defect caused by "stupidity" rather than malice.
4. Some intellectual "book smart" people are actually stupid, and vice versa.
5. People actually become stupid willingly and without any awareness of it.
6. Stupid people tend to multiply in groups, smart people practise solitude.

7. The stupid person is stubborn and unable to absorb new information.
8. The stupid person can commit evil acts easily since they don't see it as evil.
9. Stupid people view the world through personal filters, often inaccurately.
10. Children of the world inherit all the wrong things from stupid people.

"Nothing in all the world is more dangerous than sincere ignorance and conscientious stupidity." Martin Luther King Jr.

Memorable Quote:
"Neither protests nor the use of force accomplish anything here; reasons fall on deaf ears; facts that contradict one's prejudgment simply need not be believed — in such moments the stupid person even becomes critical — and when facts are irrefutable, they are just pushed aside as inconsequential, as incidental. In all this the stupid person, in contrast to the malicious one, is utterly self-satisfied and, being easily irritated, becomes dangerous by going on the attack." Dietrich Bonhoeffer

Journaling Suggestion:
Know Bonhoeffer's 10 facts about stupidity, and be smart walking the straight path.

Memo for Meditation:
"Stupid people are happy when they do foolish things. But wise people walk on a straight path." Proverbs 15:21

August 17

Motivational Idea: Attitudes to cultivate – humility (1)

A Forbes article came up with the thirteen habits of humble people. These are worthy of our consideration and can help us towards greater humility. Humble people are 'situationally aware'. This is a form of emotional intelligence and is about knowing where we are at any given time, being aware of others as well as ourselves and of the dynamics that are happening around us. Humble people 'retain relationships'. A study found that humble people in leadership positions have a more engaged and motivated workforce and are more inclined to stay for the long haul. They *"make difficult decisions with ease."* Jeff Boss says, *"Since humble people put others' needs before their own, when faced with difficult decisions they respect the moral and ethical boundaries that govern the decision and base their decision-making criteria off a sense of shared purpose rather than self-interest."* That's something quite profound. Do we make decisions in this way? Do we look for the betterment of others – the shared purpose – or are we all about self-interest? They 'put others first'.

Humble people know their self-worth, have both confidence and competence. They don't need to flaunt themselves. Jeff says that humble people realise that nobody cares how much they know until those people know how much they're cared for. *"Humility is the true key to success. Successful people lose their way at times. They often embrace and overindulge from the fruits of success. Humility halts this arrogance and self-indulging trap. Humble people share the credit and wealth, remaining focused and hungry to continue the journey of success."* (Rick Pitino).

Humble people 'listen'. You know when a person is really listening; some people are not listening but rather are just waiting to speak. Active listening is not on their agenda because they deem what they have to say as being more important, and again self-interest is to the fore. Humble people are able to paraphrase what you have said because they are interested and have been listening. We know if people are keen to understand us or not. And what about *us*? How are we doing when we reflect on these habits of humble people? Are we listening? Life is a long lesson in humility. More tomorrow.

Memorable Quote:
"Humility is the foundation of all the other virtues hence, in the soul in which this virtue does not exist there cannot be any other virtue except in mere appearance." Augustine

Journaling Suggestion:
Don't think less of myself, but think of myself less.

Memo for meditation:
"Let this mind be in you which was also in Christ Jesus, who, being in the form of God, did not consider it robbery to be equal with God, but made Himself of no reputation, taking the form of a bondservant, and coming in the likeness of men. And being found in appearance as a man, He humbled Himself and became obedient to the point of death, even the death of the cross." Philippians 2:5-8.

August 18

Motivational Idea: Attitudes to cultivate – humility (2)

Humble people have a desire for knowledge and learning. They are 'curious'; they are perpetual learners with a craving to know, to glean from others, and create opportunities to learn more. You underestimate the humble person at your detriment because they are not doormats but 'speak their mind'. They don't fear getting it wrong and have a willingness to say it as it is, and then take the necessary action to do the right thing, not necessarily the easy thing. With their 'situational awareness', they are always considerate of others, but are not afraid to name the elephant in the room. They take the time 'to say thank you' even in little things because the little things are the big things.

The humble person will take the time out of a busy schedule to send a message to that person who did something for the good, for them or others. To get a thank you from a humble person with acute awareness makes people feel good. They don't intimate or manipulate or dominate, but in their humility they raise people up to more than they can be, unlike the proud who, in their inverted shame, tear people down and have a propensity to make people miserable and question their value and validity. 'It's all about me' is their mantra. Theirs is the scarcity mentality whereas the humble person has an abundance mentality. They grow people who can be grown and don't waste time watering rocks.

The humble person can discern the difference between those who have the antecedents of the abundant mentality and need encouragement, and those who are stuck in their own proud self-aggrandisement – they're the hard-hearted rocks that cannot be changed or influenced, so don't waste your time on them. Humble people start sentences with 'You' rather than 'I'. Humble people put others at the forefront of their thoughts. Humble people boast about others, while prideful people brag about themselves. The humble 'accept feedback' and are up for constructive criticism. They actively seek it because they know that feedback is a pathway to improvement. They 'assume responsibility'. Rather than eschewing blame on 'the system' or the behaviours of others, humble people assume responsibility by speaking up and owning their part. They 'ask for help'.

Part of being humble means realising that you don't have all the answers. No one does. Humble people acknowledge what they do and do not know, and enlist help for the latter.

Memorable Quote:
"Pride makes us artificial and humility makes us real." Thomas Merton

Journaling Suggestion:
Be humble and genuine, not the proud fake who is artificial from head to toe.

Memo for Meditation:
"Be completely humble and gentle." Ephesians 4:2-6

August 19

Motivational Idea: Attitudes to cultivate – winning

Some people think they have a winning attitude but often slip at the first hint of trouble. Attitude is similar in nature to self-esteem. Someone can't give it to you. You have to build it. To develop a winning attitude, we need to think positively. Start small and don't allow the thought of some fictitious improbable future prevent you from thinking positively. We all face hardships but we need to get help from 'attitude's brethren of the faith variety'. A friend who offers me encouragement me always ends his text with the words, *"Keep going."*

Relationships make the world go round. Surround yourself with the right people. We are the average of the five people we spend the most time with. Do the maths! Relationships are meant to empower us and should never victimise us. If any relationship isn't helping us become who we want to be, we may have to walk away. We may need addition by blessed subtractions.

Another powerful way to build our positive attitude is to always be grateful. It's impossible to have a bad attitude when we have gratitude. Be grateful for everything you have. There are people who will never have what you have. And don't forget to journal! Write down your thoughts and feelings. What fires up your soul? What are you passionate about? It's so much easier to develop a great attitude when you're doing something you love. You can put your energy into it. Why not write down in 600 words what your purpose in life is? Then set high goals and monitor your progress. Be committed and don't give up.

Having faith in Jesus Christ, we find our self esteem and our winning attitude derives from Him as our Lord and Master as our perfect role model. He's the ultimate winner and has gained victory for us over every dominion, authority and power. Having said that, the following quotation reminds us that we need to work at developing ourselves; we are not passive partners in the kingdom of God, rather we need to engage and do our part in cultivating a winning attitude. *"Faith can move mountains but don't be surprised if God gives you a shovel."*

Memorable Quotation:
"Don't ever give up—being true to yourself. Let's get something straight. Winners quit. They quit the right things at the right times. They also choose the right things to start and focus only on those things. That's why you wouldn't consider thinking of them as quitters. If you've entangled yourself in something that isn't your passion, be true to yourself and find something else that is. It's your life." Andrew LaCivita

Journaling Suggestion:
Time to develop an attitude of gratitude and get back to winning ways!

Memo for Meditation:
"May the God who gives endurance and encouragement give you the same attitude of mind toward each other that Christ Jesus had." Romans 15:5

August 20

Motivational Idea: Attitudes to cultivate – believing (1)

We all believe in something. Our beliefs, however, may be accurate or inaccurate. We are influenced by opinions and assumptions and our perceptions. Beliefs tend to be formed at a very early age; our environment can play a major part in their formation. People rarely question the validity of their beliefs. Ironically, even if we are faced with evidence that challenges our precious beliefs, we tend to ignore it. One of the reasons we do this is because our belief system acts like a road map to help us negotiate life. Take the road map away and we feel lost. We would not want to admit we are using the wrong map. One of the healthiest things we can do is to examine our beliefs.

If we are to have a truly true believing attitude which shapes our belief system and is our road map for life and gives us our direction of travel, then we need to ensure that our beliefs are based on truth and not error. (See the author's book *Short Essays On Finding Hope In Our Fragile World.*) We need to ask questions; where does this belief come from? Is this my belief or have I adopted it from someone else? How does this belief help or hinder me? How do I know this belief is true? If you believe in God, *why* do you believe in God? If you *don't* believe in God, why do you not believe in Him? Get your belief right, get your belief system right, and then you will have the right road map and go in the right direction.

Memorable Quote: *"Man is made by his belief. As he believes, so he is."* Johann Wolfgang Van Goethe

Journaling Suggestion:
"I believe in one God, the Father almighty, maker of heaven and earth, of all things visible and invisible. I believe in one Lord, Jesus Christ, the only Begotten Son of God, born of the Father before all ages. God from God, Light from Light, true God from true God, begotten, not made, consubstantial with the Father; through him all things were made. For us men and for our salvation he came down from heaven, and by the Holy Spirit was incarnate of the Virgin Mary, and became man. For our sake he was crucified under Pontius Pilate, he suffered death and was buried,

and rose again on the third day in accordance with the Scriptures. He ascended into heaven and is seated at the right hand of the Father. He will come again in glory to judge the living and the dead and his kingdom will have no end. I believe in the Holy Spirit, the Lord, the giver of life, who proceeds from the Father and the Son, who with the Father and the Son is adored and glorified, who has spoken through the prophets. I believe in one, holy, catholic, and apostolic Church. I confess one baptism for the forgiveness of sins and I look forward to the resurrection of the dead and the life of the world to come. Amen" Nicene Creed

Do I believe it?

Memo for Meditation:
"And it is impossible to please God without faith. Anyone who wants to come to him must believe that God exists and that he rewards those who sincerely seek him." Hebrews 11:6

August 21

Motivational Idea: Attitudes to cultivate – believing (2)

Do you believe in aliens? Do you believe in a flat earth? Do you believe in the lunar moon landings? Conspiracy theorists are everywhere! Do we believe them? When it comes to the question, 'Do you believe in Jesus?' most people will say they do since the evidence for the existence of Jesus on earth 2,000 years ago is irrefutable. However, there are those who, with their conspiracy theory hat on, will dispel this as a myth, even when such a belief flies in the face of the evidence. The question, 'Do you believe in Jesus?' is, however, more than a question about existence. The question is really, 'Do you believe Jesus Christ is who He said He is? And do you trust Him as your Lord and Savour? Do you believe that Jesus is God in human form? Do you believe that Jesus died to take away your sins? Do you believe that Jesus is the only way to God? Do you believe that He rose bodily from the dead? Do you believe that He is going to return again because He is Lord of Lords and King of Kings?'

Believing in the historical Jesus is only part of it. Believing in Him in biblical terminology means a whole lot more. The word 'believe' in the New Testament is the Greek word *pisteuo*, which means to believe in, to entrust, to rely on, to cling to. A missionary, translating the Bible for a tribe notorious for stealing, discovered they didn't have a word for 'belief' or 'trust' in their vocabulary. One day as he sat in his makeshift chair, he thought, "I am putting my trust in this chair to hold me." He called one of the elders and asked him for the word 'to lean on', and so he translated the Bible word for 'believe' in a language that the tribe members would understand. It's our memo for today.

Memorable Quote:
"I am trying here to prevent anyone saying the really foolish thing that people often say about Him: I'm ready to accept Jesus as a great moral teacher, but I don't accept his claim to be God. That is the one thing we must not say. A man who was merely a man and said the sort of things Jesus said would not be a great moral teacher. He would either be a lunatic—on the level with the man who says he is a poached egg—or else he would be the Devil of Hell. You must make your choice. Either this man was, and is, the Son of God, or else a madman or something worse. You can shut him up for a fool, you can spit at him and kill him as a demon or you can fall at his feet and call him Lord and God, but let us not come with any patronising nonsense about his being a great human teacher. He has not left that open to us. He did not intend to. ... Now it seems to me obvious that He was neither a lunatic nor a fiend: and consequently, however strange or terrifying or unlikely it may seem, I have to accept the view that He was and is God." C S Lewis

Journaling Suggestion:
I declare that I believe in Jesus and He's my Lord, my Saviour and my God.

Memo for Meditation:
"For this is how God loved the world: He gave his one and only Son, so that everyone who leans their whole weight on Him will not perish but have eternal life." John 3:16

August 22

Motivational Idea: Attitudes to cultivate – generosity (1)

Waylon Bailey gives an account of the remarkable life of John D Rockefeller, Sr. He was born in 1839 and became a millionaire at age 33. In the 1870s, $1 million was an astounding amount of money. By age 43, he owned and ran the largest company in the world, the Standard Oil Company. He controlled 90% of the oil in the United States. By age 53, John D Rockefeller was a billionaire, the only one in the world. However, money can't buy happiness or indeed health. John's health was so bad that at the age of 53 he was on a diet of crackers because of a stomach ailment and couldn't sleep at night. He paid for the best physicians in the world but they couldn't do anything and told him that he would not live to see 54 years old. John realised that he couldn't take his money with him, so he started giving it away. It is reckoned he gave away $540 million to help those in need. He founded the University of Chicago and Rockefeller University, as well as a university in the Philippines.

He also founded the Rockefeller Foundation, dedicated to medical research. The Rockefeller Foundation was instrumental in the discovery of penicillin, the most significant medical discovery of all time, and the eradication of hookworm and yellow fever. At that point in his life, Rockefeller began to change. He became able to eat normal food. He was able to sleep well again. He also made a profession of faith in Jesus Christ and was baptised in a Northern Baptist church. He attended church every Sunday, and taught a Sunday school class until he died. After having been told he would never see his 54th birthday, John D. Rockefeller lived to be 97 years old. We may not have millions to give away but we can be generous with what God has given us. We need to be generous custodians of what God has bestowed upon us. There are no pockets in a shroud!

Memorable Quote:

"What changed? Obviously, I can't get into the mind of John D Rockefeller, but his remarkable change in health coincided with his remarkable change of heart and life. Isn't it amazing what happens when we begin to act as we were created to act? Maybe it's time we started

believing Scripture and understanding that God created us for a purpose, that when we seek to accomplish his purpose, he blesses our lives. When we die to self and seek to put God first in our lives, we experience His blessing as well." Waylon Bailey

Journaling Suggestion:
Lord, give me a generous heart like yours.

Memo for Meditation:
"My child, never forget the things I have taught you. Store my commands in your heart. If you do this, you will live many years, and your life will be satisfying. Never let loyalty and kindness leave you! Tie them around your neck as a reminder. Write them deep within your heart. Then you will find favour with both God and people, and you will earn a good reputation." Proverbs 3:1-4

August 23

Motivational Idea: Attitudes to cultivate – generosity (2)

A generous person is one who gives freely and is willing to share without expecting anything in return. A genuinely generous person is one who gives without any form of manipulation. We find people in life who seem to give with a generous spirit but then we find down the line that they have ulterior motives and were only doing so because they were expecting something in return at some point. We could describe such individuals as 'users' and 'takers', but certainly not 'givers'. Then there are the people who are known for being tight-fisted. You may have heard the saying, 'moths in the wallet' to describe those who want to keep what they have and do not want to part with their money no matter how much they have accrued. Even if they are 'filthy rich', you may well find they are even more reluctant to part with anything, unlike John D Rockefeller Sr whom we met yesterday, an exemplar of generosity.

The generous person considers 'you', but for the stingy, selfish person, 'It's all about me! What about me?' None of us want to be seen as stingy or, to use that powerful word, parsimonious. When we turn to the Bible, we find many fascinating contrasts between generosity and stinginess. Take, for example, the story of Abraham and Lot in Genesis 14. They had entered the land of Canaan, but there was a dispute between the herdsmen of the noble patriarch and his nephew. Abraham was very upset about this so in the spirit of generosity he gave Lot the first choice of the land before them. Check out our memo for today. Greed does have consequences. We do well to consider our attitude in relation to generosity given how generous our heavenly Father is with us. And God takes into account what we do with what we have because it's all from Him, and He will call us to account someday at the judgement. Salvation is free but discipleship is about sacrifice!

Memorable Quote:
"He who did not spare His own Son, but gave Him up for us all, will He not with Him also freely give us everything else." Roman 8.32

Journaling Suggestion:
Better to be like Abraham than Lot. Abraham pleased God, Lot didn't.

Memo for Meditation:
"Finally Abram said to Lot, "Let's not allow this conflict to come between us or our herdsmen. After all, we are close relatives! The whole countryside is open to you. Take your choice of any section of the land you want, and we will separate. If you want the land to the left, then I'll take the land on the right. If you prefer the land on the right, then I'll go to the left." Lot took a long look at the fertile plains of the Jordan Valley in the direction of Zoar. The whole area was well watered everywhere, like the garden of the LORD or the beautiful land of Egypt. (This was before the LORD destroyed Sodom and Gomorrah.) Lot chose for himself the whole Jordan Valley to the east of them. He went there with his flocks and servants and parted company with his uncle Abram. So Abram settled in the land of Canaan, and Lot moved his tents to a place near Sodom and settled among the cities of the plain. But the people of this area were extremely wicked and constantly sinned against the LORD." Genesis 13:5-1

August 24

Motivational Idea: Don't despise the day of small beginnings

Did Ronald Wayne despise the day of small beginnings? He may have had his reasons for selling his 10% stake in the company he was involved with at its inception. His fellow travellers were Steve Jobs and Steve Wozniak, and the company was called Apple. Two weeks after the company was formed, Ronald sold his stake in the company for $800. Today that share in the company would be worth in excess of $75 billion. In Zechariah chapter 4, the Angel of the Lord told the prophet not to despise the day of small beginnings. God was pleased that His work was underway on the temple. The circumstances of the time meant that the outlook was anything but hopeful. They were faced with a difficult and long-term project of rebuilding. There would be no overnight successes. However, the prophet and the people were encouraged to take small steps at a time and just do it. God had their back and the power of His Spirit would enable and equip them for the daily mundane tasks. They needed a different perspective on things. They needed a positive attitude and they needed to heed the word of the Lord and not listen to the gainsayers and those who sought to discourage and distract from the immediate tasks in hand.

Whatever your circumstances now, you need to know that whatever kingdom task looms before you, don't despise what needs to be done today even if your efforts seem small and insignificant. When you are having that cup of coffee with God in the morning, listen to what He is saying and write down the tasks for the day ahead and then ask for His help to do them. We need to get away from the view that bigger is always better – it's the small things that are the big things. Celebrate the small steps that you will achieve today and keep going. That vision God has given you will come to fruition but only if you attend to the small things every day. Great intentions are good but small steps are even better and are absolutely vital for reaching that ultimate goal. Make sure God is in it and it's in His plan and wait for His direction and in His timing, not yours.

Memorable Quote:

"The smallest deed is better than the grandest intention." John Burroughs

Journaling Suggestion:
Do the small things and the big things will take care of themselves in the hands of God.

Memo for Meditation:
"Do not despise these small beginnings, for the LORD rejoices to see the work begin, to see the plumb line in Zerubbabel's hand." Zechariah 4:10

August 25

Motivational Idea: Worrier or warrior

From a human standpoint, Joshua had every reason to worry: Moses had led the Israelites for forty years and had been the mediator and mouthpiece between God and the people. Now he was dead and Joshua was chosen to succeed him. Some scholars believe that the total number of Israelites who left Egypt during the exodus – women and children and old men included – was around 2.4 million people. Whatever the number, the task Moses faced was mammoth; it was his task to lead them into a harsh and barren wilderness, and then seek to keep their hunger and thirst satisfied, their needs for shelter and protection from the elements met, as well as bring them to a state of spiritual maturity and obedience. Even he cried out to God, *"I cannot carry all these people by myself; the burden is too heavy for me."* (Numbers 11:14). With God's enabling grace and strength he was able to succeed.

Numbers 26:51 says there were 601,730 family men ready to enter the Promised Land, suggesting a total population of at least two and a half million, including women and children. Joshua, too, had a mammoth task on his hands, but was he a worrier or a warrior? A reading of the first chapter of Joshua gives us a great picture of what happened to him prior to taking up the mantle of Moses, and the reason he was a warrior and not a worrier. God met with this man and God made promises to him. God said there were things He would do and there were things He expected Joshua to do. God wants to meet with you and give you the same promises. He also expects you to trust and obey, and live as a warrior not a worrier.

Memorable Quote:
The Lord is with me like a mighty warrior.

Journaling Suggestion:
One man or woman with God is a majority.

Memo for Meditation:
"Be strong and very courageous. Be careful to obey all the law my servant Moses gave you; do not turn from it to the right or to the left, that you may be successful wherever you go. Keep this Book of the Law always on your lips; meditate on it day and night, so that you may be careful to do everything written in it. Then you will be prosperous and successful. 9 Have I not commanded you? Be strong and courageous. Do not be afraid; do not be discouraged, for the LORD your God will be with you wherever you go." Joshua 1:7-9

August 26

Motivational Idea: Decide to stay

In our memo for today we can draw from the deep reservoir of King David's experiences. His encounters with fear and anxiety whilst under attack from the enemy encourage us to wait on the Lord and to take courage in Him. Be of good courage! C H Spurgeon said, *"Wait at His door with prayer; wait at His foot with humility; wait at His table with service; wait at His window with expectancy."* Campbell Morgan said, *"To wait for Jehovah is ever to find the plain path, however rough that path may be."*

One of the big problems we face in our fast-paced world is the need for instant gratification and we want it now. The words in the Queen song *I Want it All* sum up the attitude of the post-modern world" *"Here's to the future for the dreams of youth, I want it all (give it all I want it all), I want it all (yeah) I want it all and I want it now."* No time to wait, no time to stay the course – it has to be *now*. We all know that life does not work like that and this can lead to a lot of frustration and deep unhappiness.

One of the things that David does in this Psalm/song is to keep his God-focus in the midst of conflict and the impending onslaught of the enemy. We need to keep our God-focus, too, in our topsy turvy world. We need to 'stay with God,' not go off on our own path or react to the latest fad or whim. We need to cultivate an attitude of reliance upon God and trust Him. When the men of Gibeon came to the Israelites and led them to believe they were from a distant country, they believed them and were deceived. And the narrator tells us, *"But [they] did not inquire of the Lord."* Stay with God today and every day!

Memorable Quote:
"Psalm 27 is a powerful weapon against the enemy of fear and its power to enslave our hearts. Meditating on its truths provides a key to unlocking the prison of anxiety, dispels our fears, and gives us hope." Paul Tautges

Journaling Suggestion:
Prayer: Spirit of God, please direct my decision-making. Help me to make decisions in accord with your word and step with your Spirit. You see things I don't see, you know things I don't know. Your ways are higher than my ways.

Memo for Meditation:
"Point me down your highway, God; direct me along a well-lighted street; show my enemies whose side you're on. Don't throw me to the dogs, those liars who are out to get me, filling the air with their threats. I'm sure now I'll see God's goodness in the exuberant earth. Stay with God! Take heart. Don't quit. I'll say it again: Stay with God." Psalm 27, MSG

August 27

Motivational Idea: Rule of thumb

The actual origin of 'rule of thumb' is unknown. What we do know, however, is that it has been used for over 400 years for approximate measurement. It was a common practice for builders to use various parts of the body as gauges for measurement based on experience and not as an exact science. Today, a rule of thumb is used to describe a guideline, idea, or principle that helps us make decisions. The original term was thus broadened to mean any inexact but helpful rule. The first known use of the term appeared in print in a sermon by a Scottish puritan preacher called James Durham in 1685. *"Many protest Christian are like foolish builders, who build by guess, and by rule of thumb, (as we use to speak), not by square and rule."* James was taking no prisoners in his 'Heaven upon earth' publication, and we get the gist of his argument. He was referring to, I assume, the whole body of biblical truth and not only one specific principle.

Today we use the expression in modern parlance as a helpful rule for one general principle as we consider the golden rule which Jesus taught us in the sermon on the amount. This golden precept, our rule of thumb, is described in our memo for today, *"In everything, do to others what you would have them do to you."* This rule of conduct is a summary of how we are to treat others and states a fundamental ethical principle in the Kingdom of God. We are to treat others as we want to be treated. It will be a happier world when we do what Jesus says, and our own unique personal world will be a happier place, too. We will be happier when we obey the kingly rule of Jesus our Lord and Master.

Memorable Quote:
"That which you do not wish for yourself you shall not wish for your neighbour. This is the whole law; the rest is only commentary." Talmud Shabbat 31a (Judaism)

Journaling Suggestion:
"Let us regulate our conduct by the golden rule of doing to others as in similar circumstances we would have them do to us, and the path of duty will be clear before us." Adapted from William Wilberforce

Memo for Meditation:
"Here is a simple, rule-of-thumb guide for behaviour: Ask yourself what you want people to do for you, then grab the initiative and do it for them. Add up God's Law and Prophets and this is what you get." Matthew 7:12

August 28

Motivational Idea: Rise above the tit-for-tat impasse

If there is one area of our lives that will stifle and indeed cause an impasse in our pursuit of happiness it is anger, bitterness, hatred and the desire for revenge. It eats us up and can become our constant preoccupation. We are stuck in this quagmire of unrelenting hurt and we want to pay them back. We may well have justifiable reasons for feeling the way we do.

Our memo for today is set in the context of what is commonly called the 'beatitudes'. Jesus sets out the manifesto for His Kingdom and the happiness and joy that is found in proclaiming Him as our Saviour, Lord and King. The cultural norm of the day was 'an eye for an eye and a tooth for a tooth'. This was the Jewish Law. Pay them back! But Jesus raised the bar, He changed the standard and set out a new way, a different way, which was countercultural to the thinking of that time and still is today.

We are called upon to forgive and to love our enemies and to pray for them. The Message Bible (memo for meditation today) uses some hyperbole but you get the point: the thrust of the message is to live like Jesus lived. Realise today that He is able to make us more like Him. His way is the best way and in Him we can rise above the tit-for-tat mentality; we can overcome this impasse that has contorted us until we are unrecognisable with a damaged and bitter spirit. In His strength we can replace it with a different mentality – live by the rule of love, the love of God shed abroad in our hearts. In every part of our lives we are to love as He has loved us. Perhaps the Spirit of God is saying, 'Today it's time for you to deal with this massive obstacle and try God's way.' Only then can we find that happiness that has eluded us and find that joy that has been stifled in a heart full of anger. Only then will we be able to move on in the cultivation of a flourishing life and reach our true potential in a life of fulfilment as God has planned.

Memorable Quote:
"To forgive is to set a prisoner free and discover that the prisoner was you." Lewis B Smedes

Journaling Suggestion:
Today I will ask God to bring the healing that I need to forgive and move on with the plan He has for my life and the lasting joy that is found there.

Memo for Meditation:

"To you who are ready for the truth, I say this: Love your enemies. Let them bring out the best in you, not the worst. When someone gives you a hard time, respond with the energies of prayer for that person. If someone slaps you in the face, stand there and take it. If someone grabs your shirt, gift wrap your best coat and make a present of it. If someone takes unfair advantage of you, use the occasion to practice the servant life. No more tit-for-tat stuff. Live generously." Luke 6:27-30

August 29

Motivational Idea: The way to face life – and it's not with a sneer!

Theodore Roosevelt, 26th president of the USA from 1901-1909, was a man of many talents. He authored thirty-five books, he was a passionate conservationist, and a wonderful orator. The most influential and memorable speech he ever made was on 23rd April 1910 in Paris. The speech would become one of the most quoted orations of his illustrious career. It was entitled, *Citizenship in a Republic,* although it became known as *The Man in the Arena.* The speech made headlines around the world, was turned into a pocket book, and sent to all the teachers in France. The most famous section of his speech still resonates and inspires people today. Brené Brown paraphrased it in a Ted Talk, *Daring greatly.* Nelson Mandela gave it to the captain of the South African Rugby team before the world cup in 1995. South Africa went on to beat the favoured All Blacks in the final. LeBron James wrote a quote from the speech on his shoes, and Tom Brady used *The Man in the Arena* as the title of a documentary series about his time with the New England Patriots. In a tweet announcing the series, Brady wrote *"I have quoted Theodore Roosevelt's* Man in the Arena *speech since I saw it painted on our weight room wall at UM in 1995. It's a constant reminder to ignore the noise, buckle my chinstrap, and battle through whatever comes my way."* It takes courage to be the man in the arena, facing the challenges head-on. Ignore the armchair critics and just do the right thing.

Memorable Quote:
"The poorest way to face life is to face it with a sneer. There are many men who feel a kind of twister pride in cynicism; there are many who confine themselves to criticism of the way others do what they themselves dare not even attempt. There is no more unhealthy being, no man less worthy of respect, than he who either really holds, or feigns to hold, an attitude of sneering disbelief toward all that is great and lofty, whether in achievement or in that noble effort which, even if it fails, comes to second achievement. A cynical habit of thought and speech, a readiness to criticise work which the critic himself never tries to perform, an intellectual aloofness which will not accept contact with life's realities — all these are marks, not as the possessor would fain to think, of superiority but of weakness. They mark the men unfit to bear their part painfully in the stern strife of living, who seek, in the affection of contempt for the achievements of others, to hide from others and from themselves in their own weakness. The role is easy; there is none easier, save only the role of the man who sneers alike at both criticism and performance." Theodore Roosevelt

Journaling Suggestion:
Don't face life with a sneer; face it with a smile and a willingness to be the one in the arena, with courage, skill and tenacity – not sitting on the side-lines, criticising.

Memo for Meditation:
"Be strong and courageous. Do not be afraid or terrified because of them, for the Lord your God goes with you; He will never leave you nor forsake you." Deuteronomy 31:6

August 30

Motivational Idea: Kill your fear

Everyone experiences fear at some point in life. Fear can be a healthy response to danger. However, it is often irrational and can cause a lot of anxiety and prevent individuals from living their lives to the fullest – the fulfilled life. The prevalence of fear in our world today is greater than it has ever been for a multiplicity of reasons: wars, pandemics, social media hype. We can have a myriad reasons to fuel our fears and rob us of a happy, fulfilled life. Our personal insecurities can wreak havoc in our lives: we may have money worries; fear of public speaking; fear of flying; fear of being alone; fear of failure or rejection; fear of losing a loved one; fear of disease or pain; and fear of death. It may even be a fear of spiders. These are the common fears. So how do we kill it? How do we kill fear?

The world of psychology can advise us, but today we are taking a biblical approach. The Bible, the hope manual for living, gives guiding principles to enable us to overcome fear so we can live a life filled with hope and courage. God has a lot to say about fear in the Bible! Fear is mentioned over 500 times. *"Fear not!"* is the most repeated command in the Bible. In fact, it's been said that there are 365 *"Fear nots"*— one *"Fear not"* for every day of the year! The eternal God who created the universe, who created you and loves you so much is so concerned with your fear that He wants to take it away. You might think this is impossible, but God can enable you to deal with all your fears, but He wants to do this in partnership with you.

One of the best ways that enables us to combat fear is reading and meditating on Scripture. When we meditate on Scripture, we find that one of the most recurring themes in the Bible is the assurance of God's presence in our lives. Time after time we are reminded that we need not be afraid when we have the all-knowing, all-powerful Creator of the universe by our side. A strong faith in God is an effective weapon against fear. When we believe in God's promises and have faith in His power and love, anxiety and fear has no room to flourish. And that is how from a biblical perspective we learn to kill fear.

Journaling Suggestion:
"There are 366 "Fear nots" in the Bible, one for every day of the year, including Leap Year! God doesn't want us to go a single day without hearing his word of comfort: "Fear not!"' Lloyd Ogilvie

Memo for Meditation:
"When I am afraid, I will trust in you. In God, whose word I praise, In God I trust; I will not be afraid. What can mortal man do to me?" Psalm 56:3-4

"So do not fear, for I am with you; do not be dismayed, for I am your God. I will strengthen you and help you; I will uphold you with my righteous right hand." Isaiah 41:10

"He said to his disciples, 'Why are you so afraid? Do you still have no faith?'" Mark 4:40

August 31

Motivational Idea: Kill the negativity

As we draw the attitudinal dimension to a close, let's not only kill off fear but also negativity. Negativity is commonplace. It is in the nature of humans to complain when our demands are not being met. We find the world over people shouting for their 'rights', and we are not ambivalent to the fact that the legitimate rights of people should be respected and indeed honoured, but it all seems to be against a backdrop of a general spirit of negativity toward the world and life in general.

Perhaps we, too, are guilty of this negativity and grumbling. Some people seem to be determined to find the cloud in every silver lining. The world has become a place of negatives, and the positivity boat has sailed long ago. When we turn to the Bible, we find that negativity was a major problem for the Israelites: even though God brought them out of Egypt, delivered them from slavery and then parted the Red Sea, destroying their enemies in the process, as soon as they were within touching distance of the Promised Land negativity set in and they were afraid of the giants in the land of Canaan. And as they traversed the wilderness for forty years, they constantly grumbled against God. The happy, fulfilled life was theirs to enjoy and they could have rejoiced over all that God had done for them, trusting Him to continue to provide for them. Instead, they moaned and complained. *"Man only likes to count his troubles; he doesn't calculate his happiness."* (Fyodor Dostoevsky).

Memorable Quote:

"Christians can counter the doom-and-gloom mentality with a gentle, loving, faith-filled approach to life." Ephesians 4:32; 1 John 5:14

"We can refuse to be caught up in the hopelessness and me-first mentality that is too normal in the world." Philippians 2:14–15

"We can offer light in the darkness." Matthew 5:14
"Truth in the midst of Satan's deception." John 17:17
"And hope in the face of despair." Psalm 43:5

Journaling Suggestion:
Kill the negativity!

Memo for Meditation:
"But then you weren't willing to go up. You rebelled against GOD, your God's plain word. You complained in your tents: "GOD hates us. He hauled us out of Egypt in order to dump us among the Amorites—a death sentence for sure! How can we go up? We're trapped in a dead end. Our brothers took all the wind out of our sails, telling us, 'The people are bigger and stronger than we are; their cities are huge, their defences massive—we even saw Anakite giants there!'" I tried to relieve your fears: "Don't be terrified of them. GOD, your God, is leading the way; he's fighting for you. You saw with your own eyes what he did for you in Egypt; you saw what he did in the wilderness, how GOD, your God, carried you as a father carries his child, carried you the whole way until you arrived here. But now that you're here, you won't trust GOD, your God—this same GOD who goes ahead of you in your travels to scout out a place to pitch camp, a fire by night and a cloud by day to show you the way to go." Deuteronomy 1:22-33, MSG

THE BIBLICAL DIMENSION

September 1

Motivational Idea: So simple, yet beyond comprehension

To understand the Gospel, Romans 10:13 is a good place to begin. *"Whoever calls on the Name of the Lord will be saved."* The Gospel message of Jesus is that He came from heaven to earth, lived a perfect life, died for our sins on the cross so that through His death and resurrection we can experience true and everlasting life. We can choose to believe in Jesus and, through faith, experience His undeserved gift of forgiveness because of His love for us. Make no mistake, salvation is simple. The Lord Jesus Christ has paid in full the price of sin that we never could pay, and He said, *"It is finished"* (John 19:30).

Salvation is not a reward to be earned, it is a gift to be received, and it is so simple that you could receive it right now. Before we can be in a right relationship with God, we need to give up our pride and self-centeredness, and acknowledge Jesus as Lord. And we need to give up our self-righteousness and accept Jesus as Saviour and Lord of our lives. It's so simple that a child can understand it, and yet it is beyond human comprehension that the Creator God of the universe wants a personal relationship with us. Salvation is simple – call on the Name of the Lord. The simplicity of the Gospel is what makes it so controversial. We don't have to work for salvation or earn it as it is freely given as the gift of God through faith in Jesus. Have you called on Him already? If not, call on Him today. And if you have called on Him, be encouraged because you are saved and can walk in the newness of life in the power and the freedom of God's salvation and be happy and fulfilled in every way. It's so simple, yet beyond our comprehension!

Memorable Quote:

"Certain translations say. 'Whomsoever'. This means it doesn't matter your ethnicity, it doesn't matter your background; it doesn't matter your mess-ups, it doesn't matter your gender, your mess-ups have been hung

up! Everyone who calls on the name of the Lord will be saved. God says, 'I want to take your imperfect record and exchange it with my Son's perfect record, so that whenever I see you, all I see is the blood of Jesus.' Saved from God's wrath - no longer objects of wrath. When you understand what Jesus did on the cross that doesn't just give a minor shift to your life; that radically disrupts your life from self to Christ. Jesus could not stand the thought of having a sin-stricken people walk on this earth without ever knowing the most holistic, fulfilling, powerful relationship known to man, and that is to know God not as Creator to created. He wants us to know Him as Abba - Father! It literally means the Fatherhood of God. We are now children of God because Jesus saved us from wrath on the cross so that everyone who calls on His Name will be saved.'"

Journaling Suggestion:

"I will call upon the Lord as long as I live." See Psalm 116:1-2

Memo for Meditation:

*"For by grace you are saved through faith, and this is not from yourselves, it is the gift of God; **it** is not from works, so that no one can boast."* Ephesians 2:8,9

September 2

Motivational Idea: It's simple but not easy

The Gospel is simple but simple does not mean easy. The reply of some people to the simple Gospel message is, *"If it was that easy then everyone would do it."* But it's not easy at all, and here's why. If you offend someone, usually it is very simple for that situation to be remedied. To sincerely say, *"I am sorry for what I did."* It's that simple, but perhaps you will agree that's not easy! Disharmony exists and broken relationships are never mended because the guilty person cannot find it in themselves to say, *"Sorry".*

Have we said sorry to God for our sins? Our pride gets in the way. Let's say you need to do a piece of work in your home – rewiring the house. Big job, and certainly beyond the author, who is seen as only a penpusher by his beloved mother. What's the answer? Call someone who can – it's that simple, but there's something that makes it really difficult to do that. What is it? The same thing that makes it difficult to say, *"I'm sorry, I was wrong, please forgive me."* It's pride! The simple Gospel of Jesus Christ is unique in a world of religions telling us that we earn our salvation by good works. The Bible says over and over again that salvation is not by works. We have nothing to boast about. One of the misunderstandings people have of the true Gospel is this: 'If salvation is a gift, that means I can then live as I like and it doesn't matter.' Nothing could be further from the truth; once we become children of God through faith in Jesus Christ, we become a new creation. The old has gone and the new has come (see 2 Corinthians 5:17).

Another reason the Gospel is simple but not easy is because of our self-centeredness. We want to live our lives the way we please. We want to be in the driver's seat. Many would be willing to accept God's forgiveness as long as it didn't result in any change to the life they are living, but that isn't on offer. Sin is rebellion against God, and before us rebels can be forgiven, we have to surrender and give ourselves over to God, bow in allegiance and own Him as the rightful King and Sovereign of our lives.

Memorable Quote:
"This is one of the things that means it's not easy to get salvation – self-righteousness. The Bible says we are hell-deserving, and helpless to do anything to earn God's favour. Pride acts as our defence lawyer, and jumps to its feet, 'I object! My client is not that bad – this verdict is wrong, the penalty is too severe...' It is impossible to be saved while you retain pride. Give your lawyer the sack. Accept God's verdict about you, and then God's offer of salvation through Christ – it's that simple, yet people will try almost anything else if it allows them to keep their self-righteousness." Paul McCauley

Journaling Suggestion:
As a new creation in Jesus, I want to be holy

Memo for Meditation:
"Believe on the Lord Jesus Christ, and you will be saved." Acts 16:31
"This means that anyone who belongs to Christ has become a new person. The old life is gone; a new life has begun!" 2 Corinthians 5:17
"You ought to live holy and godly lives." 2 Peter 3:11b

September 3

Motivational Idea: A clear conscience

What do we do with our guilt? We feel guilty about things we have done or haven't done. Some people seek to get rid of the guilt by using the defence mechanism of 'undoing'. The person who has defrauded the tax office by cooking the books gives a large donation to charity in order to assuage the guilt. You can find umpteen ways of dealing with guilt on the net. These include acknowledging your feelings of guilt, cultivating self-compassion, practising self-forgiveness, learning from your mistakes, and making amends when possible. All very helpful, but the Bible deals with the problem of guilt in a different way and does so by pointing us to God.

We are told that God is greater than our guilt; we cannot take it away ourselves. If our hearts condemn us, God is greater than our guilt and knows everything about what we have done. Guilt can be a positive thing; it tells us we have a conscience. Being aware of our sins, our mistakes, and having a guilty conscience should drive us to the one who can not only assuage our guilt, but take it away completely. Guilt reveals our need for God and His salvation is all about forgiveness. Through Jesus' sacrificial, vicarious and propitious death on the cross we can be forgiven totally. *"Without the shedding of blood there is no forgiveness of sins."* (Hebrews 9:22).

God wants us to know today that He is omniscient – He knows everything about us, but He wants us to know that He is bigger than our sins and our guilt and our shame, and He embraces us with His tender love and invites us into a life with a clear conscience because of His beloved Son. His promise is, *"For I will be merciful to their unrighteousness, and their sins and their iniquities will I remember no more."* (Hebrews 8:12).

There is no need to wallow in our guilt. God is greater than it all. Hand it over to Him. You can't begin to enjoy a fulfilled life without a guilty conscience. So, let us go right into the presence of God with sincere hearts, fully trusting him. *"For our guilty consciences have been sprinkled with Christ's blood to make us clean, and our bodies have been washed with pure water."* (Hebrews 10.22).

Memorable Quote:
"Jesus, my great High Priest, offered his blood and died; my guilty conscience seeks no sacrifice beside. His pow'rful blood did once atone, and now it pleads before the throne." Isaac Watts

Journaling Suggestion:
No more in condemnation; here in the grace of God I stand!

Memo for Meditation:
"If our hearts condemn us, we know that God is greater than our hearts, and he knows everything." 1 John 3.20 NIV
"Even if we feel guilty, God is greater than our feelings, and he knows everything." 1 John 3:20, NLT *"My dear children, let's not just talk about love; let's practise real love. This is the only way we'll know we're living truly, living in God's reality. It's also the way to shut down debilitating self-criticism, even when there is something to it. For God is greater than our worried hearts and knows more about us than we do ourselves."* 1 John 3:18-20, MSG

September 4

Motivational Idea: It's a shame (1)

The author's dissertation for the Masters Degree in Psychotherapy was entitled: *"The Evolving Psychoanalytic Appreciation of Shame.'* One of the definitions from it that can help us in our understanding of shame comes from John Bradshaw: *"A person with guilt might say, 'I feel awful seeing that I did something that violated my values.' Or the guilty person might say. 'I feel sorry about the consequences of my behaviours.' In so doing the person's values are reaffirmed. The possibility of repair exists and learning and growth can be promoted. While guilt is a painful feeling of regret and responsibility for one's actions, shame is a painful feeling about oneself as a person. The possibility of repair seems foreclosed to the shameful person, because shame is a matter of identity."*

Shame is the 'master emotion' because as it is internalised, all the other emotions are bound by shame. We need to of course differentiate between healthy shame and unhealthy shame, or rather *toxic* shame, which is so hard to shift because it's about our identity.

We can learn all about shame but for many who believe in and follow Jesus, we can continue to live under the dark shadow of the shame identity. Yet the Bible says that God removes our shame. *"I will change their shame into praise and renown in all the earth."* (Zephaniah 3:19).

Both Paul and Peter quote Isaiah 28:16: *"Whoever believes in him will not be put to shame."* (Romans 10:11; 1 Peter 2:6). So how do we deal with this toxic shame that is like a straightjacket binding us in caverns of deep gloom and despair? To break the power of shame we need to know what actually gives shame its power. Shame's power comes mainly from a distorted view of ourselves, and such is the nature of shame that it hides in plain sight, it becomes anonymised and we see ourselves as defective, lacking dignity and of no worth; or we dress it all up in the cloak of exorbitant pride, which is really inverted shame. We need to name it and 'shame' it, and to see our true identity because our true identity is found in Jesus Christ. We need to see the cross where Jesus dealt with all our shame. The answer to the shame identity is the honour identity. Christ replaces our shame with honour. We are God's honoured sons and daughters. Live it!

Memorable Quote:
"In the crucifixion the traffic moves in the opposite direction. Jesus, who moved so many from shame to honour, is himself humiliated, embarrassed, degraded, and shamed. The great exchange takes place. Jesus takes our shame and gives us honour - Jesus bore our shame for us. He took our shame and exchanged it for His honour. He who knew no shame became shamed for us so that in Him we might become the honoured ones of God." Adapted

Journaling Suggestion:
My identity is in Christ, not the house of shame!

Memo for Meditation:
"For He raised us from the dead along with Christ and seated us with Him in the heavenly realms because we are united with Christ Jesus, in order that in the coming ages He might display the surpassing riches of His grace, demonstrated by His kindness to us in Christ Jesus." Ephesians 2.6,7

September 5

Motivational Idea: It's a shame (2)

The most important thing that we need to consider in this entire book is the cross of Jesus. What the world fails to understand is that the cross of Jesus has the answer. In this month in The Biblical Dimension, we need to grasp the fact that the entire Bible is the unfolding drama of redemption. The cross is written large upon every page of Scripture. The most momentous event in the history of the world and indeed the universe, is the death of Jesus Christ on a Roman gibbet, on the hill called Calvary outside the holy city of Jerusalem. It was here in His crosswork that Jesus died for you and me. He took our place, and John the Baptist announced it right at the beginning of the Gospel of John: *"Behold the Lamb of God who takes away the sin of the world."* (John 1:29). To accomplish this, Jesus had to take our sin and shame and guilt. The truth is, that which Jesus did not assume, He could not heal. Jesus came to reverse the curse of the fall. He did so by entering into that curse, by assuming to Himself, not just bits here and there, but all of it, and all of your stuff. All that burden you have been carrying for years – let it go! As we read in Hebrews: *"Jesus also suffered outside the city gate to make the people holy through his own blood. Let us, then, go to him outside the camp, bearing the disgrace he bore."* (Hebrews 13:12–13).

Rory Shiner of the Gospel Coalition says: *"We have been underselling a key achievement of the cross. With the rise of social media, cancel culture, and public shaming. We need to know what the cross does to address our shame."* From the cross can we hear the words of honour on the other side of shame. Only through the death of Jesus can we now stand before God, knowing Jesus is not ashamed of us but honours us before the Father as His brothers and sisters.

So, can you let go of your shame? Shame tends to be subjective. Shame is felt, and it is felt by our whole person. Guilt says, 'I did the wrong thing.' Shame says, 'I am the wrong person.' Shame takes over our sense of who we are. But Jesus has come to extinguish it in His crosswork!

Memorable Quote:
"Man of sorrows what a name for the Son of God, who came/ruined sinners to reclaim:/Hallelujah, what a Saviour! Bearing shame and scoffing rude/in my place condemned he stood/sealed my pardon with his blood:/Hallelujah, what a Saviour!/Guilty, helpless, lost were we;/blameless Lamb of God was he,/sacrificed to set us free:/Hallelujah, what a Saviour/Lifted up was He to die; 'It is finished' was His cry; now in heaven exalted high; Hallelujah, what a Saviour! When He comes our glorious King, all His ransomed home to bring; then anew this song we'll sing; Hallelujah, what a Saviour." Philip Bliss

Journaling Suggestion:
Jesus took all my sin and the shame on the cross. It's gone! I don't need to wallow in it. I need to have a greater appreciation of the crosswork of Jesus.

Memo for Meditation:
"Let us fix our eyes on Jesus, the author and perfecter of our faith, who for the joy set before Him endured the cross, scorning its shame, and sat down at the right hand of the throne of God." Hebrews 12:2

September 6

Motivational Idea: Rediscovering hidden treasure

The Ulster Museum, Belfast, as the author writes, is displaying some of the most famous paintings in the world; they are on loan from the National Gallery in London, and there is one from the National Gallery of Ireland in Dublin. *The Taking of Christ* (1602) by Michelangelo Merisi da Caravaggio (1571–1610) was discovered in August 1990 in the dining room of one of the houses of the Jesuit Fathers on Leeson Street, Dublin, by Sergio Benedetti, senior conservator in the National Gallery of Ireland. For years, the painting was presumed lost, known only through copies and from descriptions by Caravaggio's biographers. The painting was a commission for the distinguished patrician and city official Ciriaco Mattei (1545–1614). The painting remained in the Mattei family, inherited by various family members, for the next 200 years.

By the second half of the eighteenth century, Caravaggio's name was no longer attached to the painting. At this time, a number of paintings in the Mattei collection were reattributed, and Caravaggio's *The Taking of Christ* was incorrectly attributed to a Dutch artist called Gerrit van Honthorst (1592–1656). In 1802, Duke Giuseppe Mattei sold *The Taking of Christ*, along with other paintings, to William Hamilton Nisbet, a wealthy Scottish art collector in Rome. Records from this sale list the painting as *Imprigionamento del N.S. di Gherardo della Notte.* The mistake in spelling (*Notte* rather than *Notti*) was repeated on the gilt tablet made for the new frame. The painting remained in the Hamilton family for 119 years until it was sold at auction by Dowell's in Edinburgh in 1921, and again in 1922. At this point, it was in the possession of the Hon. Major Charles Hubert Francis Noel. In 1924, the painting was acquired by Dr Marie Lea-Wilson who brought it to Ireland. The first record of it being in the country is a receipt, for £20, for the restoration of its frame by the furniture restorer James Hicks in Dublin. In the 1930s, Dr Lea-Wilson presented the painting, still attributed to Honthorst, to the Jesuit Fathers of Leeson Street in Dublin. It remained in the house, hanging in the dining room, for over 50 years. In August 1990, Father Noel Barber SJ contacted the National Gallery of Ireland about assessing the works of art in the Jesuit House. Senior conservator Sergio Benedetti recognised the painting even though it was obscured by discoloured varnish. On 16 November 1993, *The Taking of Christ* went on public display in the exhibition *Caravaggio: the Master Revealed* in the National Gallery of Ireland. It's a joy and delight to behold.

Memorable Quote:
"The Bible is no mere book, but a Living Creature, with a power that conquers all that oppose it." Napoleon

Journaling Suggestion:
It's time to rediscover the hidden treasure of the Bible.

Memo for Meditation:
"And Hilkiah the high priest said to Shaphan the secretary, 'I have found the Book of the Law in the house of the Lord.'" 2 Kings 22:8

September 7

Motivational Idea: Stuck in the attic

It has been said that a book reader will never clear an attic, the inference being that they will find a book and start reading. Yet there is one book that you might well find in the attic, even though it's a stand-alone, world best-seller, and the most profound and inspired book in the world.

An art newspaper tells the story of how Martin Bailey, an art expert, discovered hidden in a London attic a Bible inscribed by Vincent Van Gogh. Martin was on the search for memorabilia in the attic in Ealing, West London. The great-granddaughter of Harry Gladwell was helping him with the search. Gladwell became a friend of Van Gogh in 1875, and they lodged together in Montmartre when they were both trainee art dealers. Martin opened a trunk and to his great delight found two leather-bound volumes, a Bible and *The Book of Common Prayer*. Amazingly, the two books had survived in the Gladwell family for well over a century.

Vincent, then aged 22, wrote about his new friend in a letter to his brother Theo: *"I live in Montmartre. Also living here is a young Englishman, an employee of the firm, 18 years old, the son of an art dealer in London... I'm very glad of his company in the evenings. He has a completely naive and unspoiled heart, and works very hard."* The two young men were both trainees at the Paris-based Goupil art gallery. The letter then added a key detail: *"Every evening we go home together, eat something or other in my room, and the rest of the evening I read aloud, usually from the Bible. We intend to read it all the way through."* Reading aloud the whole Bible would take around 80 hours in total. Martin tells the story that *"The generous great-granddaughter allowed me to borrow the Bible and The Book of Common Prayer for an exhibition on Van Gogh in England which I curated at the Barbican Art Gallery in 1992. The Van Gogh Museum's specialist, Louis van Tilborgh, later visited the show—and confirmed the exciting discovery that the handwriting of the Biblical verse is actually that of Van Gogh."* The text was from John 17:15, written out by Van Gogh as: *"Father we do not pray thee to take us out of the world, but we pray thee to keep us from evil."* This was one of Van Gogh's most cherished biblical sayings and quoted it in no fewer than eleven letters to his family. The two volumes represent both a testimony to Van Gogh's deep commitment to Christianity in his early 20s. Timothy 3:16-17 says, *"All Scripture is God-breathed. - inspired!"*

We do well to remember that the Bible is inscribed by God Himself and we should not leave it stuck in the attic – get it and read it! It has God's imprimatur!

Memorable Quote:
"The Bible is Christ, for the Old Testament leads to that culmination. Paul and the evangelists stand on the other slope of the holy mountain." Vincent Van Gogh

Journaling Suggestion:
Don't leave the Bible in that attic – get it and read it!

Memo for Meditation:
"My prayer is not that you take them out of the world but that you protect them from the evil one." John 17.15

September 8

Motivational Idea: An antiquarian curiosity seeker

François-Marie Arouet (1694-1778), known by his *nom de plume* as Voltaire, made his prediction about the Bible in 1776: *"One hundred years from my day, there will not be a Bible on earth except one that is looked upon by an antiquarian curiosity-seeker."* Many make the assumption that Voltaire was an atheist, but this was not the case. Voltaire believed in God but did not believe in a God personally involved in people's lives. He wrote, *"The astronomer who watches the motions of stars, established according to the laws of the most profound mathematics, must adore the Eternal Geometer. The physicist who investigates a grain of wheat or an animal body must recognize the Eternal Craftsman. The moral man who seeks a support point in virtue must admit the existence of a Being as fair as He is supreme. So God is necessary to the world in every way, and we can say together with the author of the Epistle to the scribbler of a vulgar book on the Three Impostors, 'If God did not exist, it would be necessary to invent Him'".*

As a Deist, the philosophical system in which Voltaire operated allowed both he and other intellectuals of the time to reconcile a belief in some form of God which incorporated their overwhelming passion for reason. In addition, Deists believe that the God who created the universe does not interfere with any natural processes on Earth. This ideology reconciles a belief in a Supreme Being with belief in scientific reasoning. As such, Deism generally rejects the concept of miracles along with any other supernatural occurrences, such as the divinity and resurrection of Jesus. Voltaire's God was an absent God, not the personal God of the Bible whom we can know.

Memorable Quote:
"After his death, the presses that were used to print Voltaire's books printed Bibles and Voltaire's house was used by the Geneva Bible Society to distribute Bibles. One hundred years from the time of Voltaire's prediction, the first edition of his work sold for .11¢ in Paris, but the British government paid the Czar of Russia half a million dollars for an ancient Bible manuscript. Research on Voltaire's vast array of writings reveal a comprehensive knowledge of Scripture, and biblical quotations permeate his works including those which have no apparent connection Christianity. He is seen to respond positively to the bible, almost despite himself and shows insights beyond the perceived wisdom of the day in terms of its composition. It's a book that must not be ignored." Taken from the author's book, *Short Essays on Finding Hope in Our Fragile World: 40 Days of Exploration.*

Journaling Suggestion:
Read the Bible for yourself and open your mind to what God is saying.

Memo for Meditation:
"Now this is eternal life: that they know you, the only true God, and Jesus Christ, whom you have sent." John 17:3

September 9

Motivational Idea: Top reading tips

Daniel Diffey from Grand Canyon University gives some top tips for reading the Bible. But, have you ever tried to read through the Bible and got stuck in Leviticus? The author concurs with Daniel when he says that Bible reading is extremely important and it is an admirable goal to read it completely within a year. Here are Daniel's seven top tips:

Firstly, we need to have realistic goals. If you are aiming at, say, nine chapters a day, you might need to rethink that. Also, why not download YouVersion, then you can listen as well as read. Secondly, be intentional. We need stickability and if we have a realistic goal each day, we are more likely to stick to it. Thirdly, Daniel suggests getting what he calls *"an accountability partner"*. This person can be an encouragement to you. Fourthly, read faithfully with the right purposeful intention. It's not about information gathering but to get to know the God of the Bible, because it's about *Him*. He gets bad press from His critics, so find out for yourself who He really is and what He is like. Fifthly, get an audio Bible; you can choose the version you prefer and you can download the app and listen to it anywhere. Number six, download helpful apps. Take for example the filament version – this allows you to scan the page and use the filament app to give you in-depth information all centred around the passage you are reading. And number seven, pray. Ask God to reveal Himself to you and to help you to persevere. Pray each day that God will help you persevere in this goal for His glory and for your good. Be encouraged because the average reader can read the Bible in about 65 to 75 hours. So, if you read the Bible for less than 15 minutes a day, you would accomplish your goal. No matter how busy we are, we can certainly find 15 minutes.

Memorable Quote:

"Don't consider this something that you have to do, but something that is a privilege to do. You should not read just to check something off of a list, but because you want to know God better. That is the goal here. You should not read the Bible so you can win a Bible trivia game or so that you can impress your friends. Read because you love God. Another part of

reading faithfully is paying attention. Don't finish your reading for the day and forget what you just read." Dr. Daniel Diffey

Journaling Suggestion:
Get a yearly Bible reading plan that suits me, and stick to it. Just *do* it!

Memo for Meditation:
"This Book of the Law shall not depart from your mouth, but you shall meditate on it day and night, so that you may be careful to do according to all that is written in it. For then you will make your way prosperous, and then you will have good success." Joshua 1:8

September 10

Motivational Idea: Inspiration demands our consideration

Jason Carlson and Ron Carlson from Christian Ministries International pose a question: *"Why should we believe that the Bible is the inspired word of God?"* And a follow-up question would be: *"What's so special, so unique about the Bible that Christians believe it is literally the inspired word of God?"*

These are great questions and demand answers. One of the ways to consider the question of divine inspiration is to look at the facts about the Bible's composition. We find that the Bible is not one book but is made up of 66 books. Then we discover that these 66 books contain a variety of genres, including history, poetry, prophecy, wisdom literature, letters, and apocalyptic literature. Then we look at authorship and we find that there are 40 different authors. When we look into the background of these authors, we find that they came from all walks of life: there are shepherds, fishermen, doctors, kings and prophets. Most of these authors never knew one another personally, so collaboration on the writing project would have been impossible. Then when we add in the timeline for the completion of the entire volume we are looking at a period of some 1,500 years. To then add into this fascinating and complex picture of the Bible – one book with 66 parts – we discover it was written in three different continents: Africa, Asia and Europe, reflecting the varied historical and cultural circumstances of God's people. Here is a challenge: go to any library in the world (choose any library you like), find 66 books which match the characteristics of the 66 books in the Bible. You must choose 66 books, written by 40 different authors, over 1500 years, in 3 different languages, written on 3 different continents. However, they must share a common storyline, a common theme, and a common message, with no historical errors or contradictions. If you can produce such a collection of books, then Christians would have to rethink the Bible as the inspired word of God. Our emphatic reply to the challenge is obvious: "But that's impossible!" The Bible claims to be God's Word, and it is! Read it for yourself today!

Memorable Quote:
"Think about the realities: 66 books, written by 40 different authors, over 1500 years, in 3 different languages, on 3 different continents. What's more, this collection of books shares a common storyline- the creation, fall, and redemption of God's people; a common theme- God's universal love for all of humanity; and a common message- salvation is available to all who repent of their sins and commit to following God with all of their heart, soul, mind and strength. In addition to sharing these commonalities, these 66 books contain no historical errors or contradictions. God's word truly is an amazing collection of writings!" Jason Carlson/Ron Carlson

Journaling Suggestion:
The Bible is unique and I need to read it every day.

Memo for Meditation:
"All scripture is given by inspiration of God..." 2 Timothy 2:16

September 11

Motivational Idea: Inspiration demands our dedication

John Piper in his *Ask Pastor John* podcast tells of a man who asked a really important question in relation to our motivational idea for today: *"I'm simply overwhelmed at how much I don't know about the Bible as a young Christian. I want to be knowledgeable about Scripture so that it can guide me and so that I can use it to guide others in the future. But there is so much. I don't know where to begin. If I were studying for an exam in a class, I would start with a list of essential topics to be tested on. But with the Bible, I feel like the test is life, and I don't know what I need to know to be prepared, if that makes sense. In other words, where do I start? What is the first and most essential thing I need to know to follow Christ by reading his word?"*

John began his answer: *"Well, my answer is probably going to be a little bit frustrating because he's asking for a particular truth in the Bible, and I'm going to say 'Bible, Bible, Bible, Bible.' I have never met a mature, fruitful, strong, spiritually discerning Christian who is not full of Scripture, devoted to regular meditation on Scripture, and given to storing it in the heart through Bible memorization. And that's not a coincidence."*

John goes on to stress that it is absolutely essential, after coming to faith in Christ, to get into the Word of God. We need to be radical about this; we need to be deeply, experientially devoted to the Scriptures of truth. We need to be unshakable and unwavering in our persuasion that the reading of and the meditating on Scripture has our total dedication. Understanding and memorising and enjoying the Scriptures is absolutely essential for the Christian life. This is the fountain of happiness and the key to the fulfilled life we all crave. Be in the word every day, with the aim that we will meet God there and, little by little, the glory of His truth will fill and transform our lives. Kill the lackadaisical attitude and make time – and take the time – for the Word of God, and be amazed at who God is and His plan and purpose for your life. The ultimate fulfilment is within your grasp.

Memorable Quote:
"'Approved unto God' signifies a standard of divine approval that transcends human accolades. This approval comes from a life that aligns with God's will, deeply rooted in the truth of His Word. Paul emphasises the importance of being a "workman" who is unashamed. This workman is one who can rightly divide the word of truth, meaning they accurately interpret and apply the Scriptures." Crosswalk

Journaling Suggestion:
Bible, Bible, Bible, Bible… and more of the Bible!

Memo for Meditation:
"Study and *do your best to present yourself approved unto God, a worker who has no reason to be ashamed, accurately handling and skilfully teaching the word of truth."* 2 Timothy 2:15.

September 12

Motivational Idea: Inspiration demands our prioritisation

We need to prioritise the Bible in our daily lives, but how do we do this? We make time in our lives for what we deem to be important. Making Bible reading and study of the Scriptures a top priority will mean carving out vital time for these pursuits. You will get out what you put in. There is no silver bullet, but making the time every day is vital. Pick a time and be consistent. It's hard to fight sleep when you leave it to the end of a hectic day. Begin with God early in the morning or at a time when you are freshest. If you miss a day, please don't beat yourself up. Pick up where you left off the next day. This isn't about legalism, but consistency. God is not a hard taskmaster, He loves you and His desire is the best for you, so don't be living in a guilt trip when you fail; the enemy loves that and wants to keep you down. Get up and get on with the task in hand.

It's a good idea to start small. You need not start by studying for an hour or more every day; but, if you do, that's great. Start with 15 minutes a day and work your way up to at least 30 minutes. It may seem hard to do at first, and it'll be difficult to find time. Just remember, 30 minutes is only 2% of a 24 hour day!

One of the best ways to get the most out of your study time is to come with a plan. Start by reading a book of the Bible, like one of the Gospels, or use one of the many reading plans available on the net. The author uses the YouVersion but there are a number of yearly plans available. Don't give up. Out of all the principles, this one is most important. There will be times when you want to give up, but push through it and keep at it. You'll hit difficult passages and sometimes you may not understand what you just read, and that's okay. Just keep at it and ask God to help you understand what you're reading. Over time, God will make it clear to you. When you hit those difficult spots, remember to make use of the tools available to you. And, inevitably, you may fall off the wagon and stop reading all together for a season. Don't get discouraged, just start again. Once you have a plan, do it daily and start small. If you do, you will have no problem making it a habit you'll keep for life.

Memorable Quote:
"We say God and faith and the Bible are important, but our time and our calendars prove otherwise. If we are going to make time for bible study , it means we have to adjust our priorities. In so far as you are serious about making Bible study a priority, that is the level to which you will find time and have success. Give God your best time, not your leftovers."
Anon

Journaling Suggestion:
Making time for Bible study , and adjusting my priorities to do it!

Memo for Meditation:
"O how I love your law! All day long I meditate on it." Psalm 119:104
"Your word is a lamp to walk by, and a light to illuminate my path."
Psalm 119:105

September 13

Motivational Idea: Food for the soul

Matthew records for us the words of Jesus in 4:4: *"People do not live on bread alone, but by every word that comes from the mouth of God."* Just as we need food for our bodies, we also need food for our souls. Here is the sustenance we need for the journey of life. Without it, we will have a spiritual hunger that cannot be satisfied anywhere else. In terms of physical food, try living on junk food for a month and see what happens to your body; better not, it's not recommended. Yet when it comes to soul hunger, so many are filling their souls with junk or alternatives to the word of God. No wonder people are not happy and do not enjoy the fulfilled life that was meant for them.

We are what we eat and we are what we feed our souls on. Scripture gives and sustains life. The words of Jesus alone are sufficient reason for us to take the Bible seriously. Here is our food for our spiritual fitness and wellbeing. We need to feed on God's word. This will be strange to many people but the proof of the pudding is in the eating. We all know that food is vital for sustaining life and without proper nourishment we will be unhealthy, even sickly, and suffer premature death as a result. Malnourishment exists in our society today because of a *lack* of food, as well as the junk food phenomenon. It's the same in the spiritual arena – unhealthy, sickly and deathly malnourished souls who have bought the lie of the enemy and think the Bible is not for them.

The words of Jesus were directed not to a human being, although the inspired words are recorded for our benefit; the truth is, Jesus directed His words to Satan, the arch enemy of our souls, and He prefixed the words with an important phrase: *"It is written."* To find the origin of the quotation, we need to go back to the book of Deuteronomy 8:3 in the Old Testament. The context is Moses preaching to the Israelites on the importance of obeying God, and the memo for today sets out the words. We normally eat every day, but many are living on starvation rations when it comes to spiritual nourishment. The food of the Word of God will not only enable us to live but to thrive and flourish, so we need to feed on it regularly and make this a daily number one priority.

Memorable Quote:
"Scripture gives and sustains life: Spiritual life, eternal life — just like physical life — must be fed, though not by bread, but by the word of God. If you think that you have eternal life as a kind of vaccination against hell, which needs no nourishment, you don't know what spiritual life is."
John Piper

Journaling Suggestion:
Daily bible food is a top priority for my spiritual wellbeing!

Memo for Meditation:
"Remember the whole way by which He (God) has brought you these forty years through the desert so that He might, by humbling you, test you to see if you have it within you to keep His commandments or not. So He humbled you by making you hungry and then feeding you with unfamiliar manna. He did this to teach you that humankind cannot live

by bread alone, but also by everything that comes from the Lord's mouth." Deuteronomy 8:2-3

September 14

Motivational Idea: More on soul food

We need to ingest food for our bodies to break it down into the different amino acids contained in protein so we can enjoy wellbeing and have the nourishment we need to live and do all the things we need to do. Our bodies need vital fuel and refuelling, so we need to fill up regularly and, indeed, on a daily basis. When we turn to the Bible, we find frequent use of the food metaphor. For example, Jeremiah tells us, *"Your words were found and I ate them, and Your word became to me the gladness and joy of my heart."* (Jeremiah 15:16).

Scripture is not only for reading and studying, it is to be 'eaten'. This means when we read God's Word, we need to pause and 'chew on it' for a while, meditating and reflecting on the meaning and application of what we've read. Take for example the paraphrased words of the Psalmist from the Message Bible: *"How well God must like you—you don't walk in the ruts of those blind-as-bats, you don't stand with the good-for-nothings, you don't take your seat among the know-it-alls. Instead you thrill to GOD's Word, you chew on Scripture day and night. You're a tree replanted in Eden, bearing fresh fruit every month, Never dropping a leaf, always in blossom."* (Psalm 1:1–3).

This use of food metaphors demonstrates the importance of ingesting God's Word. This is our soul food, this is the nourishment we need for the journey of life. Other Bible metaphors used can help to drive home the message today to feed on God's Word. God's Word is described as milk. *"Like newborn babies, you must crave pure spiritual milk so that you will grow into a full experience of salvation. Cry out for this nourishment."* (1 Peter 2:2).

The psalmist in the amazing Psalm 119, which is worth a good read and a good chew too, says, *"How sweet your words taste to me; they are sweeter than honey."* (Psalm 119:103). Paul in his first letter to the church at Corinth tells the Corinthian Christians, *"I had to feed you with milk, not with solid food, because you weren't ready for anything stronger. And you still aren't ready."* (1 Corinthians 3:2).

Are we on the milk or the meat? *Ready?*

Memorable Quote:
"Over the span of thousands of years, God gave us His precious Word. Now we have His complete revelation in our hands: the Bible. History tells us that the Bible has profoundly affected countless people throughout the centuries. It has served as a guide for how to live, and it has even been taught in schools as great literature. But the Bible isn't merely a book full of doctrines about God and the Christian faith, a work of literature, or a self-help manual telling us how to have a good life. Actually, God's intention in giving us His Word is that it would be our spiritual food to nourish us. How do we know? The Bible itself reveals this to us." Bibles for Europe blog

Journaling Suggestion:
Food, glorious Bible food, for the welfare of my soul.

Memo for Meditation:
"I have not departed from the commandment of His lips; I have treasured the words of His mouth more than my portion of food." Job 23:12

September 15

Motivational Idea: An invite to supper

The power and importance of remembering cannot be overstated. Remembering can be both a collective experience and also a very personal one. The act of remembering yields many practical and psychological benefits. We remember past successes and failures. We can learn from these and be incentivised to grow and develop in our maturity and wisdom. We remember loved ones who have gone before and we can learn from the example they set.

The power and importance of remembering extends profoundly into the realm of spirituality and faith. One of the most common words in the Bible is 'remember', and one of the most frequent exhortations in Scripture is to remember the Lord. Remembering plays a significant role in our relationship with God. Time and time again, God calls his people of every generation to remember His faithfulness. We are encouraged to remember His promises; to reflect on His goodness and mercy. We are reminded that His grace is sufficient for us in all circumstances.

Remembering God and His loving kindness towards us helps us to navigate the complexities of life and comforts us in those tough times. The psalmist says *"I remember the days of long ago; I meditate on all your works and consider what your hands have done."* (Psalm 143:3). Meditating on God's past works is an act of worship. We are invited by God to contemplate His wonders and appreciate His continuous presence in our lives. Such reflection deepens our relationship with God, enhancing our trust in His plans and provisions. We are given an important invitation by Jesus to remember His death. The invitation to participate in this event is commonly called 'The Lord's Supper', sometimes referred to as 'Holy Communion'. Significantly, it is recorded in all four Gospels. (see Matthew 26:26-29; Mark 14:17-25; Luke 22:7-22; and John 13:21-30.) The Lord's Supper is a remembrance of what Christ did for us and a celebration of what we receive as a result of His sacrifice. We eat the bread and we drink the wine in remembrance of Jesus' death for us on the cross.

Do you partake of the Lord's supper? It is a soul-stirring experience because of the depth of meaning involved. The Lord's Supper enables us to look back with thankfulness, but also to our future, with a blessed eternal hope.

Let's go to supper.

Memorable Quote:
"The purpose of the Lord's Supper is to receive from Christ the nourishment and strength and hope and joy that come from feasting our souls on all that He purchased for us on the cross, especially His own fellowship." John Piper

Journaling Suggestion:
Lord, I will partake of your supper in remembrance of you.

Memo for Meditation:
"For I received from the Lord what I also delivered to you, that the Lord Jesus on the night when he was betrayed took bread, and when he had given thanks, he broke it, and said, 'This is my body, which is for you. Do this in remembrance of me.' In the same way also he took the cup, after

supper, saying, 'This cup is the new covenant in my blood. Do this, as often as you drink it, in remembrance of me.'" 1 Corinthians 11:23-25

September 16

Motivational Idea: A strange metaphor

"Eat me!" The prophet from Nazareth caused outrage! This could well have been the MSM and social network main headline. Many would have 'unfollowed', given the nature of the bizarre statement, *"Unless you eat the flesh of the Son of Man and drink his blood, you have no life in you."* The Jews' reaction is a classic case of misconstruing Jesus's words. The context and whole discourse (John 6:25-65) needs to be taken into account, beginning with the miracle of the feeding of the 5,000. The people were following Jesus for food, they were not interested in their spiritual needs. Just as we need physical food for physical life, so we need spiritual food for spiritual life.

Jesus' teaching was explicitly symbolic about the spiritual realm. He is speaking metaphorically about our need for spiritual nourishment and He is the one who can give us this spiritual good. Only He can fill us with true joy and happiness and enable us to live the fulfilled life. He is the Bread of Life, the only one who can satisfy our spiritual hunger. Jesus often used physical elements to teach deep spiritual truths and this graphic imagery needs to be set in the context of the manna from heaven that God gave to His people in the wilderness. The reaction to Jesus' metaphor, we are told, is stark: *"After this, many of His disciples quit following Him and did not accompany Him any longer. So Jesus said to the twelve, "You don't want to go away too, do you?" Simon Peter answered Him, "Lord, to whom can we go? You have the words of eternal life. We have come to believe and to know you are the Holy One of God."'* (John 6:67)

Memorable Quote:

"The dwelling of the believer in Christ involves an utter self-surrender to him, a recognition of the supreme claims of the God-Man and his work, a complete trust in him as the Source of all life, a sound and abiding place of rest, a justification before God as one with Christ, as one identified with him in his well pleasing to the Father. The dwelling of Christ in the

believer is the fulness and riches of the Divine life. Christ liveth in him (Galatians 2:20), thinks in his thoughts, moves through his will. This is sanctification. The believer is in Christ as the members are in the body. Christ is in the believer as God is in his temple. What is the condition of this mutual indwelling? Christ puts the condition of this Divine interpretation thus: "He that eateth my flesh and drinketh my blood, dwelleth in me, and I in him." The verb is in the present tense, implying the continuous appropriation of the Divine sustenance." John 6:56, The Pulpit commentary

Journaling Suggestion:
Lord, nourish my soul as I abide in you, and feed upon you.

Memo for Meditation:
"I am the living bread that came down from heaven. Whoever eats of this bread will live forever, and the bread that I will give for the life of the world is my flesh." John 6:51

September 17

Motivational Idea: The Bread of Life

Walking down the aisle of the local supermarket, we might be in awe of the different types of bread and the vast array of produce on display by bread makers with their own unique brand for us to buy and savour. How privileged we are if we live in a land where bread is available in abundance and if we can afford to buy it. We may not be aware that bread has been a part of human history for centuries and still plays an integral role in our daily life. It's a symbol of culture, history, hunger, wealth, war and peace. It is indispensable and has been key in human survival. Bread created the structure of modern day society and gave order to our way of living. Without this seemingly simple food, civilisation wouldn't exist in the way we know it today. Bread is still a universal food and exists in every country around the world.

In Jesus' day, bread was the essential, basic food. So basic was it that in Hebrew 'to eat bread' and 'to have a meal' are the same thing. Bread was treated with great respect and many rules existed to preserve that reverence. Any crumbs over the size of an olive were expected to be gathered, never simply discarded. We can then understand more fully, given the context, Jesus' declaration" *"I am the Bread of Life."* (John 6:35). If we don't have a grasp of the context, we will miss the significance of what He said, but when we realise the importance of bread for survival, for life and living, then this is nothing short of a phenomenal statement! By equating Himself with bread, Jesus is saying He is absolutely essential for life. He is spiritual bread that brings eternal life.

So, if we are looking for the fulfilled life here on earth with a lifeforce that never dies – the life of Christ in us, eternal life – then we better take heed and embrace Jesus as the Bread of Life. Jesus then reinforces what He is saying by making a further declaration, and this is our memo for meditation today.

Memorable Quote:
"Farmers everywhere provide bread for all humanity, but it is Christ alone who is the bread of life...Even if all the physical hunger of the world were satisfied, even if everyone who is hungry were fed by his or her own labour or by the generosity of others, the deepest hunger of man would still exist...Therefore, I say, Come, all of you, to Christ. He is the bread of life. Come to Christ and you will never be hungry again." Pope John Paul II

Journaling Suggestion:
Feed the soul on the Living Bread and know the fulfilled life.

Memo for Meditation:
"Then Jesus declared, 'I am the bread of life. Whoever comes to me will never go hungry, and whoever believes in me will never be thirsty. But as I told you, you have seen me and still you do not believe. All those the Father gives me will come to me, and whoever comes to me I will never drive away. For I have come down from heaven not to do my will but to do the will of him who sent me. And this is the will of him who sent me, that I shall lose none of all those he has given me, but raise them up at the last day. For my Father's will is that everyone who looks to the Son and believes in him shall have eternal life, and I will raise them up at the last day.'" John 6:35-40

September 18

Motivational Idea: The Light of the world

Light is essential for all life on earth. It is vital for a myriad things, from the production of the very air that we breathe to the cycle of the oceans. Light is responsible for the magnetic fields around planet earth, gravity, our climate, and for the warmth we need to survive. So, we can truly say that light is life. Jesus made a startling statement in relation to light; He said, *"I am the Light of the world."* He did not say, 'a light,' He said, 'the Light'. This again is one of the great 'I am' statements found only in John's Gospel, of which there are seven.

John's Gospel is all about the deity of Christ – He is God. *"I am the light of the world,"* is rooted in Jesus' relationship with His Father. John Piper states, *"Jesus speaks from God and for God and as God."* Apart from Jesus, we live in darkness. We have limited capacity to understand who we are or what we see in the world. We need the Light, we need Jesus. In making this declaration, as with all the 'I am' statements, Jesus points to His unique divine identity and purpose. In declaring Himself to be the Light of the world, Jesus was claiming that He is the exclusive source of spiritual light. We would expect the Eternal Creator, Author and Originator of all things who desires us to escape spiritual darkness to tell us He is the light of the world.

The important question for us today is, are we walking in the Light? Many are walking in darkness today – this is the course of life. Many not only live in darkness today but *prefer* darkness; the madness of our fallen estate and distorted thinking! But Jesus is calling to all today – get into the Light! As followers of Jesus, we desire to walk in the Light and to live in His Light. In doing so we have the Light of life – this is truly the fulfilled life.

Memorable Quote:

"'The light of Christ," writes John Piper, 'Is the brightness of God shining on the retina of the human soul.' Life can be wonderful on earth, but not fully complete without Jesus. We are all created to crave the Creator, our Father, and only through a relationship with our Savior Jesus can the dark parts of our hearts brighten. 'When I admit I am not enough, I'm freed to run and cling to the God who is.'" Aimee Joseph

Journaling Suggestion:
"I want to live in the Light. But if we are living in the Light, as God is in the Light, then we have fellowship with each other, and the blood of Jesus, his Son, cleanses us from all sin." 1 John 1.7

Memo for Meditation:
"Jesus spoke to the people once more and said, 'I am the light of the world. If you follow me, you won't have to walk in darkness, because you will have the light that leads to life.'" John 8:12
"For you are all children of light, children of the day. We are not of the night or of the darkness." 1 Thessalonians 5:5
"The night is far gone; the day is at hand. So then let us cast off the works of darkness and put on the armour of light." Romans 13:12

September 19

Motivational Idea: The door

He had done nothing wrong but the elites decided to kick him out of their premises. He was barred and they thought they were the God-appointed gatekeepers. He was denied access and the door was firmly shut. Have you experienced any doors being shut in your face? There was a specific reason for the elites to close the door on this man; they were making a powerful statement. They were Pharisees and the man in question had been blind from birth, but something miraculous had occurred and he had gained his sight. This happened on the Sabbath day but because of their religious legalism, the door of the synagogue was closed to him, indicating that he could not gain access to the place of worship and therefore he could not gain access to God – or so they thought.

As he sat alone, the man from Galilee came and spoke to Him. Jesus knew he had been kicked out and that the door was closed to him. This story is very important because it sets the context for what Jesus said subsequent to these events. In John 10, He uses a powerful metaphor and guess what, it's the metaphor of 'the door'! *"I tell you the solemn truth, I am the door for the sheep."* (John 10:7). And again, for emphasis, *"I am the door. If anyone enters through me, he will be saved, and will come in and go out and find pasture."* (John 10:9).

By kicking the no-longer-blind man out of the synagogue, the Pharisees had, in their estimation, blocked his access to God. They were acting as a door to God. So, when Jesus uses the 'door for the sheep' metaphor, He is saying He alone is the door. He is the *only* door to God. He is the only way to God. The life we seek is found though this door but we need to open the door of our hearts to Him. In Revelation 3.20, Jesus said, *"Look! I stand at the door and knock. If you hear my voice and open the door, I will come in, and we will share a meal together as friends."*

Memorable Quote:
"But, 'all we like sheep have gone astray' (Isaiah 53:6) and we don't always feel satisfied with just a shepherd as our door. We look for other doors to protect us, to offer us security. Maybe a relationship will finally give us that peace we seek? Or maybe we seek financial security from a job—but it leaves us with little time to serve the kingdom? Trusting these doors will not lead to the abundant life Jesus promised in John 10:10."
Kristee Ravan

Journaling Suggestion:
I threw the door of my heart wide open to you, Jesus.

Memo for Meditation:
"Jesus heard that they had thrown him out, and when he found him, he said, "Do you believe in the Son of Man?" He answered and said, "And who is He, Lord, that I may believe in Him?" "You have already seen Him," Jesus answered. "He is the One speaking with you." "Yes, Lord, I believe!" the man said. And he worshipped Jesus. Then Jesus told him, "I entered this world to render judgement—to give sight to the blind and to show those who think they see that they are blind." Some Pharisees who were standing nearby heard him and asked, "Are you saying we're blind?" "If you were blind, you wouldn't be guilty," Jesus replied. "But you remain guilty because you claim you can see." John 9:35-41

September 20

Motivational Idea: The Good Shepherd

The idea of needing a shepherd in this day and age is somewhat strange. Who needs a shepherd? Yet in the days of Jesus on earth, the metaphor was not lost on His audience. For the original listener, a shepherd had profound cultural and historical implications. Shepherd imagery was common in many parts of the ancient world, with kings and leaders described as shepherds. For the Israelites, shepherds were integral to their history as a nation and as the people of God. The metaphor of shepherd became synonymous with leadership, both in the political and spiritual realm. In the Old Testament, God is the True Shepherd. Jesus is making a claim to deity when He declares that He is the Good Shepherd. This declaration was also a scathing criticism of the Pharisees and the religious leaders of the day who were failing those they served. There is an indirect reference to Ezekiel 34, where God reprimands the people he had appointed to be the spiritual protectors and guides for his people, exclaiming that they had only sought to care for themselves and had left the people of God vulnerable and unprotected. This statement would have resonated with the leaders who had the healed man thrown out (see previous day).

As the Good Shepherd, Jesus claims that He is the True Shepherd, guide and protector of His sheep. We need to be aware today of false shepherds. Don't fall for the false shepherds; be discerning. Jesus said of them in His day, *"You load people down with burdens that they can hardly carry, and you yourselves will not lift one finger to help them."* (Luke 11:46).

Follow the Good Shepherd today, the one who leads and doesn't push us along the way. He gave His life as the greatest demonstration of His love. As those He loves, we are able to hear His voice and follow His leadership, knowing He is good. We are not asked to measure up to some impossible standard or to earn His approval. He simply asks us to hear and follow, but that decision is ours to make. He will not force it upon us.

Memorable Quote:
"The message of this parable is that Jesus is the true shepherd. He is the Good Shepherd who was willing to die for those who put their faith in Him. Any other person who claims to be the true shepherd is a robber or thief, for they are a false shepherd. Imagine a world where people do not expect to be served but are all eager to serve and care for one another! Jesus is the Good Shepherd who cares, watches, and protects those who believe in Him. This is a wonderful message for anyone who seeks peace with God." Kristee Ravan

Journaling Suggestion: The Lord is *my* Shepherd.

Memo for Meditation:
"I am the good shepherd. The good shepherd sacrifices his life for the sheep...I am the good shepherd; I know my own sheep, and they know me, just as the Father knows me and I know the Father; and I lay down my life for the sheep." John 10:11,14, 15

September 21

Motivational Idea: I am the resurrection and the life

Nanea Hoffman, writer, dreamer, coffee lover, blanket fort dweller, cancer survivor, and Anxiety Blog founder, said, *"None of us are getting out of here alive, so please stop treating yourself like an afterthought. Eat the delicious food. Walk in the sunshine. Jump in the ocean. Say the truth you're carrying in your heart like hidden treasure. Be silly. Be kind. Be weird. There's no time for anything else."*

Nanea makes a great point; we might as well make the most of it and enjoy it. Our time on earth is limited and has an expiry date. We must all face death, our inevitable demise. All that we have accrued and worked so hard for, we leave behind. What will be our lasting legacy? Jesus made a statement that is astounding; so many of His declarations are. *"Jesus told her, 'I am the resurrection and the life. Anyone who believes in me will live, even after dying. Everyone who lives in me and believes in me will never ever die. Do you believe this, Martha?'"* (John 11:25,26). Jesus made the claim that He would rise from the dead, and He did. The evidence is irrefutable.

The resurrection of Jesus Christ is the most important event in the history of the world for a number of reasons: it means that we can be justified before God. *"He was delivered over to death for our sins and was raised to life for our justification."* (Romans 4:25). Justification means to be put right with God. The resurrection of Jesus Christ shows that Jesus defeated death. Death is the enemy of mankind and the just punishment for our sin (see Romans 6:23). The mortality rate is and will always be 100%. No amount of effort, medical technology, power or riches can help us escape the clutches of death. Christ rose from the dead because death could no longer hold Him (see Acts 2:24). We no longer have to fear death because Christ has triumphed over it. That's what led the apostle Paul to write: *"O death where is your victory? O death, where is your sting? The sting of death is sin, and the power of sin is the law. But thanks be to God, who gives us the victory through our Lord Jesus Christ!"* (1 Corinthians 15:55-57).

The resurrection of Jesus Christ confirms the truth of Scripture. The book of Job, Isaiah 53 and Psalm 16 are among the many examples of Old Testament Scriptures that prophesied about the resurrection of Jesus: *"For I know that my Redeemer lives, and at the last he will stand upon the earth."* (Job 19:25).

Memorable Quote:
"Our Lord has written the promise of resurrection, not in books alone, but in every leaf in springtime." Billy Graham

Journaling Suggestion:
It's Friday but Sunday's coming!

Memo for Meditation:
"O death where is your victory? O death, where is your sting?"'The sting of death is sin, and the power of sin is the law. But thanks be to God, who gives us the victory through our Lord Jesus Christ!" 1 Corinthians 15:55-57

September 22

Motivational Idea: I am the way

We live in a world where many are wandering aimlessly and don't know where they are going. Do you know where *you* are going? We live in a world where many are confused and don't know what to think about life and the reason for being here. Are *you* confused? We live in a world where many feel dead on the inside and don't know if they can go on. Do *you* feel dead on the inside? Can you keep on going the way you are? So, how can we find the way? How can we find the truth? And how can we find the life?

The man who has been known down through the centuries as 'Doubting Thomas' had the courage to own his confusion and ask Jesus a question. The question promoted one of the greatest answers ever given and settled everything. Thomas should be praised for honestly and clearly explaining his confusion. He thought Jesus was simply going to another place, as if it were another city. And so he asked, *"Lord, we do not know where You are going, and how can we know the way?"* Jesus said to him, *"I am the way, the truth, and the life. No one comes to the Father except through Me."* (John 14:6). This is profound! Jesus didn't say that He would *show us* a way; He said that He *is* the way. He didn't promise to *teach us* a truth; He said that He *is* the truth. Jesus didn't offer us some obtuse secrets to life; He said that He *is* the life.

Jesus is the answer for the world today; above Him there's no other – Jesus is the way. We need to know Him personally. The context of the declaration is set in a paradox. *"In light of soon events, this declaration was a paradox. Jesus' way would be the cross; He would be convicted by blatant liars; His body would soon lie lifeless in a tomb. Because He took that way, He is the way to God; because He did not contest the lies we can believe He is the truth; because He was willing to die He becomes the channel of resurrection – the life to us."* (Enduring Word Commentary). *"No one comes to the Father except through Me."* In making this remarkable statement, Jesus is claiming that He is the only way to God. He set aside the temple and its rituals; He sets aside all the religions of the world. He claims to be the exclusive way, truth, and life – the only pathway to God the Father, the true God in heaven.

Exclusivity and inclusivity! Jesus invites you to experience Him as the answer to every aspect of your life, today and every day and forever.

Memorable Quote:
"Without the way there is no going; without the truth there is no knowing; without the life there is no living. I am the way which thou must follow; the truth in which thou must believe; the life for which thou must hope." Thomas à Kempis, cited by Bruce

Journaling Suggestion:
Lord, I believe that You alone are the Way, and the Truth and the Life.

Memo for Meditation:
"Thomas said, 'We have no idea where you are going, so how can we know the way?" Jesus told him, *"I am the way, the truth, and the life. No one can come to the Father except through me. If you had really known me, you would know who my Father is. From now on, you do know him and have seen him!"'* John 14:4b-7

September 23

Motivational Idea: I am the True Vine

Are you joyful? Do you have joy in your life? Are you known as being a joyful human being? If you could get your hands on a book where the author is very explicit about living a joyful life, in fact the author talks about complete joy, would you get the book? I would buy the book! If your mind works like mine, you are probably asking the question, *"What do I need to do to get this joy?"* Here is the exact quotation from the book I'm referring to: *"I have told you these things so that my joy may be in you, and your joy may be complete."* Remember that context is everything. These are the words of Jesus, set in the context of John 15:1-17. In this passage, Jesus calls Himself the *"True Vine".* This metaphor has to do with our dwelling in Christ. Vines are among the most high-maintenance crops in all of agriculture. They need constant pruning and attention if the clusters of grapes are to grow to full maturity.

Jesus used this metaphor because our relationship with God is the same. Without constant care, maintenance, pruning and watering, our spiritual life will wither and die. In short, Jesus uses this metaphor because he knows how needy we are. As He says, *"Apart from me, you can do nothing."* (John 15:5). We are needy branches, but Christ is the true, life-giving, all-sufficient vine. Being a branch that bears fruit begins by recognizing just how needy we are and just how ready Christ is to meet every need.

Run to Him today, confess your neediness and look to Him to provide, and He will fill you with His joy, and as you bear good fruit in your life, you will know complete joy.

Pam is a vinedresser and the following is an excerpt from her writings:

Memorable Quote:
"In my role as a vinedresser, I daily walked the vineyard and my primary role, in every season, was to aid the vine in producing fruit by caring well for the branches. Right after the harvest, I walked through the vineyard looking for places to prune so the vine could produce more. When I would saw off a branch, we applied "b-lock", a mix of nutrients and sealer, to bind up the wound to keep the good nutrients in and the bad elements out. My relationship with God grew as I daily prayer-walked the vineyard. Stepping into the role of the vinedresser, I felt the attention our Father in heaven extending to us, caring for our every need, so we could become branches who bear more fruit. I also saw the vital importance of being a branch secured strong and stable into the Vine—the source of life and fruit." Pam Farrel, vinedresser

Journaling Suggestion:
Be a branch, secured strong and stable into the vine – the source of life and fruit, the dwelling place of joy!

Memo for Meditation:
" I Am the Vine; you are the branches. The one who remains in me - and I in them bears much fruit, because apart from me you can accomplish nothing. I have told you these things so that my joy may be in you, and your joy may be complete. You did not choose me, but I chose you and appointed you to go and bear fruit, fruit that remains, so that whatever

you ask the Father in my Name He will give you. This is my commandment that you love one another." John 15:5, 11; 16: 17

September 24

Motivational Idea: I am

John records the seven 'I ams' of Jesus in his Gospel. There is, however, another which can be considered at the eighth 'I am'. This one is a stand-alone 'I am'. The commonality of the eight statements concerns Jesus' self-descriptions and His self-identity. The stand-alone 'I am' is the most significant and stands out from the rest. A reading of John 8 gives the context. Jesus had described Himself using the metaphor of light: *"I am the light of the world."* (John 8.12). This was met with disdain by the Pharisees. They insulted Jesus by asking Him, *"Who is your Father?"* As the discussion continued, the Pharisees declared that Abraham was their father, the patriarch of Israel. This led to the 'I am' self-description. Such was the astounding nature of the declaration that the Pharisees tried to kill Him; they were filled with fury at Him saying such an outrageous thing. It is a radical statement: *"Before Abraham was I am."* The strangeness of the grammatical structure shows that Jesus was speaking about much more than pre-existence.

To get the full impact we need to go back to the book of Exodus and to the Tetragrammaton. In Exodus, when Moses asked God for His name so he could tell the Israelites who sent him, God said, *"I AM that I AM."* The Tetragrammaton is not a title but a name. In English *"I am"* becomes Yahweh, written in four letters. Such was the sacredness of the name that the Jews would not even say it. Jesus on the other hand was not only saying it, He was deliberately invoking the name of God as His self-description, His self-identity. He is applying the name to Himself. In other words, Jesus is declaring that He is God and His nature is the divine nature.

The Bible declares there is one God in three persons, the Blessed Trinity, and Jesus is the second person of the Trinity. This is the wonder of the incarnation – Jesus is Immanuel, God with us, the *'I Am,'* behold your God.

Memorable Quote:
"[Jesus] is the radiance of the glory of God and the exact imprint of his nature, and he upholds the universe by the word of his power. This is not the description of any angel or any man, even a superhuman man. This is a description of God. Because Jesus is God." Hebrews 1:3

Journaling Suggestion:
The fulfilled life is found in Jesus, God with us.

Memo for Meditation:
"He came into the very world he created, but the world didn't recognize him. He came to his own people, and even they rejected him. But to all who believed him and accepted him, he gave the right to become children of God. They are reborn—not with a physical birth resulting from human passion or plan, but a birth that comes from God. So the Word became human and made his home among us. He was full of unfailing love and faithfulness. And we have seen his glory, the glory of the Father's one and only Son. John testified about him when he shouted to the crowds, 'This is the one I was talking about when I said, 'Someone is coming after me who is far greater than I am, for He existed long before me.'" John 1:10-15

September 25

Motivational Idea: The Trinity

Timothy Mackie and Jonathan Collins of the Bible Project use an analogy to try to help us to better understand the Trinity. Tim says: *"We can't fully understand but perhaps we can better understand what cannot be fully understood."* It's a quote worth remembering in our seeking to understand this and other biblical truths, or axioms. The Bible Project uses the analogy of a 2D plane with an object with three dimensions passing through the 2D plane. We only see each as distinct, yet the three are one but not in a way that we are capable of understanding, nor does it fit into our limited categories of understanding.

Our hope is centred in the Triune God, His eternal Fatherhood, His eternal Sonship and His eternal Spirit, who makes truth known to us and guides us into all truth. We worship and serve one God and in so doing we are worshipping and serving the Father, the Son and the Holy Spirit.

Three distinct persons – one God. Some people who 'in their opinion' do not accept the doctrine of the Trinity, say that Christians believe in three gods. This criticism is often levelled at the Christian faith by those who do not accept the deity of Jesus Christ. 'How can He be God and the Father be God, if He was praying to Him when on earth?' The answer is simple: because there is one God and three distinct persons in the Godhead. To reiterate, we simply don't have the capacity to grasp this axiom but we accept its reality because it is biblical truth. This axiom permeates Scripture from Genesis to Revelation.

Some critics point to the fact that the actual word 'Trinity' is not mentioned in the Bible, and for them that is sufficient grounds to deny the doctrine, i.e. the axiom. The doctrine of the Trinity was first formulated among the early Christians and fathers of the Church as they attempted to understand the relationship between Jesus and God as presented in Scripture. The term, 'The Trinity' is the English equivalent of the Latin word *trinitas,* which was coined by the early Christian writer Tertullian. The word, which etymologically means something like 'the Tripleness', is used to refer collectively to the Father, Son and Holy Spirit. The doctrine of the Trinity means that there is one God who eternally exists as three distinct persons — the Father, Son, and Holy Spirit. Stated differently, God is one in essence and three in persons. These definitions express three crucial truths: (1) the Father, Son, and Holy Spirit are distinct persons; (2) each person is fully God; (3) there is only one God.

We bow in worship and adoration before our God today and acknowledge that only He can impart the joy we crave and the fulfilment in life that we desire. Jesus came to show us the way.

Memorable Quote:
"For to have the fruition of God the Trinity, after whose image we are made, is indeed the fullness of our joy, than which there is no greater." St Augustine

Journaling Suggestion:
I want to worship, trust and obey the Triune God who is near to me.

Memo for Meditation:
"May the grace of the Lord Jesus Christ, the love of God, and the fellowship of the Holy Spirit be with you all." 2 Corinthians 13:14

September 26

Motivational Idea: Making plans

We make plans for today, we plan for tomorrow, and we plan into the future. Our plans involve everyday things and also the big things. Our plans involve family, people and relationships, projects, education, career, advancement, financial security, umpteen other things, and retirement. We plan in hope, but the unexpected can happen, things we had not anticipated can throw our plans up in the air. So, from the biblical dimension, does Scripture have anything to say about God in relation to us and our plans? The Bible teaches us that God is all-knowing – He is omniscient and knows us, and He knows our plans. (see Genesis 22:14). We also learn that He is all-powerful, omnipotent. (see 1 Corinthians 6:14). He is Sovereign, which means that He is in control.

We look at a chaotic world that has abandoned God, but He is still in control and in the end all will be well. We look at things from a temporal perspective; God sees it all from an eternal perspective. Our lives are but a blink in the light of His eternity. His Word tells us that He will correct every injustice, and He will hold every individual human being to account on Judgment Day. No one gets off scot-free. *"Nothing in all creation is hidden from God's sight. Everything is uncovered and laid bare before the eyes of him to whom we must give account."* (Hebrews 4:13). We also learn from the Bible that God is everywhere, He is omnipresent. (see Psalm 139).

The implications for us are clear: we can make our plans but God is the one who has the power to change the direction of our lives. What we need to do is to bring all our plans and dreams to the Lord, and seek His will for our lives. Have we submitted and surrendered our plans to God? He may well have placed them in our hearts but we need to make sure we are going in the right direction and following His plan and purpose. Take time today to ask God to direct your steps. Ask Him to make His will clear to you. Very often the whole picture is not revealed, only the next step. Let's submit our plans to the Lord today so that we are open to following His lead. He knows what is best for us and the joy and fulfilment of being in His will.

Memorable Quote:
"For I know the plans I have for you," declares the LORD, "plans to prosper you and not to harm you, plans to give you hope and a future." God, Jeremiah 29:11

Journaling Suggestion:
I'm praising God that He has a plan for my life and is guiding me today.

Memo for Meditation:
"In their hearts humans plan their course, but the LORD establishes their steps." Proverbs 16:9, NIV.
"We can make our plans, but the LORD determines our steps." Proverbs 16:9, NLT
"A man's heart plans his course, but the LORD determines his steps." Proverbs 167:9, BSB
"The heart of a son of man plans his ways and LORD JEHOVAH orders his steps. All of the works of the Lord are done with righteousness; and the ungodly man is kept for the evil day." Proverbs 16:9, Aramaic Bible in plain English.
"We plan the way we want to live, but only GOD makes us able to live it." Proverbs 16:9, MSG

September 27

Motivational Idea: Restlessness tamed

Restlessness implies an inability to be still; the signs of restlessness abound everywhere. It's a restless world! Most of us experience restlessness as we seek to meet all the demands placed upon us. How can we rest when we have to keep so many plates spinning in the air?

Scott Jeffrey, a business coach and writer, has listed some of the signs of restlessness for us. These include a continuous need to be doing something (working, eating, drinking, watching, checking our phone or social media, etc.) Our obsession with the flavour of the month – the new and the novel. We experience restless sleep along with edginess and agitation that leads to emotional outbursts, physical pain and numbness in various regions of the body. Scott says, *"We become anxious about nothing at all. Underlying anxiety becomes a standard part of our daily existence, often accompanied by feelings of irritability, aggressiveness, or meaninglessness."*

We need to understand that restlessness is the symptom, but what is the source? Our minds are busy, constantly busy, with a million thoughts as we seek to curb the restlessness with our pet distractions. Distraction and diversion tactics can involve television, social media; some resort to pornography and other unsavoury things that are not only sinful but bad for the soul. These tactics do not lead to rest but rather exacerbate the problem; we are even more restless. Consumption consumes us and makes us even more restless. Many people turn to their addictions – food, drugs, alcohol, sugar, retail therapy, perhaps buying what they can't really afford – all to diminish that painful restlessness but to no avail.

We are even more perturbed by our inner restlessness. Blaise Pascal, the French philosopher, mathematician, scientist, inventor and theologian, said, *"Seeking diversion and distraction for its own sake only makes us miserable; humans must engage in a relentless search for something beyond ourselves, instead of the meaningless things we are running after...we cannot find happiness through pleasant self-seeking, only through seeking God."*

Memorable Quote:
"For so long as I keep choosing to try to find that satisfaction in finite, created things, I'm going to be caught in a cycle where I'm more and more disappointed in those things and more and more dependent on those things." James K A Smith

Journaling Suggestion:
You have made me for yourself, O Lord, and my heart is restless until I rest in You.

Memo for Meditation:
"Jesus said, "Come to me, all you who are weary and are carrying heavy burdens and I will give you rest." Matthew 11:28
"Be still and know that I am God!" Psalm 46:10
"In peace I will lie down and sleep, for you alone, LORD, make me dwell in safety." Psalm 4:8
"You will keep in perfect peace those whose minds are steadfast, because they trust in you." Isaiah 26:3

September 28

Motivational Idea: Going for gold

Michelle Carter, the American shot putter, is a Christian believer, who in her role as a motivational speaker talks about her faith in Christ. She won the 2016 gold medal at the Rio Olympics on the last of her six throws. In doing so, Michelle became the first United States women's athlete to win the event since the women's competition began at the 1948 Summer Olympic Games in London.

Michelle has a profound message for us today. *"Through faith and sports, I've learned discipline and self-control. In the Bible, God tells us we have to work, even if what we want is not going to happen right away. People want a platform, but with that comes responsibility. Before winning the gold medal, I needed to be in a mature place to handle the opportunities that were going to come my way, to make sure I didn't use them for my advantage. You have to put your pride aside and let God's plan come through. He has given me this platform for Him to shine."*

She also said: *"I know God allowed me to have this medal, and with it I want to glorify Him and point others to Him."* The following quote from Michelle is based on the memo for today from Joshua 1:8.

Memorable Quote:
"The Lord's message is clear. Meditate on His playbook for life - His Word. Follow it faithfully and success will follow. It's His way of saying trust me, follow my lead and watch what I can do. So let's take a lesson from Joshua and trust in the wisdom of our Divine coach. Let's meditate on His Word, obey His commands, and watch as victory unfolds in front of us." Michelle Carter

Journaling Suggestion:
Timeless wisdom – 'pure gold', given by God to Joshua, is the wisdom I need to live purposely today and every day.

Memo for Meditation:
"Moses my servant is dead. Get going. Cross this Jordan River, you and all the people. Cross to the country I'm giving to the People of Israel. I'm giving you every square inch of the land you set your foot on—just as I

promised Moses. From the wilderness and this Lebanon east to the Great River, the Euphrates River—all the Hittite country—and then west to the Great Sea. It's all yours. All your life, no one will be able to hold out against you. In the same way I was with Moses, I'll be with you. I won't give up on you; I won't leave you. Strength! Courage! You are going to lead this people to inherit the land that I promised to give their ancestors. Give it everything you have, heart and soul. Make sure you carry out The Revelation that Moses commanded you, every bit of it. Don't get off track, either left or right, so as to make sure you get to where you're going. And don't for a minute let this Book of The Revelation be out of mind. Ponder and meditate on it day and night, making sure you practise everything written in it. Then you'll get where you're going; then you'll succeed. Haven't I commanded you? Strength! Courage! Don't be timid; don't get discouraged. GOD, your God, is with you every step you take." Joshua 1:1-9

September 29

Motivational Idea: Eight lessons from the Olympics

The 2024 Olympic Games have just finished as the author writes this page. Martha Brook came up with eight inspiring life lessons the Olympics have taught us. Here they are, with a biblical dimension.

1. Someone else winning doesn't take away from your success.

"And now the prize awaits me—the crown of righteousness, which the Lord, the righteous Judge, will give me on the day of his return. And the prize is not just for me but for all who eagerly look forward to his appearing." 2 Timothy 4:8. You are worth more than any title or achievement. *He chose us in Him before the foundation of the world, that we should be holy and without blame before Him in love."* Ephesians 1:4

2. **You are valuable because of what you cost.**

"As one loved by God, you have also been chosen by God for 'adoption as sons by Jesus Christ to Himself.'" Ephesians 1:5

3. Real courage is being afraid and doing it anyway.

"I sought the Lord, and he answered me and delivered me from all my fears. Those who look to Him are radiant, and their faces shall never be ashamed." Psalm 34:4,5

4. Alone you can go fast, but together you can go far.

"And let us consider how we may spur one another on toward love and good deeds, 25 not giving up meeting together, as some are in the habit of doing, but encouraging one another—and all the more as you see the Day approaching." Hebrews 10:24,25

5. You should always stand up for what you believe is right.

"For I am not ashamed of the gospel, because it is the power of God that brings salvation to everyone who believes: first to the Jew, then to the Gentile." Romans 1:16

6. You are never too young or old to chase a dream.

"Being confident of this, that he who began a good work in you will carry it on to completion until the day of Christ Jesus." Philippians 1:6

7. A true champion keeps trying no matter how long it takes.

"Let us not become weary in doing good, for at the proper time we will reap a harvest if we do not give up." Galatians 6:9

8. Falling in life is okay, you just need to get back up again.

"For though the righteous fall seven times, they rise again, but the wicked stumble when calamity strikes." Proverbs 24:16

Memorable Quote:
"It's really all about habit-building. When we set goals, we often picture the end goal we want without thinking about the "building blocks" and "stepping stones" needed to get there. Sometimes we're subconsciously looking for a shortcut, a fast track. But when it comes to God and us, it's a relationship, a journey of a lifetime, that we need to diligently go through every day. To paraphrase a well-known quote, 'The spiritual life is a marathon, not a sprint.'" YMI

Journaling Suggestion:
Take on board the eight lessons from the Olympics.

Memo for Meditation:
"Therefore, since we are surrounded by such a huge crowd of witnesses to the life of faith, let us strip off every weight that slows us down,

especially the sin that so easily trips us up. And let us run with endurance the race God has set before us." Hebrews 12:1-3

September 30

Motivational Idea: One fruit, many flavours

For our final motivation from the Biblical Dimension, we are delving into a bowl of fruit – well, it's not a *bowl*, it's a container, and you are the container. There is ONE fruit of the spirit. A careful read of Galatians 5:22-23 shows that Paul refers to one fruit. We have one fruit and nine different flavours! More often than not we tend to focus on the fruit and not the source. We need to acknowledge the source, God the Holy Spirit.

As we reach out to God, we find that He is always reaching out to us, calling us and waiting for us with open arms to receive us, so the fruit of the spirit can grow in our lives. It is not we who produce the fruit of the spirit – they are gifts from God – but it is in our openness and submission to God that the miraculous happens, and the Holy Spirit produces the fruit of the Spirit. This involves on our part the hard work of letting go and letting God do His work in us that enables these different qualities of the spirit to grow in our lives.

Take one of the fruits: joy. Our joy comes from God. God gives us the gift of joy; our part is to make joy an active choice of attitude. It is more than simply an emotional reaction to our circumstances; it is much deeper than happiness. In a very real sense, each day we have an invitation from God; each day we can choose joy!

Henri Nouwen said: *"Joy does not happen to us. We have to choose joy and keep choosing it every day."* The gift of this characteristic involves our choice. The joy we feel has little to do with the circumstances of our lives and everything to do with the focus of our lives, God, our source of joy. We can make this choice because we know the faithful companionship of God, the source and choice of our joy, no matter the circumstances.

Memorable Quote:
"Fruit is always the miraculous, the created; it is never the result of willing, but always of growth. The fruit of the Spirit is a gift of God, and only He can produce it." Dietrich Bonhoeffer

Journaling Suggestion:
Today I choose joy and I rejoice in God.

Memo for Meditation:
"But the fruit produced by the Holy Spirit within you is divine love in all its varied expressions: joy that overflows, peace that subdues, patience that endures, kindness in action, a life full of virtue, faith that prevails, gentleness of heart, and strength of spirit. Never set the law above these qualities, for they are meant to be limitless." Galatians 5:22-23

THE CULTURAL DIMENSION

October 1

Motivational Idea: The culture of trivial pursuits

Trivial Pursuit is a popular board game in which winning is determined by a player's ability to answer trivia and questions about popular culture. The game has 2,400 questions which are set out in six categories: geography, entertainment, history, art and literature, science and nature, and sports and leisure. It's a great game for friends and family to enjoy – trivia and loads of fun. On a serious note, the world does seem to be engaged in a constant pursuit of that which is trivial in comparison to the big issues in our world: starvation, wars, abuse, discrimination and hatred. Take, for example, a squabble between two celebrities where the media becomes obsessed with the ongoing drama, and every detail and aspect is analysed to death. It may well be a coping strategy for the general public to avoid the stark reality of the cruel world in which we live. We do, however, need healthy pastimes and down-time to relax from a fast-paced world. But what is our chief pursuit in life? What floats our boat and gives us that impetus to devote every hour and every ounce of energy to the purist of that goal? Goals are good, and commitment and passion are to be commended, but our memorable quote raises the issue of the possibility of wasting our lives on the ephemeral and the chasing of the wind. And if we reach that goal – does it really satisfy? The quote is from the song, *Build Your Kingdom Here*. God wants us to put His Kingdom first and being the best that we can be in His chosen path for our lives rather than trivial pursuits. Jesus culture first – the rest follows! (See March 24 The chief pursuit.)

Memorable Quote:
"We seek Your kingdom first,
We hunger and we thirst,
Refuse to waste our lives,

For You're our joy and prize..."

Journaling Suggestion:
"But seek first his kingdom and his righteousness, and all these things will be given to you as well." Matthew 6:33

Memo for Meditation:
"So here's what I want you to do, God helping you: Take your everyday, ordinary life—your sleeping, eating, going-to-work, and walking-around life—and place it before God as an offering. Embracing what God does for you is the best thing you can do for him. Don't become so well-adjusted to your culture that you fit into it without even thinking. Instead, fix your attention on God. You'll be changed from the inside out. Readily recognize what he wants from you, and quickly respond to it. Unlike the culture around you, always dragging you down to its level of immaturity, God brings the best out of you, develops well-formed maturity in you." Romans 12:1,2

October 2

Motivational Idea: Busy culture! The 8+8+8 Rule

The 8+8+8 Rule can help you achieve balance in your life as we face the challenge of balancing our various roles and responsibilities in today's fast-paced world. Here is a simple and effective way to achieve more harmony and happiness in our lives. The 8+8+8 Rule is a time management technique that helps us distribute our day into three equal parts: 8 hours of honest hard work, 8 hours of good sleep, and 8 hours of leisure activities. The idea behind this rule is that by allocating our time wisely, we can optimise our productivity, health, and well-being.

The 8+8+8 Rule is based on the following principles:
8 hours of honest hard work
This means dedicating ourselves to our professional or academic goals, as well as any other tasks that require our attention and effort. By working hard for 8 hours a day, we can achieve more results and satisfaction in our career or studies. However, this also means avoiding distractions, procrastination, and unnecessary stress. We should focus on the quality, not the quantity, of our work.

8 hours of good sleep

This means getting enough rest and recovery for our body and mind. By sleeping well for 8 hours a night, we can improve our physical and mental health, as well as our mood and energy levels. However, this also means following a regular sleep schedule, avoiding caffeine, alcohol, and screens before bed, and creating a comfortable and relaxing environment for our sleep.

8 hours of leisure activities

This means spending time on the things that make us happy and fulfilled. By enjoying ourselves for 8 hours a day, we can enrich our lives with more joy and meaning. However, this also means choosing activities that are beneficial for our growth and well-being. We should divide our leisure time into three categories: **3Fs, 3Hs, and 3Ss.** These are the components of our leisure time that can help us balance our lives. The first – 3Fs – is: **Family, Friends and Faith**. These are the people and beliefs that support us and inspire us. By spending time with our family and friends, we can strengthen our relationships and social skills. By practising our faith and spirituality, we can connect with God and know Him. The second – 3Hs – is: **Health, Hygiene and Hobby.** These are the activities that enhance our physical and mental wellness. By taking care of our health, we can prevent diseases and boost our immunity. By maintaining our hygiene, we can improve our appearance and self-esteem. By pursuing our hobbies, we can express our creativity and passion. The third – 3Ss – is: **Soul, Service and Smile:** These are the actions that nourish our inner peace and happiness. (Credits to Robert Owen).

Memorable Quote:
"By feeding your soul, you can explore your interests and talents. By serving others, you can make a positive difference in the world. By smiling more often, you can spread joy and optimism." Robert Owen

Journaling Suggestion:
Managing the work life balance

Memo for Meditation:
"One hand full of rest and patience is better than two fists full of labour and a chasing after the wind." Ecclesiastes 4:7

October 3

Motivational Idea: The spirit of the age – influencers

The phrase 'spirit of the age' comes from the title of a book written by William Hazlitt (1778-1830). He was an English writer, drama and literary critic, social commentator, and philosopher. His book, *The Spirit of the Age: Or, Contemporary Portraits*, was published in 1825 and consisted of character sketches of 25 individuals whom he believed stood for the thought, literature and politics of the time. They included thinkers, social reformers, politicians, poets, essayists and novelists.

Hazlitt believed that individuals were able to mould and influence the spirit of the age. He saw these influencers as an active force which, by disseminating knowledge in both the sciences and the arts, could reinforce humanity towards good. One of his sketches was about the Christian social reformer, William Wilberforce. In the latter part of the 18th century, Wilberforce led a protracted campaign to end slavery. It was not an easy battle to fight as there was much opposition to his abolitionist movement from those who wanted the slave trade to continue, not least for the money they were making. Undeterred, Wilberforce continued his campaign and in 1789 he gave a three-hour speech against slavery in the London Parliament. Then in 1791, Wilberforce presented the House of Commons with another Bill to abolish the slave trade. On this occasion, he had the support of the Prime Minister, William Pitt the Younger, but the Bill failed in its passage as it was rejected by 163 votes to 88. Thereafter, every year between 1789 and 1806, Wilberforce presented a Bill for the abolition of the slave trade. He was not going to give up. Then in 1804, the House of Commons voted in favour of abolition, but Wilberforce's Bill was, alas, rejected by the House of Lords. Then in the year 1806, Wilberforce's friend James Stephen proposed a Bill that would ban British ships from carrying slaves to the French colonies. This was a clever move as the pro-slavery MPs didn't give cognizance to the significance of the Bill and were happy to allow it to pass. The upshot of this decision was that it literally halted two-thirds of the slave trade and made it unprofitable. Then in the glorious year of 1807, after eighteen long years of campaigning, the battle was eventually won, and

Parliament abolished the slave trade. Slaves were free! Freedom! Free at last. Are we influencing *'the spirit of the age'* all around us for good?

Memorable Quote:
"To live our lives and miss that great purpose we were designed to accomplish is truly a sin. It is inconceivable that we could be bored in a world with so much wrong to tackle, so much ignorance to reach and so much misery we could alleviate"..."It is the true duty of every man to promote the happiness of his fellow creatures to the utmost of his power." William Wilberforce

Journaling Suggestion:
Be a good influence and be careful who influences me.

Memo for Meditation:
"Live an exemplary life among the unbelieving so that your actions will refute their prejudices. Then they'll be won over to God's side and be there to join in the celebration when He arrives." 1 Peter 2:12.

October 4

Motivational Idea: The spirit of the age – secularism

'The spirit of the age' refers to the prevailing values, ideas and beliefs that are typical of people in a particular period in history. But what are the particular influences that have been brought to bear on our societies in the world as we know it today? What has brought about the current thinking and world views that permeate every social media platform and the lives of millions across our world? It's important for us to grasp why we are where we are, why people think the way they think, and not just take it all as fact or gospel truth. We need to delve beneath the surface to ascertain if we are being brainwashed in some way or being led like lambs to the slaughter. Are the influences behind the spirit of the age conducive to our wellbeing, happiness and the discovery of the fulfilled life? The reality is we live in a world of discontentment and dis-ease. So, what is going on, and why is it going on?

The prevailing 'spirit' today, the prevailing influence, is atheistic secularism. Secularism is really about the human kind's self-sufficiency. Whether categorically stated by some exponents, or implied by others, secularism says that the human race does not need God. It then follows that any form of religious faith, practice and worship is ruled out, at least the worship of God. The goal of atheistic secularism is to eliminate religion and faith systems from every aspect of society. This leads to an increasing desire for a society where humanism, or what we may term, secular humanism, advocates and teaches that there are no objective or absolute truths defining right and wrong.

'If it feels good, just do it,' is the motto of the age. We are reminded of the words found in Judges 17:6: *"In those days there was no king in Israel; everyone did what was right in their own eyes."* For secular humanism, man is king of the castle and can do whatever he or she likes. Any analysis of such influences on the spirit of the age needs to face the reality that we have descended to a lower level of existence in spite of all our technological advances and must-have devices. We have hardened our hearts against God and if we, *'Sow the wind, we will reap the whirlwind.'* (Hosea 8:7). On the other hand, Bible teaching lifts us to a higher moral plane and enhances every aspect of our lives. Humans are worshipping creatures, so who or what are we worshipping if we have replaced God?

Memorable Quote:
"Secularism promotes the idea that religion is nothing but a relic of the past. But the truth is, God exists, and we do need Him. Despite the claims of secular humanism, the Bible is God's truth. 'Sanctify them through your truth, your word is truth.'" John 17:17, Got Questions.

Journaling Suggestion:
"There is one King and it's not Caesar, it's Jesus, and I worship Him." John 19:15

Memo for Meditation:
"Go out into the world uncorrupted, a breath of fresh air in this squalid and polluted society. Provide people with a glimpse of good living and of the living God. Carry the light-giving Message into the night." Philippians 2:15

October 5

Motivational Idea: The greatest happiness of the greatest number

John Stuart Mill (born in 1806) was a philosopher and political economist. His development of utilitarian thought can be described as the idea that anything we do should bring about *"the greatest happiness of the greatest number"*, and that good moral behaviour is the best way to achieve happiness for as many people as possible. Personal liberty in terms of freedom of thought and speech is vital to our development and happiness as human beings. Only by experiencing freedom, Mill argued, would we be capable of achieving morality, happiness, and a flourishing in society. The only limit that he wanted to see placed on individuals was preventing us from hurting other people or infringing on the freedoms of others.

Mill was also a strong advocate for women's rights. His ideas on morality, justice, and how society should be organised are still influential today. Timothy Larsen, Professor of Christian Thought at Wheaton College, Wheaton, Illinois, wrote a book called *John Stewart Mill: A Secular Life*. This featured, however, in the Oxford University Press's *Spiritual Lives* series and is essentially a religious biography of Mill, entitled, *A Surprisingly Religious John Stuart Mill*.

Larsen notes that at the end of his life Mill was an avid supporter of a church in Avignon (where he lived). His best friend there was its pastor, and Mill gave it a large financial contribution annually. He accepted a position as an honorary member of the executive committee of its charity which supported religious schools. Whenever Mill visited a city, whether in England or abroad, he was keen to attend a worship service in its principal church. On the continent, he would sometimes wait around in a church for hours, hoping that there would be a service. In 1856, he actually left his adored wife at home and took lodgings in Birmingham so that he could attend all of the Holy Week services at St Chad's.

Larsen says Mill would have been quite happy to be thought of as 'spiritual' or 'religious'. Orthodox Christians were enthralled with Mill's *System of Logic*, and were quick to praise it and to assign it in their schools. In his posthumously published essay, *Theism*, Mill made the case for hope in God and in Christ. Mill's disciple, the agnostic John

Morley, said it was *"irreconcilable with the scientific principles which Mill inculcated,".* Mill himself did not think he had abandoned those principles. He was a thinker, a doer, and an instrument for good and positive change in the world, espousing the teachings of practical Christianity.

Memorable Quote:
"He [JS Mill] has been called everything from an atheist to a mystic. One scholar has even claimed that Mill saw himself as the founder of a new religion. Mill himself once observed that his reverence for Jesus Christ gave him the right to call himself a Christian." Timothy Larsen

Journaling Suggestion:
"It is self-evident that only Mind can create mind." J S Mill – God the eternal Creator is responsible for the existence of mind.

Memo for Meditation:
"Religion that is pure and undefiled before God, the Father, is this: to visit orphans and widows in their affliction, and to keep oneself unstained from the world." James 1:27

October 6

Motivational Idea: The spirit of the age – worship

Any analysis of our culture will take cognizance of the worship phenomenon. Human beings are natural worshippers; they have an innate desire to worship. An anecdotal inquiry by the author found that most people didn't see themselves as worshippers. However, some of the answers included, *" I take a keen interest in..." "I am totally devoted to ..." "I could not live without it," "Life would not be the same if I didn't get to see my team," "I'm a dyed-in-the-wool fan," Shopping is my thing, I would shop until I drop," "Shopping is my god."*

It could be argued that these are forms of worship. The football stadium is very often a more common worship venue than the local church. Yet the existential problem with life in a fallen world is that all common worship objects are finite realities that can't provide ultimate purpose and fulfilment for human beings. Check out the fans' response when their team loses. The spirit of the age is a consumerist, it's all about consumption, and an insatiable one; we have to have more of it and we are still not satisfied. The Bible on the other hand declares: *"Imago Dei"* – 'We are made in the image of God'. Made to know, love, and worship our Creator. We human beings are dependent upon God for our very existence, meaning, and ultimate spiritual fulfilment. The *"imago Dei"* makes us worshippers, yet the spiritual vacuum of a life that rejects God leads us to seek worship replacements instead of the true and living God. This can be manifested as egotism (self), sensualism (sex), and materialism (money). Some opt for the more developed and refined worship replacements such as the natural world, politics, and the concept of beauty. Interestingly, most of the common replacements may be good things in themselves, but those good things have become disordered and misused in the life separated from God. Who or what are we worshipping today?

Memorable Quote:
"God made us: invented us as a man invents an engine. A car is made to run on gasoline, and it would not run properly on anything else. Now God designed the human machine to run on Himself. He Himself is the fuel our spirits were designed to burn, or the food our spirits were designed to feed on. There is no other. That is why it is just no good asking God to make us happy in our own way without bothering about religion. God cannot give us a happiness and peace apart from Himself, because it is not there. There is no such thing." C S Lewis

Journaling Suggestion:
Lord, I choose to worship you and put you first in my life today.

Memo for Meditation:
"And now, Israel, what does the LORD your God require from you, but to fear [and worship] the LORD your God with awe-filled reverence and profound respect, to walk, that is, to live each and every day, in all His ways and to love Him, and to serve the LORD your God with all your heart and with all your soul, your choices, your thoughts, your whole being, and to keep the commandments of the LORD and His statutes which I am commanding you today for your good. Behold, the heavens and the highest of heavens belong to the Lord your God, the earth and all that is in it." Deuteronomy 10:12-14

October 7

Motivational Idea: The spirit of the age – Zeitgeist

The word *Zeitgeist* was used by the German philosopher Georg Wilhelm Friedrich Hegel (1770–1831). *Zeit* means 'time', and *Geist* means 'spirit' or 'ghost'. For Hegel, Zeitgeist refers to a type of supra-individual mind at work in the world, and manifests in the cultural worldview that pervades the ideas, attitudes and feelings of a particular society in a specific historical period. A Zeitgeist theory of history stresses the role of such situational factors as economics, technology, and social influences. Scholars have long maintained that each era has a unique spirit, a nature or climate that sets it apart from all other epochs. Zeitgeist is thus a way of explaining landmark social changes in any civilization. The alternative view is referred to as the *"great man/person theory"*. This refers to great persons who, with unparalleled charisma and strong belief systems, lead entire civilizations on a new course of development or to destruction. For example, Alexander the Great leading his army to India, Napoleon fighting with all of Europe, and Hitler starting a war that engulfed Europe.

Both theories take extreme positions but perhaps it's a case of some middle ground where a combination of the two lead to landmark social changes. It could be argued that Zeitgeist is the primary factor where fundamental social change happens; the change has to be part of the spirit of the time. History shows us that great changes in society can be achieved through the power of the group or the masses, rather than a hero figure. Yet there have been great people throughout history who have not acquiesced as puppets in the hands of time and have made a profound difference.

What difference can we make in our day and generation? Are we going to be puppets in the hands of time or are we going to make the world a better place? How influential is the spirit of the age upon us today? We have a different Spirit! *"For God did not give us a spirit of timidity or cowardice or fear, but [He has given us a spirit] of power and of love and of sound judgement and personal discipline [abilities that result in a calm, well-balanced mind and self-control]."* (2 Timothy 1:7, AMP.)

We have the Holy Spirit as followers of Jesus. We've got the power to change the world. God's people – God's Zeitgeist – God's fire in our hearts and in our exploits!

Memorable Quote:
"Therefore, since we receive a kingdom which cannot be shaken, let us show gratitude, and offer to God pleasing service and acceptable worship with reverence and awe; for our God is a consuming fire." Hebrews 12:28,29

Journaling Suggestion:
With God's help I can and will make a difference.

Memo for Meditation:
"But I say, walk habitually in the [Holy] Spirit [seek Him and be responsive to His guidance], and then you will certainly not carry out the desire of the sinful nature [which responds impulsively without regard for God and His precepts]." Galatians 5:16

October 8

Motivational Idea: The spirit of the age – the underbelly

The Bible makes it clear that the devil is not a myth, not a figment of the imagination. Paul tells us in Ephesians 6:12 that *"We wrestle not against flesh and blood but against principalities, against powers, against the rulers of the darkness of this world, against spiritual wickedness in the heavenly places."* Many may deny the existence of this underbelly – this unseen world, but, uncomfortable as it is to know, *"Satan, who is the god of this world, has blinded the minds of those who don't believe. They are unable to see the glorious light of the Good News. They don't understand this message about the glory of Christ, who is the exact likeness of God."* (2 Corinthians 4:5).

Satan is our arch enemy and he desires to cause as much misery and mayhem in the world today because his time is short. Satan is real. Just under the surface of our everyday interactions, hiding in the shadows, clouded in mystery and confusion, the devil works to undermine what God is doing in us and through us. Angels, demons, spiritual warfare – they all exist, but we don't have to live in fear of the supernatural. God has given us powerful weapons against the forces of darkness. He has given us His Holy Spirit and His Word, the Bible, to remind us who He is, who we are, and what is true. We need to ask God to keep us aware and sharp in the presence of our enemies, seen or unseen, without being preoccupied. What a blessing it is that *"His perfect love casts out all fear."* (1 John 4:18).

When we hone in on internalising God's love, the things that are in opposition to godliness lose their power to intimidate and undermine our faith and our plans. We can walk daily in His strength under His protection and in the joy of knowing of the glorious life to come! We can find happiness and the fulfilled life because we are serving the Lord, the Light of the world, living as lights in this dark world. *"The light shines in the darkness, and the darkness can never extinguish it."* (John 1:5).

Memorable Quote:
"The unseen realm of all that is not good coexists in our natural world with what appears good. For the most part we are often unaware of its pervasive existence. Evil is like the underbelly of a doormat. In our daily experience, we walk about in a world of seen things. What becomes familiar to our eyes is comforting. But the Bible speaks of an unseen world of 'dark principalities.' Our oblivion prevents us from seeing these battles between good and evil. Why does this world remain unseen to most? In part, it's because God protects us from what we can't handle. Not everyone is able to handle the same level of revelation that someone like, say, Daniel, experienced." Cindy LaFavre Yorks

Journaling Suggestion:
Greater is He who is in me than he who is in the world.

Memo for Meditation:
"But you belong to God, my dear children. You have already won a victory over them, because the Spirit who lives in you is greater than the spirit who lives in the world." 1 John 4:4

October 9

Motivational Idea: Therapy culture – therapist's note

Therapy is big business. 'Talking therapies' are readily accessible although going private can be an expensive one financially. Counselling and psychotherapy are offered for a whole range of issues. Brief focal therapy or prolonged in-depth therapy will depend on the nature of the problems to be talked through. Having worked in the mental health field for almost a quarter of a century, and trained in psychotherapy, I see the value of seeking professional help, if and when appropriate. But not everyone needs to go deep-sea diving to raise the Titanic. It is imperative that the practitioner is well trained and knows what they are doing. Be aware that the unscrupulous do exist in the psychotherapeutic world and can cause untold damage.

Gabrielle Pascal makes the important point that seeking help beyond prayer does not make you a bad Christian. Jesus said, *"It is not the healthy who need a doctor, but the sick."* (Luke 5:31). Jesus, the 'wonderful counsellor', made it clear that seeking professional help is okay and nothing to be ashamed of. God can use the therapist to help the sufferer. Tanya Luhrmann, Professor of Anthropology at Stanford University, visited a church where people were encouraged to think of God as their therapist. *"People expected to experience God as a person. They spoke of having a personal relationship with God. When they talked to God, they expected God to speak back."* As Christians, we believe in a personal relationship with God, and He communicates with us through His word, though circumstances and through others. Sigmund Freud set up his secular church, in a manner of speaking, so why should we as Christians not consider one of the many facets of God in terms of therapy? We can talk to Him about everything. He deals with all our guilt and shame. As a psychotherapist one is aware that shame is the clients constant companion in every session. Tanya used standard psychological questionnaires with the church people and found them to be less lonely and less stressed because of God's love. God has promised to meet our every need and so we have a Wounded Healer in Jesus our Lord.

Memorable Quote:
"When God becomes that therapist, It's obviously different from ordinary psychotherapy because The "Therapist" is more powerful than any human therapist and also more perfect. Because God is also invisible, human members of the group stand in on his behalf but one does not have to attribute their imperfections to the therapist. But whereas the human therapist coaches the client, takes the client's money, and goes away, God sticks around for all eternity. And that has its advantages."
Tanya Luhrmann

Journaling Suggestion:
God is my therapist and I talk to Him about everything.

Memo for Meditation:
"Jesus heard about it and spoke up, "Who needs a doctor: the healthy or the sick? I'm here inviting outsiders, not insiders—an invitation to a changed life, changed inside and out." Luke 5:31-32

October 10

Motivational Idea: Recognising different cultures –

guilt/innocence

We live in a world of diverse cultures. Author Nancy Lucenay says that the guilt/shame/fear model of classification has helped her make sense of the different cultures she has experienced. Most cultures are mixtures of guilt/innocence, honour/shame, and fear/power. However, one type often dominates. About 30% of the world is predominantly guilt/innocence, while 60-70% is honour/shame or fear/power. To quote Nancy, *"Most guilt/innocence cultures are individualist (i.e., Western). We measure everything with the yardstick of right and wrong. We make laws that determine innocence and guilt. Knowing and exercising individual rights is a primary concern. We teach children to be law-abiding and expect them to develop a conscience. We define innocence as being right or as righteousness. People feel guilty for what they have done or not done. Communication is direct; confrontation is acceptable."*

391

Many of us in Western culture have grown up in the context of the guilt/innocence paradigm, i.e. 'Doing the right thing and/or avoiding doing the wrong thing.' Whatever our background, one of the tools the enemy devises to rob us of the fulfilled life and experience happiness, joy and a peaceful life, is guilt. It's time for us today to learn to leave the burden of guilt behind – get rid of the guilt and move on into the blessings God has for us. Joyce Meyer says, "*Your true identity is 'not guilty'. It's so important for us to see ourselves in Christ and identify with Him as our substitute, who paid the price for the cleansing and forgiveness of our sin. Our identity is no longer 'sinner' but 'new creation in Christ', and there's a difference between our 'who' and what we do.*"

We have been justified – declared blameless by God. Don't hold on to guilt any longer – let it go because Jesus took it all at Calvary when He died for you. Let it be gone!

Memorable Quote:
"*People in guilt/innocence cultures strongly understand the penal theory of atonement. Our sin is a crime against God's righteousness. His just wrath against sin must be borne. While Jesus hanged on the cross, He carried the guilt of our sin and took the punishment we deserve as our substitute. We are justified by His blood (Romans 5:9), and His righteousness covers us*". Romans 3:22, *Got Questions*

Journaling Suggestion:
I'm no longer in condemnation – here in the grace of God I stand! Not bound by guilt anymore!

Memo for Meditation:
"*Therefore, since we have been justified [that is, acquitted of sin, declared blameless before God] by faith, [let us grasp the fact that] we have peace with God [and the joy of reconciliation with Him] through our Lord Jesus Christ (the Messiah, the Anointed). Through Him we also have access by faith into this [remarkable state of] grace in which we [firmly and safely and securely] stand. Let us rejoice in our hope and the confident assurance of [experiencing and enjoying] the glory of [our great] God [the manifestation of His excellence and power].*" Romans 5:1-2

October 11

Motivational Idea: Recognising different cultures – honour/shame

In an honour/shame culture, family is everything. Identity is about belonging to the group. The honour of the family, honour of the tribe, village, city, the nation is paramount – honour is key. The avoidance of shame is crucial in the process of advancing and preserving honour. Since honour is a shared commodity, what one person does brings honour (or shame) upon the entire community.

The most important asset any person has is their reputation. When honour is life's most important commodity, then any insult to one's honour must be vigorously defended. The reality is that people of every culture feel unworthy and fear rejection before others. The author's dissertation for the Master's degree in psychotherapy entitled, *The psychoanalytic appreciation of shame,* observed that shame is ubiquitous. It exists in all societies and resides in every personality. We have all felt defective, flawed, inferior, inadequate, incompetent, scorned and ridiculed by others.

John Bradshaw makes an important distinction between healthy shame and toxic shame. *"Shame is a normal human emotion but shame as a healthy human emotion can be transformed into a state of being. Shame takes over one's whole identity. To have shame as an identity is to believe that one's being is flawed, that one is a defective human being. Once shame is transformed into an identity it becomes toxic and dehumanising."*

Shame is the master human emotion and all other emotions are bound by shame. Removing shame requires more than forgiveness. Shame produces feelings of humiliation, disapproval, and abandonment. Shame means inadequacy of the entire person. While guilt says, "I made a mistake", shame says, "I am a mistake."

Whatever your culture, are you living with a shame identity today? It's so real and excruciatingly painful to live with day after day. The reality is, this is not your real identity. Your real identity is in Jesus who dealt with all our shame on the cross. But how do we rid ourselves of a shame identity? Here's how: *"Looking away from all that will distract us and] focusing our eyes on Jesus, who is the Author and Perfecter of faith [the first incentive for our belief and the One who brings our faith to maturity], who for the joy [of accomplishing the goal] set before Him endured the cross, disregarding the shame, and sat down at the right hand of the throne of God [revealing His deity, His authority, and the completion of His work].'* (Hebrews 12:2, AMP)

Today you can live life to the full with the absence of toxic shame, and in the place of honour that God made you to enjoy.

Memorable Quote:
"I sometimes think that shame, mere awkward, senseless shame, does as much towards preventing good acts and straightforward happiness as any of our vices can do." C S Lewis

Journaling Suggestion:
"God said, 'Those who honour me I will honour.'" 1 Samuel 2:30

Memo for Meditation
"Anyone who wants to serve me must follow me, because my servants must be where I am. And the Father will honour anyone who serves me." John 12:26

October 12

Motivational Idea: Recognising different cultures – fear/power

In power/fear societies, the focus is on the hierarchy and aligning oneself with those in power. 'Control' and 'power' are the keywords, with the focus on the leader, and the imperative is pleasing them at all costs. The leader can decide to be harsh or kind; destructive or empowering; live-giving or life-threatening.

Empowering rather than instilling fear gives a sense of belonging, and loyalty is a lot greater. But the leader can oscillate, so care is needed not to be seen as too empowered! Loyalty and compliance are important for one's welfare and security. The leader expects unswerving loyalty and compliance, and involvement in public expressions of praise, honour and respect are a must to try and keep safe or even alive. North Korea comes to mind. In organisational settings strong, dominant leaders who instil fear in employees results in toxic work cultures. Oppression and rule by fear also leads to the break-down of existing groups and of trust in relationships.

Bible history chronicles societies with a strong honour/shame worldview, but power/fear was also a dominant worldview driver. Israel had a hard time trusting God, and over and over again started following the gods of the peoples around them, wanting a god who is visible (statues and status), but also feeling that these gods were more powerful as their people were more powerful. Solomon, the wisest of all men, wrote, *"The [reverent] fear of the LORD [that is, worshipping Him and regarding Him as truly awesome] is the beginning and the preeminent part of wisdom [its starting point and its essence], And the knowledge of the Holy One is understanding and spiritual insight."* (Proverbs 9:10, AMP). The Hebrew verb *yare* can mean 'to fear, to respect, to reverence', and the Hebrew noun *yirah* usually refers to the fear of God and is viewed as a positive quality. This fear acknowledges God's good intentions (Exodus 20:20). This fear is produced by God's Word (Psalm 119:38; Proverbs 2:5) and makes a person receptive to wisdom and knowledge (Proverbs 1:7; 9:10). This good fear is reverential trust in a loving, trustworthy God. *"It is the LORD of hosts whom you are to regard as holy and awesome. He shall be your [source of] fear, He shall be your [source of] dread [not man]."* (Isaiah 8:13).

Memorable Quote:
"When the Bible refers to the "fear of the Lord," it means having a deep respect, reverence and awe for God's power and authority. Rather than causing someone to be afraid of God, a proper 'fear of the Lord' leads one to love Him."

Journaling Suggestion:
The fear of the Lord is the beginning of wisdom...

Memo for Meditation:
"And now, O Israel, what does the LORD your God ask of you but to fear the LORD your God, to walk in all his ways, to love him, to serve the LORD your God with all your heart and with all your soul. Fear the LORD your God and serve him. Hold fast to him and take your oaths in his name. He is your praise; he is your God, who performed for you those great and awesome wonders you saw with your own eyes." Deuteronomy 10:12, 20, 21

October 13

Motivational Idea: Cultural perspectives – the God delusion vs the Dawkins delusion (1)

Evolutionary biologist Richard Dawkins has sold millions of books promoting evolution as a fact, and toured universities ridiculing those who believe in a Creator because he says they have no proof of their belief. Yet Dawkins has admitted that he holds a belief that cannot be proved – evolution. Dawkins said, *"God exists, if only in the form of a meme with high survival value, or infective power, in the environment provided by human culture."*

Science is seen as omnipotent and can account for everything. Only believe what can be scientifically proven. But there are things that science cannot prove, yet belief in them is still rational. Science presupposes logical and mathematical truths, so it would be arguing in a circle to use science to prove them. Metaphysical, moral, aesthetic truths, and science itself, cannot be scientifically proven. On the other side of the delusion debate are people like Dr William Lane Craig, who runs a ministry called a Reasonable Faith. (ReasonableFaith.org). Dr Craig has presented a cumulative case of philosophical arguments to defend the existence of God, followed by the historical argument for why this God has revealed Himself to be the God of Christianity.
Peter Byrom gives a synopsis of these as follows:
1. **The Cosmological argument for contingency** - God is the best explanation for why anything exists rather than nothing.
2. **The Kalam cosmological argument** – God is the best explanation of the beginning of the universe.
3. **The Teleological argument** – God is the best explanation of the fine-tuning of the initial conditions of the universe for the development of intelligent life.
4. **The Moral argument** – God is the best explanation for objective moral values and duties in the world.
5. **The Ontological argument** – the very possibility of God's existence means that God must exist.
6. **The Resurrection argument** – *"God raised Jesus from the dead"* is the best explanation of the historical facts surrounding the life, death, empty tomb, and post mortem appearances of Jesus of

Nazareth, as well as the origin of the disciples' belief in His resurrection, which entails that God exists. *"Science can provide evidence in support of a premise in a philosophical argument leading to a conclusion that has theological significance."* (W L Craig).

Ours is a reasonable faith, not an illogical one. It is not born out of hopeless desperation, but the real truth!

Memorable Quote:
"The weird thing was that, despite Dawkins and his fellow New Atheists insistence that atheism was the superior, rational view, it was this Christian academic who was leading the way in setting the example for how such logical arguments should be conducted. The Kalam Cosmological argument - If the universe began to exist, then the universe has a transcendent cause. The universe began to exist. Therefore, the universe has a transcendent cause." Peter Byrom

Journaling Suggestion:
Faith in God is a reasonable faith.

Memo for Meditation:
"This is what the LORD says: 'Don't let the wise boast in their wisdom, or the powerful boast in their power, or the rich boast in their riches. But those who wish to boast should boast in this alone: that they truly know me and understand that I am the LORD who demonstrates unfailing love and who brings justice and righteousness to the earth, and that I delight in these things. I, the LORD, have spoken!'" Jeremiah 9:23,24

October 14

Motivational Idea: Cultural perspectives – the God delusion vs the Dawkins delusion (2)

Responding to the question, *"What do you believe is true even though you cannot prove it?"* Professor Dawkins' answer was: *"I believe, but I cannot prove, that all life, all intelligence, all creativity and all 'design' anywhere in the universe is the direct or indirect product of Darwinian natural selection."*

In an open letter to his daughter Juliet on her tenth birthday (published in his book *A Devil's Chaplain*), Dawkins advises her to accept only beliefs supported by evidence: *"Have you ever wondered how we know the things that we know?"* asks Dawkins. The answer, he says, is evidence. Dawkins advises Juliet: *"Next time somebody tells you something that sounds important, think to yourself: 'Is this the kind of thing that people probably know because of evidence? Or is it the kind of thing that people only believe because of tradition, authority or revelation?' And next time somebody tells you that something is true, why not say to them: 'What kind of evidence is there for that?' And if they can't give you a good answer, I hope you'll think very carefully before you believe a word they say."* So if Dawkins asked himself his own question, *"What kind of evidence is there for that?"* his answer when it comes to evolution as an explanation for all life is, *"There isn't enough evidence, I just believe it!"*

Is it time for you to discover or rediscover your faith, a faith that respects reason?

Memorable Quote:
"Christians believe in Christ not just on the basis of faith but also because of his bodily resurrection, witnessed by hundreds of people, many of whom laid down their lives rather than change their view. Believers also base their faith on their own personal experience of God, logical argument, and evidence from the Bible, history, archaeology, cosmology and other sciences." Andrew Halloway

Journaling Suggestion:
Strident atheism can spur us on in our Christian faith – a faith that is real.

Memo for Meditation:
"The wrath of God is being revealed from heaven against all the godlessness and wickedness of people, who suppress the truth by their wickedness, since what may be known about God is plain to them, because God has made it plain to them. For since the creation of the world God's invisible qualities—his eternal power and divine nature— have been clearly seen, being understood from what has been made, so that people are without excuse. For although they knew God, they neither glorified him as God nor gave thanks to him, but their thinking became

futile and their foolish hearts were darkened. Although they claimed to be wise, they became fools and exchanged the glory of the immortal God for images made to look like a mortal human being and birds and animals and reptiles." Romans 1:18-23

October 15

Motivational Idea: Culture and truth (1) – Veritas

'Veritas' is the motto of my youngest daughter's school, Dominican College in Belfast. It was established by the Irish Dominican Sisters in 1930. The Dominican educators draw their inspiration from St Dominic, founder of the Order of Preachers (1170-1221). Dominic based his ministry and that of his followers on the life and work of Jesus, the teacher and preacher. The 'Veritas' motto is a reminder to educators and students alike of St Dominic's mission. He believed that he had a mission to bring the truth of the gospel to the world and to remind people that this truth was an encounter with the God of love.

Veritas is not just the motto of the school, it's about the spirit of the motto, and sums up the whole purpose of being a Dominican: *"To praise, to bless and to preach the truth of the Gospel."* The emphasis is to enable each individual to grow in their relationship with Christ. Knowing the truth enables all of us on our faith journey to make the right decisions, and to go in the right direction as followers of Jesus.

We live in a world where the very definition of truth is questioned, where all 'truth' is seen as relative. A fundamental principle of philosophy is being able to discern between truth and error. Thomas Aquinas observed, *"It is the task of the philosopher to make distinctions."* The 'truth' is, Aquinas's words are not so popular among many today. Making distinctions seems to be out of fashion in a postmodern era of relativism. 'This is true,' as long as it is not followed by, 'and therefore that is false.' This is especially observable in matters of faith and religion where every belief system under the sun is supposed to be on an equal footing. Relativism says that all truth is relative and there is no such thing as absolute truth (acknowledgement – Got Questions). Jesus says, *"I am the Truth."*

Memorable Quote:
"There are a number of philosophies and worldviews that challenge the concept of truth, yet, when each is critically examined it turns out to be self-defeating in nature. The philosophy of relativism says that all truth is relative and that there is no such thing as absolute truth. But one has to ask: is the claim "all truth is relative" a relative truth or an absolute truth? If it is a relative truth, then it really is meaningless; how do we know when and where it applies? If it is an absolute truth, then absolute truth exists. Moreover, the relativist betrays his own position when he states that the position of the absolutist is wrong—why can't those who say absolute truth exists be correct too? In essence, when the relativist says, "There is no truth," he is asking you not to believe him, and the best thing to do is follow his advice." Got Questions

Journaling Suggestion:
Truth is not relative as far as Jesus is concerned.

Memo for Meditation:
"Jesus said to him, 'I am the [only] Way [to God] and the [real] Truth and the [real] Life; no one comes to the Father but through Me.'" John 14:6

October 16

Motivational Idea: Culture and truth (2) – Nietzsche

Today we take a deeper dive into the concept of truth. Friedrich Wilhelm Nietzsche (1844-1900) the German classical scholar, philosopher, and critic of culture, was one of the most influential of all modern thinkers. He influenced contemporary philosophy by pushing it in a sceptical direction. He did this by his denial of objective truth and his emphasis on personal perspective. Nietzsche described truth like this: *"What then is truth? A mobile army of metaphors, metonyms, and anthropomorphisms ... truths are illusions ... coins which have lost their pictures and now matter only as metal, no longer as coins."*

Nietzsche adds: *"Truth is the kind of error without which a certain species of life could not live."* Hendrik van der Breggen, formerly Associate Professor of Philosophy at Providence University College, Manitoba, Canada, comments, *"Should we agree? Surely not. Thinking people should be sceptical about Nietzsche's denial of truth and Nietzsche's perspectivism. Consider the following problems for Nietzsche's views. Nietzsche's denial of truth self-refutes. On the one hand, when Nietzsche says truth is mere metaphor or illusion, then Nietzsche's claim, which purports to be true, is mere metaphor or illusion—i.e., not true. On the other hand, if truth is not mere metaphor or illusion, then Nietzsche's claim is false. So if Nietzsche's claim is true, it's false, and if it's not true, it's false. Either way, Nietzsche's denial of truth is guilty of a direct self-refutation charge—and so should be rejected."*

In our world today we are increasingly surrounded by a Nietzschian culture in which the concept of truth is seen as the coin with no value, and the concept of moral right and wrong does not exist. We need to grasp the idea of 'objective truth' and 'brute facts' from our memorable quote today.

Memorable Quote:
"Historic Christianity rests upon truth - not truth as an abstract concept, nor even what the 20th century man regards as 'religious truth', but objective truth. (The contrary to this is then an antithesis to the truth of what is.) Part of this truth is the emphasis that certain things happened in history. There were, for example, the manifestations at Sinai, and Christ's propositional communication to Saul in the Hebrew tongue on the Damascus road, as well as Christ's open tomb. Historic Christianity rests upon the truth of what today is called the 'brute facts' and not just upon an unknown experience of men in past ages of which we have only a faulty hermeneutical interpretation. Behind the truth of such history is the great truth that the personal, infinite God is objectively 'there'. He actually exists (in contrast to His not being there); and Christ's redemptive and finished work actually took place at a point of time in real space—time history (in contrast to this not being the case). Historic Christianity rests upon the truth of these things in absolute antithesis to their not being true. This carries with it the possibility and the validity of that personal antithesis which occurs at the new birth, wherein the individual passes from death to life." Francis Schaffer

Journaling Suggestion:
Historic Christianity rests upon the truth of 'brute facts'.

Memo Meditation:

"And you will know the truth, and the truth will set you free." John 8:32

October 17

Motivational Idea: Culture and truth (3) – Jesus

Almost two thousand years ago, Truth stood before Pilate. Truth faced no less than six trials in less than a day; three were religious and three were civic. In every facet of these trials, lies prevailed and Truth was condemned. The first trial was before the former high priest, a corrupt and evil individual. Annas broke every rule in the book; it took place in his house, it involved striking Truth as well as seeking to coerce self-accusations. Next up was Caiaphas, the ruling high priest, Annas' son-in-law. False Witnesses spoke against Truth, but there was no evidence whatsoever of any wrongdoing. Caiaphas broke seven laws trying to convict Truth. These included the trial being held in secret, and conducted at night. Bribery was involved and the requirement of two or three witnesses was not met. Nevertheless, Truth was found guilty of blasphemy by the high priest for claiming to be God manifest in flesh. In the morning, the third trial took place when the Sanhedrim pronounced that Truth must die. The Jewish council had no legal right to carry out the death penalty and so they brought Truth to the Roman governor, Pontius Pilate. The three Roman Civic trials had begun where Jesus was proclaimed innocent. More lies were presented about Truth advocating the non-payment of taxes and the setting up of a kingdom in opposition to Caesar. However, at this first civil trial before Pilate, the decision was made that Truth was not guilty.

The second civil trial was before Herod and again the decision was not guilty. The third civil trial was before Pilate again and the decision again was not guilty. Pilate was face to face with Truth, but he turned Him over to the Jews to be crucified. Pilate was in a tenuous position with Caesar. One more mistake and he could lose his position, or very possibly, his life. Fearing for his life and social standing, Pilate relented to the crowd, and the rest is history. Pilate judged Jesus. One day the tables will be tuned and Christ will judge Pilate. Every philosophy and every worldview must stand before Truth. Jesus claimed to be the Way and the Truth and the Life – the fulfilled life is found when we bow to the Truth. This is the only Way.

Memorable Quote:
"Pilate's question, 'What is truth?' spoken 2,000 years ago has reverberated down through the centuries to this very day. If we turn to philosophy, more has been written about truth than any other subject. Worldviews are diverse when it comes to truth and many are now of the persuasion that truth cannot be known. Yet the one who stood before Pilate said, 'I am the Truth.' As the Truth stands before us today, we need to be aware that one day Pilate will stand before Him, and so shall we. Pilate made the wrong decision. May we learn from his catastrophic mistake." Author

Journaling Suggestion:
Nothing must stand in the way of Truth.

Memo for Meditation:
"The woman said to Him, 'I know that the Messiah is coming (He who is called Christ—the Anointed); when that One comes, He will tell us everything [we need to know]." Jesus said to her, "I who speak to you, am He (the Messiah).'" John 4:25-26

October 18

Motivational Idea: Culture and Christ

Relativism, scepticism, pluralism, humanism, atheism and obscurantism have left the world floundering in a sea of hopeless despair. The exponents need to be confronted with Jesus Christ. To many He's a swear word, or at best an obscure historical figure. However, this view is often held by those who have not seriously considered Jesus Christ. The facts of the case are these: the arrival of Jesus into the world over 2,000 years ago was predicted in the Old Testament. The life of Jesus was predicted. This God-man would come from the lineage of David (see Isaiah 9:7), and be born of a virgin (see Isaiah 7:14) in Bethlehem (see. Micah 5:2). He'd make the blind see, the deaf hear, the lame walk, and the mute sing (see Isaiah 35:5-6). He'd proclaim good news to the poor, comfort the broken-hearted, and set the captive free (see Isaiah 61:1).

The death of Jesus was predicted. Though innocent (see. Isaiah 53:9), he'd be betrayed by a close friend (see Psalm 41:9) for thirty pieces of silver (see Zechariah 11:12). He'd be despised and rejected (see Isaiah 53:3), beaten and spit on (see Isaiah 50:6), pierced in both the hands and feet (see Psalm 22:16), and ultimately killed (see Daniel 9:26).

The resurrection of Jesus was predicted. He would be raised to life again (see Psalm 16:10-11) and establish a never-ending covenant with God's people (see Jeremiah 31:31-34). Because He'd be willing to bear the sins of many and intercede for rebels (see Isaiah 53:12), many would be counted as righteous (see Isaiah 53:11) and He'd be a Light to all nations (see Isaiah 11:10).

The return of Jesus is also predicted. Scholars have identified 1,845 biblical references to the Second Coming of Christ (see Daniel 7:13,14). In the Old Testament, no less than seventeen books mention Christ's return. The New Testament authors speak of it in 23 of the 27 books. Seven out of ten chapters in the New Testament refer to His return (see Matthew 24:27-31).

When the angel Gabriel appeared to Mary (see Luke 1:35-41), Mary knew about the Messiah from the Old Testament. God's plans cannot be derailed. Jesus came to be the Saviour of the world; the risen Christ lives today to be our Lord and Saviour, to give salvation hope, certainty and eternal life. He's coming back as Judge. Crown Him as your King today. This is the only truly fulfilled life on planet earth as we await His imminent return. He's real in the here and now, and He is coming again as King of Kings and Lord of lords (see Revelation 11:15).

Memorable Quote:
"In a civilisation like ours, everyone has to come to terms with the claims of Jesus Christ upon their life, or else be guilty of inattention or of avoiding the question." C S Lewis

Journaling Suggestion:
Journal on the claims of Jesus Christ.

Memo for Meditation:
"Mary was greatly troubled at his words and wondered what kind of greeting this might be. But the angel said to her, 'Do not be afraid, Mary; you have found favour with God. You will conceive and give birth to a son, and you are to call him Jesus. He will be great and will be called the Son of the Most High. The Lord God will give him the throne of his father David, and he will reign over Jacob's descendants forever; his kingdom will never end.'" Luke 1:29-33. (See Isaiah 9:6,7, Daniel 2:44 and Isaiah 7:14)

October 19

Motivational Idea: Culture and poison in the pot (1)

The phrase 'poison in the pot' comes from the days of the Old Testament prophet, Elisha (see 2 Kings 4:38-41). During a famine, Elisha told his servant to put on a large pot of stew for the hungry prophets. One of them found a wild vine, gathered wild gourds, sliced them and put them in the stew. Unbeknown to him, these were poisonous. As soon as they began to eat they shouted, *"There is death in the pot."* Elisha said, *"Put meal in the pot,"* and they were able to eat because there was no more poison in the pot.

Our world today is filled with poisons that can spoil all the good there is in our lives. Discernment and courage is needed. *"The cultures of the world are at war with themselves. Civilization is boldly advancing, yet decaying, crumbling, from within with corruption and greed. Mankind is facing many of the same problems they always had. There are a bewildering array of men newly challenged, yet in the face of this, pervasive (invasive) and destructive forces are frighteningly escalating at a faster pace."* (Dr John Theodorou).

Elisha's ministry was conducted against the backdrop of the idolatrous and evil cult of Baalism and its poison in contrast to the righteousness, power and activity of Yahweh, the true and covenant God of Israel. We need a miracle today to deliver us from the poisons in our culture that will rob us of our spiritual wellbeing and the fulfilled life God has for us. The only one capable of saving us from the poisons in the pot is Jesus Himself. We need to listen to Him! What's in your pot?

Memorable Quote:

"Only if we have a steady diet of God's word, will we be able to know what brings life and what brings death. Only by drinking the milk, eating the meat, receiving the manna, and tasting the sweetness of God's word (all biblical metaphors), will we know if there is life or death in the pot. The company of prophets, who had lived daily on the word of God, knew immediately that something was wrong with the stew. They spit it out, called foul, and refused to eat any more. We are called to develop our taste buds by regularly eating the book God has given us. Only then will we easily know what is sweet and what is rancid in the world." Stephen Shaffer

Journaling Suggestion: Getting rid of the poison in my pot!

Memo for Meditation:

"When Elisha returned to Gilgal, there was *a famine in the land. As the sons of the prophets were sitting before him, he said to his servant, 'Put on the large pot and boil stew for the sons of the prophets.' Then one went out into the field to gather herbs, and found a wild vine and gathered from it his lap full of wild gourds, and came and sliced them into the pot of stew, for they did not know* what they were. *So they poured* it *out for the men to eat. And* it *came about as they were eating of the stew, that they cried out and said, 'O man of God, there is death in the pot.' And they were unable to eat. But he said, 'Now bring meal.' And he threw it into the pot, and he said, 'Pour* it *out for the people that they may eat.' Then there was no harm in the pot."* Kings 4:38-41

October 20

Motivational Idea: Culture and poison in the pot (2)

What poisons lurk in our culture today! Some are insidious and some hide in plain sight. Fear can be a major poison in our world today. Toxic fear is rampant. Yet the antidote is the Word of God. *"For God did not give us a spirit of timidity or cowardice or fear, but [He has given us a spirit] of power and of love and of sound judgement and personal discipline [abilities that result in a calm, well-balanced mind and self-control]."* (2 Timothy 1:7).

Confusion is another poison impacting our minds. People don't know what to believe anymore. Truth is diluted and lies are commonplace in governmental circles and in personal relationships. Again, the Bible is the antidote for confusion. *"Don't let anyone capture you with empty philosophies and high-sounding nonsense that come from human thinking and from the spiritual powers of this world, rather than from Christ."* (Colossians 2:8). The Amplified Bible gives us more detail on the subject. *"See to it that no one takes you captive through philosophy and empty deception [pseudo-intellectual babble], according to the tradition [and musings] of mere men, following the elementary principles of this world, rather than following [the truth—the teachings of] Christ."* (Colossians 2:8. AMP).

The Muskoka Community Church in Ontario identified five toxins we need to watch out for and which are particularly insidious: entitlement, doubt, apathy, busyness, and unforgiveness. We do live in a world where narcissistic entitlement is on the increase. *'It's all about me.'* Entitlement is the sense that God (or life, or the universe) somehow owes us a certain standard of living or quality of life. We need to realise how undeserving we are of the grace of God and live with a contentment and thankfulness befitting our standing in Christ (see 1 Timothy 6:6-8 and 1 Thessalonians 5:16-18).

Doubt is part of the life of faith but we can let our pet doubts take us out of the race. Deal with doubt at the cross and keep going (see Hebrews 12:1-3). Watch out for apathy. We live in an apathetic world and we can be contaminated. If we are lukewarm, let's deal with it (see Revelation 3:14-20). Open the door again and in fellowship with Jesus clear the toxins. Unforgiveness can be a major toxin and an obstacle to blessing and progress. Who do you need to forgive? Then there is busyness and the inability to say 'no'. Our out-of-control calendars rob us of the ability to live well, enjoy each moment and set aside time with God. (see Luke 10:38-42.)

Memorable Quote:
"What do you do if you see these toxins in your own life? The cure for entitlement is receiving everything as a gift. The prescription for doubt is stepping out in faith. The antidote for apathy is prayer; for busyness is Sabbath; and for unforgiveness it is letting go of your need for justice, declaring your forgiveness (sometimes over and over again, until it sticks)." Muskoka Community Church blog.

Journaling Suggestion:
Time to test for toxins and deal with them.

Memo for Meditation:
"Don't let the world around you squeeze you into its mould." Romans 12:1-2, J B Phillips New Testament

---

October 21

Motivational Idea: Culture and the Christian (1)

So how can we deal with the poisons and toxicity so prevalent today? Everyday living is highlighted by the Apostle Paul and is our memo for today. If we know the Truth that is found in Jesus, we can discard the old self with all its poisons and put on the new self. We will still be living in a poisonous world of evil but we will know how we are to live and not be contaminated with the toxins and poisons that confront us daily. We can be different and we can be the difference in our world as salt and light in a world of darkness. We can also help others who are being badly affected by the poisons in their pot. We know the antidote – we know the remedy for we know Him; we know Jesus.

Jesus in His prayer to the Father for His disciples, and for those of us who are His disciples, today said: *"I have given them your word. And the world hates them because they do not belong to the world, just as I do not belong to the world. My prayer is not that you take them out of the world but that you protect them from the evil one. They do not belong to this world any more than I do. Make them holy by your truth; teach them your word, which is truth. Just as you sent me into the world, I am sending them into the world."* (John 17:14-18).

Memorable Quote:
"We are in the world, not of it. So, live the way God intended and live a truly fulfilled life." Author

Journaling Suggestion:
I am *in* the world, not *of* it.

Memo for Meditation:

"You must no longer live as the Gentiles do, in the futility of their thinking. They are darkened in their understanding and separated from the life of God because of the ignorance that is in them due to the hardening of their hearts. Having lost all sensitivity, they have given themselves over to sensuality so as to indulge in every kind of impurity, and they are full of greed. That, however, is not the way of life you learned when you heard about Christ and were taught in him in accordance with the truth that is in Jesus. You were taught, with regard to your former way of life, to put off your old self, which is being corrupted by its deceitful desires; to be made new in the attitude of your minds; and to put on the new self, created to be like God in true righteousness and holiness. Therefore each of you must put off falsehood and speak truthfully to your neighbour, for we are all members of one body. "In your anger do not sin:" Do not let the sun go down while you are still angry, and do not give the devil a foothold. Anyone who has been stealing must steal no longer, but must work, doing something useful with their own hands, that they may have something to share with those in need. Do not let any unwholesome talk come out of your mouths, but only what is helpful for building others up according to their needs, that it may benefit those who listen. And do not grieve the Holy Spirit of God, with whom you were sealed for the day of redemption. Get rid of all bitterness, rage and anger, brawling and slander, along with every form of malice. Be kind and compassionate to one another, forgiving each other, just as in Christ God forgave you." Ephesians 4:17-32

October 22

Motivational Idea: Culture – dolphin or jellyfish?

John Piper from desiringGod.org uses the 'dolphin jellyfish' analogy in the context of cultural conformity. John refers to the oceans of culture that have very powerful tides and these cultural tides almost always pull us away from deep allegiance to Jesus. We have to live in the world and we have to swim in the cultural oceans of this planet. Jesus prayed in John 17:15, *"I do not ask that you take them out of the world, but that you keep them from the evil one."*

Jesus expects us to live in the world, to live in the culture in which we have been placed. You are not here by chance or by accident. You are here in this generation, at this time in history, because God has put you here for a purpose. And in terms of the culture you live in, it's not about conforming to that culture, it's all about transforming the culture you are in. We are to be embedded in our culture, not to be the jellyfish and float about with every current of the latest notion or thinking. We are to challenge as we take a biblical stance, and that is not easy, It's easier to be a jellyfish. Jesus knew that his disciples in every generation would need help. Jesus knew that we needed to be able to swim against the tide, we needed to be able to swim like a dolphin.

Jesus promised us the Holy Spirit who gives us the power to swim against the tide. *"And I will ask the Father, and He will give you another Helper (Comforter, Advocate, Intercessor—Counsellor, Strengthener, Standby), to be with you forever—"* (John 14:16, AMP).

Being full of the Holy Spirit, we are given the courage, strength, wisdom, joy and the wherewithal we need to swim against the currents of the culture. This is what it takes to be a true Christian in the world today, and even though the world thinks we have lost the plot, we find that being like the dolphin, even if surrounded by jellyfish, we have found the secret of the happy life, the fulfilled life. The memo for meditation today explains it. Let us do God's will *and* carry out His purposes and make a difference for time and eternity. The Church should be like a pod of dolphins, not a smack of jellyfish!

Memorable Quote:
"So if you are going to swim in the cultural oceans and be a Christian, you better be a dolphin, not a jellyfish, because a jellyfish just goes with the flow and dolphins can cut through the tidal currents and swim toward the truth and swim toward holiness and heaven in spite of cultural tides."

Journaling Suggestion:
Be a dolphin and not a jellyfish.

Memo for Meditation:
"Do not love the world [of sin that opposes God and His precepts], nor the things that are in the world. If anyone loves the world, the love of the Father is not in him. For all that is in the world—the lust and sensual

craving of the flesh and the lust and *longing of the eyes and the boastful pride of life [pretentious confidence in one's resources or in the stability of earthly things]—these do not come from the Father, but are from the world. The world is passing away, and with it its lusts [the shameful pursuits and ungodly longings]; but the one who does the will of God and carries out His purposes lives forever."* 1 John 2:15-17, AMP

October 23

Motivational Idea: Culture and fashion

Fashion can be conceptualised as something that is popular among a group of people. Culture and fashion overlap where fashion can be an expression of culture or can be a culture in itself. Fashion can refer to all kinds of things including: cosmetics, footwear, clothes, jewellery and other accessories. Today we are focusing on clothes.

Clothes play a significant cultural role in creating a sense of belonging, unity and coherent identity. Many of us engage in retail therapy, and we may come home with an item of clothing we had never intended to buy. The marketing agents are good at their job, and sure, it's all the rage! Not only do we have the current cultural fashion – which most people wear – but we also have the contra or counter-cultural. Take, for example, jeans that are ripped, torn, with holes in them; popular with young people mostly, and some of us not so young. Conformity to nonconformity. Whatever our fashion sense and whether we are in the cultural or in one of the countercultural camps, there is another set of clothes, so to speak, that we need to get out of the wardrobe. The Bible talks about putting on new clothes in the spiritual sense (see 1 Peter 3:3-4). It's about inward adorning. It's great to look good on the outside, it's great to take pride in our appearance, whatever we are wearing, but it's really important that we put on what is in the spiritual wardrobe; it's the New Testament shoppers' guide to show us the clothes we really need. Colossians 3.12-14 (see today's memo) gives us the wardrobe that God has picked for us.

The Greek *enduo* means to put on an item of clothing. We need to get dressed and it may be countercultural but it's Jesus' culture. Remember the vain and gullible emperor who was tricked into wearing 'invisible' clothes? Turns out he was naked. In Revelation 3:17,

Jesus speaks to the church at Laodicea. *"You say, 'I am rich. I have everything I want. I don't need a thing!' And you don't realise that you are wretched and miserable and poor and blind and naked."* They needed to get dressed in God's wardrobe of clothes. There is no need to be wretched and miserable, poor, blind and naked when the life God has for us transforms us from the inside out so that we are properly dressed and in our right minds (see Mark 5:15). Don't be afraid to be countercultural!

Memorable Quote:
"Put your energy into looking good on the inside and it will show on the outside – being a loving, kind, thoughtful, generous, wise and courageous Christ-exalting person." Adapted by the author

Journaling Suggestion:
Love is Christianity with its work clothes on!

Memo for Meditation:
"So, chosen by God for this new life of love, dress in the wardrobe God picked out for you: compassion, kindness, humility, quiet strength, discipline. Be even-tempered, content with second place, quick to forgive an offence. Forgive as quickly and completely as the Master forgave you. And regardless of what else you put on, wear love. It's your basic, all-purpose garment. Never be without it." Colossians 3:12-14

October 24

Motivational Idea: Influencer culture

Influencer culture describes the phenomenon of celebrities who use their fame to promote particular products, i.e., 'influence' their audience for money. These figures usually gain fame through social media. Awareness of influencer culture is important since there are dangers for those who do not realise that the online world is heavily edited. Influencers rarely actually lead the lives they put out for the world to see. When they do, it's often not a healthy lifestyle. Young people and children are more susceptible to pressure and likely to constantly compare themselves with the people they see on social media. As such, this edited reality is potentially more harmful for the young and the vulnerable. Influencer culture is a very superficial and artificial world, and it is important that we remain aware of this.

We must refrain from comparing ourselves with other people at the cost of our own wellbeing. Furthermore, we should avoid automatically assuming that an influencer post is authentic or trustworthy. We need to educate our young people. TikTok has evolved as a powerful influencer platform with over one billion monthly users engaged with a range of content creators. Yet with the appeal of enthralling new products and viral trends, there is a dire need to address the impact of TikTok influencers, particularly in terms of product endorsements and reviews. The rise of influencers like Alix Earle – a 23-year-old beauty guru with six million followers – marks a significant shift in the dynamics of social media.

Previously relegated to their own little niche communities, these internet personalities now boast followings numbering in the millions. What can we do in a world of sometimes dangerous cultural influencers? Did you know that God has called you to be an influencer? To announce the good news of Jesus – the Gospel. And we are called to *do* good works. We are called to show acts of love, compassion, forgiveness, patience and kindness, and in doing these things, in shining God's light through our actions, and our words, Jesus says that *"they [the people we interact with] will see your [our] good works and give glory"* to God. (Matthew 5:16.)

Be an influencer for good and for God in an artificial influencer culture! Be a countercultural influencer and be fulfilled! Happiness is found here! Go shine!

Memorable Quote:
"You have more influence than you may think. We are all influencers in our circle of friends and family. You can make such an impact by just showing up for your people time and time again. It's so easy to assume that "influencers" are the people who have a verified social media account, or millions of followers. But the truth is - every single one of us can be a powerful influencer for good and for God." The Villarrealist

Journaling Suggestion:
Be an influencer today for sure. But influence by what you do, not what you say on video. Influence with silent effective action rather than loud rhetoric and empty words.

Memo for Meditation:
"Let your light so shine before others, that they may see your good works and give glory to your Father who is in heaven." Matthew 5:16

October 25

Motivational Idea: A culture of life

A 'culture of life' according to Wikipedia describes a way of life based on the belief that human life begins at conception. All human life is regarded as sacred, at all stages of life from conception to natural death. The implication of this worldview means abortion, euthanasia and capital punishment are ruled out, since all life, and every life, is sacred. The outworking of 'a culture of life' leads to the promotion of policies, programmes and endeavours designed to lift the human spirit with love and compassion. The term originated in Catholic theology and was popularised by Pope John Paul II. *"In our present social context, marked by a dramatic struggle between the 'culture of life' and the 'culture of death', there is need to develop a deep critical sense, capable of discerning true values and authentic needs."* (Pope John Paul II). The term has also been widely used in Evangelical Christianity, particularly in relation to the pro-life movement, but not exclusively so.

The philosophy of such a culture is a consistent life ethic which means respecting human intrinsic dignity and protecting human life from conception to natural death. The argument put forward by people of faith is that to understand more fully how to defend and protect human life we need to know who we are at the deepest level. God has created us in His image and likeness (see Genesis 1.26) for fellowship and intimacy with Him. The essence of our identity and worth, the source of our dignity, is that we are precious to and loved by God who sent His Son to be the Saviour of the world. We who follow Jesus must build a culture of life that values each person as a human being, not for what they possess or have to offer.

We must seek to protect every human life, especially those who are threatened or vulnerable. We need to stand up against xenophobia and racism and hatred of any kind. We must bring the good news of the Gospel. Salvation is about saved souls and saved lives.

Memorable Quote:
"We must play our part in building a culture of life, a culture that joyfully proclaims the truth of God's love for all humanity, and that He has a purpose, and plan for each person. Changing the culture is a process of conversion that begins in our own hearts and includes a willingness to be instructed and a desire to be close to Jesus – the source of joy and love – our role model in valuing each previous soul."

Journaling Suggestion:
Love your neighbour as yourself.

Memo for Meditation:
"You made all the delicate, inner parts of my body and knit me together in my mother's womb. Thank you for making me so wonderfully complex! Your workmanship is marvellous—how well I know it. You watched me as I was being formed in utter seclusion, as I was woven together in the dark of the womb. You saw me before I was born. Every day of my life was recorded in your book. Every moment was laid out before a single day had passed." Psalm 139:13-16

October 26

Motivational Idea: Jesus' culture

The Pharisees and religious Jews hated Jesus. This is brought into sharpened focus in John's Gospel, chapter 5. Jesus was turning their culture upside down and they were furious. Jesus brought about a new culture; He undermined the symbols of first-century Judaism, so much so that they eventually had Jesus killed. In John 5, Jesus healed a man on the Sabbath day. This was a red line for religious Jews. The law of Moses taught that the Sabbath must be different from other days. On the Sabbath, people were to refrain from work and animals were to be given rest too. Over the years, the Jewish leaders had amassed thousands of rules and regulations which they imposed on the Jewish community. By Jesus' day, they had 39 different classifications of work. This included the carrying of furniture and even medical treatment on the Sabbath day was prohibited.

Jesus didn't break the law of Moses, He violated the traditions of the Pharisees which was sacrosanct to them. It didn't matter that the man had been healed; what *did* matter to them was their regulations. Furthermore, as the dialogue between Jesus and the religious ensued, Jesus claimed to be God. *"This made the Jews more determined than ever to kill Him, for not only was He breaking the Sabbath [from their viewpoint], but He was also calling God His own Father, making Himself equal with God."* (John 5:18).

God incarnate walked among them, but they rejected Him; their culture was more important than the Jesus culture that they were confronted with. *"For the Law was given through Moses, but grace [the unearned, undeserved favour of God] and truth came through Jesus Christ."* (John 1: 17).

The radical transformation of culture ushered in by Jesus meant new answers to four main worldview questions: *Who are we?* All people need to be redeemed by God. *Where are we?* The Kingdom of God embraces all creation. *What is wrong?* The ultimate enemy is not Rome, but Satan, whose primary strategy is to cast doubt on the Word of God. *And what is the solution?* Jesus is the answer in His life, death and resurrection.

The new culture revolves around the cross. God was offering these religious Jews a gift and they rejected it. What was the gift? The gift is the same gift that Jesus offers today – eternal life and access to abundant life. If you believe in Jesus, you have eternal life. But have you started to explore what having eternal life here and now means? Jesus paid for it on the cross – we have free access. Take time to explore this abundant life. It's the life of God given to us!

Memorable Quote:
"Eternal life - abundant life - explore it, walk in it, right here right now. It's a present possession to enjoy and delve into. Live life more abundantly!" John 10:10, adapted by author

Journaling Suggestion:
Jesus created a new culture – Jesus' culture is my culture!

Memo for Meditation:

"I assure you and most solemnly say to you, the person who hears My word [the one who heeds My message], and believes and trusts in Him who sent Me, has (possesses now) eternal life [that is, eternal life actually begins—the believer is transformed], and does not come into judgement and condemnation, but has passed [over] from death into life." John 5:24

October 27

Motivational Idea: The greatest cultural architect

Jesus the cultural architect is unique as He has all authority as King of Kings and Lord of Lords. Creation's amazing architect is the greatest cultural architect of all time. The most historically significant person from the dawn of civilization to the present day. Type Jesus into the Google search engine and you will get some 665 million results. A distinctive culture with a new community – the Church – came into being. Exponential growth took place. The cross was central and racial identity was supplanted with one family: the family of God.

Jesus' culture spread out, transforming cultures across the world. Because of Jesus, the history of education, architecture, art, literature, medicine, politics, religion, science, economics, society and cultures have been radically transformed and revolutionised. Jesus said, *"Love the Lord your God with all your mind."* (Matthew 22:37).

The world of education took off. Scholarship came to the fore and the establishment of halls of learning. The earliest universities in Paris and Oxford were the result of scholarship and Christianity. The Council of Nicaea (325 AD) emphasised the need to build hospitals for the sick. Egalitarianism and equality became important where children, women, the disabled and slaves were seen in terms of their human worth and dignity.

Art down the centuries has been influenced by the man from Galilee. People today can try to dismiss Jesus, but they can't ignore Him. He is the most famous and influential person in all of history. Jesus is the Lord of history. He changed the world. He wants to be Lord of your history; you have the potential to change the story and the history of others by living Jesus' culture and impact those in your world and sphere of influence.

You too can be a cultural architect following in the footsteps of Jesus. There are many obstacles with cultural assassins who want to destroy Jesus' culture. They won't win. The Lord of history is coming again and we will all answer to Him. All will be sorted then!

Memorable Quote:
"Blessed, joyful, happy, nourished are those who hunger and thirst for righteousness, for they will be completely satisfied." Matthew 5:6

Journaling Suggestion:
I will be a cultural architect for Jesus and humbly serve my King.

Memo for Meditation:
"Like an architect who knows his job, by the grace God has given me, lay the foundation; someone else builds upon it. I only say this, let the builder be careful how he builds! The foundation is laid already, and no one can lay another, for it is Jesus Christ himself. But any man who builds on the foundation using as his material gold, silver, precious stones, wood, hay or stubble, must know that each man's work will one day be shown for what it is. The day will show it plainly enough, for the day will arise in a blaze of fire, and that fire will prove the nature of each man's work. If the work that the man has built upon the foundation will stand this test, he will be rewarded. But if a man's work is destroyed under the test, he loses it all. He personally will be safe, though rather like a man rescued from a fire." 1 Corinthians 3:14

October 28

Motivational Idea: The family culture

The word 'family' can conjure up diverse emotions for many of us, depending on our experiences. Strong positive emotions can be evoked if we have experienced a caring, loving family environment. However, if we have been in a dysfunctional, abusive family environment, it may be too painful to reflect upon.

The concept of family was introduced in the very beginning (Genesis 1:28). Family members were to care and look out for each other. Cain didn't! Jesus expanded the concept of family: *"While Jesus was still talking to the crowd, his mother and brothers stood outside, wanting to speak to him. Someone told him, 'Your mother and brothers are standing outside, wanting to speak to you.' He replied to him, 'Who is my mother, and who are my brothers?' Pointing to his disciples, he said, 'Here are my mother and my brothers. For whoever does the will of my Father in heaven is my brother and sister and mother.'"* (Matthew 12:46-50). Jesus is not dismissing the biological family as unimportant, but He is making the clear theological point that in the Kingdom of Heaven, the most important family connection is spiritual, not physical. John's Gospel explains this: *"Yet to all who received him, to those who believed in his name, he gave the right to become children of God—children born not of natural descent, nor of human decision or a husband's will, but born of God."* (John 1:12-13).

Interestingly, the only occurrence of the word 'family' in the New Testament is in Ephesians 3:15. It's the family of God (memo for today) and those who believe in Jesus that are part of the family. The local church is the local family, not a hall for the self-righteous to sit in judgement, it's a family where the downtrodden, the rejected, the broken, the needy are accepted, welcomed and helped. We are family – be the brother or the sister that the family needs today. Do you want a fulfilled life? Play your part in the family of God. Your local church needs you and people need you today! And if your church is a judgement hall, find another church! (see James 1:27.)

Memorable Quote:
"Broken homes, hatred between family members, or never knowing your parents can cause an individual to be sceptical of the idea of a "family." In God's family, there is no abandonment, hatred, or abuse. Only love, forgiveness, and grace abide within God's family. He will never cast you out or turn you away." Isaiah 41:10, Christianity.com, Vivian Bricker

Journaling Suggestion:
I will play my part in the family of God. Lord help me and lead me today!

Memo for Meditation:

"For this reason [grasping the greatness of this plan by which Jews and Gentiles are joined together in Christ] I bow my knees [in reverence] before the Father [of our Lord Jesus Christ], from whom the whole family in heaven and on earth derives its name [God—the first and ultimate Father]. May He grant you out of the riches of His glory, to be strengthened and spiritually energised with power through His Spirit in your inner self, [indwelling your innermost being and personality], so that Christ may dwell in your hearts through your faith. And may you, having been [deeply] rooted and [securely] grounded in love, may be able to comprehend with all saints what is the breadth and length, and depth, and height." Ephesians 3:14-18

October 29

Motivational Idea: The hamster wheel culture

If you have ever kept a hamster, you will know that these busy little creatures spend hours on the wheel. It never seems to cross their minds that they're getting nowhere. And so the metaphor of the hamster and the wheel has come to represent us human beings in our frantic lives. Some people can be busy all the time but never seem to achieve anything. Others can be high achievers/performers, but it's the same hamster wheel and they can't get off. Others are running in circles. There is the danger of burnout. Does your life feel like a relentless cycle? If it does, then you need to take a good long look at the hamster wheel of your human existence and decide to do something about it. Some 3,000 years ago, the wisest of men, Solomon, gives his observations of the same dilemma (Memo for today). He didn't use the hamster wheel metaphor, but he did talk about the sun rising and setting – he refers to the nature of life and its repetitive tasks. No sooner are we up with sunrise than we get engulfed in our daily never-ending routine, only to fall into bed again at the end of a busy, stressful day, exhausted and dissatisfied. For some people it's not like this, but for others it's worse.

"*Stop the world, I want to get off!*" is the cry of many poor souls today. If that's you, don't despair; there is hope, and there are answers to the hamster wheel conundrum. We don't have to feel trapped – we need to change our mindset. And daily routine is not a bad thing. Having a structure to our day is not only good for our mental wellbeing, it's essential. So don't knock the routine; it's about getting off the wheel which represents excessive busyness, seven days a week, and even if we don't work seven days a week, we still have the weekend wheel to contend with.

The first step is to face up to the reality of our hamster wheel existence. Tomorrow we can start looking at the big solution. The answer is as old as the world itself, yet the vast majority miss it.

Memorable Quote:
"Solomon writes Ecclesiastes from the perspective of an atheist: what is to be made of life without God to give it significance? This life in reality is an endless, mindless cycle, whether on the wheel or not, apart from the significance and purpose Jesus provides." Adapted

Journaling Suggestion:
My hamster wheel.

Memo for Meditation:
"Generations come and generations go, but the earth remains forever. The sun rises and the sun sets, and hurries back to where it rises. The wind blows to the south and turns to the north; round and round it goes, ever returning on its course. All streams flow into the sea, yet the sea is never full. To the place the streams come from, there they return again. All things are wearisome, more than one can say. The eye never has enough of seeing, nor the ear its fill of hearing. What has been will be again, what has been done will be done again; there is nothing new under the sun. Is there anything of which one can say, "Look! This is something new!"? It was here already, long ago; it was here before our time. No one remembers the former generations, and even those yet to come will not be remembered by those who follow them." Ecclesiastes 1:4-11

October 30

Motivational Idea: The answer to the hamster wheel conundrum

You don't need to buy it, you don't need to shop online; simply put, don't shop – just stop! The answer to the hamster wheel conundrum is summed up in one word, and it's a word that may not be taken seriously by the masses. The reason for it being dismissed out of hand by many may be because it has been misinterpreted and indeed misused by the well intentioned. The word is *'Sabbath'*. The word comes from *shabbat* which literally means 'to stop'. It can also mean rest, delight, worship. For those who work, the danger is we work so many days in the week and then we have the home life admin to do too, usually on weekends. Instead of going from a place of rest back into work on a Monday morning, we are not getting time to rest, relax and recharge; we are just not stopping, seven days a week. No wonder burnout is on the increase. Big organisations have realised the importance of stopping the hamster wheel and are introducing sabbaticals for their workforces. But what can we do on a weekly basis? The most powerful thing we can do is stop! The idea of Sabbath is about stepping back. The current state of living cannot be sustained. There is a biblical mandate for Sabbath. It first occurs in Genesis 2.1-3. God actually *'sabbathed'*. Not to rest, but to delight in all He had made.

We need to stop and take delight in life, in nature, and enjoy the feeling of being alive. Sabbath is not about closing the play parks on a Sunday – it's about taking delight in life and being joyful and happy. To go without Sabbath is to go against the rhythm that God the Creator has built into our makeup. The truth is many are living a Sabbath-less life of non-stop exhaustion. Yet, today we have the choice to make it more than an aspiration – we can make it a reality and begin to practise Sabbath. The question is how are we going to do it? Perhaps we need to begin with the practice of mini-sabbaths based on our seven-day circadian rhythm. The purists advocate a full day off; great if you can, but this may not be possible for many of us. We need weekly sabbath times when we stop what we are doing and feel human again – take that walk, that run, enjoy the sun or the rain on our face. Sit and observe the world around you, a world of miracles and wonders! Breathe in the oxygen of life again, away from the toxic nature of fast-paced living and the carbon monoxide which we inhale both physically and metaphorically on a daily basis. Start practising Sabbath and find out what that means for you and what suits your weekly routine. *"The tradition of Sabbath created an oasis of sacred time within a life of unceasing labour."* (Wayne Muller). Build it in and you will be able to escape the hamster wheel conundrum. Happiness awaits!

Memorable Quote:
"If you keep the Sabbath, you start to see creation not as somewhere to get away from your ordinary life, but a place to frame an attentiveness to your life."

Journaling Suggestion:
Today is the day I begin to plan the practice of Sabbath for me.

Memo for Meditation:
"Then Jesus said to them, 'The Sabbath was made to meet the needs of people, and not people to meet the requirements of the Sabbath.'" Mark 2:27

October 31

Motivational Idea: Culture and white space

White space is dedicated time where we can pause from work and every other commitment on our plates and allow our minds to wonder again at the miracle of life and living. It's time to recharge through cycles of rest and creativity. Sabbath is about renewal and renewing, and we need this on a weekly basis. It is significant that one of the Ten Commandments is to take a day of 'ceasing' or Sabbath (see Exodus 20:8-11) each week – to create some white space, free from obligations and to-dos, in which we can just enjoy the gift of existence, of being, without the mania of the working week and the constant interruption of the mobile phone. We need proper rest and we need our Sabbath time built into our seven days each week.

We may well need to calibrate our lives to adjust to maintaining a Sabbath time of rest and putting a full stop to the weekly grind. We need to build Sabbath time in, especially if we are not used to it, and indeed it may be totally foreign to us.

Sabbath at its very essence is more than rest, it is a discipline of celebration and the delivery mechanism for happiness and joy. The Bible says God blessed the Sabbath day. The Hebrew word *barak* means 'to bless', 'to make happy'. It's a happy day. Could it be that we have so much unhappiness as a result of not celebrating Sabbath, a day when we could delight in how much goodness there is around us? Because the world is full of so many ugly things, we need to take Sabbath to fill our souls with beautiful things. We may have also lost sight of the God who made us and in whom we should delight. Sabbath is also about worship – we can even Sabbath with God every day by setting precious time aside in the morning. We have secularised this time of worship and adoration – we worship and adore other gods. But Sabbath in its purest form is the worship of the God of Sabbath.

Sabbath is a time to delight in God and His love. The Bible is a closed book to many but it's here that we learn about Sabbath. If that is the case, how much more is there to learn about ourselves and how we should live our lives on planet Earth? Sabbath is a good place to begin. The Bible has many promises about Sabbath: a gift of time (see Genesis 2:1–3); freedom from work (see Exodus 20:8–11); a blessing of joy (see Isaiah 58:13, 14); a special blessing for our children — (see Isaiah 56:2–9); security (see Ezekiel 20:20); renewal in Christ (see Mark chapter 2); and hope of eternity (see Isaiah 66:22, 23).

Let's start a true and authentic Sabbath culture! Try it!

Memorable Quote:
"If you don't take a Sabbath, something is wrong. You're doing too much, you're being too much in charge. You've got to quit, one day a week, and just watch what God is doing when you're not doing anything." Eugene H Peterson

Journaling Suggestion:
It's a Sabbath culture for me!

Memo for Meditation:
"Remember to observe the Sabbath day by keeping it holy." Exodus 20:8

THE MUSICAL DIMENSION

November 1

Motivational Idea: Music makes the world go round

On 21st June 1982, the first Fête de la Musique was inaugurated in Paris. This was the brainchild of the French Culture Minister, Jack Lang. World Music Day (WMD) is now a global event and celebrates the 1200 music genres in the world today.

Banbridge Town in County Down, Northern Ireland, has a Busker Festival every year. Musicians are on the streets from early morning and the atmosphere is joyous. Each year a specific theme is chosen; in 2023, the focus was *Music on the Intersections,* the purpose being to celebrate the power of music in bringing people together irrespective of culture or race. There is one language that unites everyone and it's music.

WMD is also a way of paying tribute to musicians who have played a significant role in the music world. Music enables us to celebrate life when we are joyful as well as those times of sadness. Songs can soothe our souls and enable us to express deeply hidden emotions; where would we be without music? Some compositions are timeless and are listened to over and over by each generation. Did you know that the Bible has a book of 150 number one hits? It's called the Psalms, composed mostly by King David. Almost everyone can quote at least a part of Psalm 23. Here we have the timeless inspired Psalter book, the song book of billions. You will find songs about every facet of life; here is the very breath and cry of the human soul, here is the language of the human spirit. It opens to us the secrets of the flourishing life, bringing lasting joy and happiness. The Psalms express the deepest passions of our humanity and lead us to our loving Creator. They are bubbling with joy for you to experience too. Get into God's hits and hear His voice as He sings over you!

Memorable Quote:
"The LORD your God is with you, He is mighty to save. He will take great delight in you, He will quiet you with his love, He will rejoice over you with singing." Zephaniah 3:17

Journaling Suggestion:
I plan to read one of the 150 number one Psalm hits every day, starting today!

Memo for Meditation:
"Hallelujah! Thank God! Pray to Him by name! Tell everyone you meet what He has done! Sing Him songs, belt out hymns, translate His wonders into music! Honour His holy name with Hallelujahs, you who seek God. Live a happy life! Keep your eyes open for God, watch for His works; be alert for signs of His presence. Remember the world of wonders He has made, His miracles, and the verdicts He's rendered - O seed of Abraham, His servant, O child of Jacob, His chosen. He's God, our God, in charge of the whole earth. And He remembers, remembers His Covenant - for a thousand generations He's been as good as his word." Psalm 105:1-8

November 2

Motivational Idea: If music be the food of love, play on

This is one of the most famous and most quoted lines in all of English literature, and first appeared in 1602 in William Shakespeare's play *Twelfth Night*. Orsino, the Duke of Illyria, is in love and as he sits in his garden surrounded by friends listening to music, he is distraught because his love is not reciprocated. The musicians seem to have paused and so he asks them to play on, his reasoning being that if music is the food of love, and if he hears enough of it, like gorging himself with food, he will become sick and lose his appetite for being in love with Olivia. As he engages in a self-indulgent monologue, he does not really believe this will work, but his unrequited love dilemma does not last long for soon he is in love with someone else. The play explores different characters being in love, and has relevance today because we still struggle with the same issues that Shakespeare's colourful characters faced. There are numerous situations in *Twelfth Night* where love is unrequited and the illusion, deception, disguises and madness, and the extraordinary things that love can cause people to do is demonstrated.

Shakespeare shows how fickle, irrational and self-serving love can sometimes be. The play does offer a happy ending in spite of the dilemmas of being in love and the various characters find one another in the end and achieve happiness.

We live in a world today that craves love and for some, if not many, the oceanic experience of being in love can lead to multiple broken relationships as there is the danger of being in love with the idea of being in love and never being satisfied. This is 'Eros' love. There is another kind of love called 'agape' love and this is the love of God that satisfies the heart and leads us into a love relationship with God. He desires to guide us into true, meaningful, loving and happy relationships, even in our brokenness, no matter how we have messed up.

Memorable Quote:
"But God demonstrates his own love for us in this: While we were still sinners, Christ died for us." Romans 5:8.

Journaling Suggestion:
Explore this agape love starting with John 3:16

Memo for Meditation:
"Speaking to one another with psalms, hymns, and songs from the Spirit. Sing and make music from your heart to the Lord, always giving thanks to God the Father for everything, in the name of our Lord Jesus Christ. Submit to one another out of reverence for Christ." Ephesians 5:19-21

November 3

Motivational Idea: Music as medicine

Research has shown that music can be a powerful medicine to the extent that it can promote our wellbeing and aid the healing processes in body and mind. In a world where doctors are prescribing self-help books, now and more so in the future, music will also be prescribed to enable us to feel happier and overcome sadness. Music is also being used to improve cognitive function and to enable us to relax. You only have to google 'happy songs' and you will find a list of the top ten that will make you feel better and put a spring in your step. We have surround sound songs these days; in the home, the workplace, shops, supermarkets and restaurants.

Research has shown that playing certain types of calming music in communal areas can significantly reduce vandalism. Happy songs have a distinctive beat. The happy song checklist has songs with a tempo of 137 beats per minute. The Gospel music genre has also been found to have a positive impact on mood, with uplifting and comforting elements. Gospel music can touch our souls like nothing else, giving hope and reducing anxiety, and it has been shown to improve self-esteem. Gospel music has been shown to increase activity in the left hemisphere of the brain which is responsible for positive emotions, and decrease activity in the right hemisphere of the brain responsible for negative emotions.

Gerontology studies (the study of ageing processes) has shown the benefits for those of older age, too, with increased energy and contentment. Music is powerful medicine and Gospel music is transformative, connecting us with the Divine and giving a heavenly joy and satisfaction the world cannot give. Try some Gospel songs today. Check out *Way Maker* by Sinach (Leeland and Passion rendition), and *Happy* by Tasha Cobbs for starters.

Memorable Quote:
"You are/Way maker, miracle worker, promise keeper/Light in the darkness/My God, that is who You are/You are/Way maker, miracle worker, promise keeper/Light in the darkness/My God, that is who You are." Sinach

Journaling Suggestion:
Make a list of some great Gospel songs from talented Gospel artists to listen to.

Memo for Meditation:
"What a beautiful thing, God, to give thanks, to sing an anthem to you, the High God! To announce your love each daybreak, sing your faithful presence all through the night, Accompanied by dulcimer and harp, the full-bodied music of strings. You made me so happy, God. I saw your work

and I shouted for joy. How magnificent your work, God! How profound your thoughts!" Psalm 92 – the song of a happy person

---

November 4

Motivational Idea: Don't worry, be happy

I used to have a singing fish and his name was Big Mouth Billy Bass. One of the songs he sang was, *Don't worry, be happy.* When strategically placed, a sensor would detect an individual and Billy would sing at the top of his sweet voice. It began to drive my work colleagues mad and Billy had to go. Here are some of the lyrics:

Here's a little song I wrote
You might want to sing it note for note
Don't worry, be happy
In every life we have some trouble
But when you worry, you make it double
Don't worry, be happy, Don't worry, be happy now
Don't worry, (Ooh-ooh-ooh-ooh) be happy, (Ooh-ooh-ooh) Don't worry, be happy

Bobby McFerrin wrote the song in 1988 and won two Grammys. Bobby says, *"Everyone has troubles, but rather than getting overwhelmed with worry we need to take a step back and realise that worry does not help, it only makes things worse."* McFerrin doesn't mean that we should have a couldn't care less attitude and have a *laissez faire* view of everything that is happening, but he does mean that we need to have a positive attitude. Even with all our problems in life, we need to deal with possible distractions and excuses or reasons for not being happy. Worrying causes double trouble. Worrying is a waste of time and energy. But how do we develop a positive attitude, especially if we are prone to negativity? We need a good foundation upon which to build, one that is firm and secure. If we can find that foundation, then we can accentuate the positive. Our memo for today gives us the answer. In short, try prayer. (See https://www.trypraying.org/)

Memorable Quote:
"Our fatigue is often caused not by work but by worry, frustration and resentment." Dale Carnegie

Journaling Suggestion:
Don't destroy today by worrying about tomorrow.

Memo for Meditation:
"Do not be anxious about anything, but in every situation, by prayer and petition, with thanksgiving, present your requests to God. And the peace of God, which transcends all understanding, will guard your hearts and your minds in Christ Jesus." Philippians 4:6,7

November 5

Motivational Idea: The Mozart Effect

Johann Chrysostom Wolfgang Amadeus Mozart was born on 27th January 1756 and died on 5th December 1791. A child prodigy, he began composing at the age of four and by the age of ten had written and performed ten symphonies. At his untimely death, he had composed over 600 works. In the 1990s, his work took on a new dimension when the 'Mozart Effect' came to the fore. Anecdotally, I have found that listening to Mozart's violin concertos can boost concentration and recall quite substantially. Also, listening to, for example, the harp and flute concerto brings about calm and relaxation – just 20 minutes a day for wellbeing. I wonder if that is why Chopin said he would listen to Mozart every day. I suggested this to clients for counselling and most came back with positive feedback. Worth a listen!

Most of Mozart's sacred works were composed when he was employed by the Archbishop of Salzburg. It can be observed that throughout his operas the theme is one of redemption and forgiveness, offering healing in the fragmented world in which humanity finds itself. *Requiem* confronts us with fearful alienation caused by our sinfulness and yet offers the promise of grace and forgiveness with the comfort of final rest. Mozart was not a 'religious' man, but he believed in the power of prayer and often prayed for guidance and inspiration. In a letter to his wife, Mozart once wrote, *"I wish to talk with you about serious matters, for I have always believed in Jesus Christ, and in his teachings."* Mozart with all his flaws and failings as a human being expressed faith in Jesus Christ, and He was a source of strength and comfort for him. He felt enabled and empowered to create some of the most beautiful and timeless music ever written. Psalm 117 was a source of inspiration to the great classical composers, and inspired Mozart to compose his famous musical setting, *Laudate Dominum.*

Memorable Quote:
"God must come first! From his hands, we receive our temporal happiness and our eternal salvation." W A Mozart

Journaling Suggestion:
Laudate Dominum – Praise the Lord.

Memo for Meditation:
"Praise the Lord, all nations/Laudate Dominum omnes gentes/Praise him, all you peoples/Laudate eum, omnes populi/Because it was confirmed/Quoniam confirmata est/His mercy is upon us/Super nos misericordia eius/And the truth, the Lord's truth remains, remains forever/Et veritas, veritas Domini manet, manet in aeternum/Glory to the Father and to the Son/Gloria Patri et Filio/And to the Holy Spirit/Et Spiritui Sancto/As it was in the beginning/Sicut erat in principio/Now and always/Et nunc, et semper/And forever and ever/Et in saecula saeculorum/Amen, Amen, Amen, Amen/Amen, Amen, Amen, Amen." Psalm 117

November 6

Motivational Idea: The happy hiatus

Taking regular breaks is essential for maintaining our wellbeing. We are constantly bombarded with information overload in our social media culture. We need to intentionally build in 'the happy hiatus' – a gap, a break, a pause, when we take a rest from it all, unplug from the 'matrix' of the everyday routine and step away from the daily grind. We find the concept of the sabbatical in the Bible: the Shabbat, the Sabbath. (See The Cultural Dimension 30th and 31st October.) It means rest and commemorates the day that God rested from creating the universe. He didn't need to rest, He wasn't tired. He stopped! It was a cessation of work, not a reinvigoration after work; He had finished His creative work.

We are human, however, and get tired so we need to rest and shift our brain states so that our minds and our bodies can bounce back! To rest and rejuvenate means that when we go back to the routine, we can plug in to what really matters. Academics and others, too, have been known to take a seven-year sabbatical. Whether you are contemplating such or simply seeking to build in that regular hiatus, make sure you do; you will reap the benefits. Matt Redman is well known as a worship leader. He decided to take a spiritual sabbatical and took a year out. This gave him time to reflect on the real meaning of worship. He realised that there was too much focus on the details such as musical style and who was leading it. He came back with a new song. We may not be in a position to take a year out but we can build in mini-sabbaticals and enjoy that happy hiatus on a regular basis. Who knows what the outcome will be when you reconnect with a fresh outlook, renewed energy and clearer vision. Unplug, then plug-in to what's really needed.

Memorable Quote:
"When the music fades/All is stripped away/And I simply come/Longin' just to bring/Something that's of worth/That will bless Your heart/I'll bring You more than a song/For a song in itself/Is not what You have required/You search much deeper within/Through the ways things appear/You're looking into my heart/I'm comin' back to 'the heart of worship'/And it's all about You/It's all about You, Jesus/I'm sorry, Lord, for the thing I've made it/When it's all about You...Jesus". Matt Redman
Journaling Suggestion:
Plan my next happy hiatus and build more into my life.

Memo for Meditation:
"Jesus said, 'Come with me by yourselves to a quiet place and get some rest.'" Mark 6:31

November 7

Motivational Idea: *The Long and Winding Road*

The song *The Long and Winding Road* has been credited to Lennon/McCartney. It was the last song released by the Beatles before they split up. The song was written by Paul McCartney in 1968. It is said that he was inspired by a road near his Scottish farm that stretched up into the highlands. It was a sad song and McCartney explained that he liked writing sad songs. It seems it was a kind of catharsis for him so he could deal with painful experiences. The song is about a sad lonely man who feels pain and is addressing the one who caused him pain, and the refrain is about not being left alone. What he desires is unattainable and the door is beyond reach. The man in his pain longs to be transported back to the happy place they once enjoyed together. We can all identify in some measure with the song because life is like a long and winding road with lots of twists and turns. One of the lessons of the song is that we should be careful who we let into our lives because they can change everything for better or worse. *"Be careful who you let on your ship, because they might try to sink you."* The lyrics include the words, *"Why leave me standing here, let me know the way,"* and, *"Don't keep me waiting here, lead me to your door,"* – the unattainable door for McCartney.

The psalmist David experienced many twists and turns in his life and bitter life experiences; his son, Absalom, is a case in point, and the restoration of their relationship to that happy place became unobtainable. But David put his trust in God and found that the God of the destination was also the God of the journey. He had the promise that God would instruct him and teach him the way he should go (Psalm 32:8). He could say with confidence, *"He leads me beside still waters"*(Psalm 23:2).

When we commit our way to God and trust Him, we find that the unattainable becomes attainable and the impossible becomes possible. He opens doors that no one can shut and shuts doors that no one can open (Revelation 3:8). Our memo for today comes from the psalter where David experiences a different kind of road with an attainable goal in the will of God. Not only does God know the road, He promises to go with us every step of the way.

Memorable Quote:
"God knows the way. Let Him drive. Sit back, relax and just enjoy the journey."

Journaling Suggestion:
"In all your ways submit to him, and he will make your paths straight."
Proverbs 3:6

Memo for Meditation:
"What a God! His road stretches straight and smooth. Every GOD-direction is road-tested. Everyone who runs toward him makes it." Psalm 18:30

November 8

Motivational Idea: Hallelujah

Leonard Cohen released his song *Hallelujah* in 1984 on the album *Various Positions*. Initially it created little interest. Then other musical artists eventually came across the song and gave their own various renditions. Its popularity began to grow and, as we all know, it is now a worldwide phenomenon. The song has its roots in Cohen's Jewish background and we find some fleeting biblical references to King David, Samson and Delilah. Cohen said he viewed the song as a celebration of life and love, but not in a religious or spiritual sense. He had laboured over the song for several years with various lyrics until he settled on the final and original version. There are, however, over 300 different variations today. The song contains the lyrics, *"It's a cold, and it's a broken hallelujah"*. Cohen said, *"You look around and you see a world impenetrable that you cannot make sense of. You either raise your fists or you say 'Hallelujah.' I try to do both."* The word hallelujah is a combination of two Hebrew words, *hallel* meaning praise and *jah* meaning God. It is usually rendered in English as 'praise the Lord'.

Hallelujah is used 24 times in the Psalms and it's all about giving tribute, praise and adoration to the Lord. It's an expression of joy in God who is seen in scripture as the source and inspiration of true joy. We are called to give praise to the Lord and focus on the God who made us and desires us to live a life of joy. In our broken world of broken hallelujahs, when many of the songs we hear on the radio are a cry for redemption, we need to raise our voices in praise to God. Scripture tells us, *"Whoever offers praise glorifies Me; And to him who orders his conduct aright. I will show the salvation of God.'* (Psalm 50:23).

The memo for meditation today tells us how to go about it; it's the antithesis of a cold and broken hallelujah, with hands lifted in praise, not raised fists. Remember too, *"The joy of the* LORD *is your strength."* (Nehemiah 8:10).

Memorable Quote:
"The climax of God's happiness is the delight He takes in the echoes of His excellence in the praises of His people." John Piper

Journaling Suggestion:
Try praise and raise a hallelujah!

Memo for Meditation:
"Hallelujah! Thank GOD! Pray to him by name! Tell everyone you meet what he has done! Sing him songs, belt out hymns, translate his wonders into music! Honour his holy name with Hallelujahs, you who seek GOD. Live a happy life! Keep your eyes open for GOD, watch for his works; be alert for signs of his presence. Remember the world of wonders he has made, his miracles, and the verdicts he's rendered— O seed of Abraham, his servant, O child of Jacob, his chosen." Psalm 105:1-6

November 9

Motivational Idea: Haydn's happiness

Joseph Haydn (1732–1809) was an Austrian composer who was instrumental in the development of chamber music such as the string quartet and piano trio. His contributions to musical form have led him to be called 'Father of the Symphony" and 'Father of the stringed quartet'. Mozart said of him, *"High esteem for true merit, and regard for the individual, influenced his judgement of works of art."* By temperament, he was deeply religious, and it is said that he gave back to Almighty God in his compositions for the services of the Church, the talent with which he was so richly endowed.

Haydn dedicated many of his works to God. He normally began the manuscript of each composition with *In nomine Domini* ('in the name of the Lord') and ended with *Laus Deo* ('praise be to God'). *The Creation*, an oratorio written between 1797 and 1798, is considered by many to be one of his masterpieces. The oratorio depicts and celebrates the creation of the world as described in the Book of Genesis. The work was inspired by the Bible and also Milton's *Paradise Lost*. Haydn was once asked why his church music was so cheerful. He replied, *"When I think upon God, my heart is so full of joy that the notes dance and leap, as it were, from my pen, and since God has given me a cheerful heart, it will be pardoned me that I serve Him with a cheerful spirit."*

Haydn discovered the secret of lasting joy: *"I think upon God."* When we think upon God, we turn our hearts and minds to His power and His love for us – we can't help but be joyful. We could take a leaf out of Haydn's music book, the 'Father of the Symphony' and 'Father of the stringed quartet', as we focus on our Heavenly Father and His Son, Jesus Christ, in the atmosphere of the Holy Spirit. Take your time today and spend unhurried time praising God. It will still your spirit and give you lasting joy.

Memorable Quote:
"God never hurries. There are no deadlines against which he must work. Only to know this is to quiet our spirits and relax our nerves." A W Tozer, *The Pursuit of God: The Human Thirst for the Divine*

Journaling Suggestion:
Journal upon God and His love for you.

Memo for Meditation:
"Summing it all up, friends, I'd say you'll do best by filling your minds and meditating on things true, noble, reputable, authentic, compelling, gracious—the best, not the worst; the beautiful, not the ugly; things to praise, not things to curse. Put into practice what you learned from me, what you heard and saw and realised. Do that, and God, who makes everything work together, will work you into his most excellent harmonies." Philippians 4:8,9

November 10

Motivational Idea: A life that sings

The inspiration for today came from our memo. It's a great way to live! Then I discovered a book with this title, hence the memorable quote. Piper Green is right; we all want a life that sings, joy in our hearts, a spring in our step, a positivity that distinguishes us, and a love that envelops us and reaches out to others.

I remember working with a mental health service user who had a metaphorical spring in her step but had been through the mill. Life events had left her in a wheelchair, and added to her burden had been the depths of depression and isolation for a prolonged period of time. *"I lost my voice,"* she said one day before we began our co-facilitation training session on an understanding advocacy course. But Julie then said, *"But I found my voice and I have written a short course to help others find theirs."* The next course we ran was Julie's course, with her taking the lead. It was called *I found my voice.* Her life truly sang. It all began when she made a decision in the realisation that her life was not defined by her circumstances and discovered God in the darkness. Isn't it time we too joined the choir? Not our voices only, but our very lives, singing in harmony in a stunning anthem to the God and Father of our Master, Jesus!

Memorable Quote:

"Everyone wants a life that sings. We all desire to have a life of beauty. Sometimes, though, circumstances cloud our vision. My circumstances were anything but beautiful; they were downright ugly. I was tired, worn out, and my eyesight had grown dim to the beauty and goodness of God. I struggled to find beauty in my life. In the midst of the mundane and madness, I had lost my song. I learned that beauty is not defined by circumstances but by my reaction to the circumstances. Each of us has a story and a song, but will we leave the world with a gorgeous melody or an off-key tune? A song of joy and thankfulness or a song of bitterness and regret? The latter leads to isolation, the former to restoration." Piper Green, *A Life That Sings.*

Journaling Suggestion:
Journal on making your life a gorgeous melody and not an off-key tune. Be a song of joy and thankfulness and not a lament of bitterness and regret.

Memo for Meditation:
"Even if it was written in Scripture long ago, you can be sure it's written for us. God wants the combination of his steady, constant calling and warm, personal counsel in Scripture to come to characterise us, keeping us alert for whatever he will do next. May our dependably steady and warmly personal God develop maturity in you so that you get along with each other as well as Jesus gets along with us all. Then we'll be a choir— not our voices only, but our very lives singing in harmony in a stunning anthem to the God and Father of our Master Jesus!" Romans 15:1-6

November 11

Motivational Idea: The sound of silence

The Sound of Silence by Simon & Garfunkel, the iconic culture touchstone of the sixties, sold 22 million copies worldwide. The imagery of light and darkness expresses how ignorance and apathy destroys our ability to communicate. We can't understand each other because we have lost the ability to communicate effectively, hence the 'neon sign'. *"People talking without speaking – hearing without listening. My words like silent raindrops fell within the wells of silence."*

The words tell us that when meaningful communication fails, the only sound is silence. It's ironic but Simon and Garfunkel had a rather troubled relationship, leading to artistic disagreements and eventually their breakup in 1970. Their final studio album, *Bridge Over Troubled Water,* was released that January, becoming one of the world's best-selling albums. They stopped speaking and it's been a lifelong feud according to those in the know. In 2016, Paul Simon said they were no longer on speaking terms. In 2023, Paul Simon, aged 81, released his *Seven Psalms* album. It's a quiet, thirty-three minute runtime. There is the whisper of his acoustic guitar as he fingerpicks his way through the arrangements. His lyrics are uncluttered. *"I lived a life of pleasant sorrows,"* he sings in one of the most memorable lines, *"until the real deal* came." Although the album is called *Seven Psalms*, they are not actual Psalms from the Bible. Simon explains that his latest work is an *"argument about belief or not".* He confronts his mortality head-on and wonders about God, the reasons for existence, and death. He mentions the Lord over forty times but not in a way readers of the Bible would recognise. These are his own psalms, not of praise, but of his search for meaning as life's little day ebbs to its close. In the sound of silence, God is the real deal and He speaks when we are still and He is not silent! Read THE Psalms!

Memorable Quote:
"If you have ever searched for the meaning of life in a pop song, you have likely turned to Paul Simon. The sacred comfort of being alone, the creeping anxiety of getting older, the haunted visitations that follow our failed relationships: For 60 years, he has explored these universal concerns in a tender, conversational voice, often accompanied by complex arrangements that suggest a busy, clattering world, already setting the stage for our next celebration or catastrophe." Sam Sodomsky

Journaling Suggestion:
Take time to be still today and speak with God. Seek Him in the silence. Listen!

Memo for Meditation:
"He [God] says, 'Be still, and know that I am God; I will be exalted among the nations, I will be exalted in the earth.' The LORD Almighty is with us; The God of Jacob is our fortress." Psalm 46:10

November 12

Motivational Idea: Nothing compares to you

Sadly, Irish singer Sinéad O'Connor died at the age of 56 on 26th July 2023. Phil Coulter said, *"She had a God-given instrument, a God-given voice, certainly one of the finest voices this country [Ireland] has ever produced."* Her signature song that catapulted her to fame was, *Nothing Compares to You.* The song was a worldwide hit and one of the biggest ballads of the 1990s. The song was written by Prince

(Rogers Nelson) in 1985. Prince never clarified the story behind the song but it has resonated with listeners as a song expressing the sadness and anger experienced in profound love loss. The first lines are, *"It's been seven hours and 15 days/Since you took your love away."* The song goes on to say, *"It's been so lonely without you here/Like a bird without a song."* It has been suggested that Prince wrote the song about his housekeeper, Sandy Scipioni, who left to be with her family after her father had died. The point is, this valued and significantly important person has gone and the disappointment is palpable. Happiness is about happenings and indeed unhappiness is about happenings, too. Here is a happening that has produced great grief and unhappiness. Given that we can have a personal relationship with Jesus Christ and He has promised never to leave us nor forsake us and isn't going to abandon us, we will never have to say that you took your love away from me, Nothing compares to Him! You are so valuable to Him and nothing compares to you in Jesus' eyes. You are the apple of his eye! Find your happiness and joy in Him today. He will give you a new song to sing! (see Psalm 40:3)

Memorable Quote:
"What a beautiful Name it is
What a beautiful Name it is
The Name of Jesus Christ my King
What a beautiful Name it is
Nothing compares to this
What a beautiful Name it is
The Name of Jesus
You didn't want heaven without us
So Jesus You brought heaven down
My sin was great Your love was greater
What could separate us now."
Hillsong

Journaling Suggestion:
"But blessed is the one who trusts in the Lord, whose confidence is in him." Jeremiah 17:7

Memo for Meditation:
"Do not be afraid or discouraged, for the LORD will personally go ahead of

you. He will be with you; he will neither fail you nor abandon you."
Deuteronomy 31:8

November 13

Motivational Idea: His eye is on the sparrow

The Canadian poet Civilla Durfee Martin (1866-1948) provided one of the most influential and often-recorded Gospel hymns of the 20th century. *His eye is on the sparrow* (1905). Its popularity has not waned over the decades. The motivation for writing the song came as a result of an encounter with a couple called the Doolittles. Civilla and her husband had developed a close friendship with the couple. Mrs Doolittle had been bedridden for many years. Her husband was disabled and used a wheelchair to conduct his business and look after his wife. Despite their seemingly insurmountable problems, they lived, in the words of Civilla, *"Happy Christian lives, bringing inspiration and comfort to all who knew them."* On one particular visit, Martin commented on their joyful and happy outlook and asked them for their secret. Mrs Doolittle responded, *"His eye is on the sparrow, and I know He watches me.'"* Civilla said, *"The beauty of this simple expression of boundless faith gripped the hearts and fired the imagination of Dr Martin and me. The hymn* His Eye is on the Sparrow *was the outcome of that experience."* The poem was written and the next day mailed to Charles Gabriel, a famous composer of Gospel songs, who wrote the music. Be encouraged today. His loving eye is upon you. He won't let you down!

Memorable Quote:
"Why should I feel discouraged
And why should the shadows, come
But why, why, why should my heart, my heart feel lonely?
And long for heaven, heaven, home, yeah, yes
When, Jesus is my portion
a constant friend, constant friend is He
Oh, oh-oh, his eye is on, his eye is on the sparrow
Oh yes, I, I know He watches, oh, over me, yeah, hey...."
Civilla Durfee Martin

Journaling Suggestion:
Journal about the knowledge that He is your counsel and guide, and He watches over you.

Memo for Meditation:
"So don't be afraid; you are worth more than many sparrows. Matthew 10.29-31 I will instruct you and teach you in the way you should go; I will counsel you with my loving eye on you. Do not be like the horse or the mule, which have no understanding but must be controlled by bit and bridle or they will not come to you." Psalm 32:8.9

November 14

Motivational Idea: Singing in the storm

We would expect a person whose house is being watched by assassins to be in a state of intense fear and foreboding. We would imagine the level of anxiety to be off the charts. Today we live in a world where some people are in a similar position and given death threats for all kinds of reasons. What would we do if we were under such an existential threat? How would we feel in that scenario? The memo for meditation was written by a man who found himself in such circumstances. King David was in the crosshairs of Saul's hatred and the dirty tricks department were busy in seeking to take David out. You can read about it in 1 Samuel 19:11-13. Rather than being at the end of his tether, David expresses a peace and a tranquillity in the storm of adversity. He is even joyous, and it's not a manic defence or a reaction formation response. No! His focus is on God as his fortress, his safe place. His life is in God's hands. In our world today we may not be facing the problems David was facing but we are in an invisible spiritual war with the arch enemy of our souls. Indeed, Peter tells us that. *"The devil goes about like a roaring lion seeking whom he may devour."* (1 Peter 5:8-9). We are to resist him and stand firm in the faith.

We too can do what David did and realise that the power of God is ours and He is our safe place and we can always count on Him. And it's a daily thing. Start the day as you mean to go on. David began the day with praise and found all he needed in the Lord, his God. We too can sing in the storm when David's God is our God and our reliance is on Him.

Memorable Quote:
"Relying on God has to begin all over again everyday as if nothing had yet been done." C S Lewis

Journaling Suggestion:
"This I declare about the LORD : He alone is my refuge, my place of safety; he is my God, and I trust him." Psalm 91:2

Memo for Meditation:
"And me? I'm singing your prowess,
shouting at dawn your largesse,
For you've been a safe place for me,
a good place to hide.
Strong God, I'm watching you do it,
I can always count on you—
God, my dependable love."
Psalm 59:16-17

November 15

Motivational Idea: Even clodhoppers can sing

Martin Luther may seem to be a strange name to include in the musical dimension but he was an ardent music lover! This is made abundantly clear when he said, *"Next to the Word of God, music deserves the highest praise. The gift of language combined with the gift of song was given to man that he should proclaim the Word of God through music."* He realised that music is a powerful gift to the Church. He even wrote a book about it: *Te Deum: The Church and Music.* Not only did he bring about a reformation in theology but he brought about a reformation in music. Luther was an able musician himself and he surrounded himself with musicians. He is also responsible for the recovery of congregational singing. It is important to point out that Luther saw music not as an end in itself but rather as an 'instrument' for delivering the greatest message in the world. An authority on Luther put it in this way: *"He [Luther] believed that the synchronisation of sound and theology served a redemptive function."* Luther said that he was not able to find words to adequately describe the wonder of music that has been infused with the message of Jesus Christ.

Our airwaves are filled with music today from many gifted musicians. There are all kinds of genres yet the recurrent themes are the search for happiness and joy; the cry for redemption and salvation; the need to be found, be saved and safe; and find that true love! We can enjoy all kinds of music. However, Luther believed that music needed to be reclaimed from what he called *"perverted minds"*. Some of the lyrics today would bear that out. His desire for its reclamation was, *"in order to taste with wonder (yet not to comprehend) God's absolute and perfect wisdom in his wondrous work of music."*

As for clodhoppers (it's in our quote for today), the word dates back to 1690 and it was usually used as a term of derision by townspeople at the expense of muddy-booted yokels. May we join in the song – it's not all about the voice, it's the song! Even clodhoppers can sing when we realise that music is a marvellous creation of God. Check out the latest Christian songs. Try Charity Gayle: *Thank You Jesus for the Blood,* and *I Speak Jesus* for a start. Also check out Luther's hymn, *A Mighty Fortress is our God.* It is based on Psalm 46.

Memorable Quote:
"A person who... does not regard music as a marvellous creation of God, must be a clodhopper indeed and does not deserve to be called a human being; he should be permitted to hear nothing but the braying of asses and the grunting of hogs." Martin Luther

Journaling Suggestion:
I am going to listen to some songs about Jesus today!

Memo for Meditation:
"God is our refuge and strength, an ever present help in trouble." Psalm 46:1

November 16

Motivation Idea: Gotta serve somebody (1)

In the late 1970s, Bob Dylan embraced the Christian faith and released his *Christian Trilogy* albums. The first of these, *Slow Train Coming* (1979), heralded Dylan's newly embraced Christianity. At the forefront of this album is the track *You Gotta Serve Somebody*, which attracted much discussion and analysis; yet at its core it conveys a very simple but profound spiritual message: it doesn't matter who you are, your status, your achievements or the wealth you have accrued; invariably you are serving something or someone.

Here we have a dichotomy between serving God or serving the devil, which represents selfishness, materialism and the hedonistic lifestyle. The reality is that we are all serving something or someone. Dylan is acknowledging that we find true meaning and joy in a life that serves God. John Lennon thought this song was *"embarrassing"* and wrote *Serve Yourself* in response, criticising Dylan's *"preaching"*, and instead asserted, *"You gotta serve yourself, Ain't nobody gonna do it for you."*

Dylan presents characters from all walks of life. In the words of one critic, *"From the socialite to the pauper, the rock star to the scientist; he emphasises that no one is exempt from this moral truth. The repeated structure of each verse—outlining a person's position and ending with the same refrain—reinforces the song's central message."* Speaking of the enduring impact of *You Gotta Serve Somebody*, the music critic goes on to say, *"Dylan captures a timeless human truth wrapped in spiritual nuance. Regardless of one's religious beliefs, the song urges self-reflection, prompting listeners to consider who or what they're truly serving in their lives."*

There is no joy or happiness on earth compared to serving the Lord Jesus, King of Kings and Lord of Lords. Spend time today reflecting on who or what you have been serving and determine from this day on to serve the Lord. Read his word daily to find out how to use your gifts and talents in His service. You may not win a Grammy but you will share in His glory (2 Thessalonians 2:13- 16).

445

Memorable Quote:
"You're gonna have to serve somebody
Well, it may be the devil or it may be the Lord
But you're gonna have to serve somebody."
Bob Dylan

Journaling Suggestion:
"As for me and my house we will serve the Lord." Joshua 24:15

Memo for Meditation:
"Serve the Lord with gladness and delight; Come before His presence with joyful singing. Know and fully recognize with gratitude that the Lord Himself is God; It is He who has made us, [a]not we ourselves [and we are His]." Psalm 100:1-3

November 17

Motivational Idea: Gotta serve somebody (2)

Would you believe that the car is now an unofficial religion and some people are ardent worshippers? Their music is the sound of roaring engines, and petrolheads (or electric enthusiasts) are lost in wonder, love and praise as they serve their gleaming land beasts. They call their cars by name and their worth is beyond monetary value. In reality, it's a modern-day Baal god. The English word 'worship' comes from two old English words, *weorth,* which means worth, denoting quality, and *scipe* – ship. We are familiar with words like friendship and relationship. We are to love God and are made to have a personal relationship with Him, an intimate friendship with our Creator. God is a God of infinite *weorth'* – worth! He alone is worthy of all our adoration and praise. We declare His worth and attribute worth to Him in our praise.

Worship is a dominant theme of the Bible. God, who created all things and has provided redemption for us through the crosswork of Jesus, He alone is worthy of all our worship and praise, and our life of service. One of the words translated as worship means to bow down, to fall down, to prostrate ourselves before our Maker. We humble ourselves in submission and obedience, offering our lives to Him as our spiritual act of worship (See Romans 12:1).

In Scripture, worship also means service; it is the orientation of our entire lives to live in awe of God and in His presence. Worship also refers to the inward posture of our spirit (John 4:21-26). In our hearts, we enthrone Him, we proclaim Him our King, and we bow before Him in spirit and in truth. Note that worship has to be in truth. It's not syncretism, where any god will do. There is only one God and only one truth. *"Jesus said, "He is the Way, the Truth and the Life, No one can come to the Father except through Him. Lets join in creation and roar His praise.""* (Psalm 98:7).

Memorable Quote:
"Christianity is the transformation of rebels into worshippers of God."

Journaling Suggestion:
I am going to ask God how to be a true worshipper. *"Every idol I have known, what ere that idol be, Help me to tear it from thy throne, And Worship only thee."*

Memo for Meditation:
"Among the gods there is none like you, Lord; no deeds can compare with yours. All the nations you have made will come and worship before you, Lord; they will bring glory to your name. For you are great and do marvellous deeds; You alone are God. Teach me your way, LORD, that I may rely on your faithfulness; give me an undivided heart, that I may fear your name. I will praise you, Lord my God, with all my heart; I will glorify your name forever." Psalm 86:8-12

November 18

Motivational Idea: From the boulevard of broken dreams (1)

Green Day's song, *In the Boulevard of Broken Dreams*, contains the words, *"Sometimes I wish someone up there would find me,"* forming part of the chorus lyric. The song is a metaphor on life and in essence is about the lyricist being all alone and his longing to be found by someone who understands and will walk with him through the boulevard of broken dreams. *"I walk a lonely road, the only one that I have ever known. Don't know where it goes, but it's only me and I walk alone."* The songwriter is expressing his experience of a life of shattered expectations, and his broken dreams mean that he is constantly revisiting all the failures and disappointments of life. The song is somewhat depressing and is also a commentary on the broken American dream. How many people live on this boulevard and are stuck in the quagmire of reliving broken dreams and the what if's and what might have been? How many today feel lonely and isolated and long for just one person who understands them, to walk with them just to make things a bit more bearable? But it's not a happy picture and not a happy road, nor does it look like a happy ending. It seems that many are confined and indeed resigned to the boulevard of broken dreams and this is as good as it gets.

And yet, it does not have to be that way anymore. The Lord Jesus wants to be your friend today and walk with you. Speak to Him and ask Him to meet you where you are. He can transform your boulevard of broken dreams into the boulevard of blessings. Invite Him today! Trust Him! Believe Him! Follow Him! Obey Him and exchange that road of hopelessness for one of hope, joy and happiness. From a languishing life to a flourishing life. He has great plans for you, and dreams too!

Memorable Quote:
"I would love to tell you what I think of Jesus
Since I found in Him a friend so strong and true;
I would tell you how He chang'd my life completely
He did something that no other friend could do.
Refrain:
No one ever cared for me like Jesus,
There's no other friend so kind as He;
No one else could take the sin and darkness from me
O how much He cared for me!"
C F Weigle

Journaling Suggestion:
Journal about inviting Jesus into every area of your life.

Memo for Meditation:
"You are my friends if you do what I command." John 15:14

November 19

Motivational Idea: From the boulevard of broken dreams (2)

In 1942, the realist painter Edward Hopper created a painting entitled *Nighthawks* which is recognised as one of the most famous artworks of 20th-century America. It depicts a bartender in a white uniform behind a triangular bar, a man in a suit and hat with his back to the observer, and a younger couple to the left of the man. The painting is a picture of lonely emptiness, which was exactly what Hopper was trying to capture. The work was completed just before the bombing of Pearl Harbour and captured the mood of the nation immediately following the attack when the fear of New York being bombed was very real. *Nighthawks* is seen as an exploration of human existentialism and loneliness in the modern age. The figures feel distant and disconnected from each other which is reflected by the viewer's literal distance from the interior of the bar. Hopper has said, *"unconsciously, probably, I was painting the loneliness of a large city."*

Gottfried Helnwein did a reworking of Hopper's *Nighthawks* and called it, *The Boulevard of Broken Dreams.* It's a powerful caricature in which Helnwein shows James Dean, Bogart, Marilyn Monroe and Elvis as the four characters. The purpose of the caricature is to communicate that they all died senseless deaths. Presley died from complications due to decades of alcohol and drug abuse; Marilyn Monroe died from an apparent drug overdose; Bogart's death was attributed to alcohol abuse; and James Dean died in a tragic car accident. All were avoidable, wasted lives and talents. The overwhelming conclusion you get from viewing any of Gottfried's work is that humanity lives in a world of violence, loneliness and emptiness, and has no lasting meaning.

Jesus was a master in painting word pictures. Our memo for meditation today gives one of these word pictures that is the very antithesis of *Nighthawks* and *Boulevard of Broken Dreams* to fill us with hope, love and optimism, and give us abundant life – life to the full, life with purpose and meaning. Walk the boulevard of blessings today.

Memorable Quote:
"The Boulevard of Broken Dreams, or the Boulevard of Blessings? You choose." Author

Journaling Suggestion:
Journal on a word picture of Jesus in the Bible where He leads someone to the Boulevard of Blessings – from brokenness to blessing.

Memo for Meditation:
"Jesus used this figure of speech, but the Pharisees did not understand what he was telling them. Therefore Jesus said again, "Very truly I tell you, I am the gate for the sheep. All who have come before me are thieves and robbers, but the sheep have not listened to them. I am the gate; whoever enters through me will be saved. They will come in and go out, and find pasture. The thief comes only to steal and kill and destroy; I have come that they may have life, and have it to the full. I am the good shepherd. The good shepherd lays down his life for the sheep."' John 10:6-11

November 20

Motivational Idea: Filling the void and the vacuum

The song *Hole-hearted* was written by Gary Cherone, lead singer with the band Extreme. The lyrics appear quite straightforward initially. The lyricist expresses his disappointment that he has been distracted by things in life that did not make him happy, describing it in what has been termed a 'heartbreak metaphor' – he has a hole in his heart and only one can fill it. The song begins:
Life's ambition occupy my time
Priorities confuse my mind
Happiness one step behind
The inner peace I've yet to find.

The refrain then repeats:
There's a hole in my heart
That can only be filled by you
And this hole in my heart
Can't be filled with the things I do.

The lyrics resonated with couples who enjoyed the romantic meaning of the song. The deeper meaning of the song is different. Cherone is a Christian and the song is not about romance but about God. The truth is there is a God-shaped void and vacuum in everyone which cannot be filled with any created person or thing, but only by God the Creator in the person of Jesus Christ. We try to fill it with what we think will make us happy but only Jesus can fill that gap, only He can meet the deepest needs of the human heart, only He can truly satisfy. Why not start reading the Gospel of John and find out more about Jesus, who He really is and what He can do for you?

Motivational Quote:
"What else does this craving, and this helplessness proclaim but that there was once in man a true happiness, of which all that now remains is the empty print and trace? This he tries in vain to fill with everything around him, seeking in things that are not there, the help he cannot find in those that are, though none can help, since this infinite abyss can be filled only with an infinite and immutable object; in other words by God himself." Blaise Pascal

Journaling Suggestion:
There's a hole in my heart, Lord, that can only be filled by you. Please fill it today, Lord.

Memo for Meditation:
"Jesus said, 'Anyone who believes in me may come and drink! For the Scriptures declare, 'Rivers of living water will flow from his heart.'""
John 7:38

November 21

Motivational Idea: Restoration in brokenness

We live in a broken world! Everywhere we look we find brokenness. And we too are not immune from this human dilemma. When we take the time to stop the hurry and the frantic pace of life and take a good look at ourselves to reflect and do some introspection, we find that we too have our 'brokennesses'. Someone once said that we are not damaged people but we are people with damaged parts, broken parts, and we all need restoration. Living in a broken world and seeking to manage our own brokenness is not conducive to a flourishing life, so we try to fix it as best we can such as tyring the latest fads that promise wholeness and healing. Again, as we look into the musical world, we find this theme over and over again. Van Morrison sang, *"Did you get healed?"* Today we are looking at a Paramore song called *We are Broken*. Here's the refrain:

Yeah, Cause we are broken
What must we do to restore
Our innocence?
And oh, the promise we adored
Give us life again
Cause we just wanna be whole.
Haley Williams

The song is actually a prayer to God. Being broken has spiritual and biblical significance as it refers to our brokenness as those who have sinned before a Holy God. Jesus came into the world and through His crosswork we can be made whole. We all have a choice: to remain in our brokenness or make the conscious choice to leave our life of sin and follow Jesus. We find our healing in Him. Divine healing and Divine health are our birthright in Christ Jesus. Our memorable quote also comes from Hayley's song and it expresses the idea of being wrapped in the arms of God as He is our Healer, our Comforter and our Tower of safety in our broken world.

Memorable Quote:
"Keep me safe inside, Yours arms like towers, Tower over me, Tower over me..." Haley Williams, Paramore, from the song *We are Broken*

Journaling Suggestion:
Journal about seeking healing from God and in those specific areas that you have ignored and denied for a long time. Lord, show me and heal me, I pray. Amen.

Memo for Meditation:
"But He was pierced for our rebellion, crushed for our sins. He was beaten so we could be whole.
He was whipped so we could be healed." Isaiah 53:5 (Check out the whole chapter)

November 22

Motivational Idea: Giving up our godship

The name Vincent Damon Furnier may not be familiar to most but he has been an iconic figure in the rock scene since the late sixties and early seventies. The name of his band is Alice Cooper and his stage name is the same. Alice Cooper has had a major impact on the music industry, not least for his theoretical performances, and that influence has gone way beyond music. Something else that is much more important to Alice Cooper is the Gospel of Jesus Christ. Jesus is the most important part of his life. In an interview with Greg Laurie, shared on Facebook, the rocker was asked why he thought that people were unwilling to surrender their lives to Jesus Christ. This was his reply: *"I think it's because they don't want to give up their godship. They believe the Hollywood version of 'Oh, I do more good than bad,' that kind of thing. And I go, 'Boy, Satan has you right where he wants you, to believe that.'"* Cooper then quoted John 14:6 and said that he, his wife and his children live their lives trusting that Jesus is the only way to salvation.*"Because 'I'm the Way, the Truth, and the Life and no one comes to the Father but by Me,' those are the truest words ever spoken,"* Cooper explained. *"How can you deny that? So, as far as I'm concerned, my life is based on that now. It's not based on my rock and roll, it allows me to be a rock and roller, but, follow me. So for my wife and I both, and our kids, it's a Christian lifestyle. But again, it's the old saying 'Why should the devil have all the good music?' Yeah, there's a lot of Christian rockers out there, I just happen to be the most vocal."*

Cooper said he grew tired of the old dead life, even with all the trappings of fortune and fame. Contrary to what most people think, there is no lasting happiness and joy found in these things, and when you get them it's disappointing to say the least – it's empty! *"When the Lord opens your eyes and you suddenly realise who you are and who He is, oh, it's a whole different world."* As for overcoming drugs and alcohol, it is because he found ultimate satisfaction and power in the name of Jesus that he knows victory.

Memorable Quote:
"Who is ruling your life—you or God? What about the way you live your life: The way you think, plan, talk, react to circumstances, respond to people, spend your money, use your time and whatever else you do in each of the 86,400 seconds that tick off the clock in each of the days the Creator has graciously provided for you." Adapted

Journaling Suggestion:
Journal about giving up ' godship' and surrendering (re-surrendering) your life to Jesus Christ.

Memo for Meditation:
"Jesus said, 'I am the way and the truth and the life. No one comes to the Father except through me.'" John 14:6

November 23

Motivational Idea: Old John knew a thing or two about grace

In 1748, a rebellious and experienced seaman involved in the slave trade was in fear of his life when a storm hit off the coast of Ireland. He did what many of us do when in deep trouble: he prayed to God for deliverance. Miraculously, he survived the storm, and subsequently this was a major turning point in his life. He had lost his faith as a teenager but now he began to explore that faith again. He left the slave trade and dedicated his life to God, serving as an Anglican clergyman, having graduated from theological studies in 1784. His life was transformed from one of debauchery and moral degradation to a life of faith and service. As you may have already guessed, this man was John Newton who wrote the hymn *Amazing Grace.* This was published in 1779 and is a powerful message of his own personal redemption and the amazing grace of God that not only saved him in his 'lostness' but kept him on the right path till his travelling days were done.

Amazing Grace has become one of the most popular songs in the world. Johnny Cash sang it with his deep resonant voice, and who can forget the renditions by Aretha Franklin with her incredible vocal range and the emotional depth she could bring to this song because of her deep faith and own experience of grace? Perhaps we can all identify with being lost; these words inspire us to find the same grace and our own personal redemption. To put it simply, the word 'grace' is the opposite of karma, which is all about getting what we deserve; grace is getting what we don't deserve. It is one of the most important concepts in the Bible and describes God's favour toward us in our sinfulness and unworthiness. In His infinite grace, God is willing to forgive us and save us even though we have fallen short. Receiving God's grace is just the start of our relationship with Him and He gives us grace to live each day the way He intended us to live. We can learn about grace from old John, who died at 82 years of age.

Motivational Quote:
"I am not what I ought to be, I am not what I want to be, I am not what I hope to be in another world; but still I am not what I once used to be, and by the grace of God I am what I am." John Newton

Journaling Suggestion:
Journal about amazing grace today.

Memo for Meditation:
"Therefore, since we have been made right in God's sight by faith, we have peace with God because of what Jesus Christ our Lord has done for us. Because of our faith, Christ has brought us into this place of grace [undeserved privilege] where we now stand, and we confidently and joyfully look forward to sharing God's glory. We can rejoice, too, when we run into problems and trials, for we know that they help us develop endurance. And endurance develops strength of character, and character strengthens our confident hope of salvation. And this hope will not lead to disappointment. For we know how dearly God loves us, because he has given us the Holy Spirit to fill our hearts with his love." Romans 5:1-5

November 24

Motivational Idea: Elton John's favourite hymn

Elton John's favourite hymn is *Abide With Me*. He said it always made him cry. Perhaps he sang it with the crowds of fans at an FA (Football Association) Cup Final in England. The tradition of singing the hymn began in 1927. The Rugby League followed suit at their Challenge Cup Final. *Abide With Me* is still sung at both matches every year. It's an emotional moment and in the midst of all the excitement it serves as a poignant reminder of our existential existence and the ephemeral nature of life. Spain's 2023 World Cup Final hero and captain, Olga Carmona, scored the only goal of the match to beat England and lift the trophy for the first time in their history. Sadly, Olga was informed a few moments after the game that her father had passed away.

Abide With Me was written by Henry Francis Lyte, born in Kelso, Scotland, in 1793. He attended Trinity College, Dublin, and during his studies won the prize for English poetry no less than three times. He was ordained as an Anglican priest in 1815 and held pastoral offices in both Ireland and West England. In 1820, he visited an elderly Anglican priest, Augustus Le Hunte, who was dying and kept repeating the words 'abide with me'. The words had a profound impression on him and it brought about a deep spiritual awakening, and from that day forward he lived in the presence of God as he carried out his work and ministry. Then in later life, when Henry himself was nearing the end of the journey in 1847, he wrote the hymn which became one of the best known hymns in the world. His last word was 'peace'. The reality for Henry was the experience of the abiding presence of Christ in his life, not just in his death. This, too, can be our experience in life and also in death. Check out all the lyrics; here is the final verse:

Hold Thou Thy cross before my closing eyes
Shine through the gloom and point me to the skies
Heaven's morning breaks, and earth's vain shadows flee
In life, in death, o Lord, abide with me.

Memorable Quote:

"Swift to its close ebbs out life's little day

Earth's joys grow dim, its glories pass away
Change and decay in all around I see
O Thou who changest not, abide with me."

Journaling Suggestion:
Journal on the words of the hymn, *Abide With Me.*

Memo for mediation:
"The Lord replied, 'My Presence will go with you, and I will give you rest.'" Exodus 33:14

November 25

Motivational Idea: Elvis' favourite music

Elvis Presley made somewhere in the region of 100 million dollars and sold more than one billion records during the course of his lifetime. Three hundred million of those were Gospel recordings. He had grown up with Gospel music and this also featured highly in his own private record collection. In 1967, Elvis released an album entitled, *How Great Thou Art*, which made number eighteen in the pop charts and has been released twice since. One of the songs on the album had a poignancy about it for Elvis and it's entitled, *Where No One Stands Alone.* The song is about a man who has everything in the world. He's rich beyond his wildest dreams and yet he feels that he's utterly alone in the world. Elvis felt alone a lot of the time and suffered depression as a result. He sang, *"With great riches to call my own/But I don't know a thing/In this whole wide world/That's worse than being alone."*

Elvis had an intimate knowledge of the Gospel – he grew up on it and he of all people knew that all material things that the world craves could not and did not yield true and lasting happiness. The song is a prayer to God to help him and be there for him because he is aware that having God in his life is better than all the riches in the world. It reminds us today that we can find true satisfaction in knowing God, and with Him standing by us we are never alone. On one occasion in Las Vegas, a woman approached the stage with a crown on a pillow. Elvis asked her what it was, and she said, *"It's for you; you're the king."* Elvis replied, *"No honey, I'm not the king. Christ is the King; I'm just a singer."* Though a prodigal son for much of his megastar years, he eventually returned to his first love, Jesus. The 'king' of rock was always happiest when singing about Jesus. With all the golden hits, the only Grammy Awards he earned were for his Gospel records, *How Great Thou Art* and *He Touched Me.* Well worth a listen and still available on LP if you search for it.

Memorable Quote:
"Hold my hand all the way, every hour, every day/Come here to the great unknown/Take my hand, let me stand/Where no-one stands alone." Elvis Presley

Journaling Suggestion:
Journal on what the metaphor means where Jesus takes your hand. Own Him today as the Lord and King of your life.

Memo for Meditation:
"Keep your life free from the love of money. Be satisfied with what you have, for He Himself has said, I will never leave you or abandon you." Hebrews 13:5

November 26

Motivational Idea: The message of the man in black

"Hello, I'm Johnny Cash." That's how the 'man in black' opened his concerts. His black clothes earned him the nickname, but it was more than just a look, it was a powerful statement of solidarity with the poor, the marginalised and the downtrodden. He wrote a song using his nickname. *"I wear the black for the poor and the beaten down/Livin' in the hopeless, hungry side of town/I wear it for the prisoner who has long paid for his crime/But is there because he's a victim of the times."*

Johnny's childhood was tough; he lived through the Great Depression when his parents could barely feed their seven children. The family gathered on the porch in the evenings after the day's work, his mum played the guitar, and they sang hymns. At twelve, Johnny was writing his own songs. He was eventually discovered by Sam Philips, who also discovered Elvis Presley, and his musical career took off. His song *I Walk the Line* was a top country hit for 44 weeks and sold over a million copies. Johnny bore the scars of hard living. Alcohol and drug addiction played a major part in his troubled life, and he hit rock bottom to the point where suicide seemed the only option. His search for redemption led him back to the Saviour his mother had sung about. In utter brokenness, he embraced Christ as his Saviour. He crawled out of Nickajack Cave in Tennessee where he had gone to die. He said, *"I thought I'd left Him (God), but He hadn't left me. I felt something very powerful start to happen to me, a sensation of utter peace, clarity, and sobriety...Then my mind started focusing on God."*

Johnny became an ambassador for Christ and brought hope to millions who had lost hope; he associated with those who society had rejected including the robbers, rapists and murderers of San Quentin and Folsom prisons. Christ lifted Johnny and He can lift anyone who responds to His voice.

Memorable Quote:
"I wear the black for those who've never read/Or listened to the words that Jesus said/About the road to happiness through love and charity/Why, you'd think He's talking straight to you and me." Man in Black/Johnny Cash

Journaling Suggestion:
God, you can reach me and lift me as you reached Johnny. I am not beyond redemption and I can reach out to others and tell them of the hope I have in Christ.

Memo for Meditation:
"He lifted me out of the pit of despair, out of the mud and the mire. He set my feet on solid ground and steadied me as I walked along. He has given me a new song to sing, a hymn of praise to our God. Many will see what he has done and be amazed. They will put their trust in the LORD." Psalm 40:2,3

November 27

Motivational Idea: Charles got rid of his chains

On Whitsunday (Pentecost), 21st May 1738, Charles Wesley said he felt his heart 'strangely warmed'; it was a spiritual awakening. He was staying with John Bray, a poor mechanic, when he heard a voice saying, *"In the name of Jesus of Nazareth, arise, and believe, and thou shalt be healed of all thy infirmities."* It is believed that the voice was most likely John's sister who felt compelled to say these words in a dream. Charles got up, opened his Bible and read from Psalm 103: *"He has put a new song in my mouth, even praise unto our God."* He wrote in his journal, *"I have found myself at peace with God, and rejoiced in the hope of the love of Christ."*

Research suggests that the first hymn he wrote after his conversion experience was, *And Can It Be.* He went on to write some seven thousand hymns. The first line of this joyous hymn is, *"And can it be that I should gain an interest in my Saviour's blood!"* Powerful imagery is used in each stanza, particularly in stanza four, our memorable quote for today. Charles experienced his dungeon flaming with light and his chains falling off, finding perfect freedom in Jesus and His wondrous salvation. This has been the experience of all those who have trusted Jesus and followed Him.

One Sunday morning, the guest speaker at our church gave his life story. He has been a missionary in Japan for over forty years and read from the Bible to us in Japanese. The congregation was spellbound as he told of being in prison as a young man for a bank robbery. He had been a loyalist paramilitary in Northern Ireland and had even been kneecapped for bad behaviour by others in the group. It was in prison that he had the same experience of Charles Wesley and came to faith in Christ. We had sung this particular hymn and he said the fourth stanza had special significance for him, having been in prison. Awesome or what!

Whatever your prison today, whatever holds you captive, perhaps a prison of your own making, you too can be free and those chains can be broken if you look to and follow Jesus! As you walk with the Lord, you will find that He has plans for you too. Who knows what wondrous plans He has for you and where He will lead you?

Memorable Quote:
"Long my imprisoned spirit lay/Fast bound in sin and nature's night/Thine eye diffused a quickening ray/I woke, the dungeon flamed with light/My chains fell off, my heart was free/I rose, went forth, and followed Thee/Amazing love! How can it be/That Thou, my God should die for me?" Charles Wesley

Journaling Suggestion:
Journal on the chains God has released you from. Ask God to break any chains that you need released from today.

Memo for Meditation:
"In my distress, I prayed to the LORD, and the LORD answered me and set me free." Psalm 118:5

November 28

Motivational Idea: You were made for this

Alfred Barnerd Smith was a boy prodigy on the violin. He was a student of Leopold Auer, and a soloist with the New York Symphony, with Walter Damrosch conducting. He studied at Juilliard School of Music. But he had a divine calling on his life. God led him to Moody Bible Institute and Wheaton College in 1943. His roommate at Wheaton was Billy Graham, and Smith was the youngest song leader of the evangelist's church. He founded the music publishing house Singspiration in 1941 and remained as president until 1962. He went on to found Encore Hymns in 1972. As well as editing and publishing many songbooks, he wrote some 500 compositions of his own.

Alfred was a man who made each day count. He was a man on a mission, and like the Apostles, Paul and Peter, he has an assignment from Jesus Christ. We need to realise that *"Our occupation is what we are paid for, but our calling is what we are made for!"* You have a calling on your life, just like Alfred, it's what you were made for and why you are here. The mission of God for you is not opposed to building a career but He wants to accomplish His mission with the opportunities He gives you and the assignment He has set for you. Below is one of Alfred's hymns. You were made for this – the Jesus assignment!

Memorable Quote:
"Show me Thy way, O Lord/And make it plain/I would obey Thy word/Speak yet again/I would not take one step until I know/Which way it is that you want me to go/O Lord, I cannot see/Grant me Thy light/Darkness bewilders me/Clouding my sight/Hold Thou my hand/and keep close by my side/I dare not go alone; be Thou my guide/I cannot see Thy face/Yet Thou art here/When will the morning chase/My doubt and fear?/When shall I see the place where day and night/Shall come not, for Thy glory is its light? I will be patient, Lord/And do Thy will/I will not doubt Thy word/My hope fulfil/How can I perish, if in Thee I hide/Jesus, my Comforter, my Hope and Guide." A B Smith

Journaling Suggestion:
Journal today about your God-given assignment. Don't know what it is? Ask Him.

Memo for Meditation:
"I [Peter] am an apostle on assignment by Jesus, the Messiah, writing to exiles scattered to the four winds. Not one is missing, not one forgotten. God the Father has his eye on each of you, and has determined by the work of the Spirit to keep you obedient through the sacrifice of Jesus." 1 Peter 1:1,2 *"But my [Paul] life is worth nothing to me unless I use it for finishing the work assigned me by the Lord Jesus—the work of telling others the Good News about the wonderful grace of God."* Acts 20:24

November 29

Motivational Idea: You are the object of His song

The rich and famous sometimes seek the services of a famous singer or group to perform for them at an intimate gig. Christina Aguilera reportedly earned $1 million to perform for an hour at investment guru Charles F Brandes' party. That's $16,666 per minute. David Bonderman, an investor from Texas, paid The Rolling Stones a staggering $7 million to play for an hour on his 60th birthday. They are singing for the person who procured their services, it's a monetary transaction and it's simply a performance. But what if a big name, someone with riches and resources beyond your wildest dreams got to know about you and decided to write a song just for you? Then they decided to surprise you by singing for you personally? That would be quite something.

In our memo today, we come across a most astounding revelation of God. Zephaniah, the writer whose name means 'hidden by God', is significant in itself in that names in the Bible convey truth. The backdrop to his short book is one of a nation that had departed from the living God and were worshipping idols. However, in humility and repentance they were reconciled to the true God and experienced His great salvation. The Mighty Saviour would delight in them and sing over them. The Creator of the universe, the God of eternity, is so very aware of you, so very sensitive toward you, and He is seeking to get ideas about His love for you into your heart and mind, so God sings over you! From just the other side of the hidden thin veil that separates the seen from the unseen, He serenades your heart, constantly whispering the truth of His love into your conscious awareness. God loves you infinitely and passionately and He writes songs for you and sings them over you. Be astounded!

Memorable Quote:
"There is some real but inaudible sense in which God's thoughts and feelings, like a song, are floating sweetly into our hearts. And as He sings over us, He is hoping we will hear His song and to know His heart. The very idea that God sings at all is actually quite an astounding revelation about the kind of Being this Almighty God must be...A God who sings must be a God who feels, a God of deep, stirring passions. If God sings— and the Bible says He does—then we find ourselves living in the presence of a Supreme Being whose heart pulsates with supreme emotion. The implications are huge." Ty Gibson

Journaling Suggestion:
Lord, I humble myself before you. Please tune my ear to hear you singing over me!

Memo for Meditation:
"Your God is present among you, a strong Warrior there to save you. Happy to have you back, He'll calm you with His love and delight you with His songs." Zephaniah 3:17

November 30

Motivational Idea: And now for the 'Good News'

Breaking news stories flash around the world in seconds; no sooner does something happen on the far side of the world than it's on social media outlets everywhere. Sadly, it's usually bad news; a major crisis, an earthquake, a tsunami, a shooting, a bombing, a mass murder. It's all about the chaos and the disasters of our fallen and broken world. There are, however, good news stories if we look for them but we have a propensity to focus on the negative – that's one for the psychological dimension to unpack. But now for the 'Good News,' the Gospel – the Godspell – good story, the *euangelion*. In the New Testament, there is a reference to the announcement that Jesus brought the reign of God to our world, through His life, death and resurrection. The word 'Gospel' as used by Jesus and the NT writers is derived from the prophetic poetry/song of Isaiah 52:7-10, where the future arrival of God's Kingdom through the Messiah is called 'Good News.' In spite of all the evil in the world, all the bad stuff, God has made a way back to Himself and salvation is found in His beloved Son. Have a good read through Isaiah 52 and 53 to see what Jesus the suffering Servant did for us to take away our sins and to build His Kingdom in us. He is coming back again for He is the King of Kings and Lord of All. *"His dominion is an everlasting dominion, Which will not pass away; And His kingdom is one which will not be destroyed."* (Daniel 7:14). Every wrong will be made right! He will redeem the entire universe and make a new heaven and new earth. Our journaling suggestion for today comes from the song, *Build Your Kingdom Here.*

Memorable Quote:

"I have tried drugs and a little of everything else, and there is nothing in the world more satisfying that having the Kingdom of God building inside you." Johnny Cash

Journaling Suggestion:

"Come set Your rule and reign/In our hearts again/Increase in us we pray/Unveil why we're made/Come set our hearts ablaze with hope/Like

wildfire in our very souls/Holy Spirit, come invade us now/We are Your Church/And we need Your power
In us/We seek Your kingdom first/We hunger and we thirst/Refuse to waste our lives/For You're our joy and prize/To see the captive hearts released/The hurt, the sick, the poor at peace/We lay down our lives for Heaven's cause/We are Your church/And we pray revive/This earth (we're prayin' for revival)" Build Your Kingdom Here

Memo for Meditation:
"How beautiful on the mountains are the feet of the messenger who brings good news, the good news of peace and salvation, the news that the God of Israel reigns!" Isaiah 52:7

THE PRACTICAL DIMENSION

December 1

Motivational Idea: Spread happiness!

An encouraging word brings joy. Joyful giving can bring a lot of joy and happiness to the recipient as well as the giver. Be the positive in a person's negative. The world is full of influencers; we are all influencers. You will influence the people in your world today by what you think and say and do. Be aware of how you are in the world; be aware of how the people in your world influence you. You are under the influence of someone or something, but are they happiness spreaders? Are they generous? Are you? Make the world a better place by being positive in it, and you can make a massive difference in the lives of others by being ready to spread happiness! You might not change the world but you can change someone else's world. One of the five-a-day for good mental health is giving to others. Happiness is found more often than not in making a positive difference in the lives of those around us. It not only has a positive impact on them, it has a positive impact on us. We have a sense of purpose and fulfilment, and the joy we give to others bounces back to us so we feel good about ourselves. Be the difference to someone's humdrum existence today and in the process you will find happiness too.

The famous celebrity, Rod Stewart, just reduced a hospital waiting list by 10% by providing scanners for a mobile scanner unit for the early detection of cancer. We find in Scripture, when it comes to giving, that God loves and approves a cheerful giver, and delights in the one whose heart is in his gift. (see 2 Corinthians 9:7). The statement alludes to Proverbs 22:9 where the wisest of human beings, Solomon, wrote, *"Blessed are those who are generous, because they feed the poor."* (see Deuteronomy 15:10; Romans 12:8).

God loves such joy-motivated giving to others because it expresses contentment in His gracious giving to us (see 2 Corinthians

9:14) and makes every good work possible, resulting in joyful thanksgiving and glory to God (see 2 Corinthians 9:11–13).

The truth is, all that we have are His gifts to us and we are custodians of the gifts. If we take the time to stop and think, we will appreciate every blessing we have. Thankfulness, being appreciative, being grateful will produce in us a joyful heart, and out of our joyousness, we can spread the joy and we can give with joy to benefit others. We can be true joy givers. The opposite of egocentricity is altruism. Perhaps we need to check our empathy bank. Are we sensitive to the concerns of others as opposed to remaining stuck in our egocentric perspective on the world?

Memorable Quote:
"Some cause happiness wherever they go; others whenever they go."
Oscar Wilde

Journaling Suggestion:
Be someone's 'pick me up' today!

Memo for Meditation:
"Worry weighs us down; a cheerful word picks us up." Proverbs 12:25

December 2

Motivational Idea: Grab life by the handlebars!

It's so easy to acquiesce in our problems and stagnate in the humdrum of everyday life and its responsibilities. Rather than flourishing, we find ourselves languishing in what Pink Floyd referred to in *The Division Bell* lyric as *"a life consumed by slow decay"*. Today let's decide to refocus and grab hold on life; grab it by the handlebars and get going again. The dreams we have lost, the aspirations we once had, let's dust them down and go for it. We need, however, to take stock of where we are at; we don't want to be going in the wrong direction. Contrary to popular opinion, happiness is not found on easy street – we have to work at it and do so on the right track! When I was involved in the mental health field, and the counselling and psychotherapeutic world, one of the words in our vocabulary was 'stuckness'. People can become stuck in particular areas of their life. One of the reasons for this can be spending hours overthinking about the magnitude and complexity of our problems.

People can become so obsessed with what seems to be a dark and dreary prison that they don't even realise that they have the choice to either stay where they are, or have the courage to open the gates. To grab life by the handlebars means to take total control of your life. It means to put life in a situation where you have complete power over it. You don't wait for opportunities to happen to you; you go and seek them. It isn't just a case of letting go and letting God. With His help, we can take responsibility and live the life we were meant to live.

Memorable Quote:
"All mankind is divided into three classes: those that are immovable, those that are moveable, and those that move." Benjamin Franklin

Journaling Suggestion:
Get on the right track and grab life by the handlebars!

Memo from Meditation:
"I'm not saying that I have this all together, that I have it made. But I am well on my way, reaching out for Christ, who has so wondrously reached out for me. Friends, don't get me wrong: By no means do I count myself an expert in all of this, but I've got my eye on the goal, where God is beckoning us onward—to Jesus. I'm off and running, and I'm not turning back. So let's keep focused on that goal, those of us who want everything God has for us...Now that we're on the right track, let's stay on it. Stick with me, friends. Keep track of those you see running this same course, headed for this same goal. There are many out there taking other paths, choosing other goals, and trying to get you to go along with them. I've warned you of them many times; sadly, I'm having to do it again. All they want is easy street. They hate Christ's Cross. But easy street is a dead-end street. Those who live there make their bellies their gods; belches are their praise; all they can think of is their appetites. But there's far more to life for us..." Philippians 3:12-21

December 3

Motivational Idea: Smile and start a chain reaction around the world

Zygomaticus major is known as the smiling muscle and, in conjunction with 43 others muscles, it enables us to smile. Smiling has loads of health benefits including the release of endorphins that give us that 'feel good' factor. Smile studies suggest that the simple act of smiling is enough to make us feel happy. Our memo today in the original Hebrew literally means to 'make the face good', that is, a healthy, favourable uplifted expression, the antithesis of a sad face. Today you can choose to either smile or frown, or sit on the fence with a blank expression. An appropriate smile at the appropriate time could make the difference to someone you meet who really needs that smile to lift them up and help them on their way. It will benefit you too! Try it. Smile!

I was driving off in the car once when a family was crossing the road. I stopped to wave them on. As they walked across the road, I smiled and they smiled back, all five of them. I was in a part of Belfast city where race hatred raised its ugly head recently. The family happened to be from an ethnic minority background. I just realised this as they walked across the road. It then impacted that this simple act of giving way to them and smiling meant much more than a faint acknowledgment; it meant much more. It was even more than a smile of approvable, it was a smile of acceptance.

You are a valued human being and precious. The Bible talks about God's smile of approvable, acceptance and love too! See Numbers 6:25-26, New Living Translation (NLT): "May the LORD smile on you and be gracious to you. May the LORD show you his favour and give you his peace."

More on this tomorrow.

Memorable Quote:
"Smiling is infectious,
You catch it like the flu,
When someone smiled at me today
I started smiling too."
Taken from Spike Milligan's poem, *Smile*.

Journaling Suggestion:
Give away more smiles and start an epidemic of happiness! Journal on smiling!

Memo for Meditation:
"A cheerful heart puts a smile on your face,
But a broken heart leads to depression.
A miserable heart means a miserable life;
A cheerful heart fills the day with song
A heart full of joy and goodness makes a cheerful face,
But when a heart is full of sadness the spirit is crushed."
 Proverbs 15:13

December 4

Motivational Idea: The smile of approval

Whether we admit it or not, every one of us likes some kind of recognition or approval. It gives us a 'feel good' factor when we know we have done a good job. For example, if our boss or someone else acknowledges us, we enjoy the recognition. We may not admit to seeking it or even needing it but we do like it. Human beings seek validation. I know of a workplace that has a RAVE portal. Colleagues can record acknowledgments of a fellow employee and for want of a better word 'rave' about them! It sure is good for morale.

When it comes to the world of relationships, to win the approval of another brings with it not a small measure of happiness. As you go about your day, think about that smile of approval and remember it's also in your gift to give it too. But in all we do today, do we have God's smile of approval? Jesus had the Father's approval and it is recorded at His baptism that God said, *"This is my beloved Son with whom I am well pleased."*

Do you need a good role model today? Jesus is the perfect role model and in following Him we can be sure of that smile of approval from God the Father. Matthew Davis has five takeaways from What Makes God Smile in *The Purpose Driven Life* by Rick Warren and inspired by Savannah Davis. Here are five ways you can make God smile so you're not solely worried about seeking approval from people:

Love God supremely (Matthew 22.37-39). Trust Him completely (Psalm 147.11). Obey Him wholeheartedly (James 2.24). Give Him praise and thanks continually (Psalm 34.1-15), and serve Him with our abilities enthusiastically (Colossians 3.23-24).

In spite of our fears and any ridicule we may face from those who are vehemently opposed to our Christian faith, we need to have the courage to defy the naysayers and stand for God in a generation that rejects or ignores our Saviour and Lord. Day after day, let us seek the smile of God's approval on the path to our eternal home. We do not seek His smile of approval for our salvation, because that is His gift to us in the death and resurrection of His beloved Son. Rather, we seek the smile of His approval on our service and live our lives to honour His Name.

Whose smile of approval do we have today? God's or the world's? *"Better is God's smile of approval than the world's loudest shouts of praise."* (Janet Slusser). God validates us and that's the primary validation we need; sometimes it may be the only validation we get, and that is more than sufficient.

Memorable Quote:
"Courage not compromise, brings the smile of God's approval." Thomas S Monson

Journaling Suggestion:
I will do what pleases God today and enjoy His smile of approval upon my life.

Memo for Meditation:
"May the Lord bless you and protect you. May the Lord smile on you and be gracious to you. May the Lord show you his favour and give you his peace." Numbers 6:24-26

December 5

Motivational Idea: The art of admonishment

The word 'admonish', depending on how it's used, can be viewed as either positive or negative. The word comes from the old French and Latin *admonere* meaning to advise, to remind, and is used with a view to improving someone else's behaviour. Happiness depends on honesty. If we are not happy with someone's behaviour, then what do we do? Do we remain silent and suffer in unhappy silence, or do we deal with it? No one likes to be admonished. Let's say you have a friend in your circle and you are not happy with their behaviour and you decide that you need to admonish them, how do you go about it? Is it a matter of scolding them? When most people think of admonishment, it tends to be seen as scolding someone; giving them a piece of our mind. Depending on the context and the person, there surely is a case for this approach on certain occasions. On the other hand, again depending on the person and the context, we need to see admonishment as something positive in nature. We need wisdom as to the kind of admonishment we undertake. We can view it as a kind instruction using reasoning. We need to see it as an affectionate admonishment. We need to learn the skill of admonishment so that we do not alienate the other person. It's about lovingly guiding them back on track and at the same time maintaining rapport. The goal is not to scold, it's not about putting the other person in their place. We all have blind spots and if we are to admonish others, *we* need to be prepared to be admonished because none of us is perfect.

When we are doing the admonishment, here are some elements to keep uppermost in our minds. Respect people – this is about natural rights. We are dealing with human beings. The raging angry admonisher can be so intent on settling scores that they dehumanise the other person to the extent that the door is now shut to any collaborative process of improvement and each person is left with the bitter dregs of resentment. You will know people who haven't spoken to each other for years – it's usually down to what someone said – and it's like a feedback loop in the mind. There is a better way if we learn the art. We need to have what Rogers called *"unconditional positive regard"* for the other.

We need to seek to retain peace and not start a war. Slanging matches do not benefit anyone, and our wellbeing can be impacted to its detriment.

Memorable Quote:
"To admonish is better than to reproach; for admonition is mild and friendly, but reproach is harsh and insulting; and admonition corrects those who are doing wrong, but reproach only convicts them." Epictetus

Journaling Suggestion:
Learning how to admonish and how to accept respectful admonishment.

Memo for Meditation:
"Therefore encourage one another and build each other up, just as in fact you are doing." 1 Thessalonians 5:11

December 6

Motivational Idea: Enemy alert

Some of us might skip this page since it's not really relevant to us – we might think we have no enemies. A revisiting of the definition of the word enemy might make us think again. We look at the news and we see enemies who are at war against another group or nation, seeking their total destruction through injury and death. We think of military adversaries. But the word enemy can also mean, 'one that is antagonistic to another'. This definition may well make us think again. Do you have someone in your life who constantly annoys or upsets you because of their antagonism? Most of us have these kinds of individuals around us at some point in our lives. People who are constantly putting us down and show hatred towards us in the way they behave and in their toxic words. They may dress it up with mixed messages, because one of the key tactics of the enemy is to cause us confusion. These people provoke anger, hatred and resentment. Enemies are a drain on our resources and they certainly will impinge on our desire to lead peaceful, happy and fulfilled lives. So, what do we do? We all remember that Jesus told us to love our enemies; easier said than done, and what does it really mean?

In ancient times, the Lex Talionis, or the 'law of retaliation' was invoked which meant 'an eye for an eye, tooth for a tooth'. Sentencing was carried out by elders who assessed the damage done and distributed a monetary punishment to the guilty party. However, Leviticus 19:18 states, *"Do not seek revenge or bear a grudge against anyone among your people."*

Jesus in our memo for meditation today says to love our enemies. Love is treating others with compassion and not contempt. This isn't to say that we shouldn't seek justice if someone does something to harm us or our loved ones. We are, however, to stamp out bitterness and not let hatred grow. Responding to evil with more evil does not solve the problem. And Jesus knew this when he said, *"Forgive them, Father."*

Memorable Quote:

"When we show respect to our enemies, we allow ourselves to become more like the Father God. This separates us from those who have evil and hatred in their hearts. This also means we don't necessarily have to stay in contact with people who have wronged us. The act of respect can often be expressed by simply saying, 'Peace be with you,' and walking away. Depending on the circumstances, we may only need to say it in our hearts, having already walked away."

Journaling Suggestion:

Journal on loving your enemies.

Memo for Meditation:

"You have heard that it was said, 'Love your neighbour and hate your enemy.' But I tell you, love your enemies and pray for those who persecute you, that you may be children of your Father in heaven. He causes his sun to rise on the evil and the good and sends rain on the righteous and the unrighteous. "If you love those who love you, what reward will you get? Are not even the tax collectors doing that? And if you greet only your own people, what are you doing more than others? Do not even pagans do that? Be perfect, therefore, as your heavenly Father is perfect." Matthew 5:43-48

December 7

Motivational Idea: Enemy at the gates

The Romans used the term 'the enemy at the gates' to describe Barbarians, and it was a rallying cry to the army to be alert, with their weapons at the ready. Barbarians at the gate were seen as an existential threat to their way of life. We are using the term today to raise awareness that we too have enemies at our gates, and we too need to be in a state of readiness, but not with military weapons, rather, spiritual ones. Our enemies can come in many guises; there are people who do not desire our welfare, and there are also the enemies within that we wrestle with: addictions, depression, anxiety and fear, to name but a few. Know your enemies today and be in a state of readiness. Then there is our arch enemy, Satan himself, who desires to damage and destroy us.

Three thousand years ago, King David wrote Psalm 18, a powerful song of encouragement for anyone under the attack of the enemy. Here is practical help for our encounters with our enemies, offering us the promise of protection and stability in a crazy and unpredictable world.

There are hundreds of names ascribed to God in the Bible. If you are feeling under attack, being threatened by the enemy at the gates, read Psalm 18:2 which gives reasons to take courage and to be confident of victory. David uses military symbols to describe God's protection and power. You may well have heard someone describe a faithful loyal friend as 'my rock'. In Psalm 18:2, David says God is *"our Rock"*; our Rock cannot be moved, no one or nothing can take away our stability and protection because God is our Rock. God is also, *"our Fortress"*. We have a place of safety where the enemy cannot follow. God is *"our Shield"*. He comes between us and harm. God is *"our Stronghold"* [High Tower], above all powers, all enemies and all the stratagems of the Devil.

Look to God today – our Rock, our Fortress, our Shield and our High Tower or Stronghold, but there is one more. He is *"the Horn of our Salvation"*.The significance of this needs a month of pages. The horn is seen as the deadly weapon of the wild ox in Psalm 92:9,10. Thus the horn in the Old Testament is a symbol of strength and a symbol of God's multifaceted power. God has conquered and will conquer every evil and every enemy, whether the opposition is physical or spiritual.

Read Psalm 18 and be empowered today. He is the Horn of our Salvation – Jesus, the all-conquering Saviour! He gives us the victory! Take heart today!

Memorable Quote:
"And He has raised up a horn of salvation [a mighty and valiant Saviour] for us in the house of David His servant— Just as He promised by the mouth of His holy prophets from the most ancient times." Luke 1:69-70.

Journaling Suggestion:
"On Christ the solid Rock I stand. All other ground is sinking sand."

Memo for Meditation:
"The LORD is my rock, my fortress, and the One who rescues me; My God, my rock and strength in whom I trust and take refuge; My shield, and the horn of my salvation, my high tower—my stronghold." Psalm 18:2

December 8

Motivational Idea: Target on your back

Have you ever suddenly felt bitter when you found out that someone was gossiping about you? Or have you suddenly felt a spirit of fear rising up about something or someone? Maybe it's a spirit of jealousy when you have heard of someone's good fortune that you decided they didn't deserve? We need to be aware that there is a target on our backs because in the background we have an archenemy, the devil, also called Satan. He wants to rob us of our joy in the Lord. When we have an awareness of Satan's nefarious activities, we are then in a position to use the weapon God has given us to extinguish Satan's attack. The Bible refers to these attacks as Satan's flaming darts. Given this knowledge – that we have a target on our backs, and we have an enemy who is hellbent on using fiery darts against us – we need to take steps to ward off these attacks. God has given us a weapon that can extinguish all of them. *"In all circumstances take up the shield of faith, with which you can extinguish all the flaming darts of the evil one."* (Ephesians 6:16).

Paul may well have got his idea from the Roman soldiers, who, when they went into battle, would have soaked their shields in water to extinguish flaming arrows, 'fiery darts'. The wet surface of the shield would put out the flaming arrows. We need to take up our shields and identify the fiery dart. This is important because we often just dismiss them as the ordinary everyday annoyances. We need to be careful, however; some people go to the other extreme and see demons in everything; we need balance and we need wisdom to know when it's a fiery dart or not.

C S Lewis said, *"There are two equal and opposite errors into which our race can fall about the devils. One is to disbelieve in their existence. The other is to believe, and to feel an excessive and unhealthy interest in them."* Once we have identified the fiery dart, we need to be confident and believe that the weapon God has provided is powerful enough to extinguish the fiery dart. The mistake we often make is that we try to quench it by trying to stop the bitterness, the jealousy, the fear, the anxiety, the doubt, ourselves, and soon we are in a state of chaos and our world can go up in flames, metaphorically. Our feeble attempts can fan the flames because we are no match for Satan.

The next time a fiery dart lands, take the shield of faith, use it and understand that the fiery dart can only be extinguished by this means. And what is the shield of faith? It is faith in Christ! We look to Jesus and we put our faith in Him; we look to His cross, the place of victory over the Devil and all his demonic forces. Use Scripture in the fight. Know your Bible and memorise key verses.

Memorable Quote:
"No matter how many flaming darts Satan fires against us, the shield of faith can extinguish them all." J Piper

Journaling Suggestion:
Identify the fiery darts that you are dealing with in this season.

Memo for Meditation:
"But when people keep on sinning, it shows that they belong to the devil, who has been sinning since the beginning. But the Son of God came to destroy the works of the devil." 1 John 3:8

December 9

Motivational Idea: Naming the fiery darts (1)

Pastor Jay Dennis on his website, *A ministry of strategies4life.inc,* identifies eight of Satan's favourite darts.

1. The Dart of Doubt

This much deployed dart of the enemy was used to disastrous and catastrophic effect in the Garden of Eden, and is still one of his favourite darts. You find it today in every conceivable context, from the academics in the halls of learning to the man in the street. The dart is delivered. *"Can you really believe what God said in a book written thousands of years ago?"* The arch arsonist watches in glee as the flames of destruction kill and destroy. It's a lie from the father of lies, the devil (see John 8:44). By the shield of faith we look to Jesus, the Messiah, who was promised in the Old Testament, and who said to the hypocritical Jewish religious leaders, *"You search and keep on searching and examining the Scriptures because you think that in them you have eternal life; and yet it is those [very Scriptures] that testify about Me; and still you are unwilling to come to Me so that you may have life."* (John 5:39). They had succumbed to the dart of doubt and suffered the consequences.

2. The Dart of Discouragement.

You can be sure that lurking in the background when we are battling with discouragement is the enemy of our souls. The purpose of this fiery doubt is to force us to look at the circumstances we are in and see all the negatives that exist in a crazy, mixed-up chaotic world. What if you have been working away and it's now feeling like a hard slog? You are ploughing a lonely furrow, you are maxed out and it seems that no one cares, and for all your labours there is no recognition? Dennis says, *"This dart most often is designed to attack the emotional areas of your life. To get anger, fear, and worry to replace joy, peace, and love. You can become bitter. Truly, this is at the top of the list of Satan's tools; perhaps it's his most favourite."*

It's time to raise the shield of faith and use the Word of God. Galatians 6:9. says, *"And let us not grow weary of doing good, for in due season we will reap, if we do not give up."* Whenever you face trials, let Galatians 6:9 strengthen you and help you to keep going. This Bible verse about not giving up shows that if we persevere in doing good, then we will eventually be rewarded. We may not see the results of our efforts immediately, but if we keep pressing on, then we will eventually reap a harvest. Don't give in to the dart of discouragement.

Memorable Quote:

"The word used for the shield of faith is 'extinguish.' The imagery here is to quench, thwart, snuff out fiery arrows – Satan's tactics. John 8:44 teaches that Satan is a pathological liar; his whole game is deception."
Nick Cash

Journaling Suggestion:
Jesus is the Truth! The devil is a pathological liar.

Memo for Meditation:
"Commit your way to the Lord; trust in Him, and He will act." Psalm 37:5

December 10

Motivational Idea: Naming the fiery darts (2)

3. The Dart of Deception

"And the great dragon was thrown down, the age-old serpent who is called the devil and Satan, he who continually deceives and seduces the entire inhabited world; he was thrown down to the earth, and his angels were thrown down with him." (Revelation 12:9). This is a vivid and disturbing description of our archenemy, Satan. Notice that he is referred to as the deceiver; he is the master deceiver. You can be sure that it is he and his demonic forces that seek to rob us of the fulfilled life and true lasting happiness which is found only in God. So, what are we to understand about this fiery dart? What is the nature of this deception? What is its ultimate purpose? The brute truth is that Satan's ultimate purpose is to rob believers of our joy, to render us useless in the role as Christ's ambassadors. For unbelievers, he wants company in hell. (See Matthew 25:41.) Nobody likes to admit that they have been conned.

Our world is filled with con artists, liars and thieves who seek to defraud us, but the Bible warns us about the greatest deceiver of all – Satan, the devil. He wants to con the lost out of the most precious possession they could receive – eternal life. One of the most pervasive forms of deception is found in religious practice. And the Bible tells us who is behind many religious deceptions. *"For such are false apostles, deceitful workers, transforming themselves into apostles of Christ. And no wonder! For Satan himself transforms himself into an angel of light. Therefore it is no great thing if his ministers also transform themselves into ministers of righteousness, whose end will be according to their works."* (2 Corinthians 11:13–15). If he can't succeed in this because we have put our trust in Jesus, then he will seek to make our lives difficult and thwart God's plan for our lives. So, what's the answer to the fiery dart of deception? It's the shield of faith.

4. The Dart of Desire

The devil tempts us to desire what our sinful nature wants. The pleasure will be fleeting and we will be even more unfulfilled and unhappy outside of the will of God. Satan operates primarily in three ways. John tells us about it in 1 John 2:16 (memo for today).

Memorable Quote:

"This is a tremendous insight into how Satan operates to get you to desire something that is outside the will of God. 'World' refers to that anti-God, anti-Christ, anti-Bible, anti-things of God system. He uses the flesh, that part of you still desiring to do wrong. 'The lust of the flesh' refers to Satan appealing to the physical part of you, doing things with your body that will dishonour God. 'The lust of the eyes' refers to Satan attempting to affect your thought life. What you see affects your thought life. 'The pride of life' refers to doing things your way instead of God's way."

Journaling Suggestion:

Using the shield of faith to extinguish satanic deceptions.

Memo for Meditation:

"For all that is in the world—the lust and sensual craving of the flesh and the lust and longing of the eyes and the boastful pride of life [pretentious confidence in one's resources or in the stability of earthly things]—these do not come from the Father, but are from the world." 1 John 2:16

December 11

Motivational Idea: Naming the fiery darts (3)

5. The Dart of Delay

Satan tries to convince us that our prayers and faith aren't working. We pray and there seems to be no answer. Yet no prayer is never unanswered; the answer could be yes, no, or wait. The waiting can be hard, and the devil or one of his emissaries comes along with the delay deception. *"It's delayed because God is not interested,"* he says, but this is a lie. God is never late. But there is another side to delay – Satan tries to delay blessings in our lives. In Daniel 10, Daniel prayed and God heard his prayer and sent an angel to answer him. The angel was held up in spiritual warfare against a territorial spirit and Daniel's answer was delayed. There are things happening in the heavenly realms that we know nothing about. But our responsibility is to use the spiritual weapons that we have been given, and again we need to raise the shield of faith to deal with delays.

Note also that Satan tries to get us to delay the decisions we need to make. Procrastination is Satan's way of preventing the blessings of God in our lives. We need wisdom and we need to seek divine wisdom to act and receive the blessings that God has for us.

6. The Dart of Distraction

You don't need anyone to make you aware of the dart of distraction – it's everywhere. We are bombarded constantly with information, news, adverts, and all kinds of unwarrantable intrusions. Just watch people at the train station, the bus stop, even in a restaurant, and the mobile phone is attached to almost everyone's arm. We can spend too much time on social media and watching TV shows. Binge-watching can take its toll. You can be sure that Satan will send all kinds of distractions, problems, people issues, work problems, money challenges, and all kinds of circumstances to get your eyes off of Jesus. He wants you to change your focus from up to around. While you are distracted, here comes a dart right at your faith. Satan is a master at using distractions as a tactic in the spiritual war to prevent us from focusing on God's purposes and plans. Distractions can include obsessing over minor details, focusing on obscure theological questions or pop culture gossip, and a million breaking news stories. Satan can use major life events, whether they be good or bad, as a distraction. Satan's goal is to turn us away from God; he will use any measure at his disposal to do this, including false philosophies, mistaken religions or deceptive cults.

Get the shield of faith ready and extinguish the darts of delay and distraction.

Memorable Quote:

"If destruction fails to entangle us, distraction will do its best." Beth Moore

Journaling Suggestion:

Delay and distraction – my watchword today is vigilance!

Memo for Meditation:
"Making the very most of your time [on earth, recognizing and taking advantage of each opportunity and using it with wisdom and diligence], because the days are [filled with] evil." Ephesians 5:16,17

December 12

Motivational Idea: Naming the fiery darts (4)

7. The Dart of Destruction
The devil by his very nature is a destroyer. He is out to destroy those who pose a threat to him. Faith poses a threat to him for sure. Jay Dennis says, *"Remember this dart is flaming, destroying everything it hits. These darts of destruction are aimed at your marriage, your home, your children, your testimony, your attitude, your body, your mind, your emotions, your spirit, your character, and your morals."*

Today, be aware of those things that you may be tempted to dabble in that have the power to destroy you and everything you have. Raise the shield of faith and extinguish this dart of destruction. When you are tempted to go your own way and do your own thing, ask yourself, "Whose influence am I under?" We read in the Bible, *"But I say, walk habitually in the [Holy] Spirit [seek Him and be responsive to His guidance], and then you will certainly not carry out the desire of the sinful nature [which responds impulsively without regard for God and His precepts]".* (Galatians 5.16).

8. The Dart of Denial
The child who steals the cookies does not have to be taught to deny that they took them. We can easily use the mechanism of denial when we are in the wrong. "It's not my fault," or "I didn't know." You can be sure that the enemy isn't too far away. Raise the shield of faith and use the word of God. *"If we say we have no sin, we deceive ourselves, and the truth is not in us. If we confess our sins, he is faithful and just to forgive us our sins and to cleanse us from all unrighteousness. If we say we have not sinned, we make him a liar, and his word is not in us."* (1 John 1.8-10).

The Roman soldier's shield was like a door (2 feet by 4 feet). When the flaming darts hit it, they would stop the darts and extinguish them. Remember you are in the Lord's army now and you are engaged in spiritual warfare. Know the enemy and his devices, use your shield, and look to the Captain of our salvation, our victorious Lord and King! Victory in Jesus!

Memorable Quote:
"Devil or Satan stands for destruction. He destroys souls. He tries to prevent people from knowing Jesus Christ our Lord. He tries to trap people from attaining salvation. He's a Pied Piper who leads people to Hell or destruction. People are not aware of the Devil's activities. We often succumb to his machinations. He's the real Machiavelli who plots and leads people to Hell. Beware of him. Don't get into his trap. Jesus Christ is our Lord. Salvation is through the Son of God alone. Depend only on the Triune -- God the Father, Son and the Holy Spirit. Let the Holy Spirit guide us. Not Satan or Devil." George Matthew

Journaling Suggestion:
I choose life in Jesus, eternal life here and now!

Memo for Meditation:
"The thief comes only in order to steal and kill and destroy. I came that they may have life, and have it in abundance [to the full, till it overflows]. John 10.10 AMP. A thief is only there to steal and kill and destroy. I came so they can have real and eternal life, more and better life than they ever dreamed of." John 10:10, MSG

December 13

Motivational Idea: Lessons from a life of idleness

F Scott Fitzgerald (1896-1940) is best known for his novels depicting flamboyance and excess. He published four novels, four story collections, and 164 short stories. Although he achieved temporary popular success and fortune in the 1920s, Fitzgerald received critical acclaim only after his death and is now widely regarded as one of the greatest American writers of the 20th century. His second novel, *The Beautiful and Damned* explores the lives of a wealthy, privileged couple, Anthony and Gloria Patch, a young couple living at the height of luxury and parties. They are prime members of the New York café society, living each day to its fullest and not caring about tomorrow.

483

They begin to overspend beyond their means, and drink to excess constantly, eventually causing a downward spiral into alcoholism and depression. Anthony joins the army, has an affair with a beautiful teenager, and can't hold down a steady job. Gloria obsesses over her looks, realises that she's too old to be an actress, and panics when Anthony's inheritance doesn't come through. Their marriage starts to break down, the money starts to run out, and before long, Anthony and Gloria begin to lose their minds. They descend into decadence and despair. One of the main lessons from the book is the danger of idleness: Anthony and Gloria's lack of purpose and refusal to work or contribute to society leads them to a life of idleness, which ultimately causes their downfall. A life without meaningful engagement can result in self-destruction.

According to the Fitzgerald scholar James L W West III, *The Beautiful and Damned* is concerned with the question of 'vocation': *"What does one do with oneself when one has nothing to do?"* Fitzgerald masterfully paints a word picture of the negative consequences of idleness. Anthony and Gloria Patch whittle away their days as they wait for the big pay cheque from Anthony's grandfather. Their idleness and lack of purpose eventually leads to poverty and self-destruction. Idleness is also the breeding ground for dissatisfaction. Today is a day to think about our purpose in life and to avoid the danger of idleness. A great example for us to follow is the woman described in Proverbs 31:27: *"She watches over the affairs of her household and does not eat the bread of idleness."* She is the personification of wisdom, and is described as a values-driven woman who lives life to the fullest and fulfils her God-given purpose. She is depicted as having many positive qualities such as being hard working, diligent and selfless.

Memorable Quote:
"Idle hands are the devil's workshop; idle lips are his mouthpiece."

Journaling Suggestion:
I will not eat the bread of idleness but be diligent and live purposefully.

Memo for Meditation:
"Go to the ant, you sluggard; consider its ways and be wise! It has no commander, no overseer or ruler, yet it stores its provisions in summer and gathers its food at harvest. How long will you lie there, you

sluggard? When will you get up from your sleep? A little sleep, a little slumber, a little folding of the hands to rest— and poverty will come on you like a thief and scarcity like an armed man." Proverbs 6:6-11

December 14

Motivational Idea: Wealth doesn't guarantee happiness

F Scott Fitzgerald's novel, *The Beautiful and Damned,* illustrates that money and luxury do not necessarily bring happiness. One literary critic says that despite their wealth, the characters remain dissatisfied and unfulfilled, showing that contentment comes from within, not material possessions. As heir to his grandfather's considerable fortune ($75 million) Anthony doesn't have the inconvenience of having to get up to go to work, and he spends much of his time pursuing Gloria, which culminates in their marriage. Initially this appears to be deliriously happy as both Anthony and Gloria live for the moment and are united in their quest to fill the empty hours with constant partying. However, inevitably (but of course!), they discover that this lifestyle is physically and emotionally unsustainable. Fitzgerald modelled the character of Anthony Patch on himself and Gloria Gilbert on his newlywed spouse, Zelda Fitzgerald. The novel draws circumstantially upon the early years of Fitzgerald's tempestuous marriage following the unexpected success of his first novel. They lived an opulent lifestyle and spent money like it was going out of fashion.

Fitzgerald's novel *The Great Gatsby* also conveys the idea that money alone is not the path to happiness. Gatsby finds out that his money can buy a beautiful home, nice cars, friends... However, his wealth cannot buy the one thing that he wants most. Gatsby's rise and fall throughout the novel show that money isn't what makes a person happy. Fitzgerald is trying to convey throughout the novel that money can buy a person many different things but cannot buy the one thing that Gatsby wants most of all: Daisy's love.

Many in the world today think that money will make them happy. Granted, in tough times when things are tight (and for many it's 'heat or eat'), it would be wonderful to be able to pay our way and to be able to afford nice things. But don't be fooled. The Bible says, *"For the love of money is a root of all sorts of evils, and some by aspiring to it have wandered away from the faith and pierced themselves with many griefs."* (1 Timothy 6:1).

Note that it's the love of money that is the root of all evil, and not money in itself.

Memorable Quote:
"Money is numbers and numbers never end. If it takes money to be happy, your search for happiness will never end." Bob Marley

Journaling Suggestion:
God is faithful and will provide for me. All I have is His.

Memo for Meditation:
"Whoever loves money never has enough." Ecclesiastes 5:10
"You cannot serve God and money." Matthew 6:24
"Whoever is greedy troubles his household." Proverbs 15:27
"Don't fix your hope on the uncertainty of riches." 1 Timothy 6:17-19
"God will supply all your needs." Philippians 4:19

December 15

Motivational Idea: The perils of excess and hedonism

F Scott Fitzgerald certainly lived a life of excess and hedonism; this was well illustrated in his drinking habits when he added absinthe to his martinis. Historically, absinthe is described as a highly alcoholic spirit. It is 45–74% ABV, or 90–148 proof in the US. Absinthe traditionally has a natural green colour but may also be colourless. It is commonly referred to in historical literature as *la fée verte* – 'the green fairy'. A bar owner in Northern Ireland once told me that he would only serve one drink if a customer were to order it, such is its potency.

As referenced in the previous two days, Fitzgerald's novel *The Beautiful and Damned* explores the hedonism of the American elite during the jazz age, through the love affair between Anthony and Gloria Patch. Their luxurious lifestyle brought them momentary and temporary happiness, but the pleasure-seeking drug meant they had to overindulge even more and more to fill the void and emptiness of their narcissistic existence and the vacant lives they led. Empty lives need distractions. Their pursuit of pleasure, indulgence and excess leads them down a path of self-destruction. The book warns against living a life solely focused on indulgence and momentary gratification. Hedonism in its extreme form is expressed by Gloria: *"If I wanted anything, I'd take it...I can't be bothered resisting anything I want."*

Some people might well identify with Gloria today and choose a hedonistic lifestyle, seeking pleasure and happiness in ways that are sometimes beyond expected and existing norms. Jesus told the parable of the prodigal son who recklessly and wastefully blew his inheritance (see Luke 15:11-32). Having obtained his share of the inheritance, he left home and proceeded to embrace the hedonistic lifestyle and indulge in wild living. Yet, when he came to his senses, he discovered that his father was patiently and lovingly waiting for him. The father forgives him and welcomes him home. In the same way, God waits for us to come home. Have you come home yet? There's a place for the prodigal ,and it's home.

Memorable Quote:
"The Prodigal Son at least walked home on his own feet. But who can duly adore that Love which will open the high gates to a prodigal who is brought in kicking, struggling, resentful, and darting his eyes in every direction for a chance of escape? The words...'compel them to come in,' have been so abused by wicked men that we shudder at them; but properly understood, they plumb the depth of the Divine mercy. The hardness of God is kinder than the softness of men, and His compulsion is our liberation." C S Lewis

Journaling Suggestion:
Far from God? There is still hope! We can never out-sin God's forgiveness.

Memo for Meditation:
"'I will set out and go back to my father and say to him: Father, I have sinned against heaven and against you.'... So he returned home to his father. And while he was still a long way off, his father saw him coming. Filled with love and compassion, he ran to his son, embraced him, and kissed him." Luke 15:18,20

December 16

Motivational Idea: The dangers of entitlement

In *The Beautiful and Damned*, Anthony's failure as a writer contrasts with his friend Richard's steady literary success, and Maury's, who is a Harvard graduate, gradually settling into a comfortable life. The growing contrast between Anthony and his friends emphasises that it's Anthony's sense of entitlement that has derailed his life – after all, Richard worked hard for his success, and Maury (unlike Anthony) pulled himself out of the carousing phase of his life years ago in order to become a responsible adult. Anthony's sense of entitlement to wealth and success without working for it prevents him from taking responsibility for his life and contributes to his downfall. One of the most prominent aspects of life in the Western world today is this widespread sense of entitlement. We believe we are entitled to happy and carefree lives without outside interference. We believe that we are entitled to own things that we can't afford instead of waiting and saving up. We believe that we are entitled to jobs and spouses that perfectly fit our interests and desires. We believe that we are entitled to both safety and freedom. We believe that we are entitled.

For Christians, this sense of entitlement can cross over into how we approach God. In basic terms, we believe that God *owes* us. The truth is, God does not owe us anything. God is good to us but God being our Creator obligates us to Him, not the other way around. We need to grasp the reality that we are not entitled; we are undeserving, but God is generous. Our response should be one of gratitude. However, if we feel entitled, we will not show the gratitude we should. A sinful sense of entitlement can be rooted in pride, and can lead to a belief that grace is due rather than being received. An entitlement mentality can also lead to conflict in relationships and gross unhappiness. Those whose sense of entitlement are extreme in nature end up like Anthony, derailing their lives and alienating themselves from others.

Jesus tells the parable of the pharisee and the tax collector who went to the temple to pray (see Luke 18:9-14). The Pharisee's entitlement meant his prayer was not heard, yet the humble prayer of the penitent tax collector was heard; God accepted him. Don't be a modern day Pharisee!

Memorable Quote:

"Feeling entitled is the opposite of feeling grateful. Gratitude opens the heart, entitlement closes it." Paul Gibbons

Journaling Suggestion:

"What separates privilege from entitlement is gratitude." Brené Brow

Memo for Meditation:

"The Pharisee stood by himself and prayed this prayer: 'I thank you, God, that I am not like other people—cheaters, sinners, adulterers. I'm certainly not like that tax collector! I fast twice a week, and I give you a tenth of my income.' But the tax collector stood at a distance and dared not even lift his eyes to heaven as he prayed. Instead, he beat his chest in sorrow, saying, 'O God, be merciful to me, for I am a sinner.' I tell you, this sinner, not the Pharisee, returned home justified before God. For those who exalt themselves will be humbled, and those who humble themselves will be exalted." Luke 19:11-14

December 17

Motivational Idea: The consequences of escapism

Another of the takeaways from F Scott Fitzgerald's *The Beautiful and Damned* is the consequences of escapism. Gloria and Anthony use the defence mechanism of escapism; they are constantly fleeing something – their feelings, their surroundings, the sober world. They are active participants in their own escape from lives they feel are oppressive. As the novel edges to a close, they frequently lament what has been missed and there is what one critic, Matthew Selwyn, has called, *"a general eulogising of youth and mourning of lost time."* He goes on to say, *"The characters feel this sense of loss, of time elapsed without significance, suggests that there is more than veiled nihilism at play. Gloria's beauty fades and she is no longer sought after by men or movie producers. Anthony's fortune is jeopardised and he cannot support his family as he might like. The novel becomes painfully fixed in the real world and the familiar concerns of Fitzgerald – of time and the rapid movement of its sands – come to the fore."*

We all use escapism to some extent and it can be a healthy coping mechanism when used in moderation, but it can also be detrimental if it's used to completely ignore reality. Escapism is the tendency to distract oneself from real-life problems or unpleasant emotions by engaging in an activity or behaviour that involves imagination or entertainment. Some examples of escapism include: daydreaming, reading, physical activity, work, overeating, oversleeping, shopping, addictive behaviours such as alcohol, drugs, pornography and gambling When healthy activities are used in moderation, escapism can provide mental respite, stress relief and a chance to recharge. It can also help us to return to our daily lives with renewed energy and perspective. However, completely ignoring reality can be detrimental. Anthony and Gloria frequently escape their problems through alcohol and reckless behaviour, avoiding the reality of their situation. The novel shows that escapism only exacerbates problems rather than solving them.

Scripture speaks of the undesirable realities of escapism in terms of slothfulness, laziness and passivity. Let's be careful about our use of escapism to get away from the harsh realities of this world by ignoring our responsibilities. By not dealing with them, we can end up in a destructive cycle that can spiral out of control.

Memorable Quote:
"Escapism isn't good or bad in itself. What is important is what you are escaping from and where you are escaping to." Terry Pratchett

Journaling Suggestion:
Healthy escapism is good but bad escapism comes with a health warning.

Memo for Meditation:
"A shiftless man lives in a tumbledown shack; A lazy woman ends up with a leaky roof." Ecclesiastes 10:18
"One day I walked by the field of an old lazybones, and then passed the vineyard of a lout; They were overgrown with weeds, thick with thistles, all the fences broken down." Proverbs 24:30-31

December 18

Motivational Idea: Keeping up appearances

Today is our penultimate observation through the lens of F Scott Fitzgerald's novel, *The Beautiful and Damned.*' Anthony and Gloria Patch are caught up in the conflict between the illusion of glamour and the reality of a meaningful existence. Their vanity is evident in their excessive partying and spending habits, and their attitude of seeking the moment's happiness at all costs. Both Anthony and Gloria are fixated on appearances – physical beauty, social status and wealth. The novel critiques this obsession, showing how it leads to superficiality and a lack of true fulfilment. Anthony sees himself as sophisticated and attractive. He expects that someday he will accomplish something of note. But until then, he is secure in his own superiority and dresses accordingly. Appearance is everything. However, if you pardon the pun, Anthony is not a 'patch' on Gloria. Gloria's total obsession with her appearance is so extensive that she has a distinct lack of interest in much else apart from high living.

While Gloria is clearly shallow and self-centred, Anthony is attracted to her by her extraordinary beauty, as are many of the other characters. The society in which they live places a high premium on beauty. It's the one quality that puts people on the movie screen, makes them famous, and allows them to earn tremendous amounts of money. Gloria's director has no interest in whether she can act, only in how she looks on the screen. So, in some sense, Gloria's obsession with beauty mirrors the value her society places on it.

Our world is also obsessed with appearances. Body image for many people is everything. We have celebrities who are prepared to endure hours of cosmetic surgery to look younger. This is not limited to the 'stars' as increasingly people even with modest incomes go under the knife to look better. For some, compulsive body-checking becomes so habitual, it dominates their lives. For many, body dysmorphic disorder (BDD), or body dysmorphia, can impact on their lives. This is not the vanity of a Gloria type but rather a mental health condition where a person spends a lot of time worrying about flaws in their appearance. These flaws are often unnoticeable to others. The world is constantly throwing mixed messages about beauty and appearance at us. With that constant bombardment, it can become difficult for our young people to have a healthy perspective of what beauty really is. It is so important to teach them God's perspective on beauty by reading Bible verses about beauty – see 1 Peter 3:3-4.

Be happy with the skin you're in. God made you, you are beautiful in His sight and He looks on the inside too!

Memorable Quote:
"Charm is deceptive, and beauty is fleeting; but a woman who fears the LORD is to be praised." Proverbs 31:30

Journaling Suggestion:
It's good to look smart, but remember, God looks at the heart!

Memo for Meditation:
"Thank you for making me so wonderfully complex! Your workmanship is marvellous—how well I know it." Psalm 139:14

December 19

Motivational Idea: *The Beautiful and Damned*

We have spent the last several days learning some salutary lessons from F Scott Fitzgerald's novel, *The Beautiful and Damned.* We have noted the dangers of idleness and its devastating results. Wealth does not guarantee happiness. Unbridled excess and hedonism is the path to self-destruction. Time and youth are fleeting and we need to redeem the time, not squander it. The relationship between Anthony and Gloria demonstrates that love alone cannot sustain a marriage. Without shared goals, respect and communication, their relationship deteriorates, suggesting that love requires effort and commitment. The novel critiques the idea of the American Dream, portraying it as an illusion that promises success and happiness but often leads to emptiness and disillusionment when pursued without substance.

We also need to watch out for the dangers of entitlement; the world does not owe us a living. And the consequences of escapism are apparent; the characters frequently escape their problems through alcohol and reckless behaviour, avoiding the reality of their situation.

Escapism only exacerbates problems rather than solving them. The novel highlights the fragility of mental health, depicting the slow mental and emotional decline of Anthony as he spirals into depression and alcoholism. It serves as a cautionary tale about the fragility of mental health when we neglect it.

Our mental health needs to be protected and promoted as we journey through life. Society's obsession with appearances is the backdrop to the sad tale. Both Anthony and Gloria are fixated on appearances – physical beauty, social status and wealth. The novel critiques this obsession, showing how it leads to superficiality and a lack of true fulfilment. These lessons from *The Beautiful and Damned* provide a critical reflection on the pitfalls of materialism, hedonism and the empty pursuit of the American Dream, warning against a life devoid of purpose and self-awareness. Anthony Patch and Gloria Gilbert are young, rich and beautiful, but damned by their reckless behaviour.

The Old Testament prophet Micah encountered people like Anthony and Gloria in his day. They had become wealthy through corruption, theft and greed, living recklessly in wanton abandon. His message is one of condemnation but also of hope, but only if such people repent and turn back to God.

We are all accountable, too, for the way we live. There is hope for all of us in God's mercy and redemption!

Memorable Quote:
"Now all has been heard; here is the conclusion of the matter: Fear God and keep his commandments, for this is the duty of all mankind. For God will bring every deed into judgement, including every hidden thing, whether it is good or evil." Ecclesiastes 12:13-14

Journaling Suggestion:
I can't change the past, but I can change the future.

Memo for Meditation:
"He has shown you, O mortal, what is good. And what does the LORD require of you? To act justly and to love mercy and to walk humbly with your God." Micah 6:8

December 20

Motivational Idea: International Human Solidarity Day

International Human Solidarity Day is an annual (20th December) observance that emphasises the importance of unity, cooperation and shared responsibility in addressing global challenges. It serves as a reminder that by working together in solidarity, nations can create a better world for all, and achieve common goals, including peace, social justice and sustainable development. This is a day when nations can celebrate unity in diversity; remind governments to respect their commitments to international agreements; raise public awareness of the importance of solidarity; encourage debate on the ways to promote solidarity for the achievement of the Sustainable Development Goals including poverty eradication; a day of action to encourage new initiatives for poverty eradication.

Solidarity Day was established by the United Nations General Assembly in 2005 to promote the concept of solidarity as a fundamental value for the advancement of humankind. It recognizes the role of solidarity in achieving international peace and cooperation. Celebrating International Human Solidarity Day involves engaging in activities that promote unity, empathy, and cooperation.

Here are some ways to celebrate: support charitable causes by contributing to charitable organisations and initiatives that address global issues such as poverty, hunger, education, and healthcare; volunteer by offering your time and skills to local and international organisations working towards humanitarian goals; advocate for change by raising awareness about important global issues; and advocate for policies that promote social justice, equality and human rights.

As Christians, we recognize that we are called to love God and to love our neighbours. Love for others cannot be limited to the level of speaking nice words; our love must extend to serious actions. Solidarity is sacred because it is the result of caring and responsible love. Solidarity is the kind of love that Jesus showed and that He calls us to share with one another. Peter, the dealer in hope, offers us a model for solidarity in a human community in our memo for meditation today.

Memorable Quote:
"There is no stability without solidarity and no solidarity without stability."

Journaling Suggestion:
The Word became flesh and blood, and moved into the neighbourhood.

Memo for Meditation:
"The end of all things is near; therefore, be serious and discipline yourselves for the sake of your prayers. Above all, maintain constant love for one another, for love covers a multitude of sins. Be hospitable to one another without complaining. Like good stewards of the manifold grace of God, serve one another with whatever gift each of you has received. Whoever speaks must do so as one speaking the very words of God; whoever serves must do so with the strength that God supplies, so that God may be glorified in all things through Jesus Christ. To him belong the glory and the power forever and ever. Amen." 1 Peter 4:7-11

December 21

Motivational Idea: How to survive Christmas

The Christmas holidays are almost upon us and many will be filled with anticipation and excitement at the prospect of a happy and joyous season. After all, the words 'happy' and 'Christmas' go together. Or do they? For many, it's an unhappy time because heightened anxiety and a sense of unease will be welling up and gaining momentum as the day approaches. The truth is that the stress of Christmas can be overwhelming and hence the term 'Christmas anxiety' is now in common parlance. So, what are the key triggers that we need to be aware of and how can we manage them? The guys at Brown Bag Packages have come up with some of the factors we need to take cognizance of – see Memorable Quote below.

Social obligations can play a big part in Christmas anxiety. We feel pressured to attend gatherings and social events; we have to have that party and invite everyone over. Then there is the financial cost of Christmas; we are expected to give gifts, never mind the expectations of immediate family. And how many children will be dreaming of the latest designer gear? Some people even take out loans to cover Christmas, with the vulnerable borrowing from loan sharks and paying big time in the Christmas aftermath. Another major trigger can be family dynamics. Families feel honour-bound to meet up, but unresolved relationship issues can raise their ugly heads.

For some, Christmas is synonymous with conflict, and anxieties can be heightened at the thought of such a prospect. For anyone who is a perfectionist, Christmas time can be a major stumbling block to happiness. Everything has to be perfect; it's like cutting sticks to beat yourself with. But here's the good news: with will power and resolve you can remove the firing pin from the triggers. We need good coping strategies, not maladaptive ones. Decide what events you want to attend and what you don't – it's your wellbeing that's at stake. Set a budget for gifts and activities and stick to it. The value of a gift is the thought behind it, not the price tag. Plan your self-care: this means taking a break, setting aside time for yourself, recharge with mini breaks amidst the hustle and bustle. Share how you are feeling with a trusted friend. Talk about it and decide what is manageable for you and what you need to avoid. If you are having family get-togethers, plan how to de-escalate potential flashpoints. Transparency is good – call it for what it is and make a contract with your nearest and dearest to keep the peace and have a 'happy Christmas', without the ghosts of Christmas past.

Memorable Quote:
"Accept that perfection is not attainable. Embrace imperfections and focus on creating meaningful moments rather than flawless experiences."
Brown Paper Packages

Journaling Suggestion:
Try praying! Make it the first thing to do, not the last thing to do!

Memo for Meditation:
"Do not be anxious about anything, but in every situation, by prayer and petition, with thanksgiving, present your requests to God. And the peace of God, which transcends all understanding, will guard your hearts and your minds in Christ Jesus." Philippians 4:6-7.

December 22

Motivational Idea: The greatest gift

Exchanging gifts is a long-established Christmas tradition. People love purchasing, preparing and giving something of value to friends and family. Getting presents is, for many, the highlight of the festive season. Gift-giving at Christmas is a Christian tradition that is widely practised around the world. However, the practice is not something that is exclusive to Christianity as several other religions mark the end of the year with a similar custom, such as the Jewish festival of lights, Hanukkah.

The tradition of gift-giving extends long before the founding of Christianity, with roots in the festivals of the ancient Romans — in particular, the festival of Saturnalia where thanks were given to the bounty provided by the agricultural god, Saturn. The festivities took place from the 17th - 23rd December, and were celebrated with a sacrifice and a public banquet followed by private gift-giving, continued partying, and a wild atmosphere where social standings were done away with. During this feast, slaves would be considered the equal of their masters and free speech was embraced.

The conversion of Emperor Constantine to Christianity in AD 312 signalled the beginning of the end of pagan celebrations in the empire, but early religious leaders couldn't simply ban the popular Saturnalia as there would have been a backlash. There is a theory that they used many of the traits of the festival when establishing Christmas, a rival feast that would take Saturnalia's place, but would commemorate a Christian occasion, i.e. the birth of Jesus. The exchange of gifts was probably one of the traditions carried over from the old to the new – the old pagan custom of gift-giving was rationalised into Christianity by attaching strong associations with the gifts of the Magi to Jesus, and was also likely influenced by the life of Nikolaos of Myra, a 4th-century saint who was famed for his fondness of giving people gifts. When he was venerated as a saint, he became more widely known as Saint Nicholas, which is recognisable as the origin of the name 'Santa Claus'.

Some Christians refuse to celebrate Christmas because of its pagan origins. However, surely the opportunity to celebrate the birth of Jesus should be celebrated, the greatest gift ever given. God is generous with us and it's an opportunity for us to be generous to others. At Christmas, let us not forget that the greatest gift was given by our Heavenly Father. It's the gift of His Son, the Saviour of the world.

Memorable Quote:
"Because our Heavenly Father loves us, He gives us many gifts. In John 3:16, we read about a most precious gift: "For God so loved the world, that he gave his only begotten Son, that whosoever believeth in him should not perish, but have everlasting life."

Journaling Suggestion:
Happiness and the fulfilled life begins by receiving God's greatest gift, Jesus.

Memo for Meditation:
"In everything I did, I showed you that by this kind of hard work we must help the weak, remembering the words the Lord Jesus himself said: 'It is more blessed to give than to receive.'" Acts 20:35, NIV

December 23

Motivational Idea: Lastminute.com

Some of us have an innate tendency to leave things to the last minute. One company that took advantage of this characteristic is *Lastminute.com.* It worked, and it became one of the most successful companies in the 1990s. They were certainly not 'last minute' in their business planning as they took advantage of the growing popularity of the internet. People could search for and book holidays, hotels and flights online. They satisfied the demands of the last minute brigade. But why do we leave things to the last minute? Our meditation for today is not meant to cause the reader added stress with presents still to be purchased, perhaps, but rather to help us understand why we have a tendency for last minute action.

Perhaps some analysis today will give us some insights into our last minute tendencies. Last minute Christmas shopping probably fits into the 'procrastination' categorisation. The deadline looms and we have yet to act and do what needs to be done. Of course, the last resort could be a gift voucher, or the excuse that Amazon did not deliver on time – a feeble excuse, and given that our family and friends know how we tick, they may well think it's a euphemism for leaving it to the last minute.

Here are some reasons why we leave it late and some suggested counteractions:

Our lack of time management can be a factor. Do the list and factor in the time required to do it and start – don't wait until you feel like doing it or it will end up as last minute again. If you are like me, you don't like taking orders or being reminded. We subconsciously procrastinate as a way to resist the interference. But personal responsibility should kick in, and we owe it to ourselves to get it done, not because of the reprimand but because someone or something is depending on us doing it on time and within the timeframe.

Another last minute philosophy is our self-talk: "It works for me; even diamonds are made under pressure". It does sound profound, but it takes 1 to 3.3 billion years for a diamond to form naturally. Lab-grown diamonds, on the other hand, typically take less than a month to grow. We can grow accustomed to the adrenaline rush of the time crunch but it's more stressful than we realise.

Another way we procrastinate is the further away the due date is, the easier it is for us to feel unmotivated to start. But if I do a couple of hours regularly, I can have mini rewards such as a flat white, perhaps. Instant gratification plays a part in delay, so mini rewards on the way can help.

And finally, excessive perfectionism can be a major problem in procrastination. Procrastination comes from fear – fear of not being able to reach the high standards you set for yourself. By not getting started, the mistakes/failures won't happen. Remember that perfection is the enemy of good enough. Just do it!

Memorable Quote:
"Time management isn't your problem, procrastination is."

Journaling Suggestion:
The good enough present. The 'perfect present' may not exist.

Memo for Meditation:
"But everything should be done in a fitting and orderly way." 1
Corinthians 14:40

December 24

Motivational Idea: The joy of anticipation

Many are waiting today in the joyous anticipation of Christmas Day.
The excitement is building and the anticipation is almost palpable.
Perhaps you too are excited; that present you have been promised is
almost within your grasp! Let's hope the joyous anticipation turns into
celebratory realisation. Remember the days of childhood when we
couldn't sleep? But eventually the day dawned and we were able to
experience what we had longed for. If we could travel back in time to
the very first Christmas Day, we would be able to gain a new
appreciation of joyous anticipation.

The promise of the gift of Jesus Christ, Mary's son, had been
joyfully anticipated for centuries. Have you ever wondered why we
have the Old Testament? Well, if we didn't, the New Testament
wouldn't make sense. The Old Testament Scriptures contain the
promise of the very first Christmas, as far back as the book of Genesis.
This momentous event had been prophesied and predicated and
promised from the day of the fall of mankind in the Garden of Eden.
God promised a Saviour, and when in God's plan the proper time had
fully come, God sent His Son. (see Galatians 4:4.) The Messiah was
promised because the world needs a Saviour. This was the message of
the angel from heaven to the shepherds: *"For unto you is born this day
in the City of David a Saviour, who is Christ the Lord."* (Luke 2:11).

The day arrived and the shepherds witnessed it. Then the Wise
Men from the East also came; they had been studying these things for
years and, in joyous anticipation, they too came and worshipped God's
Son, the one who was born to die for us. The promise came true! The
Bible promises another day, both in the Old Testament and New
Testament – a day when Jesus will make everything right. Every one of
us will give an account to Him, every wrong will be righted, and every
injustice dealt with at the judgement bar of God. This is a day for

joyous anticipation for believers and it's getting closer. There will be a new heaven and a new earth within which righteousness will dwell.

So, as we look forward to tomorrow, let us also keep an eye on the future with joyous anticipation when Jesus comes again. Are you ready? Peter tells us how in the memo for meditation for today.

Memorable Quote:
"He who was seated on the throne said, 'I am making everything new!'"

Journaling Suggestion:
"Lift up your head, redemption draweth nigh." Luke 21:28

Memo for Meditation:
"But in keeping with his promise we are looking forward to a new heaven and a new earth, where righteousness dwells. So then, dear friends, since you are looking forward to this, make every effort to be found spotless, blameless and at peace with him. Therefore, dear friends, since you have been forewarned, be on your guard so that you may not be carried away by the error of the lawless and fall from your secure position. But grow in the grace and knowledge of our Lord and Saviour Jesus Christ. To him be glory both now and forever! Amen." 2 Peter 3:13,14,17,18

December 25

Motivational Idea: The first Advent points to the second Advent

The Christmas season is known as the Advent season because it celebrates the first coming of Christ. The word 'advent is from the Latin word *adventus* and it means 'coming, approach, arrival'. Today we celebrate the day that Jesus was born into this world. We marvel at this remarkable event which we refer to as the incarnation, when God took on human flesh in the person of Jesus Christ in order to save us from our sins (see John 3:16).

As we celebrate the first Advent, let us not make the mistake that many will make today and either neglect or ignore the second Advent. Jesus is coming back again. The Old Testament predicted both Advents and the New Testament elaborates on this truth. Jesus Himself promised He would return: *"I will come again."* (John 14. 3). *"You too, be continually ready; because the Son of Man is coming at an hour that you do not expect."* (Luke 12.40).

Note that Jesus calls Himself 'The Son of Man'. He used this title for Himself over eighty times in the Gospels. See Daniel, chapter 7, where the awesome figure in Daniel's vision is Jesus. Revelation 11:15 looks forward to that day when *"the kingdoms of this world 'are' become the kingdoms of our Lord and of His Christ, and He shall reign for ever and ever!"*

As we celebrate the first Advent, we need to be mindful of the second Advent. If we want to live a fulfilled life, then we need to live it in the light of His return, fulfilling the purpose for which we were put on this earth; only then will we be truly happy as we live joyfully for Him and in the light of His return. Let's prioritise our faith and share the blessed hope we have.

The book of Revelation ends with these words: *"He who testifies to these things says, 'Surely I am coming soon.' Amen. Come, Lord Jesus."* May that be our focus this Christmas season. Happy Christmas and *Maranatha* – 'Our Lord, come!' *Maranatha* is a prayer for Christ's return, expressing the early church's longing for the end of sin and the hope of seeing their Lord. He is coming and He will not delay.

Memorable Quote:
"We must remember that the first advent of Christ points us to the second advent. We must remember that Christ's spiritual reign in the hearts of the redeemed will be fulfilled in a physical reign in the future." Tim Dinkins

Journaling Suggestion:
Today is a day of celebration and also anticipation – Jesus is coming back!

Memo for Meditation:
"I saw in the night visions, and behold, with the clouds of heaven there came one like a Son of man, and he came to the Ancient of Days and was presented before him. And to Him was given dominion and glory and a kingdom, that all peoples, nations, and languages should serve Him; His dominion is an everlasting dominion, which shall not pass away, and His kingdom one that shall not be destroyed." Daniel 7:13,14

December 26

Motivational Idea: Boxing Day and St Stephen

Have you ever wondered about Boxing Day? It's a day for sporting events. My memories of Boxing Day are of an annual football match where we all got a good kicking from even the most sanctified churches in the area. The desire to win was ferocious and it's a good job it was not an actual boxing match, although on occasions it almost became such. There are a number of explanations for the tradition of Boxing Day which came to the fore as early as the 1830s. One explanation is that it derived from churches collecting donations for those who were in need. Traditionally, alms boxes were placed in churches. These boxes were opened on the 26th and the money distributed to the poor.

"If you research the historical records of Mediaeval times and even earlier you will see that giving of alms in various forms has been a tradition on St Stephen's Day. The well-known carol 'Good King Wenceslas' is a St Stephens Day carol and traditionally sung on that day and not on Christmas Day. The carol is about Wenceslas, who was a king of Bohemia (part of modern day Czechia), giving to a person in need." (Lindsey Bradshaw).

Another explanation is that servants who were given the day off after a busy Christmas Day received boxes of leftovers from the sumptuous feasting of their masters. This explanation also suggested that employers gave boxes of gifts to their employees. The practice of giving bonuses to employees has continued to this day. So, it's called 'Boxing' Day because of the original boxes and goodies being boxed! This feast day of St Stephen, the patron saint of horses, is the reason it's associated with sporting events. Perhaps it will be overlooked by some that Stephen was the first martyr. We read about him in Acts, chapters 6 and 7. He was an amazing man, very talented, and very capable of presenting the Gospel of Jesus Christ. He was as comfortable serving the poor as he was in preaching and debating with the Jewish religious leaders. They had no answer to his apologetics and presentation of the truth, so they stoned him to death – the first martyr to die for Jesus. His faith cost him his life. On this Boxing Day – St Stephen's Day – we do well to remember the persecuted Church across the world.

Check out the most dangerous countries to be a Christian. The Open Doors organisation will give you a wealth of information. Ask God today, how can I help? How can I give? How can I pray?

Memorable Quote:
"More than 360 million Christians face persecution and discrimination for their faith. That's one in seven Christians around the world. They count a huge cost for following Jesus – but they know He's worth it."
Open Doors

Journaling Suggestion:
Today I will remember the persecuted church and see how I can help.

Memo for Meditation:
"Stephen, a man full of faith in Christ Jesus, and filled with and led by the Holy Spirit...They were not able to successfully withstand and cope with the wisdom and intelligence and the power and inspiration of the Spirit by whom he was speaking." Acts 6:5,10

December 27

Motivational Idea: It's as far away as ever

The elf will tell us there are only 364 days left until Christmas; it's as far away as ever! We have a year to wait. One man who doesn't believe in waiting decided on 14th July 1993 to celebrate Christmas every day of the year, and has kept this going ever since. Alan Park from Wiltshire, England, is known as the eccentric Mr Christmas. He has sent himself 235,500 Christmas cards and even made a single in 2005 entitled, *It's Christmas Every Day.*

The truth is we all need something to look forward to and for many, Christmas epitomises that well-earned break after a busy year. Summer holidays do the same thing – we look forward to that break and many live for a week or two in the sun if they can afford it. Perhaps there is a lesson here for us to think about, and intentionally plan regular, welcome breaks. When we arrive in the New Year and January kicks in, we get back into the usual routines and life takes on all its many responsibilities again. Let's remember the days we looked at

Sabbath (30th and 31st October), and the need to build in those times of rest and refreshment. But there is another matter we need to take cognizance of: Christmas should not be merely a once in a calendar year celebration. Pastor and author Paul Tripp says, *"I love the annual tradition, but every day we must work to remind ourselves of the stunningly magnificent truths of the birth of Jesus".*

Jesus came to die and be the ultimate sacrifice for sin, and He rose again from the dead so we can live today and every day in relationship with Him. The Christmas story confronts our delusion that we are okay. We are not – we have all messed up. We need a Saviour, a living One, and Jesus is the One that fits the bill. We need to build in, each and every day, time with Him as we read His word, pray and listen to what He has to say. You wouldn't ignore a precious and loving relationship then celebrate it just once a year. We can engage every day with Jesus and enjoy the intimacy of that relationship with Him. Don't leave Jesus in the manger; don't remember Him only at Christmas. Instead, learn to walk with Him every day as you pray and read His Word and ask Him to help you.

Memorable Quote:
"Christ didn't only come into the world that first Christmas night in Bethlehem, but He wants to come into our lives today, and every day of the year. Never forget: Jesus Christ didn't just live on earth 2,000 years ago. He is alive today, and although He's now in Heaven, He continues to work on our behalf through His Spirit. And when we put our faith and trust in Him, He comes to live within us and guide us and we submit our lives to Him. In other words, we now have a personal relationship with Him—and He wants us to walk with Him and enjoy His presence every day." Billy Graham

Journaling Suggestion:
Every day is a day to know Jesus better and walk with Him.

Memo for Meditation:
"Therefore, as you received Christ Jesus the Lord, so walk in him, rooted and built up in him, strengthened in the faith as you were taught, and overflowing with thankfulness." Colossians 2:6,7

December 28

Motivational Idea: In the waiting

It's that in-between period between the old and the new. The old year is gradually coming to an end, and the new one is about to begin. There are important lessons to be learned in the waiting. The words of Psalm 27 are worth meditating upon today. The structure of this Psalm begins with statements of confidence in God followed by prayers for rescue. David is confident, reminding himself that he can depend on God's protection. David concludes this Psalm with an exhortation to wait on the Lord (see verse 14). He gives the admonition at the beginning of the verse and repeats it at the end. Perhaps David was not only addressing himself but also his soldiers, and the assembly of Israel. The exhortation is just as applicable to us today. King David speaks to us from the deep reservoir of his own personal experience with God, and so he can encourage us to *"Wait on the LORD and to take courage in Him."* (Psalm 27:14). And: *"Wait at His door with prayer; wait at his foot with humility; wait at his table with service; wait at his window with expectancy."* (C H Spurgeon).

Our waiting is not a doing nothing kind of waiting;, it's an active waiting. We can be active and serve the Lord as we wait for answers and seek His guidance. We can pray like David: *"Teach me Your way, O LORD, And lead me in a smooth path, because of my enemies."* (Psalm 27:11). And: *"To wait for Jehovah is ever to find the plain path, however rough that path may be."* (Campbell Morgan).

"Waiting on the LORD is not a passive sitting around until the LORD does something. Wait actively, wait expectantly, wait confidently, wait defiantly in the face of adversity."

God's timetable may differ from ours. We tend to want an immediate answer to our prayers, but the Lord is never in a rush. He may ask us to wait but He is never late. We can rely on his perfect timing. Perhaps you have prayed all year and experienced what seems to be a silent heaven. *"Many of his promises bear a long date; but they are sure and infallible. Wait, therefore."* (Trapp).

The importance of waiting is given by the Prophet Isaiah: *"But they who wait for the LORD shall renew their strength; they shall mount up with wings like eagles; they shall run and not be weary; they shall walk and not faint."* (Isaiah 40:31).

As we are in the waiting for the new year to dawn, let us intentionally and purposefully decide to wait on the Lord, and do it every day. *De die in diem* – from day to day.

Memorable Quote:
"'Wait for and confidently expect the Lord.' To wait for the Lord is to demonstrate confident expectation. The Hebrews word for 'wait' may also be translated 'hope.' To hope in God is to wait for His timing and action." Amplified Bible footnotes

Journaling Suggestion:
Wait and be active in the waiting.

Memo for Meditation:
"Wait for and confidently expect the LORD; Be strong and let your heart take courage; Yes, wait for and confidently expect the LORD." Psalm 27:14

December 29

Motivational Idea: Loose ends

The idiom 'tying up loose ends' has its origins in the nautical world going back to the 1800s. When preparing his boat for departure, a sailor would check all the ropes. The last thing he would need would be for someone to trip on a loose rope and an emergency to occur, e.g. 'man overboard'. Today, 'loose ends' is an informal expression that we are all familiar with, and usually refers to a task or a project that is almost completed, but some small parts need attention. As we come to the end of the old year, do we have any loose ends to complete? This question leads to another question: are you a starter, a plodder or a finisher?

Some people are great at starting things but not so good at finishing, and vice versa. Starters get the ball rolling. Plodders toil on, keeping the project going. And finishers come along and cap it all off with an ending. If you are part of a team, it's great to have all three types involved. Starters are invaluable for their ability to have a vision and dive right into any endeavour. Starters plan incessantly. They are the creative vision in a group, with their enthusiasm at its peak in the early stages of any project. Plodders are those who actually do the bulk of the work. Their special skill is the ability to keep on working, even when the job has become overwhelmingly dull to the starter. Without a plodder, endeavours would die just after inception. Finishers are the ones who come along, have a vision for the end of a project, and just cap it all off. They like completion. Where a starter and a plodder like the project to continue, as it gives them continuity and a purpose with the work, the finisher has the unique ability to see that a finished job will provide the most satisfaction, and open the opportunity for future projects, thus beginning the cycle again.

While we are all a blend of all three of these work-styles, most of us tend towards one style more than the other two, so if you are involved in a solo task or project, it can be more difficult. Do you need to put effort into developing your 'finishing skills', envisioning the end? Do you need to find a reason for wanting something to come to completion, to find the motivation to do the work necessary to finalise a project? Mind work is needed. Imagine what it would be like to get that task or project completed, a job totally done, then perhaps you can work to see it through. And, can you also imagine how happy this will make you feel and how fulfilled you will be. You did it!

Make a list of loose ends to tie up and bring to completion. This will help clear up your mind to focus on what is really important to you in the New Year. If you are at a 'loose end', pardon the pun, you could read the book of Nehemiah and find out how he did it against impossible odds.

Memorable Quote:
"Set yourself free: tie up loose ends."

Journaling Suggestion:
Loose ends? Play to my strengths and work on my weaknesses.

Memo for Meditation:
"So on October 2 the wall was finished—just fifty-two days after we had begun. When our enemies and the surrounding nations heard about it, they were frightened and humiliated. They realised this work had been done with the help of our God." Nehemiah 6:15-16

December 30

Motivational Idea: A time for reflection

The end of the year is an opportune time for reflection. Why not set aside some time to reflect on the year that is almost gone? As the door of the old year closes and a new door of opportunity opens with a new year, it would be an act of wisdom to learn from the past and, with that knowledge, go into the future with renewed hope and confidence. If you are in the habit of keeping a journal, it's worth having a read. When I worked as a service manager in mental health, I conducted annual performance development with staff members. Some staff were not so enthusiastic about this but when they were encouraged to write down all their accomplishments, most could not believe how much they had achieved. Why don't you list your accomplishments over the year? You may well be surprised at what you have achieved. Why not revisit the goals you set for the year? What can you learn from your successes and disappointments? In what ways did you grow or did you get stuck along the way? Are you moving forward toward bigger goals? How are your relationships? The most important area to visit is to consider your relationship with the Lord, and how He is moving in your life.

Reflection on the past enlightens us with understanding for future days. Learning from the past helps prepare us for the new year. God will guide us through the new year as we look to Him. Author Nancy Kay Grace has an interesting approach to each new year. Nancy chooses one word to take her through the year. If you are like me, you may well have a page full of things to accomplish, and that's fine, but to take one overarching word might be a way to go. Here's how Nancy puts it: *"For the past several years I have chosen one word to guide me throughout the year. My word for this particular year was 'deeper.' As I read through my journal and planner, I gained insight on the events that helped me go deeper in my faith. I remembered the efforts of digging deeper and the waiting for the Lord's response. I read the questions of my heart and revelations on situations from the Lord. Going deeper in faith involves seeking God (praying and digging into the Word), waiting (allowing time for the Lord to work), trusting in His sovereign grace (resting in the assurance of God's presence), and taking the next action. When situations in the past year got intense, I knew the Lord was present* in the middle of the joys and struggles. He provided strength for the moment. In those small spaces of time, my faith went deeper because my need for the Lord was great. I'm grateful for His sustaining grace in the joyous times and in the disheartening ones."

What word will you take into the new year? Journal each day and keep a record for the next time of reflection.

Memorable Quote:
"God doesn't want to number your failures or count your accomplishments as much as He wants you to have an encounter with Him." Ann Voskamp

Journaling Suggestion:
Learn from the past and plan for the future.

Memo for Meditation:
"But watch out! Be careful never to forget what you yourself have seen. Do not let these memories escape from your mind as long as you live!" Deuteronomy 4:9a

---

December 31

Motivational Idea: Standing on the threshold

As we stand at the threshold of a new year, it's a moment ripe for reflection and forward-looking anticipation. This is a time to pause and remember the many ways God has shown His faithfulness and provision over the past year. Many of us will also have new year resolutions in mind because we want to improve, develop, grow and achieve. Don't let your enthusiasm be dampened by scepticism from past resolutions that have dissolved into the hustle of everyday life. If we make our top resolution one of aligning our walk more intimately with God and the path He has laid out for us, then everything else will fall into place.

When viewed through the lens of Scripture, resolutions are transformed from a secular pursuit of self-improvement to an act of faith and dependence on God. The focus shifts from our own strength and willpower to God's transformative power within us. So, on this the last day of the old year, and as you stand on the threshold of a new year, it's a time to look forward with hope. Wishing YOU happiness, a happy new year and a fulfilled life! Recognise that the coming year is not just another year, it's a new chapter waiting to be written, filled with possibilities for growth, resilience, perseverance and faith.

You have now spent a year considering this kaleidoscopic approach to 'happiness and the fulfilled life'. Perhaps the best way to draw everything to a conclusion is to point to Jesus, the Servant King, and His words: *"If you know these things, blessed are you if you do them."*

Memorable Quote:
"The new year ushers in an opportunity to trust in God's unfailing plans with renewed hope. While the future may hold uncertainties, our confidence lies not in our ability to predict or control what lies ahead, but in the steadfastness of God's character and His promises. As we make plans and set goals, let them be steeped in the assurance of His sovereign goodness and perfect timing. This perspective shifts our focus from worry and anxiety to a peace that surpasses understanding, grounded in the knowledge that our future is in His capable hands." Calvary Baptist Church, Kalkaska, Michigan

Journaling Suggestion:
My desire is to serve as a servant of Jesus, the servant King, the true source of happiness and the fulfilled life.

Memo for Meditation:
"When he had washed their feet and put on his outer garments and resumed his place, he said to them, "Do you understand what I have done to you? You call me Teacher and Lord, and you are right, for so I am. If I then, your Lord and Teacher, have washed your feet, you also ought to wash one another's feet. For I have given you an example, that you also should do just as I have done to you. Truly, truly, I say to you, a servant is not greater than his master, nor is a messenger greater than the one who sent him. If you know these things, blessed (happy, favoured by God, fulfilled) are you if you do them." John 13:12-17
End Matter

The Sermon on the Mount: The Beatitudes (meaning happy and blessed)

"When Jesus saw the crowds, He went up on the mountain; and when He was seated, His disciples came to Him. Then He *began* to teach them, saying,

"*Blessed [spiritually prosperous, happy, to be admired] are the poor in spirit [those devoid of spiritual arrogance, those who regard themselves as insignificant], for theirs is the kingdom of heaven [both now and forever].*

"*Blessed [forgiven, refreshed by God's grace] are those who mourn [over their sins and repent], for they will be comforted [when the burden of sin is lifted].*

"*Blessed [inwardly peaceful, spiritually secure, worthy of respect] are the gentle [the kind-hearted, the sweet-spirited, the self-controlled], for they will inherit the earth.*

"*Blessed [joyful, nourished by God's goodness] are those who hunger and thirst for righteousness [those who actively seek right standing with God], for they will be [completely] satisfied.*

"*Blessed [content, sheltered by God's promises] are the merciful, for they will receive mercy.*

"*Blessed [anticipating God's presence, spiritually mature] are the pure in heart [those with integrity, moral courage, and godly character], for they will see God.*

"*Blessed [spiritually calm with life-joy in God's favour] are the makers and maintainers of peace, for they will [express His character and] be called the sons of God.*

"*Blessed [comforted by inner peace and God's love] are those who are persecuted for doing that which is morally right, for theirs is the kingdom of heaven [both now and forever].*

"*Blessed [morally courageous and spiritually alive with life-joy in God's goodness] are you when people insult you and persecute you, and falsely say all kinds of evil things against you because of [your association with] Me. Be glad and exceedingly joyful, for your reward in heaven is great [absolutely inexhaustible]; for in this same way they persecuted the prophets who were before you.*

Matthew 5:1-12, AMP (See Isaiah 55:1-4 and the free gift offered)

ABOUT THE AUTHOR

Graham Albert Logan retired from working in the mental health field in October 2024. This is his fourth book. Having considered finding true freedom, finding true love, finding hope in a fragile world, this new book is all about finding happiness and the fulfilled life.

In reality, retirement after fifty years of employment is not an option for the author; rather, it means more time can be devoted to reading and writing.

Printed in Dunstable, United Kingdom

64684023R00299